Alternative Vegan

International Vegan Fare Straight

from the Produce Aisle

Dino Sarma

tofu hound press

First Printing 2007

For information, please contact:

Tofu Hound Press

PO Box 276

Colton, NY 13625-0276

publications@tofuhoundpress.com

http://tofuhoundpress.com

Interior Design by Tofu Hound Press

Cover design and illustrations by Elise Hartmann at Dark Faerie Creations

http://darkfaeriecreations.com

ISBN-13: 978-0-9770804-2-7

ISBN-10: 0-9770804-2-0

To amma, who is a font of wisdom, be it cooking or otherwise.

Contents

Foreword

Everyone needs a friend like Dino. Allow me to explain.

It was 2002. I was in British Columbia backpacking with a friend, cooking over an open fire, and learning how to sleep on rocks and roots. One day, we made it to an Internet cafe, and an email from a roommate read, "Hi. Hope your trip is going well. By the way, we've been evicted." The landlord claimed she wanted to renovate and move in her family. I decided to get a place on my own.

By the first day at my new digs, I realized that every utensil, pot, and skillet I used throughout university had belonged to a roommate. So I borrowed a pan from my neighbor (old habits die hard), and dug out my grubby Swiss Army knife. A friend, and vegan cooking hero, thought my minimalist kitchen was quirky and endearing. When cooking at my apartment, she'd happily exclaim, "Oh, it's like camping!" I loved food, but didn't consider myself much of a cook. Being adept in the kitchen seemed like the stuff of magicians: Their knowledge seemed too elusive, or too vast to ever grasp. Me and my pocket knife got by all right. I left the mystery-making to others.

Then, on my birthday, I received a DIY cookbook from the same friend. This refurbished address book had been covered in animal rights stickers and twisted comic strips. Inside she included a stack of her favorite sure-fire recipes. These recipes ranged from simple comfort foods to unequivocal crowd-pleasers. But, most importantly, these recipes had been tailored just to me. I'd get to the squash soup recipe and a personal note would read, "Squash doesn't have to be an intimidating vegetable. Just skip to the back of the book, read the easy instructions for preparing squash, and then try out this super delicious soup." Or, in the dessert section, she'd offer more pointed advice: Under the pecan square directions that said to chill the crust for an hour, she wrote, "I know you're thinking, 'I can skip this step...' No you can't! Seriously, it won't work." Ah, yes, she knew me well. Her cookbook was a turning point.

Like my friend, Dino is part cheerleader and part disciplinarian. He wants you to succeed, which means he's going to give you all the encouragement and support he can, but he's also going to give you a dollop of tough love to keep you in check. He wants you to have an adventure, but he wants you to pack your cruelty-free bug spray and sunscreen first. So you know you're in good hands. With his personal tone, and dangerously cheery descriptions, "Fling some chiles here... Pop these spices there... Now would be a good time to get that spray guard out if you have one...," Dino clearly knows what he's doing and wants to share all the wisdom he's honed over the years with you, his dedicated reader. All those little concerns you might have as a new, or even veteran, cook are thoroughly assuaged by detailed and friendly advice. His honest style lets you know what corners you can cut and those you can't. This is a compulsively readable and sensual text that's as fun to read as it is to cook from. As you befriend this cookbook, Dino befriends you. He's there when you need him, and makes you giddy to challenge yourself and to try something new.

Ultimately, once you've learned the skills (or if you already know the skills), like all great teachers, Dino asks you to trust yourself and take these recipes and the wonderful world of vegan cooking, and make them uniquely your own. By relying on fresh, tasty ingredients, he demonstrates that replicating meat and dairy-based recipes is completely unnecessary to make satisfying meals. This is vegan new school, which is really vegan old school, which draws on traditions that predate any of us. Cooking can be empowering, no doubt about it.

Good cookbooks give you ideas and introduce a new recipe or two into your weekly menu. Great cookbooks include family favorites and become a permanent fixture on your kitchen counter. Excellent cookbooks change the way you think about food, become committed to memory, and inspire you. This is an excellent cookbook. Thank you, Dino.

Lauren Corman
host, Animal Voices
www.animalvoices.ca
CIUT 89.5 FM - Toronto
March 2007

Acknowledgments

There are so many people that I need to thank, but I'll start off with the testers, in the order of how many recipes in total that they tested. For those whose real names I don't have, I've used their forum names.

Joanne Charlebois, for being the most active and adventurous tester. She would go in and test those recipes that others were scared to test, and would do the recipes with difficult techniques or hard-to-find ingredients. Without Joanne's feedback about the recipes, the book would not have worked out as well as it did. She'd give me help with how to tighten up the directions, and she would make different variations, and try new things with the recipes, which is exactly what I want people to do with the book!

Dana Ballantyne, for being the one who compiled all the recipes from the forums, and compiled them into a giant document from which I could make corrections and edits. Dana offered to keep the testers motivated (and did an outstanding job of it!), went through and did proofreading multiple times, and endlessly gave me feedback about the recipes. Other than that, she had me over at her house many times, and let me demolish her kitchen with all the frenzied cooking. We'd spend hours in putting together a hugely elaborate meal, only to sit around and graze for a few hours more afterwards.

Deb (AKA Mango), for doing testing even though she didn't have her kitchen for a long while during the testing period! For Lindsay (MYFAVORITEFOODISACUBE) for testing so many recipes, even though she's a young teen vegan whose kitchen is not her own, who doesn't have a car, and who doesn't have her own money to go on random shopping trips to get the ingredients.

To Gary Loewenthal, whose endless sharing of food and wisdom with his wife and coworkers gave me valuable feedback from people whose palates aren't used to vegan food. His fatherly patience is an inspiration to a young firecracker like myself.

Stephen Weierman, for being a warm, loving friend and partner. Abracapocus, who was adventurous, even though she purportedly is a finicky eater. Nell, for loving her lists and me. She was another one of those whose schedule was tight, but she still managed to test.

Amanda Sacco, whose photos of food made us drool and motivated us so much. Amanda's proofreading also made this possible, because I have been known to make some egregious errors. Her patience in going through and giving me detailed feedback about the construction and flow of the recipes, ingredients, and other content of the book was priceless.

Thanks also to Allison Dunlap for excellent, thorough, and quick proofreading!

Dr. Mary Sue Sylwestrzak for showing me that people of all ages can be wicked cool. Daniel Planteater for testing and taking plenty of photos. Melinda Getch, maddie., and Rich Bebenroth for giving me the perspective of Americans.

Of course, I couldn't have done this without Bob and Jenna Torres. It's through their podcast that I went vegan. After going vegan and joining their forums, Bob approached me about writing a book. Then, after that, he offered me my own segment on his podcast show. It's been a rollercoaster with Bob and Jenna from the first time I met them to now, and I wouldn't trade a moment of it.

Thank you to my family, for standing by my side through everything. Thank you to my friends (you know who you are) for being forever enthusiastic about the book. Thank you, from the bottom of my heart, to all the Vegan Freaks, who have been cheering me on from the time they heard of my book, and who all eagerly await its release. This book is all of ours, and I thank you for helping me see it come to fruition.

Most of all, thank you to my readers. You are the ones for whom this project was done. Thank you for believing in me.

An Introduction to My World

Whenever I or any of my good friends (and on some occasions, family) get hold of a new cooking implement of any sort, I, like a gamer with the latest console and stack of new games, feel the need to use it as soon as it has been brought home. The day I bought myself a mortar and pestle, I came home that night, bashed up some coriander seeds, poured the little shards of flavor into a bowl, then ground up some ginger and garlic with a few lumps of rock salt.

Then, I heated up my much-loved old wok—the one my mother has had since she got married 35+ years ago and that has seen the sharp side of a stirring spoon more times than I can count—screaming hot, poured in some oil, threw in some spices, and watched them pop and dance in their hot bath. Then I flung in the coriander seeds (now beautiful and ready to give the oil their all) and some sesame seeds and waited to hear the calls of the sesame seeds, exploding all over the inside of the wok, and onto my freshly clean stove. I stirred in a can of beans, and let it get to a full boil. Then I stirred in some cooked rice, and indulged myself in my newly crafted dish, which I could not have made quite this way without my brand new marble mortar and pestle.

She will see the seductive wafts of perfume that the spices wear. She will make even the most haughty garlic a smooth, creamy, salty paste. She will demand that the ginger cut her long, fibrous hair so that my soup doesn't have little strings of ginger in it. She will, like a best friend, improve with the amount of time that we spend together, teaching me, giving selflessly of herself whenever I ask. She will joyfully sing to me as I respectfully run the spices through her relentless stones. And when the two of us are finished playing in our exuberant dance of joy, she will then go back to her beloved corner of my utensil shelf, to lie in repose for the next time we speak.

This is what I want cooking to become for you. I want you to look at the recipes presented here, and be as excited as a kid with a new toy. I want your heart to race, your mouth to water, and your pots and pans to sing to you as they bring together the elements of a good dining experience. I want you ready to plunge into a recipe, headfirst, mouth wide open and ready to go. I want you to approach your food with the exuberance we reserve for eating out. Their food will never be as good as yours, because only you know your palate.

When you get my book home into your kitchen or onto your nightstand so you can pore over its pages at night and have beautiful, savory dreams while you sleep, I want you to imagine ways of adapting what I have, suiting it to your palate. Decide what you would like to tweak, and how it would taste good to you.

Once you've got ideas, get out there and do it! There's no need to worry, because all of these recipes have been tested many times over by different people of different skill levels. This is our labor of love to you, so that you may explore the gifts of nature's bounty. Now get that knife sharpened, your oven preheated, and that cutting board washed. It's time to cook.

"The beauty of the way Dino cooks is that there are no set rules. As someone who has had the opportunity to cook with him (in person) often, he has pushed me into not being afraid to alter my cooking plans at the last minute, or even during the course of cooking the meal. More than once we've started out cooking with one idea in mind, and I've turned around to find him rummaging through my cabinets, where he has found an ingredient I forgot I had, and we've totally changed gears and ended up cooking something entirely different."

-Dana Ballantyne

A Note on Being Vegan

I am a vegan for ethical reasons. This means that I consider the use of animals, for any interest that does not directly serve the animal's own interests, as wrong. This means that for ethical reasons, I will not consume or purchase anything that uses animal products. This includes meat, fish, dairy, honey, wool, leather, fur, or products tested on animals. I do not use products that contain animal-derived ingredients, such as processed foods that have vitamins or minerals that come from animal products. I also prefer to avoid foods from companies that primarily make their profits from animal exploitation, such as soymilk from a dairy company.

I am hoping that with this book, you'll all see how easy this is to do. Although I enjoy a good salad just as much as the next vegan, I don't eat only salad all day. My diet is rich and varied, and I enjoy the foods that I create. I don't have to depend on someone else to make my food for me when the things I eat are so simple to put together.

When people ask me things like, "Well what *do* you eat?" I want to point them to this book. Fortunately for me, my publisher has made this possible. I don't depend on soymilk and tofu all day—my diet is a lot more varied than that.

When I went vegan, I rediscovered my passion for cooking. It opened up a whole new world of things that I hadn't really considered before. Hopefully, with this resource in your hands, you'll also see that being a vegan isn't about deprivation; being vegan is about discovering new ways of thinking of cooking. It's a journey that has been exciting and fun. Try it out, and you'll be sure to find ways to make it work for you.

A Note About Collaboration

This book is a labor of love from a very large community of vegans. I may be the one with the author's credit, but this does not mean that I would take full credit for anything in here. Bob Torres recognized my ability to cook early on, and encouraged me to compile a cookbook. My friends that live near me, for whom I have cooked on countless occasions, kept me motivated to continue to experiment with food. My friend Liza is fond of saying, "Trust the chef!" whenever people give me odd looks while making something.

Our family friends, John and Susan Casbarro, let me raid their kitchens, their pantries, and their grocery shopping to churn out new and interesting things. Dana and Joel Ballantyne (and their daughter, who we all know as Noodle), two other vegans who live near me, along with Susan and John would get together for impromptu "cook-ins." Random vegetation would appear, rice would be cooking, beans would be boiled, and we'd attack the kitchen at full tilt either at Dana's or John's place. I cannot count the messes we made together. They never let me help clean up, and they were always enthusiastic about their leftovers.

All the while, regardless of the level of disaster, they kept coming back for more and more.

My mother let me shamelessly tap her considerable knowledge in cooking. I'd be underfoot all the time when she was in the kitchen. She would brag to all her friends that her son was such a talent in the kitchen, and they'd jealously glare at their own sons for not paying attention when mother cooks. I am quite sure that by now, all of my mother's friends, in the far-flung reaches of the globe, know about her talented little kid (who's not so little anymore).

My second eldest brother would encourage me in the kitchen and would have me cook for his friends when they came over. After tasting the food, he would shamelessly brag about his baby brother's cooking prowess. We'd make unlikely dishes, like fettuccine with tomato sauce and diced potatoes, ramen noodles with Indian pickles, and random rice concoctions which were always so good.

My father was a willing guinea pig (animal testing is NOT VEGAN) for countless dishes I made. He would eat them with a smile, and didn't complain even when they were disasters. When my mother dashed off to India for a year and it was just the two of us, I would make him his favorite aubergine (eggplant) dishes, which he ate with relish. Little did he know that my brain was quietly taking notes on all of it, and storing it away.

My sister and brothers were equally patient and forgiving with my culinary adventures. I've made some rank disasters in the past, which they would basically re-spice and eat. Even when I would make a very simple dish, like pasta with garlic and olive oil and a diced tomato (quite delicious, if I do say so myself!) they'd crave exactly that and be willing participants in eating it.

My grandfather would spoil me senseless with delectable delights. Murukku (a south Indian snack), pakora, bajji, anything my little junk-food loving tongue could ask for was mine for the feasting. My grandmother would swear up and down that he was going to ruin my health and doom me to being that way for life, but he would chuckle and give me more.

Then there are the people on the Vegan Freak Forums. Bob invited me to get a cookbook done, and I started producing recipes quite rapidly. Unfortunately, being a college student living alone at that time made it difficult to ideally test about ninety percent of the recipes I was cranking out. Bob put the pressure on to get them tested. Instead of being a good Dino and actually doing the work myself, I ran to the forums and asked for help. Within an hour of posting the request for help, we had most of our first round of testers, eager to jump on board. With round two, it barely took one night to get many of the vegans from the forums to rush in and offer their help.

"Watching Dino crank out a recipe in IRC is like reading poetry. His passion for food shines through in every line. He is also one of the most compassionate individuals I've ever known, one who genuinely cares for people and other living creatures. I feel truly blessed to call him a friend."

-Stephen Weierman

They tested the recipes, then popped onto the forum to give me excellent, detailed feedback. There were mishaps, such as when I messed up the wording of the instructions, forgot ingredients, and there was that garlic incident that I'd rather not get into. The omisubi was originally a disaster and a half. It was bland and lifeless. The pakoras were equally disastrous in the beginning. I won't even get into the pain that was the dipping sauce for the appetizers.

Yet, even with all of that, my vegan friends kept coming back for more. "More recipes!" they cried. They kept me motivated when I was feeling down about things in real life. They made me want to show them different and interesting things. They continued to rally around me to create. They inspired me with their trust. Here are people whom I've never met, and they'll probably never get a chance to meet me either. Based purely on the faith they have in my ability, they put their dinners on the line.

There was the IRC chat room too. The vegans hanging out in there would ask, "Dino—I have a can of black beans, some leftover vegetables from that party I was at where they only served a stupid not-vegan dip with raw vegetables, and some rice. What do I do?" I would respond with, "Got any peanuts, walnuts, pecans, onions, or garlic?" I'd get a "Sure, I've got it all." I would crank out a recipe right there on the spot. Often times, it was a combination the person hadn't considered.

Then, the person would dash off to the kitchen, cook whatever it is I told him or her to cook, and come back and rave about it to the others, who all would demand that the person share.

I am not an island—I am the product of the thousands of years that vegetarians the world over have been cooking. I am a culmination of all the friends, family, animals, and people I've met in my life. I have the ability to create, because there is beauty in this world, and I can appreciate it.

What does all of this mean?

It means that I, as the "author" of the book am no more solely responsible for the creation of it than you who read it. If it wasn't for the fact that Bob spotted my abilities at the time that he did, I wouldn't have bothered to compile this mad stack of ravings. If it weren't for the fact that the world is such an amazing place, with so much beauty and so many adventures waiting to happen, I would not be the person that I am. I don't own these ideas—they're all of ours to share.

So take this book, and share it!

Basic Kitchen Tools Guide

This is the "what you need" section. Also known as "Dino is a diva meanie head who wants us all to be like him"

I was being facetious with the subtitle, but it's sort of a mentality that I used to have when a cookbook told me that I *need* a tool or something along those lines that I didn't have. Here, I give you the heads-up as to the bare essentials, how not to spend a fortune on it, and how to take care of it so that you're not cursing me out next week when your cast iron skillet turns into a rusted hole-riddled thing. So let's get started.

On Skillets

The first and foremost thing to discuss is the cast iron skillet. It's perfect for frying. It's perfect for cooking. It'll get your vegetables roasty and toasty, and after using it for a while, it becomes (through what I know to be magic) nonstick. It's dark and heavy and slippery slick. It's also cheap. You can generally find one at the store for less than $12, and this thing will last you forever (if treated right). A good, seasoned nonstick skillet is *Some people are lucky enough to inherit a cast iron skillet, and those people can go away.* worth many times its weight in (cruelty-free, sweatshop-free, evil corporation-free) gold. Hold on to it for dear life (when it's not blazing hot), as your family members will jealously eye it if they know how you got those stunning results on the dinner table.

To care for your new best friend (sorry dog, but you don't know how to get those herbed potatoes all crusty) is far simpler than you'd think. After you're done with your cooking, drain off any excess fat from the pan. Into the pan, sprinkle some kosher salt. Let it sit for a minute or so, scrub it around with a paper towel and then discard the salt and the paper towel. Rub in some extra oil, and leave it alone. Don't wash it. Don't put it in the dishwasher. You want to develop that fat coating, and washing it will just wash away all your work.

Some people are lucky enough to inherit a cast iron skillet, and those people can go away because I'm jealous. Others, like me, need to start from scratch. Now what?

Internet!

Go online, and find a pre-seasoned cast iron skillet. They will tell you up front that it's been seasoned from vegetable sources, and you're set. Cooking.com has a 10.25 inch skillet seasoned by Lodge that's $14, and they say right there that it's from a vegetable oil blend that's heated in industrial ovens.

For the more DIY types, go to the local hardware store, snag a cast iron skillet for $10 – $12, and swing by your local grocery store. Why? You need shortening. I'm really not joking here. We don't have industrial strength ovens that can force vegetable oil in its unsaturated form to accept the fat properly. Besides, with the shortening, you can go home and make your own puff pastry later on.

Go home, and preheat your oven to 275° F. Rub the shortening on the pan. Wear plastic food service gloves or use a sheet of parchment paper to help keep your fingers clean, because I don't think you'll be too fond of solidified fat sitting in the crevices of your hands. Make sure to coat every inch of the pan's insides (not outsides) with the grease. You might even want to overdo it and have a little bit of excess. This can't harm the pan.

Once coated, put your pan into the oven, and let it sit there like that for about 20 minutes or so. Take out the pan, and pour off the extra grease. Put it back into the oven, and drop down the heat to 200° F. Leave it there for five or six hours (or overnight). Do not waste the oven's heat while this is going on. Take a few 6 quart pots that are oven safe, and pour in one variety of bean into the bottom of each pot. Fill to the top (leaving about 5 inches of head room) with water and put on a lid. Put these pots of beans into the oven with the skillet so that you have hot cooked beans in the morning, along with a seasoned skillet. The low heat of the oven will allow the beans to cook slowly, as in a crock pot situation. Keeping the water just below boiling point will prevent too much water evaporating as steam.

On Knives

If it were a more perfect world, they would have figured out how to clone me, and you could have your very own Dino to cook for you all the time. But, we're not in a perfect world, so you have this book instead.

Similarly, in an ideal world, we would all be able to afford top quality knives. We'd go to our local knife sharpener, where he would sharpen our knives for us, and we'd have beautifully working knives all the time.

Enter: reality. You're a college student who couldn't give a flying cabbage about perfect situations. You want something you can afford, and you want it yesterday, darn it. You're a single mother, without the time, energy or patience to go trawling through second-hand stores, stalking the knife section. You have actual bills to pay. So what do you do? You get what you can afford immediately and move on and tell me to cram it.

Don't do this. If you cannot afford top quality knives, just go the next best step down—never needs sharpening knives. Before the real chefs reading this come chasing me with aforementioned knife for such blasphemy, hear me out. A dull knife is a dangerous thing.

If it slips, it will cut you (but not the vegetables) badly. And your hands, being very sensitive parts of your body, will not thank you for this mistreatment. Instead of asking you to blow $100 – $300 on a top quality knife that you can't or won't care for, I'd prefer that you just get a never needs sharpening twelve inch chef's knife, and move on. You can generally get one for a few dollars.

But I still wish you'd get a good one.

On Pots

This is where you cannot compromise. Don't worry about brand names, celebrities on the cover, or the fancy garbage they try to tell you about the pot that means nothing to you. So much of it is marketing, rather than actually showing you differences in the meal you'll end up serving. If you're in a professional setting, you'll have to invest in the top quality pots and pans and there is no room for compromise.

This would also mean that you have perfectly calibrated stoves, top-quality steel counters that can handle the high heats these pots get to, and equipment fitting of these pots. You aren't in a professional kitchen, though; you're at home, and you need to be prepared to work within the constraints of your own budget.

I would rather have you find an OK pot that you will use and can afford than a horrible one that won't work. So in that spirit of compromise, let me tell you this: conventional wisdom is anything but.

What do I mean? Ideally, you'd all have copper cooking pots. They're excellent conductors, and they hold heat well. Meanwhile, I don't have a full time maid to clean them, which is what using copper cookware would require. They take stains extremely easily, and hold on to their stains. Copper cookware is also very expensive. Once I make my first billion, I'll be sure to get out there and buy copper cookware for all my friends and all you readers out there. Until then, I'll have to keep looking.

Then you've got cast iron. Ideally, all my cookware would be cast iron, so that I could get that perfect distribution of heat and the maintenance of heat that cast iron offers. I love cast iron with all my heart, but frankly, I can't be bothered to wait for a cast iron Dutch oven to heat up, and I don't have an unlimited budget to spend on propane for the gas stove. Unfortunately, I'm not a power lifter either.

Then they have all the fancy metals that a stock pot can come in, and they use all these fancy terms like "sandwiched" and "anodized" and other such rot. I'm sure that someone out there somewhere has bought this sort of thing, and noticed a significant difference in the quality of the food she or he has turned out. When I meet that someone, I'll let you know.

You as the home cook won't really notice that much of a difference. All that stuff is just ... stuff to justify the exorbitant cost. I'm not producing world-class cuisine for the Emperor of America's mom. I'm making myself a pot of soup because I'm hungry and I want to eat something comforting to me. I'm not sitting in my million dollar restaurant and hoping that some VIP is going to throw me some piddling praise. I'm making a pot of pasta with some simple olive oil and basic ingredients.

For me, the home cook, a good, heavy-bottomed, large 12-quart stock pot does wonders. I can boil water quickly. I can sauté my onions in the pot till they're a golden, caramel-y brown, then trust the heat to sustain the sweat later on. I can control the heat enough so that the soup sustains a nice, steady simmer. I can pour in some oil, and fry up some delicious, crispy yucca fries. That's what I care about.

Get yourself a pot larger than you think you need. The extra space allows for steam to move around and prevents bubbling over when you have starchy ingredients. Get a pot that feels heavy on the bottom, but not so heavy that you can't lift it easily. Carrying a steaming hot pot of doom will be your own downfall if it's too heavy. Get one with metal handles so that you can transfer it to the oven if needed. And, make sure the pot has a nice tight-fitting lid. It shouldn't run you more than $20.

My mother has always been a huge fan of second-hand stores, garage sales, rummage sales, and other such reuse initiatives. If I tell her I got something on sale at the store, she'll go out on a Saturday morning, find pretty much the same thing, and show me up by getting it for a fraction of what I paid on the *taxes*. She'll shoot me a smug look and say something like "You won't outdo the master, my dear." I then hang my head and return what I bought.

My grandfather was fond of saying, "Only a fool learns from his own mistakes. A wise man learns from the mistakes of others." Let's combine the wisdom of both my mother and my grandfather. Get out to those second-hand stores, the thrift stores, the yard sales, the rummage sales, the swap meets, and all the rest. Get into websites like freecycle.org, which are all about sharing what we don't need with others. Be on the lookout for a bargain, because you will most assuredly find one.

I don't think I own any cookware with a pedigree. They're all of indiscriminate origin, dug up by my mother in her adventures. Why not make it an adventure? Cooking is certainly an exciting adventure—why not get yourself into it headfirst? When you do find that real bargain, you'll have earned bragging rights with me and my family. Just don't brag to Mom, because she'll promptly show you up and send you packing with a whole bunch of food.

There you have it. Those are the three essential parts to a kitchen. With those three basic tools, you can produce a dizzying array of impressive and delicious foods. I will go into more detail about other useful products in the next section.

Cooking Techniques

If sautéing makes you sweat ...

Different cooking techniques will bring out different aspects of your food. Depending on the flavor and texture of the food that you desire, you will be using one, or many, of the techniques I am presenting here. I'll explain briefly the reasons for using each method with its preparation instructions. The reason I'm spending time on this here isn't so I can shorthand the techniques later—it's about giving you an arsenal of tools for your vegan toolbox.

By understanding the different techniques, you will first and foremost be a more skilled cook. However, more than that, you will also become a more independent cook. If you are familiar with a particular technique, you'll notice errors right away.

An example of this is when I was younger, and I was making a pot of soup for my sick sister. I wanted it to come out just right. When the recipe called for 5 tablespoons of salt to be sprinkled over my 3 cups of sweating vegetables, alarm bells went off in my head. I knew from watching the food channel that sweating happens at low heat and with just a little bit of salt.

This also leads me to a note about this cookbook. I keep repeating the fact that you should do things that suit you, so that you will want to keep cooking. If you see something in here that seems a bit extreme for your liking, trust your instincts and cut back on it. If you think that one pound of beans is going to be way too much for your family to finish, you're most likely right. (However, to be fair, I have seen one pound of beans disappear, like lightning, before my very eyes when I have cooked at friends' houses.)

I tend to err on the side of more salt, fat, and chili than a majority of people are comfortable with. If something seems like it'll burn off the first layer of your tongue, cut back on the heat to suit your needs. I would think nothing of flinging a few tablespoons of red chili flakes into a pot of soup—that's just how my family eats. I also wouldn't mind having a heavily-spiced snack just before an equally heavily-spiced meal. Not everyone will be comfortable with that. As long as you give yourself permission to experiment, you'll be fine.

Sautéing

Sautéing is specifically meant for drawing out the sugars from aromatics (such as onions or bell peppers) and other ingredients, to get that food browned. It's a high-heat cooking method that yields a concentrated flavor that's slightly sweet. To sauté a vegetable of any kind, start preparing the vegetables. The French call the arrangement of your ingredients *mise en place*, and it's one of the first things that you will learn in a cooking school.

Have all your ingredients cut up into small pieces. Try to keep them as uniformly sized as possible, so that everything gets cooked evenly. Were I to make a hierarchical list about the importance of cutting, I would begin with uniformity in size. Too many times there will be different sized chunks in the pot, all of which cook at different times, and the end result is ghastly. Do the best you can to get the pieces the same size. Have them arranged in front of you in an area near the stove. Also arrange close at hand any spices you'll be using, in the order that you add them to the oil. Open any jars, bottles, or other containers, and have spoons ready to measure out your amounts of spices.

Turn your stove to the highest setting that it has, and put on a wide, shallow frying pan. Coat the bottom of the pan in oil, and heat up your oil until a little wisp of smoke escapes the surface. Immediately toss your vegetables into the hot oil. Once the vegetables are in the pan, stir them around to evenly coat all the pieces in the oil. You want the pieces looking shiny.

"Dino reminds me of a story that I read with my second graders during my student teaching. It was called "Gino Badino" and it was about a sweet, little mouse whose family made noodles for a living. Gino took some weird noodles and turned them into a new, amazing shaped noodle that ended up helping his family's business prosper. Dino, like Gino (ha-ha that rhymes), loves to take ordinary ingredients and turn them into something new and wonderful. His recipes are full of a deep love for cooking and life!"

–Sarah Preston

Once all the ingredients you want to sauté are evenly coated with oil, sprinkle in a little salt and any of the dry spices you will be using (such as turmeric powder, curry powder, or any other dry spice powder), and stir around all the ingredients in the pan to coat them evenly in the spices. Drop down your heat to medium high. Forgetting to turn down your heat will result in burned spices.

Leave the ingredients sitting in the pan for 2 – 3 minutes, or longer (depending on the recipe) until desired brownness is achieved. You may deglaze the pan after this step for a rich sauce to form around the vegetables.

This basic sauté gives you an excellent starting point for any number of vegetables you want to cook. It works very well for dark leafy greens, root vegetables, and beans. This would also be an outstanding point to start a soup. Oh no! I'm getting hungry. Let me go hammer out some baby spinach in this sauté, and I'll come back to show you how to deglaze. I promise I'll be back. In the meantime, what are you waiting for? Get out a pan, and sauté yourself some lovelies.

Deglazing

Deglazing is a method of loosening up the sugars in the bottom of a pot or pan. Usually, it is a step performed after sautéing, but this is not always the case. Deglazing helps liberate any flavors that are lurking about in your pot or on the surface of ingredients and dissolves them in the liquid. After you have sautéed your vegetables or aromatics in the pan, you may deglaze the pan with alcohol, juice, water, stock, or other "wet" ingredients. This is one of the essential techniques to have, as it will prevent your spices from burning. Wet heat is gentler than dry heat, because water will not rise above the 212° F boiling point. Your metal pot, on the other hand, will get far above that. OK, I'll shut up and get on with it.

Other wet ingredients would be things like tomatoes, cooked beans with some of the cooking water, or even fresh fruit. Citrus is a wonderful bet for deglazing, since it leaks out its juices so quickly, and coats the other ingredients so well. You may have even been deglazing your recipes all this time but just didn't know what to call it! Now you've got a fancy technique to impress your friends.

Use other "wet" ingredients when you would like to deglaze something that's only aromatics. If all you have in your pot is garlic, onion and some herbs, tomato would be your best bet. Deglaze with liquid when there are other vegetables in the pot already. These two rules aren't hard-and-fast, but they do help form a basis for deglazing.

To deglaze with a liquid, sauté the vegetables as you normally would. Turn the heat back up to high. Wait about 15 – 30 seconds for the pot to catch on that the heat has been increased. You should hear the vegetables begin to sizzle excitedly, telling you that they're ready for what you're bringing.

Pour in about a cup of liquid into the pan, and quickly begin to scrape down the bottom of the pan with a wooden spatula to free up all the little bits of browned goodness that got stuck to the pan. If it looks too dry to be able to scrape up all the bits, add in another half cup of liquid, and keep scraping. You'll have to work even more quickly if you're using alcohol, because alcohol evaporates more quickly than water.

For an impressive trick, under safe conditions (no loose sleeves, no flammables nearby, fire extinguisher close by), after you've added the alcohol, you can remove it from the heat (and turn off the stove, please) and take it to the table. With the stick of a long lighter, set the surface of the alcohol on fire, and watch the ooooohs and aaaaaahs. The flambé technique does very little to actually add any flavor and is more for show than anything of significance besides burning off the alcohol. Use it on special occasions.

In a very short time, you should start seeing the liquid get thicker and thicker. When it's gotten thick enough to cling to the vegetables quite possessively but still coat the stirring spoon, you're done. The liquid should all be about as thick as a rich gravy.

When you want to deglaze with a "wet" ingredient, have that ingredient diced or minced ahead of time first. Sauté the vegetables as normal. Turn the heat back up to high. When you hear your vegetables (or, in this case aromatics) sizzle and sing, quickly add your chopped up "wet" ingredient and stir around. Keep stirring around for about a minute. Drop down the heat to medium, and let the mixture cook for five to ten minutes, depending on the ingredient.

These examples are just to illustrate in your mind the techniques and are not to provide a basis for any recipes, real or implied.

Sweating

Sweating is a gentle method of cooking vegetables that allows the flavors to slowly leak out of the vegetables and into the surrounding fat. It's a very simple method, because it doesn't involve too much "baby-sitting" like sautéing and de-glazing. It's also ideal for beginning cooks, because it doesn't hold as high a risk of burning something. If you're starting out as a cook, sweat your vegetables in lieu of sautéing them the first couple of times you try out a new or unfamiliar recipe. It will save many fires both in frustration and in kitchen!

To sweat a vegetable (classic example is the basis of many soups, a *mire poix*: carrots, onions, celery), chop up all the pieces of vegetables into roughly 1/2-inch cubes. You want all the pieces of vegetable to be as close to the same size as possible. When they're chopped, each vegetable should measure about a cup.

"Providing more of an outline than a formal recipe is the best way for vegans to learn to cook. With Dino's guidance you know what you're making will be good and he lets you tune into your intuition to make it great."

-Kris

Once you have them all evenly chopped, prepare yourself a *bouquet garni* (bundle of herbs) using a small bunch of fresh parsley, two or three sprigs of thyme, and 2 bay leaves (or whatever fresh herbs you like), and tie them up together with a piece of heat-proof string. You may use a dried bay leaf, but the parsley and thyme should be fresh.

In a large stock pot, pour in some oil, until there is about half an inch of oil in the bottom of the pot. Turn the heat up to medium high, and wait for the oil to heat. You may be nervous about placing your hand over the heating fat, so here's an easy trick to check the temperature of the oil. Take a chopstick (or the thin end of your wooden spoon) and poke the bottom of the inside of the pot (almost like you're using a long thermometer to take the oil's temperature). Let it sit there for 10 seconds or so. If you see little bubbles forming around your stick, the oil is just the right heat.

When the oil reaches optimal heat, pour in the combination of vegetables. Stir to combine, so that every piece of vegetable gets coated in the hot fat. Sprinkle in some salt, and stir to combine once more. Drop down the heat to a low setting (not as low as it'll go), and put on the lid to the stock pot. For a new cook (and even some experienced ones), this may be a nerve-wracking moment for you, but remember that the vegetables are at a relatively low heat.

Wait for a minute, and listen to what you hear in the pot. Is it sizzling away? If so, the pot is too hot, and the temperature needs to be reduced. Drop down the temperature to a lower setting, and open up the lid to vent off the excess heat. Stir the vegetables around, and spread them out flat. Put the lid back on, and listen again. You should just barely hear noises coming out of the pot. It will sizzle, but only gently.

Once you've found the optimal temperature, leave the sweat to sit there in the low heat for about 10 to 15 minutes. Every five minutes or so, come back in and stir the vegetables around to redistribute the flavors. When you're done stirring, make sure to lay them flat in one layer again, like you did at the beginning, to promote even cooking.

After fifteen minutes of cooking, the vegetables will be soft and ready to take in anything you can give them. Pour in about one liter of stock, and let it come up to a full boil. At this point, put in your *bouquet garni* and the rest of the ingredients for your soup. You can use anything from vegetables (green, leafy vegetables are always good) or even beans or other legumes.

Some popular sweats, like the *sofrito*, the *mire poix*, and the ginger-garlic-onion mixture (as yet unnamed, but it'll have its day in the spotlight!) of India are so popular that they form the basis of a dizzying variety of dishes. Bear in mind that a sweat is not a sauté. It is a gentle form of cooking. Sautéing is delicious in a variety of foods, but it doesn't give the food enough time to leak out its flavors into the oil.

"Popping" Whole Spices

Throughout the book, you'll likely see me refer to getting oil very hot, then adding whole spices and waiting until they pop. What is meant by this is that the whole spice that's cooking in the fat should explode, releasing its essential oils into the surrounding fat. It's a very potent method of flavoring a savory dish, and I use it often. There are a few points to remember, and you will be popping away like mad in no time!

For one thing, don't expect this to be clean and neat. Even my deepest stock pots manage to get a few stray seeds out of the pot and onto my counter, my hair, my face (ouch) or the surrounding stove. Those spices are going to go out with a bang, and they'll let you (painfully) know it if you're not careful. For me, this is the most thrilling and exciting cooking method of all time. The end product is so delicious, and things move FAST, so preparation is a key component. I am completely serious on this one. It's fun, but you want to be safe, and you don't want to waste money on burned spices.

I've watched little old grannies transform into super heroes with lightning quick, deft, (if a bit wrinkled) hands. As a little boy, I perfected the technique of the "grenade method" of spicing. I watched my mother and aunts do it, and I do it myself. I myself have startled my mother's friends as they watched me transform, in the space of five minutes, a pot of humble, boiled lentils into a dark, smoky, soupy, hot, and oh-so-good pot of love.

Before you try this, make sure you have a clean kitchen, free of stray children, pets, or (in the cases of married folk) spouses. Have plenty of counter space ready. Make sure you've got on a full apron. Clear the room, and warn your friends. If you own a splatter screen (a piece of wire mesh with a metal ring around it that you can hold over things that tend to splatter) get it ready to go.

Before starting, have ready 1 teaspoon of cumin, 1 teaspoon of mustard seed, and a handful of curry leaves. Have a chopped onion sitting in a bowl in eager anticipation. Have your salt shaker next to the onion bowl, and have a teaspoon of turmeric at the ready. Next to the onions, also place some minced ginger (about 1 tablespoon's worth) and two cloves of garlic, minced up really finely. Behind the onion bowl, have two medium tomatoes chopped up into small, even pieces at the ready. Behind the bowl of tomatoes, have a pound of cooked lentils, soaking in about 2 cups of their cooking liquid while they wait to be added to the pot.

Here's how it works. In a large wok, get about 3 tablespoons of oil screaming hot. You want a little wisp of smoke to escape the surface. Once it's hot like that, stand slightly back, with a small amount of the spice you would like (in this case, the cumin and mustard seeds) in your hand. You wait for the smoke. You see it. Bingo. Time to blow this stand. You fling the spices dead center into the wok, and jump back. If you have the splatter screen, now would be the time to employ it.

The spices will begin to EXPLODE very shortly. Once you hear them popping like crazy, fling in the curry leaves, ripping them in half as you go. As soon as the curry leaves explode, immediately throw in the onion, the ginger and the garlic. Sprinkle about a teaspoon of salt and 1/2 teaspoon of turmeric. Stir around immediately to coat in the fat. Cook at the very high heat until the onions are softened but not browned. This should be about a minute or two.

Throw in the tomato, and stir around to coat in the fat. Let it cook at the high heat, making sure that you stir it frequently, for about one or two minutes. When the tomatoes have broken down a bit, pour in the pound of cooked lentils that you'd soaked, along with their liquid. The water will boil almost instantly. Stir around, and scrape down the wok (remember deglazing?) to release the brown bits from the bottom of the wok. When the water comes to a full rolling boil, drop the heat to a simmer, and let it sit that way until you're ready to serve it. You can eat it immediately, or later. I choose now, with rice.

And that, my friends, is popping spices.

Pasta Cooking

Pasta can be a fun and interesting way to add some zing to your consumption of grains each day. There are a dizzying variety of shapes, colors, and sizes in the pasta world, and I will leave it to your local store to show you those, as I don't have the time to go into all of them. I will, however, give you a baseline for cooking pasta, from which you can build your own dishes using different shapes and ingredients, based on what you can find. Even the most basic garlic, oil, and salt pasta is a treat.

First and foremost, you should make sure that you are cooking your pasta (regardless of the amount) in plenty of water. If you're making one pound at a time, use six quarts (or liters) of water. If you are making half of a pound (8 ounces, 250 grams), you should still use four quarts (or liters) of water. If you are making more than one pound, use a separate pot with its own four to six quarts. Why? There are a variety of reasons.

For one thing, the water is going to receive the starch from the pasta. When you have a high quantity of starch in a small amount of water, the water will thicken up and start forming bubbles. Those bubbles will then start stacking up on each other, and before you know it, you've got boil over and a disgusting burned smell when the starch burns on the hot stove. For another thing, those starches are responsible for sticky pasta. If you've ever had mushy rice with nothing on it, you'll know about how sticky starch can get. Using a large quantity of water gives the pasta enough space to move around and prevents sticking.

Another thing to remember is to liberally salt the water (salty like the sea). Why? This is the only chance you'll have of getting the pasta to take some salt in. Salt loves water dearly, and will cling to water as much as it can. When this clingy pair meets pasta, the three form a sordid love triangle of flavor. It's a beautiful thing. What happens when you don't salt your water? The starches on the surface of the pasta aren't as receptive and don't let the salt in. Also, in the absence of water, the salt is like a rejected lover; salt just lies there and doesn't do much of anything. Salt becomes the party pooper. Salt your water.

"Dino loves food, cooking, and people. He has the innate ability to take seemingly random ingredients and come up with a feast!"

-Mary Sue Sylwestrzak

If you're cooking pasta, and you're nervous about sticking, citrus can be your friend. Oil, in its slippery slickness, cheats you out of proper pasta because having oil on the surface of the pasta doesn't let it take to sauce very well. The sauce, much like the rejected salt, will sit there in a pool by itself, shunned by the smoother, slicker oil. Instead, when you add lemon, (about a tablespoon per four quarts) your pasta tumbles around in joy in the pot and marries rather well with the sauce when you're done.

The draining of pasta can be a tricky thing. You don't want it to be so well drained that it's dry, because then it'll stick together. You also don't want it too wet, because that will dilute the flavors in your sauce. Instead, you have to find a happy medium that lets the pasta be mellow, but not so mellow that it falls down. When you pour your pasta through a colander to strain it, just shake the colander once or twice, and pour it into a receptacle immediately. You'll have just enough water hanging around to keep the pasta chaste, and enough will evaporate off so the sauce can come in and do its work.

You can make sauces as you're waiting for the water to boil. This is actually the perfect time to do so, as your pasta, the main attraction, is a very big Diva. It will not be kept waiting. Sauce waits for pasta, but not the other way around. By the time you drain your pasta, you should be immediately ready for the sauce to meet the pasta on the serving dish. The moment that the pasta slides out of the colander and onto a serving dish is when it's most receptive to flavor. After a long bubble bath in the boiling water, it'll take anything that comes along. Make this anything be the flavor, and you won't be sorry!

Now comes the part about cooking time. I can't give you an exact time here, or you may end up over or under-cooking your pasta. The only way to tell if your pasta is done is to taste it. There are some pastas that take two or three minutes to cook, and others that take much longer. You have to test it. Pull out a noodle (with a slotted spoon, please), and bite into it. Throwing it onto random kitchen spots will just give you a messy kitchen, and you still won't know if it's cooked. You have to touch it and taste it. Give the noodle a little squeeze. Does it give at all? Does it feel hard in the center? Bite into it, and chew it around. Does it taste cooked? Can you see completely uncooked pasta in the center? Do you think it could do with more time? Are you going to be cooking it some more in some other dish? In the recipe below, I'm going to give you a VERY ROUGH cooking time. Do not use this as a hard and fast rule; know your food.

I've prattled on forever on this, so let me get to the program.

Boil the water over the highest heat that your stove has (you will not be turning down the heat again) in a large stock pot. You want it to be at a full, rolling boil. Sprinkle in salt by taking your salt shaker, and generously sprinkling in salt from one side of the pot to the other until you've sprinkled "all over" the pot's surface. This is the method I find simplest, which is why the salt isn't a measurement. The salt will dissolve almost instantly.

When the salt does dissolve, dip a clean spoon into the water, and take some out to taste it. If it tastes salty enough to you (should be as salty as sea water), you've salted it perfectly. If it's too salty, now would be the time to pour out some of the water, and replace it with fresh water. Remember: You can correct not salty enough, but not too salty.

Once the water is at the proper salt and boil, put a wooden spoon in the pot. Pour in your pasta in one quick motion, and immediately start stirring it around so that it doesn't make a giant clump in the bottom of your pot. Stir until the water comes to a full boil. Pour in your lemon juice.

Your pasta will begin looking larger and be more flexible as time goes on. Again, this is not a hard and fast rule, but wait about five minutes after the water has come to a full boil, and begin testing your pasta by removing one or two noodles from the pot with a slotted spoon.

When it's cooled down, bite into the noodle, and see if it seems done enough. Squeeze it between your thumb and forefinger to see if it gives enough. It probably won't be done yet, but you will now have a starting point. Ladle out some of the pasta water into a serving dish and swish it around. This warms up the plate. Dump out the water. Ladle on a second washing of this water to maintain that heat. Leave it there. Put a colander in the sink.

Test your pasta again. If it's not cooked to your liking (note: your liking, not mine or anyone else's), let it go for another minute and test again. Keep going like this, tasting and waiting for a minute or so, until your pasta is done to where you'd like it to be done. Dump out the pasta and the water into the colander, and shake once.

As soon as your pasta is shaken out, feel free to throw it in a bowl, and add your herbs, spices, sauces, oils, or anything else you like to eat on pasta. An important thing to remember is that you want to add the sauce while the pasta is still hot, to facilitate maximum absorption of the flavors. You may be tempted to toss on some oil before you add your sauce. Resist this temptation. All it's going to do is give the pasta a slippery surface to which sauce will not adhere. Just have your sauce ready when your pasta is done. You have plenty of time to prepare, especially since the water takes so long to come up to a boil.

Cooking Rice

If you're going to be making rice regularly, go out and get yourself a rice cooker. You can generally find one in a thrift store. If you can't find one used, a new one shouldn't run you more than $30 for a basic model.

Not convinced, eh? I tried. What I'm about to tell you breaks most major rules for cooking rice the traditional way, which is to start it off with a quantity of water and allow it to absorb into the rice. Unfortunately, that traditional method often leaves me with a burned pot, ruined rice, and hours of cleaning. It also manages to demolish my manicure every single time. Let's avoid the drama, shall we?

Start off with one cup of uncooked long grain brown or white rice. I personally prefer brown rice, because the grains take longer to cook and are far more forgiving than white rice, so you've got a fair bit of wiggle room when you're in the process of boiling it. Brown rice is also better for you, since it retains the high fiber and nutrients that rice is good for.

In a medium sized pot, pour in the cup of brown rice, and about five cups of cold water. Sprinkle in one teaspoon of salt. Put the pot on your stove, and turn on the heat to high. Let the water come to a full rolling boil. Drop down the heat to medium high. Let the water continue to boil. In about 30-45 minutes, the rice should be cooked. Test a grain and see if it's cooked to your liking. If it is cooked, the rice is finished boiling.

In a colander, drain the rice of the excess water. If you're going to put it in the fridge to use later, toss it with a little bit of oil, and put it away. If you're using it immediately, feel free to use it immediately. Either way, your rice is finally done!

If you're using white rice, the rice should take roughly twenty minutes to cook through. Test the rice at halfway in to the cooking, to make sure that you don't end up with mushy rice. If you do end up with mushy rice, don't fret—just throw it into a soup, and nobody will know any better.

Coincidentally, rice is also an excellent way to bulk up a soup that you've added too much salt to.

What to do with day old hard bread

A lady at the store who was standing in line behind me was complaining that the French bread she bought from there (because they don't add weird dough conditioners and preservatives) would always go hard in a day. She wondered aloud what to do about it if you don't need breadcrumbs. I grinned, because I'd used this trick to revive killed bread before.

Take the loaf of bread, and wrap it in a damp towel. Leave it in the fridge overnight. The next day, unwrap the towel, and preheat the oven to 350° F. Lightly mist the surface of the bread with some water. Put the bread in the oven for about five to ten minutes. The steam from the water will reconstitute the bread.

Substitutions & Explanations

I've heard a lot of "Dino I don't have _____, so can I try something else please," and I want to encourage that. It all flows into the Dino Philosophy of making recipes your own. Go right ahead and make the substitutions to make foods suit your kitchen and your budget. I'll also be including notes for certain ingredients throughout, so that you can use exactly what's indicated if you want. So here we go.

Chili powder: In this book, when I call for chili powder, I mean ground red cayenne chiles, not the darker red Mexican chili powder.

Curry leaves: No substitutes, unfortunately. Curry leaves have this earthy, smoky flavor that you cannot replicate with any other herb or spice combination of any sort. They grow in a tropical climate, which probably explains why I've got trees of the stuff growing in my yard. As much as I would love to send you a batch of my special leaves, I'd soon denude all my trees if I did that. You are, of course, more than welcome to come to my house, where my mother will feed you senseless with dishes smothered in the stuff. Barring that, you can find curry leaves at Asian groceries or online.

Cilantro: I've sometimes heard people describe cilantro as having a soapy taste to it. I have no idea what they're talking about, but in the interest of helping people, I'll see what I can come up with. Italian flat leaf parsley has a milder taste in comparison to its curly cousin. You should be able to get away with Italian parsley in most applications, although in Mexican foods, it won't taste quite as authentic. Does that mean you grin and bear a taste you don't like? Never! Have I taught you nothing? You make it the way you like it, and if people complain, they can get their food elsewhere.

Asafetida: (Also spelled asafoetida; it is a spice that comes from the sap of an herbaceous plant in the same family as carrots and fennel.) No substitute. Use good quality sesame oil to compensate for the flavor difference. Asafetida has been described as one of the most vile smelling things on the planet, and I would almost concur, but for the fact that I love it so much. It's an integral part of my childhood smell memories, and I can't imagine South Indian food without it. For those who have kids, I'll make an analogy to Pokémon. When Ash was in the perfume city, they used essence of Vileplume to make their more distinct scents. That little bit of nasty smell made the final product smell divine. Similarly, even though asafetida by itself is quite rank, you don't smell it in the final dish if you use it properly.

Sesame oil: Do not use toasted sesame oil in Indian dishes. The flavor would be overpowering to the spices, and the final dish will taste off to anyone who's eaten Indian food before. Use toasted only for things like Japanese, Chinese, Thai, and Vietnamese dishes. Besides that, toasted sesame oil can get pretty pricey. Save it for dishes where you can use it uncooked, and where its subtle undertones have a chance to play. Try it drizzled onto cucumber slices with a little lemon. For cooking, use regular (untoasted) sesame oil. If you can find it, get what's called "Gingelly" or "Til" oil at the local Indian store for an authentic Indian food flavor.

Oil: Use regular vegetable oil, unless specified. For frying, use peanut oil. For sautéing, a good corn oil is fine. Try avoiding olive oil for Asian dishes and sesame oil for Mediterranean dishes. Nothing tastes weirder than a long simmered tomato sauce with a sesame oil taste. If you can't afford to have a large variety of oils on hand, a clean and simple canola or corn oil is a good multipurpose oil for most dishes.

Spices: Use whole, unless powder is specified. If substituting a ground spice, use 1/2 the amount, and add with your aromatics (onions, peppers, garlic, etc.). The reason to avoid ground spices if you can help it is that as soon as you grind a spice, it begins to lose its potency and its more complex undertones. Someone who dislikes a particular spice blend most likely dislikes it because eating already ground spices is akin to carving Michelangelo's David with war hammer and a spatula—it can be done, but the results won't be the same because you would miss out on the subtle details. Freshly ground black pepper is not only hot, but it's also slightly smoky and a little bit earthy.

Similarly, freshly pounded coriander seeds have a mildly sweet smell to them. Cumin, when it is used whole (and popped in oil) has the same smokiness it is known for, but it also has a distinctly nutty smell too. There is no comparison between ground and whole cumin. With the exception of cinnamon, it's best to get whole spices, and grind them down yourself.

If you do use powders, make sure to have them in airtight containers. This means that you might have to change the container that the spice came in, but that's fine. The containers they sell spices in are there to attract your eye and make you want to buy them, but they are not suitable for storing the spices. Unless you're in need of fresh spices every week, get some airtight containers; it's worth the extra few cents.

Herbs: When using fresh, add at the end. When using dried, add with aromatics. The reason for this is because the different forms of herbs have different purposes. A dried herb needs to be added at the beginning, so that the flavors have time to leak into the rest of the dish. If they don't have enough time, they'll overpower the dish, and stand out too much. You want dried ingredients to cook down as much as you can.

Fresh herbs, on the other hand, are added at the end to round out whatever flavors you have already developed. They're a bright, vivid addition to a dish, and having little bursts of fresh herbs on your tongue gives the dish a little "something else" that you wouldn't quite find with dried. Nobody is going to convince me that the light minty taste that fresh basil contains is preserved in the dried version. This doesn't mean that one is better than the other, but more that each has its own purpose.

Olive Oil: When cooking, go for regular olive oil. When using in dressings, dips, or uncooked, use extra virgin. Don't use light olive oil, as it's basically a marketing ploy to palm off cheap oil that's got no flavor. The method for getting good quality olive oil is called "cold pressing," and it involves some fairly expensive machines to slowly press out the oil from the olives. Good extra virgin olive oil is obtained from the "first pressing" and is not refined.

Extra virgin olive oil has a floral, green aroma, and the taste is light and delicate. It is sensitive to heat and light, which is why it may be sold in dark-colored bottles. White truffle oil is olive oil that's been steeped with truffles. Truffles are very expensive, so it's often cheaper for the home cook to snag a $20 bottle of truffle oil than shell out $50 an ounce for truffles.

Chilies: Use Thai bird chilies. They're hot and have multiple levels of heat inside the chili itself. If you can't get them, use Jalapeño or Serrano. Experiment with different types to see what you like. If you need something milder, go for a banana pepper. If you want something hotter, increase the amount of Thai bird chilies.

DO NOT use Scotch Bonnet or Habanero chilies in Indian food. Save them for the more Latin American inspired dishes. The comment that chilies have flavor always greatly amused my less heat-inclined friends, but they do have flavor. They each have unique characteristics that blend with your foods in different ways.

If you want a milder chili experience, pop on a pair of those food service gloves before you get started. If you're in need of milder chilies, chances are that your skin is sensitive to them too. Let's not risk it. Cut the chili in half lengthwise. With the tip of your knife's blade, scrape away the seeds and the inside membranes of the chili. If you're afraid of demolishing a chili, you can practice the technique on a bell pepper. Its seeds come in a neat package, and its membranes are large and easy to see.

If you dislike hot food in general, or your stomach is sensitive, try using a very small amount of black pepper, and work your way up as your tolerance increases.

Potatoes: Sweet potatoes work just fine in place of white potatoes in any of these recipes.

Pickles: An Indian pickle is nothing like its similarly named western counterpart. It's a something that's been preserved in spices, salt, and oil, not vinegar. They generally involve large amounts of salt and chilies, although milder pickles are quite common. Use them VERY sparingly, as they are meant to be enhancements to flavor, not an actual dish. Never use more than 1 teaspoon on your plate to accompany your meal. I have included two pickle recipes (Indian pickles p. 90 and mango relish p. 91) in this very book, so feel free to experiment.

One Pot Meals

The following dishes are what I would consider to be meals all by themselves. They're not the traditional "American" meal per se, but usually after just one bowl you're full. These are also amongst the easiest to customize. If you're a beginning cook, make sure to read through the section on cooking techniques. Once you've finished that, you're ready to try customizing these recipes on your own.

There's more than enough "wiggle room" in these dishes than you would have in a dish that requires stacks of ingredients. What do you need to complete the one pot meal? Usually, just some rice will complement these dishes well. Many of the recipes in this section make big portions, and I often pack the leftovers for my lunch when I'm headed out to work and the like.

Because they're so customizable, these are the dishes that I'd like you to try first. Try the variations, or even make up your own and give those a shot. These are the ones that are so easy to make all yours that your friends will get used to your version of things, and wouldn't ever suspect that you could have creatively borrowed the recipe from someone else!

That One Soup Dino Makes...

Total time: 1½ hours

I sometimes get a request for "That one soup like how Dino makes." Aside from being grammatically cringe-worthy, it's also highly useless when trying to describe what the soup is, what goes in there, or much of anything else. All I know is that it's good.

This is a sort of default soup for when you don't really know what you're in the mood to eat, or are going to feed a person used to eating dairy or meat — the creamy texture and the smoky flavors help this to happen. The vegetables in here are fairly neutral, and don't really bring in too much flavor. This is essentially what I like to call a "mother soup" (much like the Mother Sauces found in European cuisine), because you're supposed to add stuff to it. It tastes lovely all by itself, but it leaves something to be desired in terms of variety.

Make this soup your own by adding your favorite blends of frozen vegetables (i.e., you're not doing any of the work, and just have to reheat it from the freezer and dump it in), favorite quick-cooking green (spinach, arugula) or your favorite canned vegetables or beans. The base flavors take a while to lie down, so you can play fast and loose with the other ingredients.

Or, take it totally gourmet, and add roasted butternut squash, roasted red peppers, caramelized onions, garden fresh herbs, sun dried tomatoes, olives, marinated artichoke hearts, whatever you can think of. How about some morel, shiitake, oyster, crimini, and cloud ear mushrooms? Add some black beans, avocado, huitlacoche, and fresh tomato for a Tex-Mex like thing. Basically, you can make the final product as fancy or plain as you'd like. This is a concentrated soup, meant to be ready for storage. A lot of the water has boiled off, and the final product will seem like it's fatty. That's normal.

» 2 Tablespoons oil
» ½ Tablespoon (either yellow or black) mustard seeds
» 1 Tablespoon cumin seeds
» 1 Tablespoon coriander seeds, lightly crushed
» 1 large onion, chopped fine
» 2 teaspoons turmeric
» 1 Tablespoon salt
» 2 bay leaves

» 1 lb carrots, scrubbed and chopped
» 6 roughly chopped potatoes
» 5 small summer squash, chopped
» small bunch watercress
» small bunch Italian parsley
» Up to 6 cups water
» 2 cans coconut milk
» Any other ingredients you're adding (pre-cooked)

This soup starts off in layers, and builds up step by step. Start by chopping up your onion finely. When it's chopped, heat up the oil in a large stock pot on high heat. When the oil is hot, pour in the mustard seeds. When they pop and crackle, add the cumin. When you can smell a strong cumin smell in the air, and the cumin is popping, add the crushed coriander seeds. Wait about 10 seconds, and add the onions. Stir around immediately to coat in the oil. Sprinkle in the salt and turmeric, and add both bay leaves. Stir around until the onions are all yellow.

Drop down the heat to medium low and put on the lid. You want it to cook for about 15 minutes, covered, to slowly sweat. Every five minutes, come back and stir the onions around to redistribute the spices. While the onions are sweating, chop up the carrots. If you have time, start in on the potatoes as well. Check the onions at the end of the 15 minutes.

If they're completely softened, increase the heat to high. Stir around the onions until evenly coated in the oil. Add the potatoes and carrots. If you still have more potatoes to chop, don't worry about it—we can add those as soon as they're chopped. Stir around the vegetables to coat evenly in the oil and the spices. Drop down the heat to low, and cover. Finish chopping your potatoes (and add them to the pot as you complete them). Let the potatoes cook in the pot dry for about 15 - 20 minutes.

While the potatoes are cooking, chop up the watercress, parsley, and squash. At the end of 15 minutes, open up the lid of the pot, and pour in just enough water to barely cover the vegetables. Allow the water to come to a full boil. Turn down the heat to a simmer, and allow the soup to simmer, covered, an additional 5 minutes. You may stop the soup at this point, and freeze it. Then, later on, when ready to serve, you would reheat the soup to come back to a simmer.

Open the lid, and layer on the squash, watercress, parsley, and coconut milk (in that order) AND DO NOT STIR. Just let it sit like that in layers, and cover the lid. Let it sit for 10 minutes, at a low simmer, covered. At the end of the 10 minutes, the soup will be ready for any other additional vegetables you'll be adding to dress this up. After the addition of any such ingredient, make sure to let the soup come together in a medium boil for about 5 minutes before serving.

Serve with a side of beans, and a green salad. Have plenty of croutons ready to grab.

Uppuma

Total time: 30 minutes

Uppuma is a south Indian dish that uses a wheat product called sooji (in Hindi). In the US, most people wouldn't know what you're talking about, so I've found that Farina (cream of wheat) works perfectly well. This recipe isn't as tricky as it seems, because you develop a knack for it once you've made it a couple of times. Figure on the texture of the stuff in the pot being a little bit wetter than a couscous. You don't want it to be too wet like a porridge. You want it to finish on the dry side. If you cannot pour with one hand, and stir with another hand, ask for help!

- » **2 cups sooji or farina**
- » **2 Tablespoons oil**
- » **1 teaspoon mustard seeds**
- » **1 teaspoon cumin seeds**
- » **⅛ teaspoon asafetida (optional)**
- » **1 handful curry leaves (optional)**
- » **salt to taste**
- » **¼ teaspoon turmeric**
- » **1 large onion, diced**
- » **Fresh chopped chiles to taste**
- » **¼ cup diced carrots**
- » **¼ cup corn**
- » **¼ cup peas**
- » **1 ½ cups water**
- » **1 cup water, reserved**

What is Cumin?

Cumin is a brown seed that grows well in tropical climates. Its smoky, pungent aroma adds a distinct flavor that cannot be replicated by any other spice.

It is popular in Latin American and Asian cuisines. It is especially common in Indian cuisine, where it can be found in everything from the fiery curries of the North to the quiet soups of the South.

In a skillet, pour in the sooji, and roast over a gentle flame. You want the stove at medium low to medium, so that you don't burn the sooji. Roasting enhances the flavor, and lends an extra dimension to the dish. It's also the only way I know how to make the stuff, because that's how my mother taught me, and I'm not comfortable with trying to use unroasted sooji.

Make sure you constantly stir the sooji to avoid burning, and drop down the flame if you notice any smoke coming up from the pan. This should take anywhere from 10 - 15 minutes. When the sooji smells lightly nutty and looks tan, remove it from the heat, and pour it into a bowl to cool. Rinse out your pan, and place it over high heat.

When the water evaporates, pour in the oil, and wait for it to heat. Add the mustard seeds. In about 30 seconds, they should be exploding. Add the cumin seeds. They should be popping before long.

Add the asafetida, and wait 5 seconds for it to sizzle. Add the curry leaves and step back, because they will explode! Immediately add the onions and chiles. Generously sprinkle in salt and add the turmeric powder.

Stir the onions and chiles around the pan to combine with the oil and the turmeric. When all the pieces are yellow, you've combined enough. Let the onions soften, but do not brown them. When the onions are soft, add the carrots and corn. Stir to combine all the ingredients. When the carrots are soft, add the peas. Stir everything to evenly coat all the vegetables with the oil and spices.

Pour in the 1 1/2 cups water. The water should come up to a full boil very quickly. Start stirring everything together, and make sure to scrape the bottom of the pan to release any particles stuck onto the bottom of the pan.

This would be the time to ask for help if you can't stir and pour simultaneously. While constantly stirring the ingredients in the liquid in the pan, pour the roasted sooji into the pan in a steady stream. Everything should start coming together very quickly. If it looks too dry, add a little bit more water, until it's at the consistency of a very thick porridge. Keep stirring, until the excess water evaporates, and you're left with a dry final product.

This is a stand-alone meal, because it has everything you'll need in one bowl!

Basic Kale Soup

Total time: 1 hour

This is a soup of kale and spices, and on its own, it is a bit simple. Be sure to use one of the variations following the recipe for the best possible results. Try one or two different variations and experiment a bit!

» 1 Tablespoon oil
» 1 teaspoon cumin seeds
» 1 large onion, minced fine
» 1 clove of garlic, minced
» 1 teaspoon black pepper, ground

» 1 bunch kale, chopped. (Chop the stem pieces finely, and treat as leaves)
» Salt to taste
» 1 quart (4 cups) of water
» 1 bunch parsley, minced (about 1 cup)

Add the oil to the bottom of a heavy bottomed, large pot. Turn on the stove to high heat. When the oil is hot, add your cumin seeds. In about a minute or so, if you made sure to get the oil good and hot, you'll have the cumin seeds popping and cracking. At this moment, add your onions. Sprinkle in some salt. Stir around to evenly coat in the oil. Cook for about 5 minutes, until soft.

Add garlic and pepper. Add the chopped kale. Stir around in the onion mixture, so that the pieces of kale are evenly coated in the oil. You may have to add the kale in batches if your pot isn't that large. Add one batch, stir it around, and wait for it to wilt down. When there's more room, add subsequent batches, and continue to stir around and wilt the kale. Sprinkle on salt. Toss through over the heat for about five minutes. Add the water. Bring up to a full boil, and then drop down to a simmer. Allow to cook for about 20 minutes. When cooked, sprinkle in parsley, and let sit about five minutes.

Variations

» *1 lb diced, cooked potato, stirred in at the end*
» *8 ounces mushrooms, sliced, added in 10 minutes before removing from heat*
» *1 head of cabbage, sliced, added in 10 minutes before finishing*
» *1 lb zucchini, cut in half, and cut into half moons, added in roughly 5 minutes before removing from heat*
» *A teaspoon or so of chili oil, added in right at the end of cooking*
» *In each bowl of soup, 1 Tablespoon of kimchee*
» *Add 1 lb of cooked garbanzo beans in the last 10 minutes of cooking*
» *Add 1 lb of cooked kidney beans in the last 5 minutes of cooking*
» *Combine all the variations to make a very filling soup*

Butternut Squash

Total time: 30 minutes

This stuff is not only mindlessly easy to make, but pulses up to make a creamy, rich, decadent soup. I'm including multiple variations, because I love the stuff, and I'd like to get people to at least try it. Because it stands alone (for the most part) you can use this soup as an appetizer before starting the rest of your meal.

» **1 butternut squash**
» **2 cups vegetable stock**
» **Sage**
» **Rosemary**
» **Thyme**

The easiest way to peel squash for soup is to microwave it. Roughly cut the squash into eight large chunks and put it in a microwave safe bowl with 1/4 cup of water. Cover loosely with a plastic lid. Nuke it until the squash is tender (it takes about 15 minutes in my microwave). Now, you should be able to easily scoop out the seeds and flesh with a spoon. Scoop out and discard the seeds, then scoop out the flesh of the squash, and simmer over medium-low heat with the finely chopped herbs for about 10 minutes. Remove from the heat, and blend until smooth.

Variations

» *For a smoother texture, strain through a sieve before serving it piping hot with a side of croutons.*
» *For those who like some heat in their food (such as myself) add in a red chili or two before simmering, and grind it along with the squash (I find Tabasco sauce to have an offensive flavor with butternut squash).*
» *If you want your soup thicker, stir in a little bit of hummus.*
» *If you like it a little sweeter, add some carrots to the microwave with your squash.*
» *If you want extra protein in it, add ¼ lb of cooked red lentils to the blender along with the squash.*
» *To make it a dressing, take ½ cup of the soup, ¼ cup olive oil, and ¼ cup of balsamic vinegar, and whisk vigorously. Then, stir in some fresh dill, parsley, and basil for a really nice zip.*

QUICK Garbanzo Soup

Total time: 20 minutes

Just about every weekend, I make a giant lot of beans, and I often end up using some of them for this soup. Since we're looking for speed here, you should use canned beans. The key to this recipe is finding the balance of tomato to garbanzo. You can use larger or smaller cans as you wish, but make sure to adjust the flavorings.

- » **1 teaspoon canola, peanut, or safflower oil**
- » **¼ teaspoon cumin seeds**
- » **½ teaspoon sesame seeds**
- » **Curry leaves (if available)**
- » **1 medium onion, chopped**
- » **¼ teaspoon turmeric**

- » **Salt**
- » **1 lb canned chopped tomato, drained**
- » **1 lb canned garbanzo beans, drained**
- » **1 ½ cups water (this is a thickish soup)**
- » **Fresh chilies, chopped (to taste)**

Heat oil over high heat in a wide, shallow pan. Sprinkle in cumin. When you hear the cumin popping (about 30 seconds, if the oil is hot), add in sesame seeds. When the sesame seeds brown, toss in the curry leaves (if available) and the diced onion. Drop down the heat to medium high, and sprinkle in turmeric, and a little bit of salt. Sauté onions until soft (about a minute). Bring back the heat to high, and add in the can of tomatoes. Stir around vigorously for about 3 - 5 minutes (you'll see the tomatoes breaking down a little — this is a good thing). Add the garbanzo beans. When the beans are coated with the tomatoes, add the water. Add the chopped up chilies. When water comes up to a boil, you're done!

Serve over brown rice, or with your favorite short pasta, or Asian-style noodles.

Variations

- » *For a creamier texture: Strain out some of the beans from the soup at the end, and blend them in a blender with a little bit of the soup water.*
- » *Grind all of the soup: Add a Tablespoon of tahini at the end, and stir through.*
- » *For heartier soup: Add a pound of frozen vegetables along with the garbanzos.*
- » *After the onions soften, add two Tablespoons of tomato paste, and cook for a minute or two. If you notice a tinny flavor in the tomatoes from the can, add ½ capful of vanilla extract when you add in the tomatoes. This goes for paste, puree, or pieces of tomato from a can.*

Green Leafy Soup

Total time: 1 ½ hours

This freezes beautifully, so I'm giving large proportions. A lot of people like to remove the stalks from the greens, and you may do so if you want, but it's best to cut up the leaves with the stalks on. Just cut the rougher portions really finely so that everything will get cooked at the same time. Your local grocery store will most likely have pre-mixed, pre-washed, pre-cut greens that come in a bag. These are perfectly acceptable, as long as they still look fresh and green.

» 1 lb kale
» 1 lb collard greens
» 1 lb mustard greens
» 2 Tablespoons olive oil
» 1 large white onion, diced fine
» 1 large red onion, diced fine
» 1 head garlic, minced finely

» 1 teaspoon salt
» 1 Tablespoon red pepper flakes
» 1 teaspoon ground black pepper
» 1 ½ cups water
» 1 ½ cup stock
» 2 cans coconut milk
» Salt to taste

Chop up your greens to bite-sized pieces. Take the stems, and chop them finely, and treat them like you would the leaves. Heat the olive oil in the stock pot. When the oil gets hot, add the onions and the garlic, and sauté until softened. Add the chopped greens and sprinkle with salt (to leach the water out). Stir the greens around in the aromatics to get them coated (roughly ten minutes). You will likely have to add the greens in waves, let them cook down a bit to make some more space, and add the next batch. Add in the chili flakes and black pepper, and stir around an additional five minutes. Pour in the water and stock, and cover with the lid.

When the soup comes to a full boil, drop it down to a simmer, and let the greens cook for about an hour. About ten minutes before removing from the heat, stir in two cans of coconut milk. If the soup looks too thick to you, or too creamy, add some water until it gets to the desired thickness. This is when you want to taste the soup. If it's not salty enough, not hot enough, or needs something more, this is where you'd do that. In between additions of chili flakes, you're going to have to let them cook for a few minutes to get integrated in the soup.

Serve hot, by itself, or over brown rice. Offer wedges of lime to each diner when serving.

If you would prefer other vegetables in this soup, you can add potatoes, pumpkin, green beans, carrots, cabbage, spinach, parsnips, winter melon, or artichoke hearts without disturbing what's already there. Believe me, that amount of green leafy vegetables can take it. You may scale this down if you cannot acquire that many greens, or if you prefer to make a smaller quantity.

Venn Pongal

Total time: 1 hour

During the month of Thai (which usually hits in early January) in Tamil Nadu, the women dress themselves up in bright yellow saris with red borders, get the house sparkling clean, and begin cooking up savory pots of rice stew, called pongal. (There is also a "chakkarai," or sweet pongal, but I don't care for it, and the recipe here is for the savory version.) These three days, the harvest festival of Pongal is celebrated. (Incidentally, this is how you can tell whether I'm talking about the dish or the celebration—the celebration is capitalized.)

To symbolize the harvest, the family finds all their old, worn out clothing, and creates a large bonfire to burn the clothes. The father gives his family and servants new clothes, money, and other gifts. This also marks the time for old, unclean thoughts to be scrubbed out of the mind, and for new, spiritual thoughts to enter. It's a time of mental and physical renewal, and is celebrated with equal exuberance across the caste and religious lines.

In the north, it's known as kichdi, but as we all know, nobody north of Chennai knows the first thing about pongal! They add weird things in there, like cloves or cardamom. Ew. Take it from someone who is from the Indian south: you cannot find a decent pongal unless it's made properly. The main flavor components of a good pongal are the cumin, the black pepper, and the ginger. The curry leaves and asafetida help, but the stars here are the three I just described.

If a south Indian can afford nuts, she will use them. This means that if cashews are a little out of your price range, leave them out. They're not integral, but they certainly add a very nice contrast to the mushy consistency of the rice. That's the other main thing to remember about pongal: it needs to be very mushy. If you have to chew it too long (aside from the cashews, of course), you haven't cooked it long enough. This is the type of thing given to young children (without the nuts) and older people. That being said, people of all ages enjoy pongal.

My mother, being the kitchen innovator that she is, would always make the stuff in a rice cooker, because it's easier to just dump everything in and forget about it. To be honest, I do the same thing. When you don't want to be bothered with keeping track of ... stuff, just dump everything in a pot, and pretend it doesn't exist until everything is cooked.

The reason I use two separate pots (one large, one small) for the rice/daal and the spices is mainly because of my mother's trick with working everything in a rice cooker. You could technically do the spices in oil, add the rice and daal to the spices, then add the water. I don't know if it would taste the same, though. Either way, I like pongal quite a lot.

- » 1 cup white or brown long grain (not basmati) rice*
- » ½ cup moong daal (or yellow split peas)
- » 1 teaspoon turmeric powder
- » 1 Tablespoon ground black pepper
- » 6 cups water
- » ⅛ teaspoon asafetida
- » 1 Tablespoon grated ginger
- » 2 Tablespoons oil
- » 1 teaspoon cumin seed
- » 1 teaspoon mustard seeds
- » 1 cup curry leaves
- » ¼ cup of cashews
- » Salt, to taste

* And for heaven's sake, please don't use basmati. This requires a good sturdy rice that can stand up to the hard boiling you're going to give it.

Boil the rice, daal, turmeric powder, and ground black pepper in the water until the rice and daal both reach the consistency of a thick oatmeal. Don't be fooled into thinking it's done if the rice just pretends to be mushy enough. This stuff needs to be MUSHY. On my stove, this took around forty minutes at a medium simmer.

If you're nervous about the daal getting cooked, feel free to cook the daal in the water until it's soft first. Then add the rice, turmeric, and black pepper along with extra water (to replace what's evaporated), then cook it down until the rice is mushy. This will take slightly longer, because you're waiting for two things to cook completely, but it does more or less guarantee that the daal will be soft enough. Add a little less salt than you think you need to your liking after the rice and daal are cooked through. I know that the rice smells good already — that's the point! It's supposed to be tempting you far before it's anywhere near complete.

When the rice and daal are cooked, start preparing the seasoning. It takes just under two minutes, so you can't have it prepared ahead of time. In a small saucepan, heat up the oil until a small wisp of smoke comes out of the top. Add the mustard seeds, and wait for them to pop and explode (roughly 30 seconds). When the popping has subsided a bit, add the cumin seeds and asafetida. Wait for the cumin seeds to pop (about another 30 seconds). The seeds will turn a darker brown. At this point, add the curry leaves, and let them explode. Immediately after the curry leaves explode, add the cashews and ginger. Stir the cashews around, and continue to stir them until the nuts become lightly toasted.

Pour in about a cup of the rice and daal mixture from the other pot, and stir it around. Wash out the spice pot with some water, and pour the spiced water into the rice pot.

Stir the rice, daal and spices around in the pot until they're fully combined. Allow the spices and rice and daal to cook in the pot over medium heat for another fifteen to thirty minutes for everything to get combined.

Taste for salt and heat. If it's too bland, add some extra ground black pepper, or some extra grated ginger. Definitely make sure there's enough salt, because you want everything incorporated when it's hot.

Erissey (Avial, Kootu)

Total time: 1 ½ hours

Thousands of years ago in Kerala there was a great asura (demon) king named Mahabali. Although he was from the race of demons, he was a just and kind king. So kind was he, that any person who stood before him to make a request immediately got what he wanted. His people were happy, and Mahabali loved them with all of his heart.

One day, the god Vishnu, in the guise of a small beggar came to Mahabali, and asked for a request. Being the loving king that he was, Mahabali wanted to know what that request was. Vishnu said, "I want enough land to put three [of my] feet on." Mahabali laughed, and immediately told the little beggar that the request would be happily granted.

Suddenly, Vishnu began to grow, and grow, and grow. He grew to his full, massive size. With one foot, he covered all of the Earth. With another foot, he covered all of the skies. Vishnu then looked down at Mahabali, and said, "I still need one more foots' space." Mahabali offered his head as the third foots' space.

Vishnu was touched by how humble the good king was, and revealed his identity as a God. He granted Mahabali anything that his heart desired. Mahabali loved his people so much that he only asked that he be allowed to return to visit them once a year. For ten days around August or September (Indians use a Lunar calendar), the festival of Onam is celebrated.

Keralites the world over celebrate this harvest festival with plantain chips, stewed vegetables, and a LOT of coconut. This particular dish showcases the love that the region of Kerala (in the south of India) has for its coconuts. The women and men use the oil on their hair and skin. The food is bursting with coconut. Everything from sweet to salty has lots of the delicate snowflakes of coconut in it. It must work, because Malayali women don't have grey hair until very old age, and both men and women don't get wrinkles until they reach their twilight years.

This particular dish should be served piping hot, over rice. Make sure to have enough of it for second and third helpings, because it will go rather quickly.

- » 1 pound black-eyed peas (soaked overnight)
- » 1 Tablespoon oil
- » 1 Tablespoon mustard seeds
- » 1 cup curry leaves (omit if you don't have)
- » 3 quarts water
- » 1 teaspoon turmeric powder
- » 1 pound yellow squash
- » ½ cup grated coconut
- » 1 Tablespoon cumin seeds
- » 3 dried chilies
- » 3 quarts water, reserved
- » Salt, to taste
- » Black pepper, to taste

In a heavy bottomed stockpot, heat the oil over high heat until a small wisp of smoke escapes the surface. Add the mustard seeds, and wait for about 30 seconds for the seeds to pop and explode. Add the curry leaves. Immediately add the black-eyed peas, and about three quarts of the water. Reserve the other three quarts to add in case you need more later. Add the turmeric powder, and stir the beans and spices to combine. You will boil these covered for about 45 minutes to an hour.

While the water comes up to a boil, slice the squash in half, vertically. Slice the halves in half again, vertically. You should be left with four squash sticks. Cut the sticks (horizontally this time) into quarter-inch sized pieces. Set them aside.

In a skillet, combine the grated coconut, the cumin, and the dried chilies. Gently toast them over a medium flame until you smell the aroma of the cumin seeds intertwined with the lightly browned roasted coconut. The coconut will become just a light woodsy brown. That's the perfect color.

Once the spices and coconuts are roasted to perfection, pour them all into the jar of a blender, along with about three cups of water. At this point, the water in the pot that's cooking the beans should have reduced considerably.

By now, the roasted coconut and roasted spices should have had enough time to release some of their flavors into the water in the blender. Add a generous dose of salt (you can adjust later, as needed). Grind the water and coconut and spices on high speed, until everything is ground down. You'll never get it down to a paste, but you can get the coconut finely ground. This will also work if you cheated, and didn't manage to get the coconut finely ground the first time around.

About forty minutes into the bean boiling, check one of the beans, and see if it's getting cooked. If it's almost there, you're ready to add the squash. If it's still not quite there, get a glass of water, and relax until the beans are cooked through, because you're most likely sweating a little bit by now.

After 45 minutes to an hour (depending on your stove), the beans should be mostly cooked through. Add the squash, and boil for another ten minutes. Add the coconut spice paste, and drop down the heat to a simmer. Stir everything around to combine all the ingredients, and simmer for another ten minutes.

Test the Erissey for salt. If there isn't enough, add enough to suit you, taking care not to over salt the food. Add ground black pepper to taste. Serve the Erissey over hot white or brown rice. It's perfect as a meal in one pot. Always have plenty of fiery hot pickles on the side, as some diners may want things hotter than the few scant chilies we've added to this dish. Have plenty of icy cold water and cold cucumber (shredded, tossed in lemon) at the ready for those whose tongues need more bland flavors.

Chipotle Garlic Risotto

Total time: 45 minutes

Risotto is a dish that should have been vegan to begin with. The texture of the rice and the flavor of your stock should be more than ample to get your tastebuds dancing, and your tongue begging for more. Adding nonvegan ingredients to risotto just dilutes out those experiences and overpowers the delicate little rice grains. Use this recipe, but suit it to your own tastes. If you don't like hot food, then use roasted red peppers instead of chipotle peppers.

The chipotle is actually just a jalapeño pepper that's been smoked and dried. Chipotles in adobo are the chipotle chilies sitting in a spicy sauce. It's a unique flavor, and I would recommend it to anyone who hasn't ventured into Mexican cuisine very often.

The sort of "Rolls Royce" of risotto (to quote Mario Batalli) is arborio rice. It's a short grain Italian rice that works beautifully with a good vegetable stock and crisp white wine. I suggest using a Pinot Grigio, because an Italian wine will marry well with the arborio, and won't overpower anything. You do have a lot of discretion, however. Don't use a sweet white wine, like Gerwurstraminer, because it'll just taste weird at the end. If you don't like having alcohol in the house, just use stock. It'll still be fine.

Why Arborio?

For most rice dishes, a nice long grain rice should do just fine. In certain rice dishes, like risotto, you're looking for a particular texture and starch content. Arborio rice is a short-grain rice with a lot of starch. These starches are liberated from the surface of the rice when the rice is stirred. The grains rub against each other and release their starches into the surrounding liquid. It wouldn't quite work with regular long grain rice.

Stirring is what develops the starches in the risotto, so don't skimp on it! If your arms are prone to getting tired, you can cheat, and invite all your friends for a "risotto party" and say that everyone gets a "turn" at stirring the risotto. Then you can pretend to be this wicked creative host, and have out a bunch of different ingredients out, so that people can customize their own individual bowls of risotto. Have many rolls of crusty bread, oil with some fresh herbs and sea salt (I like a mix of basil and oregano), and a couple of bottles of the wine that you'll be making your risotto with. You'll have them talking about the party for years!

If you want to, you can serve little accompaniments, like roasted vegetables, fresh tomatoes, sliced red onions, or any other side dish you deem to be a contrast to the rich creamy risotto. I like to give my guests a choice in their risotto toppings. Try having sautéed mushrooms, interesting olives (without pits), cherry tomatoes tossed in lemon juice, field greens salad, and different kinds of nuts. People will have fun building their own individual risottos.

The addition of chipotle and cumin to risotto is my little nod to that fusion cuisine thing everyone is so excited about. You can leave them out if you want to, but you'd be missing out.

- » 2 Tablespoons olive oil
- » 2 cups arborio rice
- » 1 clove garlic, minced
- » 1 scant teaspoon cumin
- » 1 quart vegetable stock (low sodium), simmering
- » 1 quart Pinot Grigio, at room temperature, poured into a bowl and reserved
- » 1 quart water, simmering and reserved
- » 1 chipotle in adobo, minced fine
- » Salt to taste

Start with a wide skillet. A paella pan works for this just fine. In the bottom of the skillet, pour in your olive oil. Heat up the olive oil over medium high heat. When it gets hot, pour in your rice and garlic. Stir everything very well with a wooden spoon to combine it with the oil and spices.

Continue to stir the rice around until you see it getting a little puffed looking and it smells nutty. It might get a little bit browner in color, which is a good thing. Add your cumin powder, and stir everything around to get it all combined. Pour in 2 cups of stock, and one cup of wine. You can eyeball it, because this isn't baking. A standard ladle is usually about a cup. Don't bother trying to avoid cross contamination with the wine—you'll most likely end up using all the liquid and more.

Stir the rice around vigorously, to get everything combined. As the rice begins to absorb the water, continue alternating between the wine and the stock. You'll notice a sort of gravy forming around the rice, which is what we're looking for. Continue to stir the rice around with your wooden spoon.

It will continue to absorb the water, and the gravy will get thicker and thicker. This is also a good thing. After about the third addition of wine or stock (by this point, I've had a few glasses from the other bottles of wine, so it's rough to keep track), taste one of the grains of rice. If it's still not done, just keep alternating your stock and wine.

This is where the water comes in. Some people's stoves treat rice differently, and I find it best to have reserved water in dishes like this. Nothing is worse than ruining a whole pot of risotto at the eleventh hour. You may not need it, but having it will save angry phone calls to me. If you run out of the stock and wine, use water until the rice is cooked to your liking.

When the risotto is done, let it sit (if you can resist, that is) for about five minutes. Taste it for salt. If it's not salty enough, you can add more salt on top, and stir it through. Because the stock should have had enough salt in it, I doubt that you'll need to. I, being a salt fiend, however, tend to have salt sitting on the table in any case.

When you're ready to serve it, arrange a neat little pile of the chipotle chiles on top of the rice, and serve. This goes great with a fresh green salad, dressed with lemon juice and a lot of garlicky croutons. Serve it with a bottle of white wine to give the meal a nice rounded feeling.

Lentils and Chickpeas

Total time: 1 hour

In July 2006, I went to Ithaca, New York to hang out with a large group of my vegan friends. We went to Buttermilk State Park and were having a potluck. Since most of us would be traveling in from various corners of North America, we were expecting mostly simple food without too many frills. I decided to knock everyone's socks off, and serve them something that they would remember me by.

Before heading to Ithaca, I was staying at my friend Rich Bebenroth's house in New York, where I invaded his kitchen. In addition to making a vat of soup the night before, I whipped up some puri and roti, along with this dish to take to Ithaca. The lentils were the only thing to survive. It was a series of accidents!

Originally, I was supposed to be making a daal-like thing with the chickpeas. Unfortunately, the can of chickpeas was far outstripped by the tomatoes. In a panic, I flew around Rich's small New York kitchen, and searched for something, ANYTHING to get me out of this bind. In went the rest of the lentils he had. Then, by the time the lentils were cooked, it was missing something, so in went the cashews and lemon juice. Rich had a whole bunch of thyme, so that went in as well.

By the time we got the food to upstate New York, I was horrified that it would be a giant flop at the potluck. At the potluck, I was chatting away with my friends. They wanted to know what to do with the "lentils thing," so I advised that they just use it like a dip for tortilla chips. I laid back on the cool grass, and continued chattering on. I got up to take a look in the cooler to see if I could snag a bit of my mishmash of beans.

Oops! It was finished in the space of 15 minutes.

People were eating it straight up, over hummus, with tortilla chips, and pretty much every other manner you could imagine a thick salsa-like chickpea and bean dish to be eaten. After testing this recipe, my team of tried-and-true testers and I found that there's a LOT of wiggle room with the beans, the tomatoes, and water. The other neat thing is that this is one of those "wing it" dishes. If you don't have vodka, use red wine, or leave it out all together.

If you do somehow end up with leftovers, it will definitely taste better the next day. Use it between two slices of bread as a sandwich. Try it thinned out a bit with some water, and served with rice. Try it tossed with pasta. Take it straight up, and watch your coworkers drool as the lovely smells fill the room as you heat up your lunch in the microwave. Or, freeze the leftovers! They keep rather well.

If you're out of cilantro, use basil. If you can't for the life of you find where you put those bay leaves, it'll be fine without. The spices and nuts are the key to this dish turning out a success. It's that subtle interplay between the different spices and the tomato and beans and nuts that gives this dish its signature kick. But again, if you can't find cashews, peanuts or pistachios would be just fine.

» 3 Tablespoons oil
» 1 teaspoon mustard seeds
» 1 teaspoon cumin seeds
» 1 large onion, minced fine
» 2 cloves garlic
» 2 medium carrots, chopped
» ½ teaspoon turmeric powder
» Salt to taste
» ½ teaspoon clove powder
» ½ teaspoon cinnamon powder
» ⅛ teaspoon nutmeg
» 1 Tablespoon thyme

» 2 dried bay leaves (or 3 fresh)
» 1 whole dried chili
» 3 cups chopped tomato
» 1 cup vodka
» 8 oz chickpeas, cooked (i.e., a can of chickpeas)
» 8 oz of lentils, uncooked
» 6 cups water, reserved
» 1 cup raw cashews
» 1 lemon, juiced
» ¼ cup chopped cilantro (optional)
» Black pepper to taste

In a wok or large pot, pour in the oil, and heat over high heat. When it gets hot enough that a small wisp of smoke escapes the surface, add the mustard seeds. Wait until they pop and explode. Add the cumin seeds. Wait for the cumin to pop and explode, and subside. This should take only a few seconds.

Once the cumin settles down in its popping a little, add the onions, garlic, carrots, turmeric powder, salt, clove, cinnamon, nutmeg, thyme, the bay leaves, and dried chili. Stir the ingredients in the pot to combine everything. When the onions are all turned evenly yellow (from the turmeric), things are properly combined. Turn down the heat to medium, and begin chopping the tomatoes finely. If the tomatoes are canned, drain off the liquid, and reserve it.

After about five minutes, the onions should be softened. Pour in the tomatoes and vodka. Stir everything around in the pot to combine the ingredients thoroughly. When the liquid comes up to a full boil, pour in the reserved tomato liquid (if using canned). Let cook for about five minutes, until the mixture of tomatoes and spices thickens.

Add the cooked garbanzos, uncooked lentils, and about three cups of the reserved water. Add the cashews, and cover the pot. Turn up the heat to high, and let it come to a full rolling boil. Leave the water boiling until the lentils are cooked through, adding more water as the pot dries out. This should take thirty minutes.

Finish the dish with the lemon juice, cilantro and black pepper to taste. Continue boiling, until you reach the consistency of a thick salsa.

Sopa Lorca

Total time: 1 hour

While I was in the mountains in Quito, Ecuador, I stayed at a decidedly upscale hotel called La Ronda. The service was stellar and the people were as friendly as anyone could hope for. That night, after going out to some clubs and coming back feeling a little drained, I wanted to order something from room service that was vegetarian and that would calm my dancing stomach.

Lorca de papa. Papas, aguacate, ajo (potatoes, avocado, garlic). All three of those words leapt off of the pages of the room service menu, and my mouth watered as I anticipated what was to come. I called down and ordered a bowl with a side dish of garlic bread, and a spinach salad. It arrived. I opened up the little brown crock, and the punchy garlic leapt out and greeted me. I tasted it. I was in heaven.

It was rich and creamy. My mouth savored the contrasting textures of the potatoes and the avocado. The garlic was just perfect—adding a gentle counterpoint to the smooth creamy textures.

Traditional Lorca de Papa contains both milk and butter. In my version, the roux mimics the texture and gives you a much lower-fat version of the traditional butter and milk laden soup. It's so rich and delicious as a starter. However, the potatoes and avocado are so filling that it would work just fine as a main course as well. The avocado gives the soup a creamy texture that you cannot replicate with anything else.

If you're making this at home, please do not use too much else in the way of seasoning. The charm of this soup is its simplicity in flavor. I would personally prefer an even simpler mode of making the soup, but this is (in my opinion) a good primer for a beginning chef, as it combines a variety of basic techniques. I find recipes that are so simple to be a testament to a talented cook, because the ingredients must stand bare without any major flavorings to hide behind.

> » 3 cups, or 3/4 liter of water
> » 5 small red new potatoes, diced into ½ inch cubes
> » 1 small red onion, chopped finely
> » 1 clove of garlic, minced (or more to taste)
> » 2 Tablespoons of oil, split into 2 separate Tablespoons
> » 1 Tablespoon flour
> » salt to taste
> » black pepper to taste
> » 1 small Hass avocado, thinly sliced
> » 4 - 6 leaves of cilantro (optional)

In a pot, let the water come to a boil. While the water is boiling, chop the potatoes, the onions, and garlic. In a skillet, heat up 1 Tablespoon of oil over medium high heat. When the oil is hot, sprinkle in the Tablespoon of flour, and whisk or stir through to combine. When the roux has reached a light blond color, pour in 1 cup of water from the pot of water on the stove. Whisk vigorously to combine. Allow the liquid in your skillet to come to a full boil, then turn off the heat, and set aside.

When the water in the first pot comes to a full boil, drop in the potatoes.

In a separate skillet, pour in the second Tablespoon of oil. Sauté the garlic and onions until softened. When they are soft, add them to the pot of boiling water and potatoes. Add the "gravy" (oil, flour and water mixture) to the pot as well, and stir to combine. When the potatoes are tender, remove from the heat. Add salt and pepper to your taste.

In each diner's bowl, pour in about 1/2 cup of soup. On top of the soup, lay on 3 - 5 avocado slices. Garnish with a leaf of cilantro (optional). If you're a garlic fiend, like me, mince up a clove of garlic really finely, and stir into the soup in the last minute or two of cooking. You'll get a very strong garlic flavor.

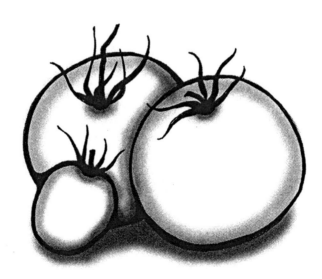

Green Split Pea Soup

Total time: 3-6 hours in a crockpot

For this recipe, I just put these ingredients into a crockpot and turned it on. What resulted was a thick, rich soup that tasted fantastic all by itself. I ordinarily loathe sweet potatoes, but this recipe made it possible for me to eat them. Unlike regular potatoes, sweet potatoes don't get gummy when you grind them in the blender, and the split peas control the gummy texture even further. You may or may not want to thin this out with more water.

» 1 lb yellow split peas
» 1 medium sweet potato, cut into 1 inch rounds
» 2 - 3 Tablespoons Italian seasoning
» 1 teaspoon olive oil
» ½ teaspoon turmeric
» 1 teaspoon salt
» 1 teaspoon ground red chilies
» 1 Tablespoon ground black pepper
» 1 teaspoon cumin powder
» 2 quarts water

Cook until sweet potatoes are soft (anywhere from 3-6 hours). Remove from crockpot, put in blender, and blend it until smooth.

If you don't have a crockpot, take all the ingredients and put them into a large roasting dish in the oven. Bake at 375° F until the vegetables are all cooked through. This can take anywhere from two to three hours. Make sure to cover the dish, so that the water does not evaporate.

Caldo Verde

Total time: 1½ hours

Kale is a lovely vegetable. This soup will technically work with any hearty green, such as collard greens, mustard greens, or radish greens, but for some reason, the kale just feels right. Caldo verde is a staple dish in Portugal, and is eaten with corn bread. Because it's got a mix of potatoes and leafy greens, you're eating something that will fill you up and still be a pleasure on the palate.

If you are out of potatoes, chickpeas work just as well. Just make sure to cook the chickpeas before hand, or use canned. Beans like chickpeas take a long time to cook, and you'll be hungry far before dinner is served!

» **2 tablespoons olive oil**
» **1 large onion, diced**
» **1 teaspoon salt**
» **3 garlic cloves, minced**
» **¼ teaspoon coarsely ground black pepper**
» **2 pounds red potatoes (about 5 medium), cut into 2-inch chunks**
» **6 cups water**
» **1 pound kale, chopped finely**

Start with the olive oil in a large, deep pot. Heat the oil over high heat until a small wisp of smoke escapes the surface of the oil. Add in your onion, and a healthy pinch of salt. Stir the onions in the oil to get all the pieces coated in the oil, and then turn down the heat to medium. Allow the onions to slowly develop a brown color. This should take about five to ten minutes, depending on how often you "check in" on them and stir them around. The longer you let the onions be left alone, the easier it is for them to get properly brown.

Add the garlic to the browned onions, and stir through until just combined. Add your black pepper. Stir everything in the pot to combine it. Add the chopped potatoes and the water. Put the lid on your pot, and turn up your heat to high. Let the water come to a full, rolling boil. Once you reach a boil, drop it down to a simmer, cover the lid of the pot, and let it simmer away for 30 to 45 minutes (until potatoes are soft). Using a potato masher or large wooden spoon, break up the potatoes as if to mash them. Leave enough chunks of potato (you don't want this to be smooth) but make sure to break up the large pieces. Add the kale to the potatoes in the pot, and stir the ingredients to combine. Let the kale and potatoes simmer together for another twenty minutes, or until the kale is cooked to your liking. Taste for salt, and adjust as needed.

Wintermelon Soup

Total time: 1 ½ hours

Wintermelon is a giant gourd-like thing traditionally grown in China, but is also available in the USA. The texture, when cooked, is unmatched to anything else. It's a very mild, soothing experience to eat this vegetable.

» **2 lbs wintermelon peeled of the outer skin, and diced**
» **1 lb potatoes, diced**
» **1 lb carrots, diced**
» **1 lb kale, roughly chopped**
» **2 Tablespoons whole fenugreek seeds**
» **1 Tablespoon chili powder**
» **1 Tablespoon salt**
» **2 cans coconut milk**

Dump the wintermelon, potatoes, carrots, kale, fenugreek seeds, chili powder, and salt into a large pot. Pour in just enough water to cover the vegetables. Bring the water to a full rolling boil, then drop to a simmer.

With a spoon, take some of the cooking water, and taste for salt. If it seems a little bland, this is OK, because a lot of the water will evaporate and concentrate the flavors. Cook 45 minutes. Taste the water again. If it's still not salty and spicy enough for your liking, add more salt and chili powder until you have as much heat and salt as you like. Add coconut milk. Bring up to a boil. Turn off the heat, and allow it to sit until you're ready to eat.

Serving Suggestion: *This is perfect with a warm, crusty baguette. Simply wrap the baguette in a slightly damp towel, and bake in the oven at 350° F during the last 10 minutes of the soup's cooking. When the soup is ready, remove the baguette from the oven, and take it out of the towel. Use oven mitts to do this, because the bread is hot. Slice the bread in half, lengthwise, and drizzle on a little olive oil. Sprinkle some sea salt and fresh parsley onto the halves of bread. Turn off the oven. Lay a dark-colored napkin or kitchen towel into the bottom of a basket. Put the basket into the oven to warm. Cut the bread into 2-inch pieces. When you're done cutting, remove the basket from the oven, and put the bread into the basket. Lay the edges of the towel over the bread. When you serve, lay the basket of bread next to the soup tureen, and let each diner share the communal breadbasket while eating the soup.*

cook's notes:

Salads

Some people dislike salads because they've only ever had boring iceberg lettuce or mixed baby greens with a few vegetables thrown on top. The salads in this section bring together beautiful colors, textures, and flavors that will satisfy even the biggest salad skeptic. Most can be full meals in themselves (a variation on the one-pot meal), or a nice, fresh accompaniment to a main course.

Dino Salad

Total time: 40 minutes

This is a salad I used to take with me for my lunch at school, because it's really filling! I have expanded this to use as a party dish, because it makes a beautiful, dramatic presentation on the table. You can either make this a layered salad (stack the layers from the bottom up), or toss everything through and get it well-mixed. Both make for interesting presentations. I personally prefer to chop up the lettuces and all vegetables to the size of my mouth, so that there's no … awkward moments with errant dressing or people struggling with the thing. To make it easy on you, I've listed the ingredients in the order that I stack them. It's best to stack them on a very large platter, but if serving tossed, it looks best in a large salad bowl. I've included a dressing because it's complementary to the salad.

- » ½ lb romaine lettuce
- » ¼ lb mixed field greens
- » ¼ lb watercress
- » 1 lb garbanzo beans
- » ¼ cup cilantro, chopped finely
- » ¼ cup flat leaf parsley, chopped fine
- » ½ lb Roma or plum tomatoes, cut into quarters lengthwise, then sliced
- » 1 large English cucumber, sliced in half lengthwise, then sliced thin
- » ¼ lb chopped olives
- » 2 Hass avocados, sliced thin, and arranged around the edges (or placed onto each serving if the salad is tossed)

Layer or toss salad ingredients as described above.

Dressing:

- » 1 cup lemon juice
- » 1 Tablespoon tahini
- » 2 Tablespoons olive oil
- » 1 Tablespoon red pepper flakes (optional)
- » 1 teaspoon salt (or more, if desired)
- » 1 teaspoon fresh ground pepper

Combine all ingredients in a blender or food processor on high.

Brutus Salad

Time: 30 minutes for reduction; 5 minutes for salad

Just as Brutus killed Caesar, so shall this salad destroy that limp, watery mass they call a Caesar salad (which I don't eat, because Caesar dressings contain eggs and anchovy). The last time I dealt with this monstrosity was when I was at my company's annual banquet.

I had requested a vegetarian meal, and they served me Caesar salad. Unfortunately, back in those days, I was a lacto-ovo vegetarian, so I ate the limp, squalid greens that were swimming in their eggy dressing. It was so disgusting that I couldn't take another bite without wanting to emit the contents of my stomach all over the jerk who was saying "In France, we would have some real meat, like beef, to start the meal. This is so cheap." I seriously wanted to do very not vegan things to his face at that point, but civility prevailed.

By the time I got home, I was so livid at the whole farce that they called a banquet, that I immediately invented this dish on the spot. I figured that I could definitely do better in my sleep than the inept cooks at the hall. Apparently, I was right.

» 1 whole romaine head, chopped into bite-sized pieces
» ½ lb watercress
» 1 teaspoon lemon juice
» 1 Tablespoon orange reduction (1 carton of orange juice reduced to ¼ the original volume on low heat or just use frozen orange juice concentrate)
» Salt and pepper to taste
» 3 Tablespoons olive oil

Chop lettuce. Dump on the washed watercress. Pitch the mix into a bowl.

Combine the lemon juice, orange juice, and the salt. Whisk until dissolved. Add black pepper. Combine. Add olive oil. Whisk vigorously to make a dressing.

Fusion Sandwich

Total time: 45 minutes

I used to take this sandwich on those four and five hour road trips Mom and Dad loved to dash off on. Whenever we would go on vacation, it would be for long drives, instead of flying like sane people. To deal with the monotony of the road, my parents would encourage us to come up with interesting foods to take with us. This sandwich is a modified version of a salad. Fortunately, because of its portability, it makes the perfect travel food. Unfortunately, if you're driving to a large family gathering where there is bound to be food, you'll already be too sated to bother eating! Make this at your own risk, but know that you've been warned.

» 1 Tablespoon red wine vinegar
» 1 clove garlic, minced finely
» 1 teaspoon sea salt
» 1 clove garlic, sliced in half lengthwise
» 1 large baguette
» 1 eggplant, sliced into long planks (half inch thick)
» 1 zucchini, sliced into long planks (half inch thick)
» 1 Portabella mushroom, sliced into strips (half inch thick)
» 2 Tablespoons olive oil
» 3 drops of white truffle oil
» 1 Tablespoon chopped thyme
» 1 Tablespoon chopped oregano
» 1 Tablespoon chopped basil

Why roast?

The vegetables in this dish are fairly benign. They have their own flavors, but they're too subtle to come out in a sandwich. Roasting gives the vegetables an unmatched smoky flavor that you won't get with steaming or boiling. It is a relatively low – fat cooking technique, and a nice way to get your needed servings of vegetables for the day.

In a bowl, combine the vinegar, minced garlic, and salt. Allow it to sit for the duration of your preparation. Take the garlic clove that you have sliced in half lengthwise, and rub it all over the baguette. This imparts a subtle garlic flavor that will permeate the bread. Preheat your oven to 350° F.

Slice up your vegetables into long planks or strips, as needed. To make it easier on yourself, use a serrated knife on the zucchini and the eggplant, because it will grip the vegetables better than a smooth-edged knife.

When all your vegetables are sliced, toss them in the olive oil and herbs, and lay them onto a wire rack. Place the wire rack over a baking sheet and bake in the oven for 20 – 25 minutes, or until they're golden brown. Some ovens heat better than others, and will take more or less time. You want to check on your vegetables ten minutes after heating initially, then once every five minutes after that. Depending on how thick you cut the vegetables, you may or may not need to adjust the cooking time.

In the last five minutes of roasting the vegetables, rub some water onto your bread, and wrap it in foil. Place the loaf of bread into the second rack of your oven.

When the vegetables (and bread) are done cooking, remove them from the oven. The bread will be especially hot, so handle with care. With a bread knife, cut the baguette loaf three quarters of the way down (so as to leave a "hinge" on the loaf) and neatly stack your vegetables into the pocket you've formed. Drizzle in the garlic and vinegar mixture over the vegetables.

Close your "pocket" and wrap it up tightly with either a kitchen towel or plastic wrap. Place a large board over the loaf. Then, get some weights on top of the board. I use a few large cans of beans. In about an hour or so, your traveling sandwich will be ready to eat.

Mixed Greens Composed Salad

Total time: 30 minutes

My friend Jenna in New Jersey was getting married. What should have been a happy occasion was quickly turning ugly, because her omnivorous mother, family, and caterers were giving her grief over her desires for a vegan menu. Fortunately for the cows and chickens and fish, Jenna knew that what should be a celebration of life should have nothing associated with death in it. Instead of caving in to the pressures from others, Jenna stuck to her guns.

Caterers can be rather clueless when it comes to serving vegans. Rather than take a chance and end up having the caterers serve tofu burgers and soy hot dogs, Jenna asked me for help. I compiled a menu for her that involved ingredients that the caterers could get a hold of easily, and in a way that would be easy for them to do. I didn't include any of the fake meats, because that's not how I work.

This salad is very simple to put together, but it looks fancy on the plate. It would be a very filling starter to a formal dinner, and a great way to make your co-workers or school mates jealous. They'll be eating air bread (bread that's mostly air, and not actual bread), and some dead thing. You'll be having what looks like nature's bounty exploding onto your plate.

If you have any nice greens that you like eating raw, feel free to add those as well. This is the time to experiment and see what you like.

The dressing, while not integral to the dish, is a good starter dressing for anyone who isn't familiar with making salad dressings that involve strictly vegan ingredients. The creamy sesame seeds and tahini don't weigh the salad down—instead, they enhance the fresh green textures in the leaves.

As with any composed salad, you want to have the vegetables cut up into pieces that are just big enough to fit onto the end of your fork. It looks really gross to see little bits of vegetables dangling out of peoples' mouths as they eat, and having to cut up your salad at the table takes far more effort for the diner. Be considerate to the people who you're serving, and they will thank you by coming back for more and more!

Because of the amount of nuts in this salad, you don't really need croutons. If you absolutely must have croutons, feel free to use your favorite recipe (or the one in this book). Additionally, you could add things like falafel, toast points, potato patties (also in this book), or any other crispy sort of thing you like. I have had good results with stacking bajji or pakora on top of my salad. There is something about fried foods on salad that seems so sinful, yet so tasty.

- » 1 lb romaine lettuce
- » 1 lb mixed field greens
- » ½ lb watercress
- » 2 lb garbanzo beans
- » 1 lb Roma or plum tomatoes, cut into quarters lengthwise, then sliced
- » 1 lb large English cucumber, sliced in half lengthwise, then sliced thin
- » ½ lb chopped olives
- » 2 Hass avocados, sliced thin, and arranged around the edges (or placed onto each serving if the salad is tossed)
- » Sprinkling of lemon juice.
- » ¼ cup cilantro, chopped finely
- » ¼ cup flat leaf parsley, chopped fine
- » ¼ cup walnut halves
- » ¼ cup pecan halves
- » ¼ cup cashew halves

Stack the vegetables in layers, and sprinkle on the herbs, nuts, and lemon juice on top. Serve dressing on the side (to follow). Scale up or down as needed.

Dressing:

- » 1 cup lemon juice
- » 1 cup sesame seeds
- » 1 Tablespoon tahini
- » ¼ cup cashews
- » 2 Tablespoons olive oil
- » 1 Tablespoon red pepper flakes (optional)
- » 1 teaspoon salt (or more, if desired)
- » 1 teaspoon fresh ground pepper

Combine all ingredients in a blender or food processor on high, until smooth.

Palm Hearts

Total time: 30 minutes

Palm hearts are good cold, but grilling them gives a beautiful contrast in color. The insides will be blindingly white, while the outsides will be mildly darker. This salad, with its bursts of cooling freshness, will provide considerable workouts for those who like to sink their teeth into their dinners. However, if you cannot grill the palm hearts, just use them plain, as the dish will still be delicious.

» 1 lb palm hearts, grilled lightly, and diced
» ¼ cup frozen grated coconut
» ¼ lb tomatoes, diced
» 1 small carrot, grated
» ½ medium onion, diced
» ¼ cup lemon juice
» Pepper and salt to taste, reserved until the end
» ¼ cup cilantro, chopped and reserved, for garnish

Awaken the coconut from its frozen state by heating it over low heat on the stove. Some fat will render out of the coconut, but if you're nervous about the pan being that dry, you can throw some water in. You just want to smell the coconut, and it'll be done.

Combine all the ingredients (except salt), and toss with the lemon. Chill in the fridge until cold. Serve cold. Add salt and pepper to taste. Scatter on the cilantro leaves for a garnish. You may use more or less as your taste decrees.

cook's notes:

Back to Basics

These recipes are generally simple to make, and involve making things in their most stripped down manner. I would use these as a primer for any beginner vegan cook to get him or her started in her or his adventures. They're the sort of thing I'd call "mixed company" food. If you don't know what the rules are to begin with, how can you break them with any level of confidence? This section can be your baseline from which you can deviate as much as you want, once you master the technique.

Once you work with these recipes a bit, you'll certainly find your own way of doing things that works for you. My mother was never a fan of the oven, and she would avoid it like the plague. Instead of making leavened breads, she would make flatbreads, delicious and steamy directly from the stove. Instead of casseroles, she would make these complex stews and soups from a variety of vegetables, then serve them over piping hot rice to give that satisfaction.

I'm hoping this section will help you get your feet wet, then see how you can make it work for your own comfort level. Not comfortable with the stove? Use an oven or microwave! Don't like using the large oven? The toaster oven is the ideal tool for any person pressed for space, and people wanting to avoid using so much gas or electricity. Improvise as needed whenever you can.

Dry Cooked Garbanzo

Total time: 30 minutes

I love this served either with some good basmati rice, or mashed up and spread onto my bread when I make sandwiches. It's also excellent with any Indian flat breads. It's a large-ish quantity, because there's really no sense in using that many different spices and then having this tiny little dish of food to show for it. Ground spices will not work in lieu of the whole ones in this particular recipe. I use cooked garbanzo for this, so you may substitute canned. There are a lot of ingredients, so I've grouped them together for easy reference in the steps. This dish works well in nonstick cookware, so if you have it, use it.

» 2 lbs cooked garbanzo beans (canned is ideal—just drain the water).

Whole spices

» 1 teaspoon cumin seeds
» 1 teaspoon black mustard seeds
» 2 teaspoons whole coriander seeds, crushed (throw the seeds into a zip lock bag, and run a rolling pin over them until they're crushed)

Ground spices

» 1 teaspoon turmeric
» 1 teaspoon red chili powder

Aromatics

» 5 cloves of garlic, minced
» 1 large onion, chopped fine
» 2 stalks of curry leaves (if available)

Fresh herbs

» ¼ cup cilantro, chopped finely, for garnish

Oils

» 2 Tablespoons peanut, canola, or safflower oil
» 2 Tablespoons sesame oil
» Salt and pepper to taste

Heat both oils in a wok, or large, shallow pan on high heat. Add the whole spices. When the whole spices begin to pop, wait 10 more seconds, and add all of the aromatics. Sauté until the onions are soft. Add the ground turmeric and 1 teaspoon salt and stir through. Cook for another minute. Add the beans. Toss gently, until all the beans are yellow. Cook for five more minutes. Add chili powder. Toss through until thoroughly combined.

At this point, taste a bean or two. If it needs more heat, add some ground black pepper. If it needs more salt, sprinkle on some more salt, and cook for an additional five minutes.

Remove from the heat, and sprinkle on the chopped cilantro over the top as garnish. You may use more or less as your tastes dictate. This will also work with Italian flat leaf parsley instead of cilantro.

Generic Accompaniment to dry-cooked anything

Total time: 30 minutes

» 1 large English cucumber
» 5 Thai bird chilies
» 1 small onion
» Lemon juice
» Salt

Dice up the cucumber, and sprinkle lightly with salt. Set aside to drain. Dice the onions finely, and mince the chilies. Marinate the onions and chilies in the lemon juice. Strain out the cucumber after 1/2 hour of "soaking" in the sprinkling of salt. Toss through to combine.

You may omit the chilies, or reduce the amount, but having that kick along with the cooling refreshing cucumber is a really nice contrast.

Why dry roast?

Soups, stews, and sauces are all well and good. However, there are times when you want a dish to be dry cooked, so it can be incorporated into different applications. This is what I did with the dry cooked garbanzo beans. I wanted to get a recipe that I could easily use with bread, rice, or salad, without making everything a huge mess. The dry cooking technique is good for any bean you can drain and wash off.

The accompaniment I have provided here works just as well with dry roasted potatoes.

Basic Broccoli

Total time: 40 minutes

I was at some function or another for work, and they had this really bad menu for vegans. It consisted of limp, dead-looking romaine lettuce smothered in Caesar dressing, some steamed broccoli, and pasta with steamed vegetables. I got really annoyed that something as tasty as broccoli could be messed up to that level. Instead of stewing in my juices, I came home, and whipped up a couple of easy, basic recipes. This is what I came up with for a basic broccoli.

> » 1 head broccoli, cut into florets
> » 2 Tablespoons oil
> » Zest of one lime
> » Juice of one lime
> » ½ teaspoon cayenne powder
> » 1 teaspoon garlic powder
> » 1 teaspoon cumin powder
> » Salt, to taste
> » 1 Tablespoon sesame seeds (optional)

Preheat the oven to 350° F. Take the oil, lime zest, lime juice, chili powder, garlic powder, and cumin powder and blend in a bowl to make a loose paste. Toss broccoli florets in the oil, lime and spice mixture, and sprinkle with salt. Bake in the oven, covered for 30 minutes. Remove the cover, sprinkle on the sesame seeds, and bake for five more minutes, uncovered. This is a perfect side dish, but it also does really well when added to creamy pasta dishes.

Basic Spiced Cauliflower

Total time: 20 minutes

Sometimes, you just want to have the simple flavors of the vegetable by itself without a lot of other complex flavors getting in the way. I like this cauliflower when I'm having warm flat bread.

It's funny, though. I don't think that once it's cooked, cauliflower has much of a taste in general. With this particular vegetable, I find that I'm looking for the texture more than anything else. Be careful not to overcook your cauliflower, or you'll end up with a disgusting mash which is decidedly unpleasant.

Another neat thing about this recipe is that since cauliflower is so neutral in flavor, it absorbs all the spices and tastes even better the next day.

> » 1 head cauliflower, cut into florets
> » 2 Tablespoons oil
> » ½ teaspoon curry power
> » Salt

Toss cauliflower in the oil and curry powder. Sprinkle with salt. Cook in a 400° F oven for 15 minutes. Serve with flat bread.

Fast Cauliflower

Total time: 20-40 minutes

I can't really call this a proper aloo gobi, which is an Indian potato and cauliflower dish that involves a long list of spices, multiple cooking techniques, and an iron will while making the dish (as it is prone to burning, and is fairly easy to have a disaster with). This is my college dormitory answer to the "proper" Indian version. Try this in warmed pita bread, or just by itself.

> » 1 head cauliflower
> » 2 medium potatoes
> » 1 teaspoon cumin powder
> » 1 teaspoon coriander seeds, crushed
> » 1 teaspoon sesame seeds
> » 2 teaspoons oil
> » ½ teaspoon salt
> » ½ teaspoon pepper
> » ¼ teaspoon turmeric powder
> » ¼ cup water

Separate the cauliflower into medium sized florets, and cut the potatoes into 1/2 inch cubes. Combine the cumin powder, coriander seeds, sesame seeds, oil, salt, pepper, turmeric powder and water in a blender, and pulse until all the ingredients are combined. If you don't have a blender, just mixing it together with a fork or whisk will do just fine.

Toss the cauliflower, potatoes, and spice mixture together until combined. Microwave on high for 8-10 minutes, or until the potatoes and cauliflower are cooked through. If you don't have a microwave, you can cook this in the oven at 350° F for 30 – 45 minutes. Tastes great in pita bread as a sandwich, over rice, or as a simple side dish.

Basic Mushrooms

Total time: 15 minutes

These are basic sautéed mushrooms. You can serve this as a side dish, or add it to other recipes.

> » **3 Tablespoons olive oil**
> » **4 large Portabella mushrooms (stems too, please), thinly sliced**
> » **Salt, to taste**
> » **1 teaspoon Italian seasoning**
> » **1 clove of garlic, crushed and minced**
> » **¼ cup flat leaf parsley, chopped fine**

Heat oil in a wide, shallow pan. Get it very hot. Add the mushrooms, and sprinkle on some salt. Allow to get cooked for about 10 seconds before disturbing (you want it to sear). Toss around in the pan. Add Italian seasoning. Add garlic. Stir around for about ten minutes (to allow it to get less watery). Remove from heat, and stir in the parsley.

Basic Potatoes

Total time: 30 minutes

With small red or new potatoes, you want to have the mildly sweet, delicate flavor and texture of the potatoes all by themselves. This dish showcases the potatoes beautifully, and allows you to enjoy them fully.

> » **5 lbs small red or new potatoes**
> » **Salt**
> » **3 Tablespoons olive oil**
> » **Parsley, minced**

Add the potatoes to a pot and fill with cold water. Bring the water to a full boil, and liberally salt the water (salty like the sea). Drop down to a simmer, and simmer for about 10-12 minutes. Remove from heat, and drain off the water. Toss with oil, and sprinkle salt on top. Put in a 500° oven for up to ten minutes to develop crispy skin. Remove from heat. Toss with parsley.

Asian Roasted Potatoes

Total time: 30 minutes

As you can probably tell, I really enjoy potatoes in every form that I can find. This is another one of those basic, simple potato recipes that looks pretty on the plate, and tastes interestingly good.

- » **5 lbs red new potatoes**
- » **2 Tablespoons sesame seeds**
- » **2 Tablespoons sesame oil**
- » **3 Tablespoons rice wine vinegar**
- » **Sea salt**
- » **Cracked black pepper**

Toss all ingredients together, coating the taters evenly. Spread out on a baking sheet in one layer. Bake at 350° F for 20 minutes, then 500° for another 5 minutes. Toss the potatoes gently with the vinegar. Serve as an accompaniment to a light stir-fry meal.

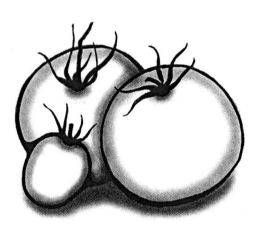

Baked Potato Rounds

Total time: 30 minutes

For the "potatoes and potatoes" vegan in your life. While baked potatoes taste really good, they're a mess to eat, and often require margarine or other unsavory ingredients. These can be eaten in one or two bites. Choose potatoes that are long and slender to avoid having people get messy. You may vary this with Yukon Gold or Fingerling potatoes for a different texture, but make sure to adjust your cooking times, because these tender potatoes cook more quickly. There's no need to peel the potatoes as long as you clean them thoroughly.

I talked to a friend of mine, who is the mother of a four-year-old, about this recipe. She told me she has made it multiple times, because it is a very easy way to give her child a snack without making a giant mess in the kitchen, paying a small fortune for something heavily processed, or having something that is too complicated for her child to eat. Because they can easily picked up with your hands, these rounds go beautifully for children still exploring food.

- » **1 Idaho baking potato, cut into ½ inch discs**
- » **2 Tablespoons olive oil**
- » **1 teaspoon paprika**
- » **Salt**
- » **Pepper**
- » **Chopped chives (reserve)**

Preheat oven to 350° F. In a large zip top bag, combine potato rounds, the 2 Tablespoons of olive oil, paprika, salt, and the pepper. Close the top and make sure it's sealed. Shake the bag around, and rub the potato rounds through the bag to make sure they get well coated. If you don't have a zip top bag, you may coat the potatoes with a pastry brush, and evenly sprinkle on the spices.

Lay onto a baking sheet in one layer. Bake until tender (about 20 minutes). Sprinkle on chives.

Variations

- » *You really don't want to combine these variations. Mix the spices with the potatoes in the zip top bag. Instead of just salt and pepper, here are some other spices that go well with potatoes:*
- » *1 Tablespoon of curry powder*
- » *1 teaspoon each of cumin, black mustard, and coriander seeds ground*
- » *¼ cup of finely minced parsley*
- » *1 Tablespoon minced thyme*
- » *Sprinkling of cayenne pepper*
- » *Broccoli floret on top, with an extra drizzle of olive oil and sprinkle of sea salt.*

Herb Crusted Potato Patties

Total time: 1 hour

This was one of those recipes that began its life as a colossal disaster, but after serious tweaking and retesting it became a good, solid recipe that people really enjoy.

» 3 lbs potatoes, baked and gently mashed (½ bakers, and ½ red)
» 1 Tablespoon of sea salt
» 3 Tablespoons dried basil
» 3 Tablespoons dried thyme
» 1 Tablespoon ground black pepper
» Roughly 1 cup breadcrumbs (more may be needed)
» Oil for shallow frying (about 2 inches up the sides of a saucepan)

Sauce

» ¼ cup oil
» 1 tomato, diced finely
» Up to 1 teaspoon salt (to taste)
» 2 Tablespoons red chili flakes
» 1 clove garlic

For the potatoes, bake and gently smash them (you want some lumps in there). In a food processor, combine the spices and toss with the breadcrumbs. Combine with the potatoes. You want a mixture that's on the dry side and will hold together in a ball. You may need to add more breadcrumbs to make the balls take and hold their shape. Make the potatoes into balls, about 1/4 cup in size.

Let them cool down to room temperature. Gently toss the potato ball in the spice blend. Roll it around in your hands to make sure that the spices get stuck onto the ball properly. Set aside, and allow to cool in the fridge for one hour.

Remove potatoes from fridge, and gently press down the center of the potato ball to make a flat patty. Fry in the heated oil for 2 – 4 minutes per side (until browned). Drain on a wire rack.

Make the sauce as soon as the potatoes come out of the fridge, and keep simmering gently until the potatoes are ready. Heat the oil in a pan. Add the tomato to the pan, and add the salt. Allow to cook down for about five minutes. Drop the heat down to as low as it will go, and allow to simmer until all the potatoes are done.

When ready to serve, add the chili flakes and garlic to the hot tomato mixture, and throw in the blender until smooth.

Indian Roasted Potatoes

Total time: 45 minutes

Back in India, the only people to own an oven were the bakers, and those who were mind-bogglingly wealthy. This means that the Indian cook needed to improvise and make this dish over the stove, constantly watching it, and fearing that the whole mess won't form a crust, and won't get properly cooked.

If you have the luxury of an oven, use it! This is my own variation on the classic dish which uses russets, because I find that the contrasting textures of the potatoes and the other vegetables is really a change from anything you'd get elsewhere. It's a personal preference that you can do without if you don't want to bother with it. Just plain Idaho baking potatoes work perfectly. But be careful – these things go as fast as homemade croutons!

These sorts of dishes are eaten as one of many accompaniments to one main bed of rice/bread, and many little cups of different foods. Good point to mention: if this had been a typical meal, you would have had a small bed of rice on your plate, surrounded by sambhar/rasam, some steamed vegetable, some fresh raw vegetables, some Indian pickles, and some small amount of stir-fried vegetables.

- » 1 lb Yukon Gold potatoes
- » 1 lb red potatoes
- » 1 lb white potatoes
- » 1 lb Russet potatoes
- » 1 lb Idaho baking potatoes
- » ¼ cup peanut, canola, or safflower oil
- » 2 teaspoon cumin seeds
- » 2 teaspoon black mustard seeds
- » ½ teaspoon split yellow peas (this is to be used as a spice, not an ingredient)
- » Handful of curry leaves (if you can get them)
- » 1 whole chili (sliced lengthwise)
- » 1 teaspoon salt
- » 1 teaspoon turmeric powder
- » 1 teaspoon ground coriander seed

Preheat oven to 375° F. Dice all potatoes to about 2 inches square. In a roasting dish on the stove, heat the oil. Add the cumin seeds and mustard seeds. Wait until they crackle and pop like mad (about one minute). Add the split peas. Roast gently for 5 seconds. Add the curry leaves. Immediately add the potatoes and chili. Sprinkle on the salt, coriander powder, and turmeric powder. Toss through until the color is all yellow. Remove from stove, and bake until fork tender (about 30 minutes).

Serve with rice, roti, or puri.

Beeten Potatoes

Total time: 1 hour

I strongly dislike beets. This is more or less the only way I'll eat them, because they have a smoother taste and texture than canned beets. The potatoes and dill just round out the flavor enough that you can take advantage of the pretty color of the beets without having too much of their taste powering through the dish. I do like this over a salad, because the colors and textures look so nice on a white plate.

- » **15 small red potatoes**
- » **375 mL wine (about half a bottle)**
- » **¼ cup red wine vinegar**
- » **¼ cup raspberry preserves**
- » **½ cup water**
- » **3 medium sized beets, sliced ¼ inch thin**
- » **3 Tablespoons sugar**
- » **Salt**
- » **½ teaspoon allspice**
- » **3 Tablespoons grated ginger**
- » **2 – 5 Tablespoons olive oil**
- » **Large handful of chopped dill**

Fill a large stock pot 3/4 of the way with cold water. Add the potatoes to the pot, and place on a stove over high heat. In a skillet, pour in the wine, red wine vinegar, raspberry preserves, and the water. Turn the heat up to medium high. If you don't have the raspberry preserves, you may use apple jam, strawberry jam, or marmalade. If you don't have any of those, feel free to use some pineapple juice instead.

Both these liquids should take anywhere from 10 – 15 minutes to come up to heat. While they're going, remove the stem and root from the beets, and slice them about 1/4 of an inch thick*. Don't bother peeling them, because they will stain everything and make a mess. It's not worth it.

When your beets are all sliced up, slide them into the skillet that has the wine and vinegar and water. Don't worry if the liquids haven't boiled yet. Sprinkle in the sugar over the beets. Grab two large pinches of salt, and sprinkle over the beets as well.

Start chopping the dill as finely as you can get it. When the dill is chopped, grate up the ginger.

By now, the water (with the potatoes) should be boiling, and the wine and beets should be bubbling. Turn down both burners on the stove to medium low. You want them to simmer, not boil.

Boiling makes the beets bitter, and makes the potatoes fall apart.

You may or may not want to stir the wine around—this is a matter of personal choice. Once the liquid in the pan with the beets and wine has come down to a gentle simmer, add the ginger and the allspice.

In a large bowl, combine the dill and olive oil. Have it waiting for when the beets and potatoes are finished cooking.

With a fork, poke one of the beets. If you feel no resistance, the beets are finished cooking**. Make sure that the liquid never reaches a boil. If, by mistake, the pan gets too hot, and the liquid has been boiling for any length of time, add some additional sugar to round out the flavor.

Remove the beets from the skillet, leaving behind the liquid, and add the beets to your bowl with the dill and oil in it. Toss gently to combine the beets with the oil and herbs.

Place the skillet back on the stove, and turn the heat up to high. Whisk vigorously until the liquid gets thick and syrupy. When it's at the desired consistency, remove the skillet from the heat, and pour it over the beets. Toss the beets and liquid to combine.

With a fork, poke one of the red potatoes. If you feel no resistance, the potatoes are done. Drain the potatoes in a colander. Liberally sprinkle them with salt. Toss the potatoes to combine with the salt.

Add the potatoes to the bowl with the beets. Gently toss the ingredients to combine.

You might serve this as one appetizer in a series of appetizers. This dish also works well in a salad. If you take some out, mash it, and stuff it into a pita bread, all you'd need is some lettuce and tomato to make a smashing sandwich. Toss with some cooked brown rice for a nice comforting side dish. Chill it, and serve cold for a lovely potato salad. Experiment with other juices, wines, and liquors to find a combination that works for you!

*If you're a beet lover to the max, feel free to add a few more beets. Don't worry about it too much, because you've got a lot of potatoes to beet up!

**If you find that the beets are taking too long to cook, give them a quick spin in the microwave for 7 – 10 minutes (without the liquid) to get them all the way tender.

Jimmy Crack Corn Crack

Total time: 30 minutes

These are godly good. These are so good that I know for a fact we ate roughly four apiece while I was making them. We were supposed to have wound up with around 4 dozen, but I think maybe 2 dozen actually survived to reach the table. And then at the table, we ate more. This stuff is like crack, but in corn form. They're delicious in the plain version, but we noticed astronomical flavor from the addition of just a few simple spices.

- » **3 cans (12 oz per can) of sweet corn, drained**
- » **4 cups cornmeal**
- » **¼ onion, finely chopped or grated**
- » **Around 2 cans (use the cans from the corn to measure) worth of water**
- » **salt to taste**
- » **Spices, to taste (optional, see suggested variations below)**

Preheat your cast iron skillet over medium-low heat. If you're using a nonstick skillet, heat it up over medium heat. You want it hot enough to be able to sear the corn for an extended browning time without burning it.

Mix the canned corn, salt and cornmeal together in a large bowl (about double the volume of the three ingredients to avoid making a mess), tossing evenly with your hands. We didn't add any salt at all, because the corn was not fresh, and it still tasted wonderful.

Pour in your first can of water. Mix the water and cornmeal and corn mixture with your hands as much as you can. There will still be a lot of dry cornmeal in the bowl. This is a good thing. Add the onion and any additional spices, if any, and mix in to the best of your ability. Add the second can of water, and stir through. You'll notice the batter feeling fairly thick. You want it to be about as thick as a bread dough, but too wet to be an actual bread.

What is cornmeal?

There is a difference between corn flour (also known as Maseca in some Latin American stores), cornmeal, and cornstarch. Please do not confuse them! Cornstarch is a very fine white powder, and is used to thicken sauces and make glazes. Corn flour is used in dishes like tamales, and is about the consistency of all-purpose flour. Cornmeal is ground corn, and has the texture of grits or farina (cream of wheat). All are versatile!

Grab a small handful in your palm, and roll it around to make a ball. Press down gently to form into a soft patty approximately 2 inches wide and 1 inch thick. If the round patties aren't sticking together, stir in some extra cornmeal until they do form wet, soft patties.

Lay the patties flat onto the hot skillet. With a small teaspoon, drizzle a few drops of oil around the edges of the corn fritter. If the fritters are browning too quickly, or you smell a burning smell or see too much smoke, remove the pan from the stove to allow it to cool down, and drop down the heat to a lower heat.

About a minute after laying the corn fritters onto the hot skillet, the bottom side should be lightly browned. Flip fritter over, and drizzle on a few more drops around the edges. In about another minute or two, the cake should be cooked on the other side. If you would like them to be a darker brown, cook them for a longer amount of time.

Drain on a wire rack.

Leftovers may be frozen, and reheated in the toaster oven.

Variations

» *1 Tablespoon paprika*
» *1 Tablespoon coriander powder, 1 Tablespoon cumin powder, and 3 Tablespoons coconut milk. Add an additional 3 Tablespoons cornmeal to even out the added liquid.*

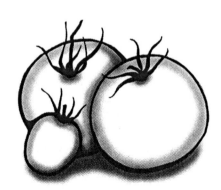

Eggplant Version 1

Total time: 30 minutes

Eggplant is one of those things that I am finicky about, because I don't like its texture or mouth feel. I don't like to eat it at all, but I know how to make it because I've watched my mother cooking it and I know how it's supposed to smell and look in the pot. I haven't had a single complaint. This particular version is quite excellent on bread or over pita bread. The different spices are what give the dish character, because eggplant in itself has little flavor.

Look for the smaller, thinner eggplants when you're shopping. The thinner ones have fewer seeds. This was made using a large eggplant, so if you're using the Japanese eggplant, double the quantity. You want to end up with roughly one pound of eggplant going into this dish for the amount of spices and oil.

» 1 teaspoon cumin seeds
» 1 teaspoon mustard seeds
» 1 teaspoon coriander seeds, lightly crushed
» 1 Tablespoon sesame seeds
» ½ teaspoon fennel seeds, lightly crushed
» 2 Tablespoons peanut oil
» 2 cloves garlic

» 1 Tablespoon minced fresh ginger
» 1 eggplant roughly chopped
» ½ teaspoon Chinese 5 spice powder (star anise, fennel, clove, white pepper, cinnamon)
» ½ teaspoon cinnamon
» ⅛ teaspoon nutmeg
» Up to ¼ cup water

In a small bowl, combine the cumin seeds, mustard seeds, crushed coriander seeds, sesame seeds, and crushed fennel seeds. In a wok or large skillet, heat up oil over high heat. When the oil is hot, pour in the mixture of seeds. Wait about 30 seconds. When they all begin to pop and crack, add the garlic and ginger, and stir for 1 minute. Add the chopped eggplant, and toss to combine with the spices and oil.

Drop down the heat to medium low, and cover. In a small bowl, combine the Chinese five spice powder, the cinnamon, and the nutmeg. Stir to combine. Let the eggplant cook, covered, for about 5 minutes. Open the lid of the pot, and pour in the powdered spice blend. Toss completely to combine all the spices, and to let the spices cook in the oil for a few more minutes. If you notice the bottom of the wok getting too dry and too many spices sticking, just pour in some of the water and stir to combine, scraping up the bottom of the pot (this will most likely happen).

Eggplant Version 2

Total time: 30 minutes

- » 5 Tablespoons peanut oil
- » ½ teaspoon coriander seeds, crushed
- » ½ teaspoon cumin seeds
- » 1 medium onion, minced fine
- » 3 cloves garlic, minced fine
- » 1 bay leaf
- » 1 Tablespoon ginger, grated
- » ½ teaspoon curry powder
- » 2 lbs Japanese eggplants (the long, thin versions), diced
- » ½ lb tomatoes, chopped fine
- » 1 teaspoon garam masala
- » 5 chilies, minced (may be adjusted for your tastes)
- » 1 bunch cilantro, minced
- » Salt to taste

Heat oil in a wide, shallow pan, until a small wisp of smoke escapes. Add the coriander and cumin seeds. When the cumin starts to pop, add the onion and garlic. Add bay leaf. Stir for one minute. Add the ginger, curry powder, and eggplant. Allow to cook for 5 more minutes over medium high heat. Add the tomatoes. Cook for 5 minutes. Add the garam masala. Add chilies. Cook for 1 more minute. Remove from heat. Sprinkle in the cilantro as a garnish, and stir it through.

This dish is perfect with both flatbread and white rice.

Aubergine Planks

Total time: 45 minutes

The aubergine (eggplant) planks look so fancy when they're perched atop a bed of basmati rice. If there's no leftover oil in the pan after baking, feel free to add in an extra Tablespoon or two to the gravy recipe. You can scale this recipe up easily. The spices given here are for one large eggplant—if you're using more, just scale up the spices accordingly.

Alternately, some people prefer if the eggplants are cut into discs, rather than planks, because it makes a nice appetizer as well. Feel free to do this, and to experiment with different toppings if you are going to make this an appetizer.

» **1 large eggplant, sliced lengthwise into ½ inch thick planks**
» **1 red bell pepper**
» **1 teaspoon cumin seeds**
» **1 teaspoon coriander powder**
» **1 teaspoon cinnamon powder**
» **1 teaspoon clove powder**
» **1 teaspoon turmeric powder**
» **1 teaspoon salt**
» **½ teaspoon ground black pepper, or red chili flakes**
» **2 Tablespoons peanut oil**
» **Cooked basmati rice**

Preheat the oven to 400° F. Start roasting the red bell pepper until the skin is blackened (on a gas stove burner or in the oven). While the pepper roasts, pour cumin, coriander, cinnamon, clove, turmeric, and salt into a spice mill, and grind until very fine. Combine the spice blend and oil to make a loose paste. Rub each plank of eggplant with the spice and oil blend on both sides. Lay the spiced eggplants onto a wire rack. Lay the wire rack onto a baking sheet, and drizzle any remaining oil/spice mixture onto the aubergines. Bake, uncovered, until tender (about 15 – 20 minutes). The roasted red peppers should be ready by the time the eggplants are cooked. Serve each diner with 2 planks of aubergine, 2 slices roasted red pepper, and 1/2 cup of the cooked basmati rice.

Aubergine gravy

Pour the extra oil and spices from the bottom of the baking sheets into a saucepan. Add extra peanut oil until you have 1/4 cup of oil total. Sprinkle in 1/4 cup of flour to make a roux. Turn on the heat to medium high. Stir the flour and oil together to make sure it's blended well. The heat will slowly permeate the mixture. You want to continuously stir the flour and oil, so that you work out any lumps and keep the flour moving. When the flour reaches a blonde color, pour in 2 cups of vegetable stock. Whisk until thickened, and set aside until needed.

Hot Penne

Total time: 20 minutes

I like for my hot penne to be really hot, so one Tablespoon of chili flakes doesn't nearly cover my needs. I like this with about three or four generous Tablespoons of red chili flakes. The presentation is simple, but beautiful looking. The red tomatoes with the fresh green parsley and the little red flecks from the chili flakes make the final dish look rather pretty on a clean white plate. Definitely serve this with some kind of steamed or roasted vegetable on the side, because it's fairly plain on its own. Granted, when I make this dish, I keep sneaking more pasta, and pretending like I can't see the vegetables.

> » 1 lb penne pasta
> » 3 Tablespoons olive oil
> » 3 cloves garlic, sliced
> » ¼ cup sun dried tomatoes packed in oil, diced finely
> » ½ cup Italian flat leaf parsley, chopped finely
> » 1 Tablespoon chili flakes (less if you don't like lots of heat)

Cook pasta. (See pasta cooking guide on p. 19 for tips.)

While the pasta is cooking, heat oil in a pan, and add garlic. Cook for a few seconds, and add the tomatoes (you may also want to add some of the oil from the tomato jar). Cook for a few more seconds, and add the parsley and chili flakes. Add pasta to the pan. Toss to combine. Serve hot.

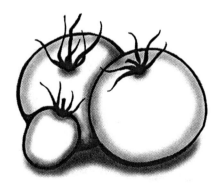

Basic Pasta with Garlic

Total time: 20 minutes

> » 6 quarts water
> » 1 lb pasta (ziti, penne, or rotini all work well on this one)
> » 4 teaspoons of olive oil
> » 2 cloves of sliced garlic
> » red chili flakes (adjust to your own taste)
> » 2 Tablespoons lemon (optional)
> » generous sprinkling of salt

Put the water into a large pot on high heat. While you wait for the water to boil, slice up your garlic into thin rounds. Heat some olive oil in a pan over medium high heat, and add your garlic. Let it sizzle in the oil until the garlic gets a very light brown (this happens quickly). Remove from the heat, and sprinkle in some red chili flakes. Set this aside next to your serving plate.

Once the water has come to a boil and is salted accordingly, add pasta and cook until done. Drain the pasta and drizzle on the garlic sauce. If you want to, you may add in some lemon juice at this point to brighten up the flavor of the pasta. Toss the pasta to coat it with the oil, garlic mixture, and lemon.

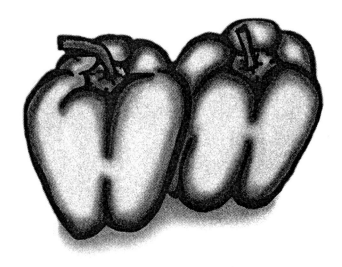

Steamed, but not Angry, Vegetables

Total time: 20 minutes

This recipe came together after I got frustrated at yet another genius who managed a thundering failure at steamed vegetables. I was fairly irritated when I put this recipe together, but the taste calmed my tension. I definitely like this one as a base for other flavorings. This is just where you get started—you can always add other things like paprika, chili flakes, or fresh chopped herbs to this, and have a more complex taste. This is what I'd call the bare minimum for steamed vegetables.

Say it with me: THERE ARE NO BORING VEGETABLES, ONLY BORING COOKS.

- » **5 cups water**
- » **¼ lb baby carrots**
- » **¼ lb snow peas**
- » **¼ lb green beans**
- » **2 Tablespoons lemon juice**
- » **Salt and black pepper, to taste**

In a large stock pot, boil the water. Place a metal colander over the top of the pot. Place the carrots into the bowl of the colander, and cover the pot. Cook for fifteen minutes. Add the snow peas and green beans. Cook for an additional five to ten minutes. Remove the vegetables from heat. Toss with lemon. Sprinkle salt and black pepper, and toss. Serve hot.

Cucumber Invasion

Total time: 15 minutes

I love the flavor of cucumbers with something smoother and darker in the center. Try this with your own favorite spices or seasonings. I call it the cucumber invasion, because the little bites of cucumbers are called (in my brain, anyway) cucumber boats.

The neat thing about these little bites is that they look so cute on a platter and work well as appetizers. Whether you serve it as a side dish at a sit down dinner or as an appetizer at a party, cucumber boats are bound to be a hit.

» 2 lbs large cucumbers
» ¼ lb lentils, cooked
» 1 teaspoon cumin powder
» 3 shallots, minced
» 1 clove garlic, minced
» ¼ cup cilantro, minced
» Splash of lemon juice
» Splash of olive oil
» Sea salt
» Cracked black pepper

Peel cucumbers, and cut in half, lengthwise. If you're using small pickling cucumbers, like Kirby cucumbers, don't worry about peeling off the skin. Remove the seeds with a spoon, making sure to get every last bit of the central pulp out. Toss together the lentils and the cumin, garlic, sea salt (to taste), lemon, and olive oil. Add the lentil mixture to the hollowed out cucumbers, and sprinkle on pepper. Slice the cucumbers into bite sized pieces. Make sure that you cut up the boats into pieces that are small enough to be eaten in one or two bites.

This dish can be topped off with cilantro and minced garlic.

Lentils

Total time: 30 minutes

I love lentil soup, but it doesn't allow me much leeway for creativity. I prefer to cook the lentils, drain them, and use them like regular beans. Then after that, I'll use them in soups and the like. What really irritates me, however, is how easy it is to find nonvegan lentil soup. It does not need bacon, people! Lentils are so creamy and delicious all on their own that you just need a few spices to brighten up their texture.

» 1 Tablespoon peanut oil
» ½ teaspoon cumin seeds
» 1 Tablespoon sesame seeds
» 1 large onion, chopped
» 2 cloves of garlic, crushed
» 1 handful curry leaves (optional)
» pinch of asafetida
» 1 teaspoon turmeric
» 16 oz can whole tomatoes
» 1 lb cooked lentils
» Salt and chilies to taste
» 3 cups water

Heat the oil and add the cumin seeds. When they pop and crack and make a lot of noise, add the sesame seeds. Wait 5 seconds, and add the onions, garlic, and optional curry leaves (tearing them as you add them). Add the asafetida and turmeric powders. Sauté until the onions are softened. Drain the canned tomatoes, reserving the liquid. Crush the tomatoes over the onions with your hands. Cook on medium high heat for about 10 minutes. Add the lentils, and stir around until coated with spices. Season with salt and chili powder. Add the water and the liquid from the can of tomatoes, and simmer for 5 minutes. Serve with brown rice or crusty toasted bread.

This method can be used to make any daal (Indian legume) that you'd like to make, and can be used for any beans as well. It won't taste the same, because the beans will all react differently to the flavorings. For a variation in spices, try garam masala (add along with turmeric), or chana masala (ditto). Or, if you'd prefer to experiment with your own spices, try adding a pinch of ground cloves and a pinch of cinnamon powder. Both are considered warming spices in Indian medicine. For a very fragrant soup, omit the turmeric, and use a small pinch of saffron instead (bloom in a Tablespoon of water, and add towards the end of the cooking).

Banana Bread

Total time: 1 ¼ hours

Looking up recipes for banana bread on the Internet is a frustrating experience for me, because they all seem to call for some stupid egg replacer. Let me just clue those people in to a little factoid that vegans the world over have used since ... forever: BANANAS ARE USED AS AN EGG REPLACER. To put egg replacer into a recipe that's rife with bananas seems utterly pointless to this little vegan. If you don't have peanut butter, you can use any neutral flavored oil as a substitute.

The dough for the bread will be relatively thick. Do not get nervous and decide to deviate from the recipe. That's a bad idea when you're baking. Just go with the (lack of) flow, and move on.

> » **3 medium-sized, ripe bananas**
> » **2 tablespoons peanut butter**
> » **2 cups flour**
> » **½ teaspoon salt**
> » **1 teaspoon baking soda**
> » **½ cup coarsely chopped nuts**
> » **¾ cup sugar**

Mash the bananas. Add the peanut butter, salt, baking soda, sugar, and nuts. Stir together to combine. Add the flour, and stir to combine. Pour into a greased baking pan. I used a small casserole dish, and had excellent results. You can try using a loaf pan, but I think that it would make the center be a bit uncooked.

Let the bread bake for one hour in the oven. Let it cool for 15 minutes before removing from the dish.

cook's notes

More Complex

You've baked. You've boiled. You've sautéed, simmered, sweated, and soaked. You're familiar with how a vegetable cooking in not enough oil sounds, and you know what smells to be aware of so that you don't burn things. You're ready to take things to the next level. While the recipes in this section aren't exactly complicated, they do combine a variety of techniques.

This does not mean, however, that these particular recipes are reserved for some elite cook out there. It does mean that you need to be careful before you embark on these journeys. Read the recipe from start to finish carefully. If you don't know how to make a particular technique work, look up instructions on the Internet, or call that one friend you've got in your phone book who knows food. If things get too daunting, remember that the health food store can be an outstanding resource for cooking advice. If you have a decent one locally, swing by there, and ask about cooking techniques. Someone is bound to know.

Whatever you do, don't think that because you're not the best cook in the world, you can't make this. They are workable, even for novices. Just take your time, go slowly, and have fun experimenting with your new abilities!

Indian Pickles

Total time: 45 minutes preparation, 2 weeks fermenting

A pickle, in India, is something (vegetable, fruit, etc.) that is preserved in salt, oil, and spices — not vinegar. Think of it like a sort of combination pickle/relish/other preserved food. It's meant to be a hot/salty addition, and is meant to be eaten in VERY small amounts (no more than a teaspoon per meal). They're ideal to take with you on long trips and the like, because they taste great just spread onto some flatbread, or stirred into a soup that seems bland. This pickle in particular is not one you'll find elsewhere; it's an amalgam of different pickle recipes that I've liked in the past.

When you make pickles, you're investing a fair bit of time and labor. Double or triple this batch as needed. You really can never have too many pickles. Homemade pickles make excellent gifts for family or friends. They also do very well with freshly minted college students. When I went away for seven weeks in a residential college program while I was in high school, my mother sent up some pickles with me to save my life. It really came in handy when I was stuck in the middle of nowhere with very bland food to eat.

I remember making pickles with my mother as a child. The whole house would fill up with the smell of the toasting spices and the cooking food. We'd immediately have to try some, even though you're technically supposed to let it sit for a week or so to let the flavors meld properly.

Pickles and Water are Mortal Enemies!

When you're making Indian style pickles, be aware that water is the enemy of good pickles. Water allows mold to grow in the jar, and gets things nasty. Make sure that you have absolutely no water in the jars that you store your pickles in. When my mother would store pickles, she would put a sheet of plastic (usually a clean zip top bag works) over the mouth of the jar before closing the lid tightly. Then, every time one of us would dig into the jar, we would make sure to use a clean, dry spoon ONLY. Then, when closing the jar, the plastic was replaced, and the jar was kept in a cool, dry place at all times.

» 1 cup oil (peanut or corn)
» 1 teaspoon mustard seeds
» 1 Tablespoon sesame seeds
» 1 small onion, minced fine
» 1 head garlic, minced
» 1 Tablespoon curry powder
» 5 Tablespoons salt
» 1 lb tomatoes, diced finely
» 1 lemon, minced and de-seeded
» 1 cup chilies, minced finely
» 1 Tablespoon chili powder
» extra oil to add to jar (sesame or canola)

Add 1 cup oil to a wide shallow pan, and allow to heat on high. Add mustard and sesame seeds, and allow to pop like mad. Add onions, garlic, curry powder, and 1 Tablespoon salt. Allow to cook for about 10 minutes, until the water is mostly evaporated from the onions.

Add the tomatoes and lemons and stir vigorously. Add the rest of the salt. Drop down the heat to as low as it'll go. Cook 20 minutes. Add the fresh chilies and chili powder. Cook five minutes. Allow to cool to room temperature.

Pour the cooked pickles into a jar, and fill the jar until it's about 90% full. Pour oil over the pickles to fill out the rest of the jar. Place a sandwich baggie on top. Screw on the lid. Allow the pickles to sit in a cool, dry place (not the refrigerator) for about two weeks before eating.

This is lovely mixed with rice, pasta, or noodles. It also perks up any dish that's too bland. It can be spread onto roti, with some vegetables for a quick wrap on the go.

Manga Thokku (Mango Relish)

Total time: 45 minutes preparation, 2 weeks fermenting

Manga thokku is a south Indian pickle that my mother makes in enormous quantities. Those enormous quantities would be decimated by the time the next mango season rolled around, so she was forever foraging unripe mangoes wherever she'd get a chance. When I say a large amount, I mean that she'd process, single-handedly (for a long time, until we all began pitching in to help) multiple kilos of the stuff at one go. Because the green mangoes are grated, you don't really have to worry about soaking them in salt for a week.

If you are using very small unripe mangoes, key limes, or cut up lemons (roughly the size of a golf ball) you can salt them for a week, and follow the rest of the recipe as stated. All you do is put the tiny mangoes (or key limes or lemons) into a glass or plastic bowl. You then pour on enough kosher salt to cover all the mangoes (or key limes, etc.) completely. Yes, this is a LOT of salt. I know this. If following this method, don't add salt to the recipe, as the soaked fruit will be plenty salty enough. Regardless of what you're using, don't bother peeling the mangoes, the key limes, or the lemons. When preserved in salt, then preserved in salt and spices, the flavor is incredible.

I have considerably cut back on the amount of salt for this recipe, because I know there's someone out there who's going to try to eat these like American pickles, and then call me screaming. You may or may not want to increase the amount of salt to help preserve it longer. If you do add more salt, it will stay for a much longer time, and prevent the growth of bacteria and mold.

» **1 medium sized green mango (unripe), grated**
» **½ cup oil (peanut, sesame, or canola)**
» **2 teaspoons mustard seeds**
» **1 teaspoon fenugreek seeds, ground in a spice grinder**
» **1 teaspoon turmeric powder**
» **3 fresh chilies, finely ground**
» **¼ cup salt**
» **⅛ teaspoon asafetida**

In a wok, or a large skillet, heat up the oil over high heat, until a small wisp of smoke escapes the surface. Pour in the mustard seeds. Wait about 30 seconds or so, until the seeds pop and explode. When the popping subsides a few seconds later, add the grated unripe green mango. Stir around to combine in the spices and oil.

Add the salt, the turmeric powder, the fenugreek powder, and the asafetida. Stir the grated mango to combine completely. When all the mango mixture turns yellow, you've stirred it enough. Drop down the heat to as low as it will get. Add the ground chilies to the top, but DO NOT STIR. Let the mangoes sit, simmering in the heat, until they become a thick paste.

After about 15 – 30 minutes (depending on your stove), the mixture will resemble a thick sauce. Turn off the heat, and let it cool to room temperature before storing in a jar. The relish will keep indefinitely. Let it sit for two weeks before eating.

Bear in mind that water and oil do not mix, so be very careful to only use dry spoons when serving the relish, and to leave the jar at room temperature to avoid condensation of water on the inside of the jar. If you happen to get any mold in the relish, just scoop it out, and discard it — the rest of the stuff will not be harmed.

Serve as a spread for bread, as an accompaniment for fresh vegetables, or use it as a kick in your regular food.

Tostones

Total time: 40 minutes

Depending on what part of Latin America you're from, you'll call them patacones or tostones. These little fried pieces of gold are delicious when served piping hot. Instead of oil, if you use shortening, you'll get a totally different experience; the shortening can get much hotter than oil can, and will give a better crust. Be liberal with the salt and chili. Use a canola or peanut oil, so that the second frying won't overheat the oil.

Tostones are the perfect appetizer to any meal, because they're so easy to eat. They're a fair bit more fancy looking than something like potato chips, but give that same satisfying crunch. If you feel up to it, you can serve them atop a fresh garden salad as croutons, or with some guacamole.

> » **1 Plantain, cut into ½-inch thick discs**
> » **Oil for frying**
> » **Salt**
> » **Chili powder**

In a large pot, heat up the oil to 375° F. While the oil is heating, peel and slice the plantains. You want them to be 1/2 – 3/4 of an inch thick. If you make them too thin, you'll end up with hard plantains that are difficult to bite through. You want these to be crispy outside, and tender inside, so stick with a thick enough plantain. You don't, however, want them too thick.

When the oil has reached the 375° F, gently slide in the plantain slices. The plantains will begin to bubble. The best way to tell when one of them is cooked enough is to look around the edges of the slice. If the large bubbles have stopped forming, you're ready to remove it from the oil. This should take roughly 5 – 7 minutes. You want the plantains to be tender at this point.

When cooked, remove the plantain slices from the oil, and drain them on a wire rack, standing upright. While they're still hot, liberally sprinkle on some salt. You will now want them to come down to room temperature. While you wait, mix up equal parts salt and chili powder as an accompaniment to the plantains when they're ready. When all the plantains are fried, turn up the heat on the oil to 475° F.

Set one of the cooled plantain discs onto a flat surface (a cutting board or your counter will work fine). Take a spatula, and pressing down with your palm, flatten the disc into a patty. Gently slide the patty into the 475° degree oil. Continue to flatten and fry the rest of the plantains. When the patties of plantain are golden brown, they're ready to serve.

Drain on a wire rack for a few minutes before serving.

Curried Plantains

Total time: 30 minutes

These are delicious over steamy hot bowls of rice. It's another one of those dishes that my mother came up with when we were younger, when we found plantains for really cheap. Make sure to use green plantains. You don't have to peel them, but you can peel them if you want to. You want the plantains to be a fairly small dice, so that they cook more quickly.

» **2 large plantains, diced**
» **5 Tablespoons oil**
» **1 teaspoon cumin seeds**
» **2 teaspoons coriander seeds**
» **¼ teaspoon turmeric powder**
» **½ teaspoon chili powder**
» **Salt, to taste**
» **Water (optional)**

In a wok or skillet, pour in your oil, and turn up the heat on your stove to high. While you wait for the oil to heat, quickly bash up your coriander seeds in a mortar and pestle. If you don't have a mortar and pestle, throw the seeds into a paper bag. Fold the top of the bag to close it, and run a wine bottle or rolling pin over the bag to crush the seeds.

When the oil is hot, add the cumin seeds. Wait about 15 – 30 seconds. The seeds will begin to pop. At that point, add the coriander seeds. Wait about 10 seconds, for the popping of the cumin to go down a bit.

Add the diced plantains, and stir to combine them with the spices and oil. Sprinkle in the turmeric powder and salt. Stir the plantains again, until all of them are yellow from the turmeric.

Turn down the heat to medium low, and cover your wok or skillet. Cook undisturbed for about five minutes. Open the lid, and toss all the ingredients together to redistribute the oil and the spices. If you think that the pan looks too dry for your liking, and you're nervous about burning the spices, feel free to add a little bit of water to the pan, and stir it through. You want the dish to be dry, but you also don't want to burn anything!

Continue to cover, let sit, uncover and stir in increments of five minutes until the plantains are done. This can take roughly 20 minutes in total.

When the plantains are cooked, serve them as a free-standing side dish, or serve them atop cooked rice for a filling meal.

Split Pea Croquettes

Total time: 30-40 minutes, plus overnight soaking

I came home one night and fried up a batch of frozen falafels I had prepared the week before. My mother took a taste of one, and commented that while the crispy texture was nice, she was displeased with how dry they seemed. The texture wasn't working for her. I explained that you're supposed to eat a falafel combined with a tahini sauce, or in a sandwich, but she wasn't pleased with that answer.

The next week, when I soaked some beans for my next batch of falafel, she convinced me to leave out the chickpeas all together, and just to use yellow split peas. Then, once we started to get down to business, we started pitching in grated ingredients that we thought would cut through that dry texture. The first to go in was a large, grated onion. When that worked really well for the first batch, we began adding more and more ingredients to the base recipe. Eventually, we came to the conclusion that while patties of beans taste great, they can be improved infinitely by the addition of vegetables. They become like little portable meals.

The croquettes are not only comforting, they also store really well. If you make up a large batch, and freeze the leftovers, they reheat most impressively in the oven. The best tasting ones are the ones that aren't perfectly smooth on the outside. The jagged edges and craggy outside allows the croquette to get more crispy, and gives you extra surface area to hold dipping sauce.

If you want a shortcut to getting all the vegetables prepared, a perfectly reasonable method is to use a basic box grater, and grate everything down. Feel free to add the garlic along with the split peas when you grind them down in the food processor. Avoid using a blender for this recipe, because you want the patties to hold up firmly.

» 1 cup yellow split peas, soaked in water overnight
» ¼ cup shredded cabbage
» 1 small onion, minced
» 1 small carrot, shredded
» 3 cloves garlic, minced
» Salt, to taste
» Water, reserved
» Oil for deep frying

Drain the yellow split peas and grind them in a food processor until they're the consistency of a grainy hummus. You'll never get it smooth, but you want it to be ground down. If it's not grinding down enough, add a couple of tablespoons of water, and keep grinding.

In a wok or skillet, pour in your oil, and turn up the heat on your stove to high.

Combine all the remaining ingredients (shredded cabbage, carrot, garlic, and onion) with the split peas. Form into rough patties. Drop the patties into the fat, and fry until a dark brown. This will take roughly 7 minutes per side, depending on how hot your stove gets. Serve with hummus or ketchup.

» *SIDE NOTE: If you want to pan-fry these, it does work with a healthy dose of oil, heated over medium high heat, in a wide, shallow skillet.*

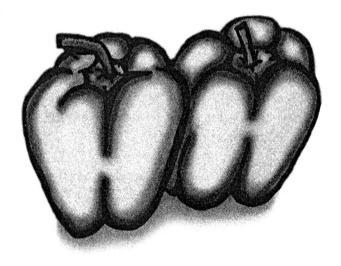

I Must Be Nuts!

Total time: 20 minutes

I love roasted nuts, but most of the ones from the store are honey roasted! This makes me sooo mad! I've developed these to roast on top of the stove, so that you're not trusting the oven to do the deed. The amounts of these nuts are only suggested. As long as you end up with 1.5 lbs of nuts in the end, you'll be fine. Use raw nuts for this recipe, so that you don't end up with overcooked nuts!

» 2 Tablespoons oil
» 1 teaspoon mustard seeds
» 1 Tablespoon cumin seeds
» 1 Tablespoon sesame seeds
» ¼ lb raw almonds
» ¼ lb raw hazelnuts
» ¼ lb raw cashews
» ½ lb raw peanuts
» ¼ lb raw pistachios
» Salt to taste
» 2 Tablespoons chili flakes

In a large skillet or wok, heat the oil. When the oil is hot, add the mustard seeds. Wait for them to pop. When they begin popping, add the cumin seeds. When both the mustard and cumin seeds are popping and exploding, add the sesame seeds. Once the sesame seeds get lightly browned, add the almonds. Drop down the heat to medium high. Toss the almonds to combine with the spices.

Roast the almonds with the spices for about 3 minutes, making sure to stir frequently to avoid burning. Add the hazelnuts. Toss the nuts to combine with each other and the spices. Roast the two together for 3 minutes. Add the cashews and peanuts. Toss to combine, and roast the four nuts together for 3 minutes. Add the pistachios. Toss all the nuts together to combine with the spices and nuts. Generously salt the nuts. Roast the nuts together for about 3 more minutes.

Sprinkle in the chili flakes, and turn off the heat. Toss all the ingredients to combine thoroughly. Remove one of the nuts, and blow on it to cool it down. Taste it for salt. If you need more, this is the best time to add more.

Omisubi ... Sort of

Total time: 1½ hours

The Japanese rice ball (omisubi) usually involves meat or fish. In my version, you're using all plant ingredients. They look very pretty when laid out on a platter with the sauce. Caveat: These tend to be very bland on their own. Make sure that you serve them with some form of dipping sauce, or people will start to think that vegans eat like invalids. You can use your favorite Asian-style dipping sauce, or use the one I have in the sauces section (p. 118).

» 1 cup uncooked short grain brown rice
» 1 Tablespoon oil
» 1 red bell pepper, minced finely
» 1 shallot, minced finely
» 3 red potatoes, boiled and mashed
» 1 Tablespoon ginger, finely grated
» 1 Tablespoon chopped cilantro

» 2 Tablespoons rice wine vinegar
» 1 teaspoon red chili flakes
» Up to 1 teaspoon salt (to flavor the rice)
» 3 Tablespoons white sesame seeds
» 3 Tablespoons black sesame seeds

Cook the brown rice. In a shallow pan, heat the oil, add the bell pepper and shallots, and cook until softened. Remove from heat, and let it cool down slightly. Mix with the mashed red potatoes. Add the ginger. Shape into teaspoon-sized balls.

Take the rice and combine with the cilantro, the rice wine vinegar, and the chili flakes. Sprinkle in the salt, and toss to combine. Taste the rice. If it tastes too bland to you, it's going to need more salt. Without a decent amount of salt, it's going to be horribly bland. This would also be the time to add any extra seasoning that you feel the ball would do well with. Because the bulk of the rice balls are the rice itself, you have to flavor it now.

In the palm of your hand, take some of the rice, and press it into a roughly 2 inch disc. Take the small ball of potato mixture, and lay it in the center. Bring up the disc around the potato ball, and roll it around in your hand. This should give you about a one inch ball.

Combine the black and white sesame seeds together, so that you can see equal amounts of both seeds. Pour the seeds onto a plate. Coat the rice balls with the sesame seed mixture by rolling them around in the sesame seeds.

You want them to be lightly coated so that you can see the color contrast between the sesame seeds and the cilantro and chili flakes. Lay on a wire rack, and spray with sesame or canola oil spray. Bake at 375° F until lightly brown (about twenty minutes). Serve with dipping sauce.

Winter Rolls

Total time: 1 hour

Try this with your own favorite blend. This dish is a palate cleanser, giving you a refreshing burst of pure vegetable flavor. These are not like your traditional spring rolls, which are short and thick, but rather, they're long and thin. They should be no fatter than the size of two fingers. Depending on where you live, the spring roll wrappers may also be called rice paper.

You can do these in the oven or fried on the stove—they taste lovely either way.

> » **12 spring roll wrappers**
> » **pot of hot (not boiling) water**
> » **4 oz snow peas, lightly steamed, and sliced into long strips**
> » **4 oz carrots, lightly steamed, and cut into long, thin sticks**
> » **1 cup finely shredded red cabbage, steamed lightly**
> » **¼ cup finely sliced red chilies (optional)**
> » **Oil for frying (Neutral flavored oil, like canola, peanut, sunflower or safflower), or, if baking, a few Tablespoons for brushing on**

The vegetables I have listed here are just a start for the recipe. Anything you have lying around the house that you think might taste good would work. If you have some leftover Chinese stir-fry from the night before, you could use that too. This also works very well with rice noodles. As long as you like the flavor of the food before it got wrapped up and fried, you'll be fine.

Dip the spring roll wrappers in hot water to soften, and lay flat on a cutting board. On one end of the wrapper, mound (in small doses, please) the vegetables and chilies. Roll it up, making sure to close both ends, and deep fry for about three minutes, until lightly browned. If you'd rather not deep fry things, just brush it with peanut oil, and bake in an 375° F oven for about 20 minutes. Serve with soy sauce with chopped scallions in it.

Flautas

Total time: 2 hours

- » 1 large red potato
- » 3 cups water
- » 1 cup salsa verde*
- » 1 red onion
- » 1 red bell pepper
- » 2 teaspoons oil
- » 1 teaspoon fresh Mexican oregano, chopped
- » ½ teaspoon chili powder
- » salt to taste

- » 8 corn tortillas (the small ones)
- » 1 8 oz can black beans
- » 8 oz canned corn, drained
- » 2 avocados, thinly sliced
- » ¼ cup chopped cilantro
- » 6 Tablespoons vegetable shortening or daalda
- » 2 limes
- » toothpicks

In a small pot, bring the water to a boil. Add the red potato, and cover the lid. When you hear the water come to a boil again, turn down the heat to a simmer. It will need to cook for about thirty minutes.

Set your oven or toaster oven to 175° F. Next, assemble the salsa verde* (see below). You want to begin with this part, so that it has time to sit around and let the flavors meld. Chop the onions and bell peppers. Drain the corn.

In a saucepan, heat the two teaspoons of oil. Add your onions and peppers. If you have it, add the Mexican oregano. Add the chili powder, and a good pinch of salt. Stir all the vegetables to combine them. Cook the onions and peppers until they are soft. While they cook, wrap the tortillas in foil, and keep them in a warm oven or toaster oven. The oven should not be hotter than 175° F.

When the onions and peppers are cooked to your liking, drain the can of black beans, and stir it into the pan with the onions and peppers. Feel free to bash the beans around in the pan to mash them up a bit. Cook over low heat for five minutes. Turn off the heat, and cover with a lid.

By now, the potato should be cooked. Drain the water from the potato pot, and discard it. Quickly give the potato a good smash with a wooden spoon to break it up into smaller pieces.

Add the potato to the beans and onions pan. Using a potato masher, mash the whole mixture until everything is relatively smooth. Mix while you mash to speed the process along. Remove the tortillas from the oven, but leave the oven on.

Arrange the tortillas, potatoes and beans mixture, the corn, and the avocados in front of you like an assembly line (in that order). Take a tortilla in the palm of your hand. In the middle, pile on about two or three generous Tablespoons of the potato mixture. Spread the mash around on the tortilla shell in one line down the middle. Take about a tablespoon of corn, and gently sprinkle it over the mash. Lay on a slice of avocado. Lay the tortilla, open faced, aside on a cookie sheet and return it to the oven to keep it warm as you assemble the rest of the flautas. Assemble the remaining flautas.

In a large high sided skillet, heat the shortening over medium heat. As the fat begins to melt, remove the cookie sheet with the warmed tortilla disks from the oven. Carefully roll the tortilla up around the stuffing. If you are using a corn tortilla, you might have some cracking. This is not a problem. Place it seam side down on the cookie sheet. If you want to be on the safe side, secure the rolled up flauta with a toothpick.

Once the shortening is melted, and gets good and hot, you're ready to start frying. Pick up one of the flautas, and place it seam side down into the hot fat. If it sizzles and bubbles in the oil, you know that the fat is hot enough to fry the flautas. If it doesn't sizzle and bubble, remove the flauta from the oil, and allow it do drain as you wait for the oil to come up to heat. When the shortening is hot enough to sizzle your flautas, slowly lower all the rolled up, secured flautas into the fat, seam side down. Let them cook until they are a deep golden brown.

Try not to disturb them too many times, as they need to be left alone to develop a strong color. After about five minutes (or when the big bubbles start turning clear and subside), when the flauta is browned on one side, flip it over with tongs or a spatula to allow it to cook on the other side. Let it brown on both sides. Remove the flautas from the heat, and allow them to drain in the warm oven for about 30 minutes.

Drain off all but one teaspoon of shortening from the skillet. Place the skillet back over high heat. When the oil is hot, pour in the cup of salsa verde. Let the salsa warm through, and remove it from the heat.

When it's time to serve, arrange the flautas on a platter, and drizzle on the salsa verde. Sprinkle on the chopped cilantro. Cut the limes into wedges, and serve on the platter, so that each diner can squeeze on some lime as needed.

* Salsa Verde

» *6 tomatillos, husks removed and quartered*
» *1 bunch of cilantro, stems discarded*
» *1 teaspoon fresh Mexican oregano*
» *1 jalapeño chili, seeded*
» *1 bunch green onions*
» *1 lime, juiced*

In the bowl of a food processor, combine the tomatillos, lime juice, the jalapeño, green onions, and Mexican oregano. Pulse until the tomatillos are roughly chopped. Add the cilantro, and pulse until the leaves are combined.

Bajji

Total time: 1 hour

I am a firm believer in the concept that pretty close to anything that you dip in batter and deep fry will taste good. In the case of bajji, it's usually just potatoes, but I want you to experiment with other ingredients. When I was visiting Chicago, I even managed to use zucchini!

This is one of those dishes that I've managed to teach my mother something about. She used to make her bajji using chickpea flour or all purpose flour. The bajjis were still delicious, but they would lose their crispiness rather quickly. In my version, with the rice flour, the bajji has a chance to get very crispy and stay crispy. If you can't find or afford rice flour, go ahead and use the all purpose flour. It won't be a huge loss, but it won't be as crispy as with the rice flour.

When you're done frying the bajji, save the oil! It's now been spiced with all those delicious spices you used in the batter. You now have a spiced oil to use in cooking other dishes.

A Note on Rice Flour

If you're using rice flour, I would suggest trying to find it at your local Indian store. For whatever reason, the texture of the rice flour found in most health food stores is too coarse for the bajji application, whereas the ones you find in an Indian store will have a finer grain, almost like all purpose flour. If you have success with the flour you normally buy, then by all means stick with it.

» 1 lb potatoes, sliced into discs
» 1 lb red, green, or orange bell peppers, seeded and sliced into discs
» 1 lb onions, sliced into discs (you may use them as rings or as slices)
» 1 lb Anaheim chilies, tops removed, and seeded
» 2 cups rice flour, sifted
» 1 Tablespoon curry powder
» 1 teaspoon cumin
» 1 Tablespoon chili powder
» 1 Tablespoon salt
» ¼ teaspoon baking soda
» 1¾ cups ice cold water
» Oil for frying (in preferred order: peanut, sunflower, safflower, canola)

Prepare all vegetables, and set aside. Combine the flour, spices, salt, and baking soda, and sift together. Slowly pour in water, stirring constantly, until you have a batter that's slightly thinner than pancake batter. You'll want the batter to coat the vegetables, but not coat them thickly. This is a matter of personal preference, and you might want to experiment with the batter slightly thicker than you think it should be. You can add more water if you feel it's too thick, but you can't take it out if you think it's too thin. Be very careful about water content, because adding more flour to the batter throws off the flavorings that you've worked so hard to achieve.

Heat the oil to 400° F, and dip the vegetables in the batter. Deep fry in batches, until golden brown. This works best when you have someone helping you. If one person dips the vegetables, and the other person baby-sits the oil, the process runs very smoothly.

When golden brown, remove from oil, and allow to drain on a wire rack. Serve as soon as possible. This particular dish doesn't need accompaniments, but here's a sauce in case you demand one:

Dipping Sauce

- » ¼ cup oil
- » 1 tomato, diced very finely
- » 1 Tablespoon chili powder
- » ¼ cup lemon juice
- » 2 Tablespoons chopped cilantro

Heat oil until very hot. Add tomato. Cook for 10 minutes. Add the chili powder, and cook for about a minute. Pour the mixture into a blender with the lemon juice and cilantro, and puree.

Comforter

Total time: 1½ hours

What could be better than creamy potatoes and a nice contrast of colors and flavors all wrapped up in flaky tender puff pastry? Creamy potatoes and a nice contrast of colors and flavors all wrapped up in a flaky, tender puff pastry with gravy! This particular gravy is essentially the veloute gravy. I have included it here for quick reference, because this dish is totally not the same without the gravy.

> » 1 Tablespoon vegetable oil
> » ¼ cup minced shallots
> » 1 clove garlic
> » ¼ teaspoon cumin powder
> » ¼ teaspoon coriander powder
> » ¼ teaspoon turmeric powder
> » 1 teaspoon curry powder
> » 1 cup finely diced potatoes
> » 1 cup finely diced carrots
> » ½ cup green peas
> » ½ cup yellow and white corn
> » 1 sheet puff pastry

Gravy

> » 1 Tablespoon flour
> » 1 Tablespoon oil
> » ¾ cup vegetable stock
> » ⅛ cup each white wine and sherry

Preheat oven to 375° F. Heat oil in a pan over high heat, and add the shallots and garlic. Drop the heat down to medium low, and add the cumin powder, the coriander powder, the turmeric powder, and the curry powder. Cook shallot garlic spice mixture until softened.

Increase heat to high. Add carrots and potatoes. Stir until all the vegetables are evenly coated in the oil and spices. Drop down heat to medium. Put the lid on your pan, and cook covered until potatoes and carrots are softened. Add peas and corn. Cook for an additional 5 minutes. Remove from heat, and refrigerate.

Split puff pastry into four equal parts. Roll each part out into rectangles until it's 1/8 inch thick. If you're buying pre-made puff pastry, it is most likely already 1/8 of an inch thick. Refrigerate.

Start preparing gravy. Add oil to a saucier or shallow pan, and heat over medium high heat. Sprinkle in flour. Stirring constantly, allow it to cook for 30 seconds, or until light brown. Pour in the vegetable stock and alcohol, whisking constantly. If you're not using alcohol, you may use all vegetable stock. Bring the mixture up to a full boil, then remove from heat. Set the saucier on a cool burner to allow it to drop in temperature more quickly. Turn down the heat to low. If you're using a gas stove, you may replace the pan now. If you're using an electric range, wait until the heat of the range has come down to the lower heat. Replace the pan onto the stove, and simmer for about three minutes, whisking all the time.

Remove the chilled vegetables and puff pastry from the fridge. Onto the 4 rectangles, arrange the vegetable mixture in the center, leaving about 1 inch all around. Spoon on about 1 Tablespoon of the gravy. Lightly spread water around the edges of the puff pastry. Fold the puff pastry in half, to cover the vegetables, and gently press the pastry shut. Cut out small holes onto the top in the middle to allow for venting of excess steam. Brush the tops of the puff pastry with oil, vegetable shortening, or margarine to facilitate browning. Bake at 375° F until the puff pastry is browned (approximately 20-30 minutes). Let it sit for 20 minutes to cool and to allow the juices to settle. Serve with the rest of the gravy.

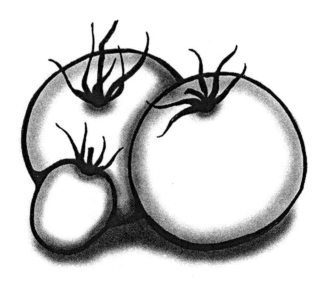

Pakora

Total time: 1 ¼ hours

- » 1 head cauliflower
- » 3 Tablespoons oil (in preferred order: peanut, sunflower, safflower, canola)
- » 1 teaspoon cumin seeds
- » 1 teaspoon coriander seeds, crushed
- » 1 teaspoon curry powder
- » ½ Tablespoon salt

- » *Batter*
- » 3 cups rice flour
- » 1 teaspoon cayenne pepper
- » ½ teaspoon garlic powder
- » 1 teaspoon chili powder
- » 2 ½ cups water
- » 1 teaspoon sesame seeds
- » 1 teaspoon ajwain seeds (optional)
- » 2 quarts oil for frying

Break up cauliflower into florets. Add the oil to a wide, shallow pan, and allow to get hot. Add cumin and coriander seeds. When they start to pop, add cauliflower. Sprinkle in the curry powder and salt. Toss to coat. Drop down the heat to medium high, and continue to stir as needed.

Cook covered, for roughly 15 minutes, so that the cauliflower is cooked ¾ of the way through, but not softened. If you find the pan getting too smoky, you may add a Tablespoon or two of water and stir it around.

Sift together the flour, the cayenne, garlic powder, and chili powder. Add water to the flour. Mix through. It should be the consistency of a loose pancake batter. Add the ajwain seeds and sesame seeds. Stir through. This is your batter mixture.

Allow the cauliflower mixture to cool to room temperature.

Pour about ½ gallon of oil into a 1 gallon pot. Allow the oil to reach a heat of 375° F. Dip the florets into the batter, and deep fry until golden brown. Alternately, you may want to just dump the entire amount of cauliflower into the pakora batter, stir everything around to combine it, and drop it by the spoonful into the oil. Allow the pakoras to drain on a wire rack, and serve hot with a sauce that's good with fried foods (like the one on the next page!).

Basic Fried Food Sauce

Total time: 10 minutes

This is really my mother's invention, so I'm crediting her, and tweaking it to meet the tastes of a wider audience. I like mine to be screaming hot, but for people who are less inclined to call in the fire trucks, you may adjust this to your own liking.

» **¼ cup ketchup**
» **Up to 1 Tablespoon ground chilies (to taste)**
» **Up to ¼ teaspoon salt (to taste)**
» **Up to 1 Tablespoon black pepper (to taste)**

Stir to combine. Serve with the pakoras as a dipping sauce.

Kashmiri Biriyani

Total time: 1 hour

Decadent, yet surprisingly light, this dish is best served with more mildly spiced accompaniments and palate refreshers, such as thinly sliced cucumber, tossed with lemon juice. The flavors in this dish are so complex and delicate that having strongly flavored things in close proximity would be a waste of the ingredients. This is not cheap, but it is worth every penny.

One of the people testing this recipe said that she wishes she could wear the fragrance from the dish as a perfume!

» **1 cup basmati rice, uncooked**
» **1 cup sliced lotus root**
» **1 cup sliced carrot**
» **4 Tablespoons vegetable shortening**
» **1 Tablespoon sesame oil**
» **¼ teaspoon clove, whole**
» **¼ teaspoon black peppercorns, whole**
» **½ teaspoon cumin, whole**
» **3 – 4 green cardamom pods**
» **2 sticks cinnamon**
» **⅛ teaspoon fennel seeds**
» **½ teaspoon coriander seeds, gently crushed**
» **¼ cup cashews**
» **¼ cup pistachios**
» **1 pinch saffron, steeped for 5 minutes in 3 Tablespoons hot water**

A note on spices

Because this dish depends on its spices so heavily, make sure that you buy your spices from a store that has a high turnover rate. This goes double for any sort of spice that you're using that is ground. If you go to a store where the spice bottles are gathering dust, you can be sure that you will miss out on the full, robust flavors of fresh spices.

I personally prefer to buy my spices whole, and grind them myself as needed. This is because as soon as you grind a spice, its oils begin to release. Just be aware of spices!

Get the basmati rice cooking first.

Slice up the lotus root into ½ inch discs. Slice up the carrots into ½ inch discs. Set aside. Heat up a wide, shallow pan over high heat. In the pan, melt the shortening, and pour in the sesame oil. You will need this much oil. Do not reduce the amount of oil. When a wisp of smoke escapes the surface of the oil, it is hot enough for the spices to be added.

Add the clove, the whole black peppercorns, the whole cumin, the cardamom pods, the sticks of cinnamon, the fennel seeds, and the crushed coriander seeds. When cumin starts to pop in about 30 – 45 seconds, pour in the cashews and pistachios.

Drop down the heat to medium. Cook the nuts and spices over the medium heat for 3 – 5 minutes, or until you smell a light nutty smell. Stir constantly to ensure that the nuts get thoroughly coated in oil and spices, and so that the nuts don't overcook.

Add the carrots. Stir to combine in the oil and spices. Drop down the heat to medium low, and put on the lid. Cook 5 – 8 minutes, until the carrots are half done. Add lotus roots, and stir very gently to combine (you want to maintain the look of them). Put the lid back on, cook 10 – 15 minutes. The lotus is going to be a little bit on the crispy side, so don't worry about this. They just need time to cook.

Remove the pot from the heat, and allow it to cool slightly. Add the steeped saffron to the pot. Stir very gently to combine. Lay out the rice onto a platter. Evenly coat the rice with the spiced carrot and lotus root combination. With two salad forks, gently toss the rice through the spice and vegetable mixture, being careful not to smash up the rice or break up too many of the delicate, long grains.

Sauces

Sauces are good to know, if for no other reason than the fact that they are useful in covering up mistakes. When a soup turns out too watery for my liking, I'll often add a bit of gravy to it. If a dish is looking a little oddly colored, a bit of a roux based sauce will hide any blemishes. With these basic sauces, go ahead and expand your existing repertoire.

Buerre Mani

Total time: 5 minutes

Buerre mani is traditionally made with butter, which is disgusting and not vegan. The purpose is to have starch suspended in oil that will slowly release into a soup or sauce. Any thing with a buerre mani needs to be cooked for extra time after being incorporated to avoid the raw flour taste. Use these in soups that have long-cooking vegetables that you don't have time to thicken with a roux. Because the base is so easy and quick to make, you can perform food first aid almost immediately. The repeated boiling alternated with the simmering allows the soup to gradually accept the thickener, get to the full thickening strength and then allow the thickener to mellow out, and let you see roughly how thick the soup will become. Bear in mind that any thickened soup or sauce will get thicker as it cools down.

> » **1 Tablespoon shortening**
> » **1 Tablespoon flour**

Take the flour and shortening, and massage them together, kneading the shortening through the flour as well as you can. Make sure that the flour and shortening are thoroughly combined, so that the resulting dough ball is tight. Use the buerre mani to thicken soups that you have mistakenly added too much water to.

Here's how:

1 pot of overly watery soup

1 recipe's worth of beurre mani, divided into 10 equal parts

Drop in one of the balls of beurre mani, and stir to combine into the soup. Let the soup come up to a full boil. Drop the soup back down to a simmer. Stir to combine all the ingredients. If the soup is thickened to the desired thickness, stop now. If not, continue adding extra balls of the beurre mani, and repeat the stirring to combine, the bringing up to a boil and dropping down to a simmer, and stirring to combine to gauge the thickness.

Once the soup has reached its desired thickness, let the soup continue to simmer for an additional 20 – 30 minutes, to cook out the raw flour taste. Taste the soup, and check for salt and seasonings at this point. If you need to add additional salt or seasoning, do so now, and let the soup simmer for an additional five minutes, to allow the seasonings to permeate.

Roux

Total time: 15 minutes

A roux is also traditionally made with butter, which should show you how gross traditional cuisine can be. Roux are meant to be bases for sauces, such as gravies, where you want thickness and a lightly roasted flavor. For a sweeter sauce, please use something like a slurry instead. The darker you make your roux, the less it will thicken your sauce or soup. The blonde roux is the most basic one. I use olive oil, because it imparts a clean flavor. Use regular All Purpose flour to avoid weird flavors.

» **1 Tablespoon olive oil**
» **1 Tablespoon flour**

In a wide, shallow skillet, heat up the olive oil over medium high heat. Sprinkle in the flour evenly over the skillet. Immediately, with a whisk or a wooden spoon, stir the flour completely through to coat in the oil. Make sure that all the flour is well coated.

Over medium high heat, continually stir the flour/oil mixture until the flour reaches a light blond color. Depending on your stove, this can take anywhere from 5 – 10 minutes. Remove the pan from the heat, and reserve until your liquid to make the gravy, sauce, or soup is ready.

Veloute (Gravy)

A veloute is a classic French sauce that involves stock with bones in it. I use vegetable stock to provide superior results. You don't have to use your own homemade vegetable stock; a good quality, low-sodium one should work just fine. Use a white wine or a sherry to avoid overpowering the rest of the veloute.

> » **1 cup vegetable stock**
> » **½ cup wine**
> » **1 recipe roux (p. 113)**

Place the pan with the roux over high heat. When the flour sizzles, pour in the stock and wine, and whisk. If you don't have wine, you can use more stock instead. Whisk the sauce vigorously until all the lumps are whisked out. Bring the sauce up to a full boil, and then drop it down to a simmer. Simmer for about 5 minutes, or until the sauce reaches desired thickness. Remove from the heat, and serve.

Gravy-thickened soup

> » *1 pot overly watery soup*
> » *1 recipe of gravy*

In the last five minutes of cooking, pour gravy into the soup pot. Allow the soup to come up to a full boil, then drop it down to a simmer. Let it simmer for five minutes in total. The soup will get even thicker as it cools.

Slurry

Total time: 10 minutes

A slurry is for when you want a clear, shiny sauce. When you go to an Asian restaurant and you see a shiny glazed looking sauce over the food, the chef used a slurry to make that glaze. You may use arrowroot, kudzu, tapioca starch, or cornstarch in slurry types of dishes. Do not allow a slurry dish to come to a boil, as the starches will get overcooked, and won't thicken properly. If you see bubbles, the heat is too high.

Slurry-based sauces can be a lot of fun to experiment with. Try using pineapple juice or orange juice instead of straight water, and you'll have a sweet glaze. Throw some lemon onto the finished dish, and you'll have a sweet and sour sauce. Toss that sweet and sour sauce with sautéed or steamed vegetables, and you've got a cool looking Asian-looking dish, ready to go over rice or noodles.

» **1 Tablespoon cornstarch**
» **1 cup plus 3 Tablespoons (reserved) water.**

In a saucepan, heat up 1 cup of water to a bare simmer. Do not allow bubbles to form, as this means that the water is too hot. In a bowl, combine 3 Tablespoons of water and cornstarch. Mix well to form a loose batter. Pour in a few Tablespoons of the hot water. Stir vigorously to combine. Pour in a few more tablespoons of the water. Stir to combine. This is your slurry.

Pour the slurry into the remaining water in the pot. Stir to combine, and allow it to simmer for about 3 minutes. Turn off the heat, and remove the pot from the stove to cool. It will come down to room temperature in minutes.

Spicy Soup Cream

Total time: 5 minutes

If you've ever made a soup that looks like it needs a little something more, you've found the perfect recipe here. The problem with cooking with peanut butter, almond butter, cashew butter, or any of the other nut butters is that they're too sweet. Use tahini, and you end up with bitter undertones. Commercial nut milks are far too thin for making a soup more creamy, and they lack the actual nuts themselves, which lend an interesting and pleasurable texture.

Try this both at the stove and at the table. You can add the soup's cream towards the end of a recipe, or have a small bowl of it at the table for people to blend into their own bowls. This is quite a versatile recipe, and can be used as a creamy salad dressing as well. You can use my recipe for roasted nuts, or use your favorite commercial mixed nuts. If you're using a commercial variety, add a teaspoon of cumin powder to the recipe.

> » **1 cup roasted nuts**
> » **1 ½ – 2 cups water**
> » **1 clove garlic**
> » **Salt to taste**

In a blender, add the nuts, garlic, and 1 cup of the water. Begin pulsing in short bursts, to get the nuts coarsely ground. Pour in an additional 1/2 cup of water, and pulse for longer periods. If the sauce looks too thick and the blender can not handle it anymore, add more water, and continue to pulse. In the last stages, when the sauce looks smooth, let the blender grind the sauce at full speed until it's completely smooth.

Orange Molested Sauce

Total time: 30 minutes

Jenna made a comment in the Vegan Freak Radio podcast, about yuppie names for food, which make the white middle class folk salivate. She referred to "chipotle-kissed sweet potatoes" and my brain followed the line to the next logical step (after kissing), which is what inspired this title.

» **4 cups orange juice (or 1 can frozen concentrate, in which you can skip the reducing part)**
» **1 Tablespoon lemon**
» **2 Tablespoons ginger, grated**
» **2 Tablespoons sesame oil**
» **1 teaspoon sesame seeds**

Bring the orange and lemon juices to a rolling boil. Drop down the heat to a gentle simmer, and allow the juices to reduce to 1/4 the original volume (down to a cup). Add the ginger, and simmer for 5 more minutes. Add sesame oil, and whisk vigorously. Pour the sauce into a blender, and blend on high with the sesame seeds for 1 minute.

This sauce is excellent on grilled food: grilled eggplants, grilled zucchini (you can even use it as a marinade, but it's perfect as a sauce) grilled portabella mushrooms, or pretty much any vegetable you grill. Try the sauce poured over fresh berries for a dessert that bites back. This would also be pretty good on salad. If adding to a salad, try some chopped cilantro.

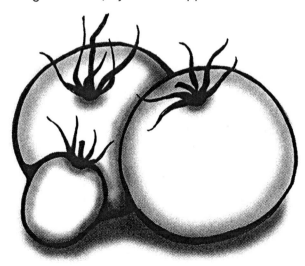

Asia Sauce (for Asian Appetizers)

Total time: 10 minutes

I put this sauce together to go over the omisubi recipe (p. 98), because the rice balls are fairly plain on their own. You can use it with other Asian-style appetizers that you're serving with rather good results.

» 1 Tablespoon rice wine vinegar
» 1 Tablespoon tamari or soy sauce
» 1 Tablespoon grated ginger
» 1 Tablespoon scallions, chopped
» 3 Tablespoons toasted sesame oil
» Salt to taste
» Pepper to taste
» 1 Tablespoon kimchee (optional)
» 1 clove garlic

Combine these ingredients in a small bowl, and whisk vigorously to make a vinaigrette. If it seems a little bland, add the kimchee as well. If it's still too bland for you, add some extra ginger. If it's still a bit tame, increase the pepper, mince up the garlic clove, and blend those in. If you're still feeling underwhelmed, you've got no tastebuds left. For a slightly creamier-looking sauce, you can add all the ingredients to a blender and blend on high until it's combined. This particular recipe should be able to serve two to four diners, depending on the amount of sauce each person likes.

cook's notes

Dished to Impress

These dishes, while not complicated per se, do look and taste impressive, as if you had spent multiple hours on making them. Serve these to those guests who are not used to vegan food as a sort of invitation to try something new. I've included dishes from when I was growing up and new ones that I developed on my own. In both cases, the food is so different from the run-of-the-mill that the diner will begin to develop the understanding that vegan food is not only delicious—it's diverse as well!

Asian Pesto Tomatoes

Total time: 20 minutes

This is the perfect appetizer to serve as a refreshing palate cleanser between the heavier snacks you'll be serving alongside them. If you want a more complete dish, you can just serve this over pasta, and it tastes outstanding. Use a short pasta, like a farfalle.

> » ½ cup sesame oil
> » 1 clove garlic
> » 1 Tablespoon salt
> » ½ teaspoon black pepper
> » 1 Tablespoon chopped cilantro
> » 3 oz cashews
> » splash of rice wine vinegar (to make the pesto loose)
> » 1 lb cherry tomatoes
> » Italian flat leaf parsley, leaves separated from the stems.
> » Endive leaves or other greens

Prepare the pesto. Pour oil, garlic, salt and pepper into a blender. Blend on high until the garlic is smooth. Add the cilantro. Pulse two or three times until the sauce becomes green. Add cashews. Pulse until the cashews are chopped up. Add just enough rice wine vinegar to loosen up the pesto until it becomes possible to pour (roughly 2 Tablespoons). Pour out, and chill.

Cut off the tops of the tomatoes, and scoop out a centimeter or so of the meat with a grapefruit spoon, melon baller, or the tip of a paring knife. Fill the vacated space with Asian pesto. Tie a parsley leaf around the tomato with its stem. Chill until ready to serve.

Because of the sheer riot of colors, you want to serve this on a white plate with some pretty greens that you find pleasing, such as curly parsley or kale. If you serve it in the bowl part of an endive leaf, you'll be able to have a sort of salad on the go.

Rasam

Total time: 30 minutes

This one's my own version, because I find the original version to be kind of weak in flavor. My mother used to make huge batches of rasam, and use it whenever one of us would have an upset stomach. We'd eat it over mushy white rice as a soup, and it was so comforting on rumbling tummies.

Rasam powder

» 1 Tablespoon dry toor daal or yellow split peas
» 5-6 dry red chilies
» ½ Tablespoon cumin seeds
» 1 Tablespoon coriander seeds
» 1 teaspoon peppercorns
» 1 teaspoon dry curry leaves

Roast all the spices in a small pan, and grind in a coffee grinder.

Rasam

» 1 cup dry yellow split peas or toor daal
» 1 Tablespoon oil
» 1 Tablespoon black mustard seeds
» tiny dash asafetida
» ¼ cup curry leaves
» 1 lb tomatoes, chopped
» salt to taste
» 1 Tablespoon ground black pepper
» 2 Tablespoons tamarind paste
» 1 gallon water
» 1 cup cilantro, minced for garnish

Boil the split peas or daal in a separate pot for 20 minutes. Heat oil in a pot, add mustard seeds, and allow to pop. Add a dash of asafetida. Wait 3 seconds, and add the curry leaves. Add the tomatoes, and sprinkle on salt. Cook for about five minutes. Add the black pepper, the rasam powder, and the tamarind paste. Add the water and cooked, drained split peas. Bring to a full boil, and keep it boiling for 15 minutes. When cooked, sprinkle on cilantro for garnish. Serve over mushy rice.

Sambhar

Total time: 1½ hours

Sambhar is essentially a wet curry. It's excellent as a side dish for dosa, vada, or idli. It's really spicy, and the tamarind paste gives it a dark, earthy flavor that cannot be matched by anything else. That mix of hot, slightly salty, and sour, along with the ground texture of the daal is quite an interesting sensation.

Sambhar powder

- » 1 teaspoon salt
- » 1 Tablespoon fenugreek powder
- » 1 teaspoon turmeric powder
- » 1 teaspoon coriander powder
- » Tiny dash of asafetida powder (optional)
- » Ground black pepper or chili powder, to taste (optional)

Combine in a small bowl and set aside. Freshly ground spices work well here, but be sure to double the amount of each whole spice before making it into powder.

Sambhar

- » 1½ cups dry toor daal (or yellow split peas)
- » 6 cups water
- » 3 Tablespoons oil (in preferred order: peanut, sunflower, safflower, canola)
- » ½ Tablespoon black mustard seeds
- » ½ Tablespoon cumin seeds
- » ½ Tablespoon coriander seeds, crushed
- » ½ lb onions, roughly chopped
- » ½ lb carrots, roughly chopped
- » 1 tomato chopped coarsely
- » 1 eggplant, roughly chopped
- » 1 potato, roughly cubed
- » ½ cup curry leaves (optional)
- » 5 green chiles, chopped
- » 1 Tablespoon of red chili powder
- » 2 Tablespoons tamarind paste (if using tamarind concentrate, ½ Tablespoon)
- » Up to 1 cup coriander leaves, chopped

In a stock pot, pour in six cups of water, and close the lid. Place the pot on the stove over high heat, and wait for it to come to a full boil. While the water comes to a boil, measure out your toor daal, and have it ready to place in the pot when the water starts boiling.

Begin to chop the onions, cube the potatoes, slice the carrots, and roughly chop the eggplant and tomato. Set them aside. By the time you're done chopping the vegetables, the water in the stock pot should be at a full boil. Add the toor daal to the boiling water. Close the lid of the pot, and wait for it to come back up to the boil. At this point, remove the lid of the pot, and set it aside. Allow the daal to cook, uncovered, for around 45 minutes, or until cooked through and tender.

While you wait for the daal to cook, finish chopping your vegetables and chilies. Combine the two Tablespoons of tamarind paste with some of the hot cooking water from the pot of toor daal. This will allow it to integrate more easily into the pot. As soon as you are finished chopping the vegetables, set another large stockpot on the stove.

Pour your oil into the pot over high heat. Wait for the oil to get very hot. Have your mustard seeds, coriander seeds, cumin seeds and onions nearby. When the oil gets hot, add the mustard seeds. Wait for about 30 seconds or so, until they pop and explode. Add the cumin seeds. Wait another 30 seconds for them to pop and explode. Add the crushed coriander seeds and onions at the same time.

Stir the onions around in the pot, until they are combined completely with the spices and oil. Allow the onions to brown lightly, about five minutes. Instead of stirring the onions around constantly, make sure to let them sit still for a minute or two at a time, then continue to stir them around to avoid burning the onions.

When your onions are lightly browned, add the carrots to the pot, and stir the carrots around to evenly combine them with the spices and oil and onions. If you feel that your pot is looking a little dry, feel free to splash in some water from your cooking toor daal to allow it to calm down the heat a bit. You want the carrots to get cooked in the pot for about three to five minute before adding the next ingredient, so that they get lightly caramelized as well.

Add the tomatoes and sambhar powder to the pot, and stir around vigorously to combine. Drop down the heat to medium high, and cover the pot with a lid. Let them sit at the lower heat for about five minutes. The tomatoes should cook down a bit (but not completely) to a loose saucy consistency.

Add your potatoes and eggplant. Add the curry leaves. Stir the vegetables around in the pot to combine them thoroughly. Cover the lid again, and let the vegetables cook for about five to ten minutes. Every couple of minutes, open the lid of the pot, and give the vegetables a stir. When the potatoes begin to get softened (but not quite completely cooked yet), you are ready to add in the fresh green chilies. By this point, the toor daal should be cooked through. Pour the contents of the daal pot, along with the water, into the pot with the vegetables. Add in the chili powder.

Turn the heat on the stove to high heat, and let the vegetables come up to a full boil. Add the chili powder and tamarind paste that you have mixed with water. Let the vegetables continue to boil until the potatoes and eggplant are cooked through. You want the consistency of the sambhar to be that of a thick stew. If it seems too loose for your liking, feel free to let the sambhar simmer until some of the water has evaporated off.

Garnish the top of the sambhar with the chopped coriander leaves.

Black-eyed Peas Daal

Total time: 45 minutes (not counting cooking time for beans)

Black eyed peas are common in the American and Indian south. They are creamy, and have a distinct flavor all their own that you won't find in other beans. I'd describe the texture as somewhere between a lentil and a black bean. It cooks up much more soft than a black bean, but stays together better than lentils do.

» 1 lb. dry black-eyed peas, cooked in 10 cups water, with water reserved
» 4 Tablespoons oil
» 1 Tablespoon mustard seeds
» 2 Tablespoons cumin seeds
» 1 large handful curry leaves
» 2 cups chopped onion
» 1 Tablespoon turmeric
» Generous sprinkling of salt
» 5 plum tomatoes, chopped

Begin in a large stock pot. Add the 4 Tablespoons of oil and put over high heat.

When the oil is hot enough that you see it get more viscous when you move the pot around, immediately add the mustard and cumin seeds. After 30 seconds to a minute, they should be popping and cracking. At that point, add the handful of curry leaves and step back while they explode. Add the onions immediately, and stir around to combine. Sprinkle in the salt and turmeric. Stir to combine.

Drop down the heat to medium low, and cover the pot. Walk away for about 5 minutes. Start chopping up your tomatoes. After 5 minutes, check the pot, and stir the onions around to redistribute the spices and oil. If they're ready, you can turn up the heat to high. If they aren't ready, give the onions another 5 – 10 minutes, until they're softened.

When the onions get soft, turn up the heat to high, and add the chopped tomatoes. Stir around to coat in the oil, and sprinkle in a little salt to draw out the water. Stir around until all the oil and spices are mixed thoroughly. Drop down the heat to low. Put on the lid to the pot. Set a timer for 15 minutes.

In the meantime, drain the beans. In a separate pot, boil the bean cooking liquid to reduce it down to 1-5 cups, depending on how thin you want the final daal to be. You'll leave it at a medium boil (over medium heat) until you're ready for it. When 15 minutes have passed for the tomatoes, check the pot to see if they're fairly well broken down, and slightly browned around the edges. This is good.

Pour in the beans, and stir around to combine. When completely coated in the tomato mixture, pour in the bean cooking liquid from the other pot. Stir to combine. Turn up the heat to high. Wait for it to come to a full, rolling boil. Allow the beans to boil like that for about five minutes. Remove from heat, and serve over brown rice.

Spinach, Indian style

Total time: 20 minutes

Served with a basmati rice, this fragrant spinach dish will make mouths water before even hitting the table. I was always shocked at how my friends in the United States treated spinach. I'd see it in a gray mass that was limp and smelled vile. Why did it smell bad? Because the lot of it was just boiled and served straight up. There wasn't any flavoring added. There were no spices. It was horrible stuff.

Fortunately, my mother loves spinach, and knows just how to make it. I have modified her recipe and the recipe that I've eaten in various Indian restaurants over the years.

» 1 Tablespoon peanut oil
» 1 Tablespoon sesame oil
» 1 teaspoon cumin seeds
» 1 teaspoon coriander seeds, crushed gently
» 1 Tablespoon sesame seeds
» 1 large Spanish onion, diced fine
» 2 lbs spinach (yes, you'll need that much; this stuff goes FAST)

In a bowl, combine the following spices:

» 1 teaspoon Garam Masala
» ½ teaspoon kosher salt
» 1 teaspoon ground black pepper
» 1 teaspoon chili powder
» Grating of fresh nutmeg
» 5 cloves garlic, minced fine

Heat the oils in a wok or large shallow pan on high heat. Add in the cumin seeds. When they begin to pop (up to a minute), add the coriander seeds. These won't need to pop, so only wait 5 seconds. Add the sesame seeds. Wait until they pop (up to a minute). Add onions. Sauté the onions until softened.

Add the spinach in batches (wait for the first batch to wilt a little before adding the second batch), and all the other spices (Garam masala, pepper, chili powder, nutmeg). Stir to coat. When most of the spinach has started to wilt, add the garlic. Cook three more minutes, until all spinach is wilted.

Serve over a bed of basmati rice. Accompany with roasted vegetables and a fresh garden salad for a complete meal. Can also be served with Indian flatbread (roti or naan).

Roti

Total time: 1 hour

Roti is ideal for travel, because it keeps so well. I like adding spices to mine, because then I can eat it all by itself. The spices also help preserve the roti for long trips. Add ground herbs for a different effect. Use garam masala or curry powder for a wholly different taste. This recipe will work perfectly well as a plain roti if you leave out the spices. The spices, however, give it a kick that complements any meal.

When you're traveling, make a large stack of roti, and keep it one of those insulated boxes. Pack a box of either daal, dry cooked garbanzos, Indian roasted potatoes, pickles, or any other thing you think would go well with a flatbread. You'll find yourself slowly sneaking more and more of the roti along with whatever accompaniment you brought. This particular version that I have here is quite good all by itself.

» **2½ cups whole wheat flour**
» **3 Tablespoons wheat germ**
» **1 teaspoon salt**
» **1 teaspoon ground black pepper**
» **1 teaspoon coriander powder**
» **1 teaspoon cumin powder**
» **¼ teaspoon cinnamon powder**

» **¼ teaspoon clove powder**
» **grating of nutmeg**
» **¼ teaspoon green cardamom**
» **1 cup + 3 Tablespoons water, warm**
» **flour for dusting**
» **oil for spreading and to prevent drying out**

Mix all dry ingredients together. Add water, 1/4 cup at a time, and knead the resulting dough. Use flour to dust your counter if the dough ball feels too sticky. You don't want it to stick to your hands.

Divide dough into 2-Tablespoon-sized portions. Take each lump of dough, and roll it into a tight little ball. You may want to use a little oil when rolling the ball to prevent the ball from sticking to your hands, and to prevent the dough from getting dried out.

Toss each ball in flour, and generously dust your counter. Roll each ball into a disc with a rolling pin, liberally dusting with flour as needed. You want them to get into discs about 1/8 inch thick. The discs should be lightly coated with flour. Lay them all out on one layer on your counter, avoiding overlap.

On medium heat, preheat a heavy-bottomed skillet (cast iron is ideal). Lay the disc of dough onto the skillet. When little bubbles appear on the surface of the roti, flip the disc over. Let sit on the other side for about 30 seconds. You should be able to move it around in the pan. With a kitchen towel that's been rolled up, gently press down all over the roti to encourage it to puff. Once your puff is achieved, remove from heat and place in an insulated container. Spread a little bit of oil over the top to make the roti moist.

Fill the roti with your favorite roasted or dry-cooked vegetable, and roll up for a quick snack on the go. Spread on some agave nectar and brown sugar to an unsalted, plain roti for a sweet snack. Top off with fruit, and fold in half for an easy to eat dessert. Make the dough with an extra healthy dose of spices to have a stand-alone roti. Try it smeared with roasted garlic and ground sun dried tomatoes. Use it like a tortilla shell for your favorite cooked beans, rice, and vegetable mixture.

» *Freeze it!*

Yes, you may make your roti disks ahead of time. Freezing roti is an easy way to avoid going through all the work and effort of making roti every single time you have a yen for flat bread. Roll out the roti and cook them. Stack them with sheets of parchment paper between each roti (to prevent sticking), wrap them up, and freeze them.

Total time: 30 minutes

In its simplicity, puri is (in my opinion) the easiest flatbread to crank out en masse. If you really care how the thing looks, do what my mom does: roll out the dough in one fell swoop, cut into equally sized sections (with a pizza cutter), and fry the sections. Rolling out each one separately is a pain, but does make a nice presentation

> » **1 cup whole wheat flour**
> » **up to ½ cup water**
> » **Peanut or canola oil for frying**

Combine flour and water until the consistency of Wonder bread (doughy, pasty, that sort of thing). It should be able to hold its shape, and you should be able to roll it out. Separate the dough into about 8 – 10 equal parts. Roll the lumps of dough into little balls. Liberally dust your work surface with flour, and roll out the balls into discs. Each one should be about as thick as a CD. Fill a deep pot or wok about halfway with oil, and heat to 375° F. The oil should fill about half of the pot or wok. Fry as described below:

» *How to fry Puri*

The idea behind puri frying is to achieve a puff. The dough takes little to no time to cook, so the technique is important. Gently slide the disc of dough into the hot oil. It will sink to the bottom, then try to float back up. Gently take your slotted spoon and push down on the disc to dunk it under the hot oil. Continue to do this until it becomes puffed. Then, flip over the puri to cook on the opposite side. When lightly golden brown, remove from the oil, and drain on a wire rack (paper towels just make it swim in its own fat — ew).

Coconut Rice

Total time: 45 minutes

This is a dish that my mom used to serve up on those days when we'd get fresh coconuts from the market and she didn't particularly feel like spending hours in the kitchen. It's very simple because it's meant to be a quick dish.

It's best if you use freshly grated coconut, but not imperative. However, do NOT use sweetened coconut, because the sugar preserves it, and allows them to sell you an inferior (less fresh) product.

One method for using fresh coconut: remove the coconut meat from the shell, and throw it into the blender with about a cup of water. Blend on high until finely grated. Then, squeeze out the liquid AND SAVE IT. This is coconut milk, and it's worth its weight in gold! It's perfect as an addition to soups when the soup is almost done cooking, as it allows you to add lemon to the soup, and still have a creamy flavor. Then, use the coconut that you've drained in this recipe.

This is not to be confused with tender coconut, which comes in a coconut with the husk still on it, and has a slightly gelatinous texture. You want mature coconut, that's thick and white. There is a lot of water in the coconut, and this tastes good all by itself (to drink).

» 3 ½ cups cooked basmati rice
» 1 ½ Tablespoons peanut or canola oil
» ¼ teaspoon cumin seed
» ¼ teaspoon black mustard seed
» ½ teaspoon coriander seeds, crushed
» Tiny dash of asafetida (optional)
» 1 bunch curry leaves (if you can get them)
» ½ cup whole cashews, unsalted (optional)
» 1 whole chili, sliced in half (scrape out seeds for a milder flavor)
» 1 coconut, grated (or 1 ½ cups grated coconut)

When the rice is done cooking, dump out onto a wide, shallow serving dish to come down to room temperature.

Add your oil to a wide shallow pan, or a wok. Allow to heat up. When hot, add the cumin seeds, mustard seeds, and the coriander seeds. When they start to crackle and pop, add the dash of asafetida powder. Add the curry leaves, which will immediately pop loudly.

Throw in the optional nuts and roast for a little less than a minute. Add the chili. Add the coconut, and roast over medium high heat, stirring constantly. You may add salt while roasting, but it's not completely necessary. When the coconut turns light brown in color, turn off the heat, and pour the mixture over the room temperature rice.

Using salad serving forks, gently toss the mixture through the rice, being careful not to break up the long fragrant grains of basmati rice. Serve immediately as a main dish, with some kind of steamed or grilled vegetables.

Saffron Rice

Total time: 30 minutes

My friend Dana had some saffron in the house, along with some basmati rice that we'd just bought earlier that day. We had finished cooking a particularly large and somewhat exhausting meal. I didn't have the patience for a proper biriyani, but I still wanted a rice dish with saffron in it. Granted, the saffron would not have gone to waste, because the stuff is gold to me, but that's not the point. What we ended up with was a light, delicately perfumed dish that went well with the heavily spiced foods we made that night. It's been a favorite of ours ever since.

- » **2 cups uncooked Basmati rice**
- » **½ teaspoon saffron threads (usually one small packet)**
- » **¾ cup hot water**
- » **1 cup unsalted raw cashews, roughly chopped**

As the rice is cooking, heat up the ¾ cup of water so that it's very hot but not boiling (microwaving it in a coffee mug works great for this). Dump the saffron threads in the hot water and set the mug aside to steep.

Lightly roast the cashews in a pan over medium heat until they're slightly browned.

When the rice is done, mix in the saffron-water very, very, carefully so as not to mangle the rice, then add the cashews.

Tomato Rice

Total time: 1 hour

This is one of my favorite rice dishes of all time. It's funny, because Mom didn't make this as much as her friend did. We had professed love for that kind soul's version, which Mom took to mean that she was saved from having to bother making it anymore. Every time we'd visit this friend in any context, the dear woman would cook up a batch especially for us to eat.

Of course she made enough for everyone to eat, but that minor detail never got in the way of both of us feeling really special. If you ever do come into contact with children who like a particular dish that you make (not your own, that is), be sure to do it as often as possible, because it's a memory they'll cherish for their entire lives. I know I still think about my mom's friend to this day, and it's been years since we've seen her.

> » **3 cups of uncooked long grain rice**
> » **2 Tablespoons peanut oil**
> » **1 teaspoon sesame oil**
> » **1 teaspoon black mustard seeds**
> » **½ teaspoon coriander seeds, crushed**
> » **Dash of asafetida**
> » **1 bunch curry leaves**
> » **1 large Spanish onion, chopped fine**
> » **2 cloves garlic, minced**
> » **½ teaspoon salt**
> » **¼ teaspoon curry powder**
> » **2 lbs tomatoes, diced fine**
> » **1 Tablespoon crushed black pepper**

Cook the rice ahead of time. Spread the cooked rice onto a wide shallow serving dish.

If you have non-stick pans, this would be the time to use them. Add both oils to the pan, and allow to heat well. Add the black mustard and coriander. When the spices pop (up to a minute), add the asafetida. Immediately add the curry leaves, followed by the onions and garlic. Sprinkle on about 1/2 teaspoon of salt, to allow the water in the onions to evaporate faster. Add the curry powder. Stir through constantly to avoid burning.

When the onions have shrunken down in size, add the tomatoes and immediately turn down the heat to medium. Add in an additional 1/2 teaspoon of salt to facilitate water evaporation. Stir the tomatoes around, and allow to cook on medium for about 3 minutes. Drop down the heat to low, and allow the tomatoes to simmer very gently, until the tomatoes break down enough so that you have reduced the water by half. Add pepper. This isn't an exact science, and you've got some wiggle room, so it's OK if your first batch or two turns out a little on the watery side.

When done, pour the mixture over the rice, and mix gently to avoid mashing the rice. Serve at room temperature, but not cold. If it feels a little too cold, you can warm it up in the microwave (sprinkle on some water) for about a minute or so per serving. Serve as a main dish with a side salad to be a counterpoint to the heat of this dish.

Easy Peasy!

These are recipes that you crank out quickly when you're running late but need some food, or that you cook when you're still learning to cook. Without these kinds of recipes, any cookbook would seem incomplete.

Garlic Bread

Total time: 15 minutes

I've seen people pay exorbitant rates for "Texas Toast," which is essentially giant slabs of bread with partially hydrogenated vegetable oil. Often times, these margarines contain whey, casein, or any number of other disgusting dairy products that we most assuredly will do well to avoid like the plague. On top of that, they've been sitting there in the packaging for who knows how long!

However, garlic bread is a passion for me, because the marriage between the hot steamy bread—crusty on the outside and fluffy soft on the inside—with the sharp pungent garlic and the little bursts of sea salt is a pleasure to be experienced, not a food to be eaten. Without the humble loaf of garlic bread, most meals seem empty and pointless. Why did you even bother to roll out of bed if you don't have a warm, crusty baguette waiting for you?

Do not relegate yourself to substandard garlic bread substitutes made by corporations just salivating at the thought of sneaking yet another evil ingredient onto your dinner plate. Fight the power! Eat your own garlic bread! And now that you think I'm a raving lunatic, onwards to the recipe.

> » **1 crusty baguette**
> » **1 clove of garlic, cut in half lengthwise**
> » **1 clove of garlic, minced finely or crushed**
> » **Salt**
> » **3 Tablespoons olive oil**

Cut the bread almost in half, lengthwise. You want there to be a bit of a "hinge" on the bread. In a small saucepan, add the garlic and the oil together. Heat the garlic and oil over a gentle flame, until the garlic just sizzles. While you await the sizzle, take the halves of garlic you have, and rub them all over the baguette. This imparts a garlic flavor to the outside of the bread.

When the garlic in the pot is sizzling, remove it from the stove. Spoon the garlic-oil mixture into the "pocket" you've created in your baguette. If you got overzealous with the knife, and didn't leave a hinge, it's OK. Just spoon on the garlic oil mixture onto the bottom half of the baguette. Then, firmly press on the top loaf, and handle it that way. If you have a spray bottle with water, spray on some water. If you don't, lightly sprinkle some water over the loaf. If you do still have your hinge, close the "door" of the baguette, and wrap it in foil.

Bake at 350° F for about 5 – 7 minutes. You just want the loaf warmed through.

Herb Garlic Croutons

Total time: 15 minutes

I tried making my own croutons for myself because I wanted a salad and didn't want to go to the store. When I finished composing my salad, I arranged the croutons in a little pile on the edge of my plate. I flipped on the TV to watch *Finding Nemo* (my favorite movie of all time), and distractedly munched through my pile of greens. I was in veg-out heaven. When it got to the part where Nemo finds out about the evil niece Darla, I realized that I forgot to eat the croutons with the salad.

I still wanted a little something to take that last lingering edge of hunger away, so I just munched on the croutons, and was shocked by how delicious they were all by themselves! I happily devoured the remaining croutons in what seemed to be the space of one second flat, and have been making them as a snack for myself and my mother ever since. Be sure to make more than you think you'll need, because they go FAST.

» **1 loaf baguette**
» **1 clove of garlic, sliced in half lengthwise**
» **2 Tablespoons Italian seasoning (you may need more if it's a large loaf)**

» **Olive oil flavored cooking spray**
» **Sea salt, to taste**

Take a garlic half and rub it onto your baguette. This adds a gentle backdrop of garlic to the croutons that won't dominate the other flavors. Use up the whole clove – you never want to waste yummy garlic!

Slice the baguette into ½ inch rounds. If it is a very fat loaf, simply slice the loaf into half, lengthwise. Slice each half lengthwise again, so that you have four large sticks. Slice those sticks into ½ inch pieces.

Arrange the bread on a cookie sheet so that it's only one layer high. Rub the Italian seasoning in between your palms (releases the herbs' oils) and sprinkle evenly over the bread. Give the bread a very light mist of the cooking spray. Sprinkle on the sea salt. Bake until golden brown.

The thing about making croutons is that you want them to be cooked, but not brittle. There should still be a little bit of softness in the center of the crouton. Start the oven off at 350° F, and bake them for about five minutes. Remove the baking sheet from the oven. Pick one crouton up with tongs, and blow on it to cool it down. Pop it into your mouth and eat it. If it's still too soft, increase the temperature of the oven to 375° F, and let it go for a couple of more minutes. Test another one like you did before. Still not ready? Let it go a little longer. It'll involve some tweaking until you're able to come up with an approximate time for how long your oven takes.

Plain Hummus

Total time: 15 minutes

In most hummus that you'll buy or make, there's all sorts of extra bells and whistles like different aromatics, vegetables, olives, garlic, or even finely chopped truffles. This, however, is a recipe for what makes a hummus a hummus. From this base hummus, you can then begin to experiment with different bells and whistles. If you use canned chickpeas, drain the chickpeas, reserve the liquid, and use it in place of the water below.

> » **1 lb cooked chickpeas, drained (roughly 2 cups)**
> » **¼ cup olive oil**
> » **¼ cup tahini**
> » **¼ cup of lime or lemon juice**
> » **1 clove garlic**
> » **1 teaspoon cumin powder**
> » **1 teaspoon salt**
> » **1 cup of water, reserved**
> » **Extra salt to taste**
> » **Chopped parsley**
> » **Olive oil for garnish (optional)**

In the bowl of a food processor, add the chickpeas, olive oil, tahini, lemon juice, garlic, cumin, and salt. Pulse in short bursts for about a minute. The chickpeas should be broken up fairly well, but will be rather thick. Add in a bit of the water (about ½ cup).

Pulse for another 15 seconds, in short bursts. Open up the food processor, and taste the hummus. If you feel like it needs salt, sprinkle in some salt. If the hummus looks too thick for you, you may want to add more water. Replace the lid of the food processor, and blend. If the paste still looks too thick, drizzle in more water, ¼ cup at a time, until it looks like the consistency you want.

When the hummus is smooth, set on a platter. Sprinkle with parsley and lightly drizzle with olive oil. This is just a personal preference, but when I make my hummus, I prefer to serve the pita bread toasted lightly. It makes for a really nice textural variation.

IF YOU DON'T HAVE A FOOD PROCESSOR!

You can still make very delicious hummus if you don't have a food processor or blender. In most Latin American stores, you can find large wooden mortar and pestles. Find the largest one you can find, and pound the ingredients in the mortar and pestle. This also makes a fun party dish! All you do is place all the ingredients in the bowl of the mortar and pestle, and have your guests pound out fresh hummus right there on the table. If you don't have the money for a mortar and pestle (even though you can snag one for a few dollars), use a potato masher. If you've managed to lose your potato masher, get all the ingredients into a high-sided pot, and stir everything around vigorously with a large wooden spoon. Hummus is a delicacy that nobody should have to do without.

Black Olive and Truffle Oil Hummus

Total time: 20 minutes

» 1 lb cooked chickpeas, drained
» ¼ cup olive oil
» ¼ teaspoon ground cumin
» ¼ cup crushed garlic
» ¼ cup tahini
» Splash of lemon
» Generous pinch of salt
» Chili powder to taste (¼ teaspoon)
» 1 can black olives, chopped
» 1 teaspoon White truffle oil
» Chopped parsley

Sauté chickpeas in olive oil until lightly browned. Add cumin powder and crushed garlic, and toss through until combined. Blend in food processor until smooth with tahini, lemon, all the olive oil in the pan, salt, and chili powder. When smooth, remove from food processor and stir in the olives (1/2 of the can) and the white truffle oil. Put hummus on a large platter, so that it's 1 inch thick. Make 3 slight indentations that span the length of the hummus in the center. Drizzle olive oil into the middle one, and sprinkle a mixture of parsley and chopped olives. VERY lightly sprinkle chili powder over the olive/parsley mixture.

Roasted Red Pepper Hummus

Total time: 40 minutes

» 2 large red bell peppers
» ½ cup olive oil
» 1 lb cooked chickpeas, drained
» 1 teaspoon cumin powder
» 3 or 4 cloves garlic, crushed
» Salt, to taste
» ¼ cup tahini
» ¼ cup of lemon
» Chopped parsley

Preheat the oven to 400° F. Cut the red bell peppers in half, lengthwise, and remove and discard the seeds and stems. On the inside of the peppers, sprinkle in some sea salt and drizzle a few drops of olive oil. Rub the sea salt and olive oil into the insides of the bell pepper. Lay the four halves of bell pepper, skin side up, onto a baking sheet and place in preheated oven. Set the timer to 10 minutes.

In a wide, shallow pan, heat up the oil over medium high heat. Add the chickpeas, cumin, garlic, and a good sprinkling of salt. Cook until the chickpeas are roasted and lightly browned, for about 10 to 15 minutes. You may stir every couple of minutes to redistribute the flavors.

Check the peppers after 10 minutes. If the skin isn't black yet, bake for another 5 minutes. When the skin is completely blackened, remove from the oven, and put a large bowl over the top of the red peppers. The beans should be ready by now. Set the beans and peppers (with their bowl top) aside for roughly 10 minutes.

Set up your food processor, and juice your lemon and chop the parsley. In the bowl of the food processor, add your cooked chickpeas, tahini, and lemon juice. Set aside.

By now, the peppers should be ready. Remove your bowl. The peppers should be soft and pliable, and the skin should easily rub off with a paper towel or kitchen towel. Do NOT wash under water to remove every last bit of blackened skin. If a few pieces remain, it's not a problem. They add to the roasted flavor. Set aside the peppers for now.

Pulse the food processor four or five times until the ingredients are roughly chopped. Open the food processor, and taste the mixture for salt. If you need more salt, add more. If it tastes a little too salty, add some additional tahini, and increase the amount of lemon by double. If it's too dry, add some water or lemon juice as your own taste dictates. Pulse a few more times. Taste again. If it tastes right, blend until smooth. Add your roasted red pepper.

Pulse until the red peppers are evenly combined. Spread on large platter so that hummus is 1 inch thick, sprinkle with chopped parsley, and drizzle lightly with olive oil. Serve with wedges of tomato, wedges of lemon, and a basket of warmed pita bread.

Hummus Canapés

Total time: 15 minutes

This is another one of those recipes that just looks really pretty on a plain white plate. The color isn't a sharp contrast, but it is nice enough that a "busy" plate with a lot of patterns will detract from the dish's beauty. Try serving this on a stainless steel or silver plate. Or, for a very interesting and beautiful presentation, serve them atop a mirror. The reflections and the bright lights shining around the little canapés will give an impressive looking presentation.

> » **1 lb cucumbers, sliced into discs**
> » **Your favorite small crackers**
> » **8 oz hummus**
> » **4 oz black olives, sliced**
> » **1 small bunch dill**

Lay 2 overlapping cucumber discs onto a cracker. Spread hummus onto the cucumber discs. Lay on a slice of olive. Top with a little sprig of dill. You may also drizzle on a tiny bit of olive oil.

In lieu of, or in addition to the olive, you may also want to add:

» *Thin slice of sautéed mushroom*
» *A grape tomato (tiny tiny tomatoes)*
» *A curl of carrot (make these by curling off slices from a carrot with a vegetable peeler)*
» *A thin slice of red chili*
» *A small piece of red bell pepper*
» *A "sword" of chive, laid on top*
» *A leaf of flat leaf parsley*
» *Tiny sprinkle of lemon zest*

Hummus Bites

Total time: 20 minutes

- » 1 can (8 – 12 oz) of chickpeas, drained and washed
- » 1 Tablespoon olive oil
- » 1 teaspoon cumin seeds
- » 1 Tablespoon sesame seeds
- » 1 teaspoon salt (adjust up or down to personal preference)
- » ¼ cup water or lemon juice
- » 1 teaspoon paprika
- » 1 Tablespoon tahini (optional)
- » 20 – 30 (depending on how you stuff them) mini pita breads OR
- » 20 – 30 (depending on how you stack it) crackers or bread discs

Drain and rinse the chickpeas. In a wide, shallow skillet or wok, heat up the olive oil over medium high heat. Sprinkle in the cumin seeds. Wait for 30 – 60 seconds, until they begin to explode and pop. Sprinkle in the sesame seeds. Add the chickpeas and salt, and toss to combine all ingredients evenly. Toss continuously for 3 – 5 minutes, or until chickpeas are golden brown.

Pour in the water or lemon juice, paprika, and tahini, and stir the chickpeas to combine with the liquid, paprika, and tahini. Increase the heat to high, and toss the ingredients in the skillet until the liquid mostly evaporates, and the chickpeas have the creamy coating of the tahini. Turn off the heat, but leave the skillet on the stove.

» *Method one: Mini Pita*

Cut open the pita bread via a small slit measuring about 1.5 inches across along the side seam of the mini pita bread. Stuff with a small spoonful of the chickpeas, depending on what you can fit. Serve on a large platter as appetizers.

» *Method two: Crackers*

Between your two fingers, smoosh one to two chickpeas. Lay the smooshed chickpeas on top of a cracker. Sprinkle on a couple of the sesame and cumin seeds. Serve on a platter as appetizers.

» *Method three: Toast points, bread discs*

Using your thumb and forefinger, split 2 – 3 chickpeas in half horizontally (their natural split should let this happen), and arrange the halves on top of the toast point or bread disc. Sprinkle on some of the sesame and cumin seeds. Serve on a platter as appetizers.

Vizza

Total time: 10 minutes

This is a quick, easy, and tasty vegan pizza recipe that avoids omni subs. This also works wonderfully with thinly sliced (cooked) red bliss potatoes in place of the tomatoes, thinly sliced olives, or even thinly sliced cucumber. If you don't have lavash (see p. 144), you can also use a flour tortilla. What I like about this recipe is that it is eminently customizable. If the variations I have presented do not look appetizing to you, make up your own! The important thing is to stack up ingredients that will taste good together with the hummus.

> » **1 sheet of lavash**
> » **2 Tablespoons hummus**
> » **1 plum tomato**
> » **1 Tablespoon chopped parsley**
> » **Splash of lemon**
> » **Sea salt**

Spread hummus onto the lavash. Slice up your tomato into thin slices. Arrange them onto the lavash in concentric circles. Sprinkle on some parsley, lemon, and sea salt. Cut the vizza into eight slices, and eat like regular pizza.

> » *Level 2 Vizza:*

Onto the regular vizza, add sliced kalamata olives and marinated artichokes.

> » *Level 3 Vizza:*

Bake Level 2 for five minutes at 475° F.

> » *Level 4 Vizza:*

Drizzle on Vizza oil (1 teaspoon olive oil mixed with truffle oil).

> » *Level 5 Vizza:*

Slice up some portabella mushrooms as thinly as you can get them. Toss with thyme and rosemary and some olive oil. Bake the mushrooms at 450° F for about 10 minutes, so that they get crisp. Lay onto the vizza, and serve as normal.

> » *Level 6 Vizza:*

When making your hummus, peel the garbanzo beans. Once peeled, press the beans through a strainer. With a large wooden spoon, vigorously mix in 4 Tablespoons of extra virgin olive oil. Grind in some white pepper. Thinly slice some garlic, and bake at 400° F until dried out. Grind in a spice grinder. Sprinkle into the bean mixture and stir in completely. Use this instead of regular hummus.

Lavash Buddy

Total time: 10 minutes

I found some Kosher Pareve Lavash (imagine that it's soft matza, but with leavenings and fat) at a dollar store near my house. I've been having fun making different dishes with it. This recipe is perfect for those mornings when you're horribly late and you have to take your lunch, and thank goodness you just happen to have some hummus on hand.

> » ¼ cup hummus
> » 2 sheets of lavash
> » 1 Persian cucumber (you can also use Kirbys instead, but just use 2)

Spread hummus onto lavash sheets. Slice the cucumbers in half, lengthwise, then make the halves into strips. Lay half the cucumbers onto each lavash sheet, and roll up tightly. Slice the lavash in half at a steep angle. Pack tightly into a box. Take a small baggie of hummus for dipping. Run out the door. When you get to work, pop into the fridge.

Pita, Not Pizza

Total time: 25 minutes

> » 1 pita bread
> » 2 Tablespoons hummus
> » 1 red potato, sliced into very thin rounds
> » 1 red onion, sliced into thin rounds
> » 1 tomato, sliced into thin rounds
> » 1 clove of garlic, minced
> » ¼ teaspoon cumin powder
> » Olive oil

Spread hummus onto the pita bread. Lay down one slice of potato. Next to it, overlapping most of the potato, lay down a slice of onion. Then, next to the onion, overlapping most of the onion, lay down the slice of tomato. Alternate this way until the pita bread is covered. Sprinkle on the minced garlic and the cumin powder, and lightly drizzle with the olive oil. Bake at 350° F for about 15 minutes, or until vegetables are browned.

Pita Pockets

Total time: 25 minutes

Although the traditional falafel and tahini is divine, I'll leave that up to the professionals. I like my homemade pita bread to have other ingredients that I find interesting to me. I don't cut the pita in half, to make two little half-moon looking pockets. I prefer to make an opening in one end about a few fingers wide, so I can tuck in my ingredients. Try your own favorite combinations for an interesting and varied menu. Or, have a party where guests can choose from piles of delicious looking ingredients, and make their own.

Red ingredients make for a nice rich flavor.

» **1 pita bread**
» **1 small beet, roasted and sliced thin**
» **2 slices red onions**
» **3 sun-dried tomatoes packed in oil**
» **1 plum or roma tomato, thinly sliced**
» **1 whole red pepper, seeded and roasted.**
» **1 red chili, roasted**
» **2 Tablespoons Italian flat leaf parsley**
» **2 or 3 basil leaves**

Slice the pita bread open about halfway. Place the roasted beets on the bottom layer. Then stack on the tomatoes, the peppers, the onion, the chili, and the herbs. Complete it with two or three grinds of black pepper, and a sprinkle of sea salt.

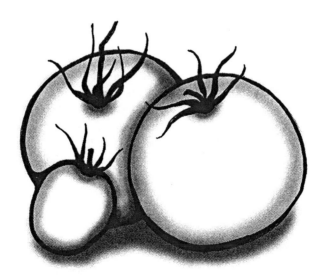

"Heart"y and Hearty

Total time: 20 minutes

» 1 Tablespoon olive oil
» 2 cloves of garlic, minced finely
» 1 medium red onion, chopped
» ¼ teaspoon cumin powder
» 2 lbs beefsteak tomatoes
» ¼ cup finely chopped mint
» ¼ cup finely chopped cilantro
» ½ cup lemon or lime juice (if you can get them, use key limes)
» Salt
» 1 package or 1 cup uncooked couscous, prepared (follow package instructions) in vegetable stock instead of water.

In a wide, shallow pan, heat the olive oil, and add the garlic, onions, and cumin powder. Sauté until the onions are soft. Add the tomatoes, and toss through very quickly. Cook for about a minute, then remove from heat. Toss with chopped herbs. Mix in the lemon or lime juice, and add just enough salt for the entire dish.

On a plate, spread out your couscous to form a sort of bed. Spoon on the tomato mixture over the top. Delicious as a side dish. It can also be served over toasted bread with a garden salad to make a really interesting and filling lunch.

Okra Buried Treasure

Total time: 30 minutes

The purpose of using a large amount of oil in this recipe is to virtually deep fry it is so that you reduce the slimy texture that okra is so infamous for. The tomatoes, in their acidic goodness, cut through further sliminess. Meanwhile, okra is good for you, being rich in B and C vitamins and essential minerals. This is a good way to get people who aren't usually fans of okra to eat the stuff.

I still hate it though.

I'm calling it buried treasure, because you're cutting the okra into thin, round discs, that are shaped like little okra coins. This dish tastes fine on its own, or over bread or rice.

- » **1 lb okra, cut into coins**
- » **¼ cup peanut or other high heat tolerant oil**
- » **1 teaspoon cumin seeds**
- » **1 teaspoon sesame seeds**
- » **2 stalks curry leaves, ripped**
- » **1 teaspoon salt**
- » **2 cloves garlic, minced**
- » **1 large tomato, chopped**

Preheat a wide skillet on medium heat. Slice the okra into thin, coin-shaped rounds. Discard the stems. Pour oil into the skillet, and turn the heat up to high. When the oil is hot, pour in the sesame seeds and cumin seeds. After they start popping, throw in the curry leaves and step back, as it will explode loudly. Immediately add the okra to the skillet. Arrange the okra medallions in such a way that they are almost submerged in the oil, and sprinkle in the salt. Do not stir. This almost deep frying method allows the okra's mucilaginous texture to be suppressed or even removed. When the okra begins to brown lightly (this can take up to 5 minutes, depending on how hot your skillet is), add the garlic and tomato to the pan, and stir to combine in the oil. Cook for 3 more minutes, or until the tomato has broken down slightly. If the pan looks too dried out, you may add some water, as needed.

Collard Greens

Total time: 35 minutes

- » 3 Tablespoons peanut oil
- » 1 Tablespoon yellow mustard seeds
- » 3 stalks curry leaves
- » 1 cup onion, finely chopped
- » 1 Tablespoon minced sage (½ Tablespoon dry)
- » 1 Tablespoon turmeric
- » 1 Tablespoon chopped thyme (½ Tablespoon dry)
- » 1 Tablespoon dried marjoram
- » 1 Tablespoon fresh basil
- » 1 Tablespoon coriander powder
- » 1 Tablespoon paprika
- » salt to taste
- » 1 bag (16 oz) collard greens, finely chopped in a food processor
- » 2 cups walnuts, roughly chopped
- » 2 cloves garlic, minced
- » up to ½ cup water

In a wide, shallow pan, heat up the oil over high heat. When a little wisp of smoke rises from the surface of the oil, sprinkle in the mustard seeds. Wait for about 30 seconds. When they begin to explode, rip in the curry leaves. Immediately add the onion, and stir around to coat in the oil. Add the sage, turmeric, thyme, marjoram, basil, coriander powder, paprika, and a few dashes of salt.

Stir the spices and the onions in the oil for about 5 minutes, or until the onions are translucent. Pour in all the collard greens into your pot. Since they're minced up so finely, you don't have to add them in batches if your pan is big enough. Add the nuts and garlic. Toss through to coat in the oil, spices, and onions.

Stir fry the collard greens for around ten minutes, or until the greens get brighter. About half way through, you might notice some crusty bits forming in the pan, and some of the greens sticking. This is perfectly normal, and may be combatted with the addition of up to 1/2 cup of water. This will allow the collards to get steamed slightly (and cook faster, so watch out), and avoid having burned bits in the final dish. Most if not all of the water should evaporate off by the time you're done.

Serve over a bed of hot rice or pasta, or in between slices of bread as sandwiches.

Dino Sandwich

Total time: 20 minutes

» 1 pita bread
» 1 teaspoon stone ground mustard
» 2 Tablespoons hummus
» 1 Kirby cucumber, sliced thinly lengthwise
» 1 plum tomato, sliced thin
» 1 shallot, sliced thin
» ¼ cup Kalamata olives, smashed and pitted
» ¼ teaspoon cumin powder
» ½ teaspoon chili powder
» 1 teaspoon lemon juice
» Olive oil

Split the pita bread to make two rounds. On one side, spread the mustard. Atop this, spread half the hummus. Layer on the vegetables. Smash the kalamata olives until they sit relatively flat. Lay them down on top. Sprinkle on the cumin, chili powder, and lemon juice. Drizzle with olive oil. Spread hummus on the second round of pita. Lay on top of the sandwich. Slice in half. Optionally, you may tuck this into another pita half to avoid falling vegetables, but I think that it makes it all too bready.

California Veg Wrap

Total time: 20 minutes

I made this recipe to have enough fillings for two wraps, because leaving behind a half of a cucumber is annoying. If you do not have lavash, simply use a regular wheat tortilla wrapper.

» **2 lavash sheets, or tortillas**
» **3 Tablespoons hummus**
» **1 romaine lettuce heart**
» **1 English cucumber, cut into long, thin slices**
» **2 plum tomatoes, sliced thinly lengthwise**
» **2 Tablespoons alfalfa sprouts**
» **Handful of spinach**
» **Sliced black olives**
» **Sliced marinated artichoke hearts**
» **Sea salt**
» **Ground black pepper**
» **Chili powder**

Spread hummus over each lavash sheet. On one edge of the sheet, layer the ingredients in the order listed. Heat up a griddle, and spray with cooking spray. Roll up as desired, making sure to fold in the left and right sides of the wrap before rolling up (to make the thing closed). Lay the wrap onto the hot griddle, and press down with a spatula. Cook 1 minute, then flip to cook the other side. Press down on this side. Remove from heat, and allow to settle. Wrap in tin foil, and you're ready to go! Keep cold if you're keeping it for more than 1/2 hour.

Variations

» *Thinly sliced zucchini or eggplant, roasted and spread with olive oil*
» *Thin slices of avocado*
» *Pitted olives, sliced*
» *Roasted garlic cloves*
» *Thin strips of carrot*
» *Snow peas, lightly steamed*
» *Your favorite pickle, chopped finely and sprinkled on*
» *Sprinkle of sunflower seeds*

Jackfruit Granité

Total time: 3 hours freezing time

A granité is essentially flavored shaved ice. I've made this dish to be a cooling, calming end to a fiery meal. You will most likely end up using canned jackfruit if you live outside of the regions where it grows, because it can get extremely expensive and hard to find. If you're not a fan of jackfruit, feel free to use pineapple, carambola, or oranges. I like to serve the granité in a chilled martini glass, with a sprig of mint to garnish.

> » ½ lb jackfruit
> » 2 cups water

Puree the jackfruit and water in a blender until silken smooth. Strain. Pour into a cookie sheet, and freeze. Every hour, go in with a fork, and break up the ice crystals to make tiny shards, until all the liquid is frozen. Serve in a chilled martini glass, with a sprig of mint.

Pomegranate and Wine Slushy

Total time: 30 minutes

> » ½ cup pomegranate juice
> » ½ cup Pinot Grigio (or other white wine)
> » 2 Tablespoons of sugar
> » Dash of cinnamon
> » Dash of nutmeg
> » 2 cups frozen strawberries or cherries
> » 6 ice cubes

Over medium heat, simmer the pomegranate juice, wine, sugar, cinnamon, and nutmeg down until it reduces down to half of its original volume (½ cup). Pour the juice and wine mixture into a blender along with the berries and ice, and blend until smooth. Spoon the mixture into wine glasses and chill in the freezer for 15 minutes.

Peanut Butter Banana Smoothie

Total time: 5 minutes

Ever had one of those mornings when you need something five minutes ago, because you're about to miss your bus/carpool/traffic jam avoidance? This is so fast to put together that I can do it even during crunch time. If you make enough for the others in the carpool, they won't be annoyed at the extra couple of seconds you took to bring on breakfast. If the smoothie is too sweet, dilute with more ice. Also, the liquid amounts here are merely suggestions. You may want to adjust them to your own liking.

If you find yourself running low on peanut butter, feel free to substitute any other nut butter. Or try a small handful of nuts. This does work with other juices as well: apple, mango, apricot, or white grape juice, etc. The purpose of the orange juice is to give a slightly sour kick.

To remove peanut butter from your spoon, just use another spoon (or your finger) to swipe it off. Do not (as certain people in an unnamed restaurant do) stand there with the peanut butter on the spoon, forever tapping away at the edge of the blender. You'll manage to irritate everyone in the vicinity of your kitchen, and you'll make this thing take much longer than it needs to. For shame.

> » 1 medium banana
> » 2 tablespoons peanut butter
> » 1 cup water
> » Handful of ice
> » ¼ cup orange juice

In the order that I've listed the ingredients, combine everything in a blender. You may want more or less ice, depending on whether or not your bananas are frozen. Blend on high speed until everything is smooth and consistently blended.

Strawberry's Dream

Total time: 5 minutes

If you can't find vegan graham crackers, just use a slice of bread with a little cinnamon on it, and toast for longer than 30 seconds to be sure it gets crispy.

> » 2 strawberries
> » 1 vegan graham cracker square
> » Dark chocolate
> » Sprig of mint for garnish

Slice your strawberries thinly, and lay on top of your graham cracker square in a circle, overlapping the slices. Shave some chocolate on top with a vegetable peeler. Pop into a toaster oven for about 30 seconds at 350° F. Garnish with mint. Enjoy.

Poached Pears in Mulled Wine

Total time: 40 minutes

This is a dish I created for a friend of mine who was getting married. Her caterer had no clue what to serve after the dinner, and she wasn't about to spend a small fortune on soy ice cream or something along those lines. She wanted something easy to make in quantity, and with ingredients that the caterer would have on hand. If you don't drink alcohol, thin out some concord grape juice with a little water, and use that instead.

> » 1 star anise
> » 1 stick cinnamon
> » 5 cloves
> » 1 green cardamom pod
> » 2 cups wine
> » 2 pears, peeled, and sliced in half, lengthwise,
>   then cored

Gently poach the pears in the wine and spices until wine has reduced by half. When the pears are cooked, remove them from the liquid and place in the refrigerator in a tightly sealed container. Return the wine to the stove over low heat and reduce it to a thick syrup. If it isn't thickening fast enough, add sugar to facilitate thickening. Serve each diner half a pear with a few drops of the sauce.

Brandy Married Man...darin

Total time: 10 minutes cook time, overnight in the fridge

This is one of those desserts that rounds out a nice, long dinner. You can use it as an appetizer, but be careful about how much you serve!

- » ¼ cup brandy or amaretto
- » 2 Tablespoons sugar
- » 1 star anise
- » 1 small can mandarin orange sections, drained

Put the anise seed in a small pot. Over the anise seed, pour in brandy. Bring up brandy to a bare simmer. Pour in the sugar, and heat and stir until the sugar is melted. Pour the brandy syrup over the orange sections. Macerate (let soak) in the fridge overnight. Cover tightly if you have many things in the fridge. Serve chilled with your favorite fresh fruits.

Hot Cock...tail

Total time: 15 minutes

It's good, I swear. I personally like my martini to be very dry, so I use a spray bottle to get my vermouth in my glass. If you don't have the vermouth in a spray bottle, measure out the 1/8 of a teaspoon, because much more than that, and your drink is destroyed.

- » 1 oz vodka
- » 1 red chili, sliced 3/4 of the way in half lengthwise
- » 1 cup cranberry juice cocktail, chilled
- » ⅛ teaspoon dry vermouth

Pour the vodka over the chili, and allow it to sit for about 10 minutes. Pour in cranberry juice, and stir to combine. Remove the chili, and perch onto the edge of a martini glass. Spray one or two sprays of vermouth into the glass, or pour in the 1/8 teaspoon. Pour the vodka and juice mixture into the glass slowly, being careful not to disrupt the vermouth too much. Serve.

Special Edition Coffee

Total time: 15 minutes

I personally love my coffee black, but you're welcome to splash in some vegan milk if you'd like. However, since this the coffee already has a complex flavor profile, you can be adventurous and try it without creamer. It's worth the effort.

» **1 pot AA Arabica coffee, brewed**
» **3 Tablespoons cocoa powder**
» **6 Tablespoons sugar in the raw**
» **1 Tablespoon panela (unrefined cane juice, whose water has been evaporated off)**
» **1 ½ Tablespoons cinnamon powder**
» **The zest of one orange**
» **pinch of salt**

Mix the cocoa with double the amount of boiling water, and dissolve. Mix in the sugars, the cinnamon, the orange zest, and the salt (salt *really* brings out the flavor in chocolate). When the coffee is done brewing, stir your mixture into the pot. Strain it through a fine strainer, and pour into pre-warmed cups to serve.

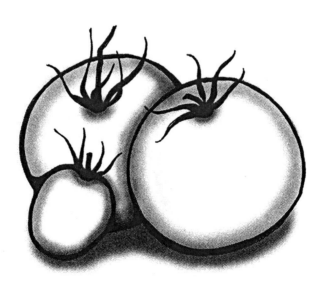

Index

Printed in the United States
89151LV00004B/55-170/A

Adobe®
Photoshop® Elements 2.0

User Guide

Contents

Installing and Learning Adobe Photoshop Elements 2.0

Welcome to the Adobe® Photoshop® Elements application, an easy-to-use, yet powerful image-editing, photo-retouching, and Web-graphics solution. Photoshop Elements offers robust features designed specifically for amateur photographers, hobbyists, and business users who want to create professional-quality images for print and the Web.

Registration

So that Adobe can continue to provide you with the highest quality software, offer technical support, and inform you about new Photoshop Elements software developments, please register your application.

When you first start the Adobe Photoshop Elements 2.0 application, you're prompted to register online. You can choose to submit the form directly or fax a printed copy. You can also register by filling out and returning the registration card included with your software package.

Installing Adobe Photoshop Elements 2.0

You must install the Photoshop Elements application from the Adobe Photoshop Elements 2.0 CD onto your hard drive; you cannot run the application from the CD.

Follow the on-screen installation instructions. For more detailed information, see the following file on the CD:

- (**Windows**®) *HowToInstall.wri*
- (**Mac**® **OS**) *HowToInstall.txt*

Learning Adobe Photoshop Elements 2.0

Adobe provides a variety of options you can use to learn Photoshop Elements, including a printed user guide, online Help, Hints, Recipes, tutorials, and tool tips. You can also use the free Adobe Online service to easily access a number of continually updated Web resources, from tips and tutorials to technical support information.

To view the Adobe Portable Document Format (PDF) files included on the Photoshop Elements CD, you must use Adobe Acrobat® Reader™ or Adobe Acrobat. Acrobat Reader software is included on the CD.

Using the printed documentation

A printed user guide, *Adobe Photoshop Elements 2.0 User Guide,* is included with the application.

The user guide assumes you have a working knowledge of your computer and its operating conventions, including how to use a mouse and standard menus and commands. It also assumes you know how to open, save, and close files. For help with any of these techniques, please see your Microsoft Windows or Mac OS documentation.

Using online Help

The Adobe Photoshop Elements 2.0 application includes complete documentation in an accessible HTML-based help system. The help system includes all of the information in the *Adobe Photoshop Elements 2.0 User Guide.* It contains essential information on using all Photoshop Elements commands, features, and tools, as well as tutorials, keyboard shortcuts, and full-color illustrations.

The accessible HTML format allows for easy navigation and reading using Web browsers. To produce a handy desktop reference, you can print the HTML file or an included PDF copy.

Online Help requires Netscape Communicator 4.x or Microsoft Internet Explorer 4.0 or 5.x.

To start online Help:

Do one of the following:

- Choose Help > Photoshop Elements Help.
- (Windows) Press F1.

Note: To properly view online Help topics, you must open them in Photoshop Elements.

Using Hints, recipes, and tutorials

Photoshop Elements provides Hints, recipes, and tutorials to help you learn the application quickly and work knowledgeably.

The Hints palette displays an illustration and brief description of any palette or tool your mouse pointer is on. The How To palette provides recipes that guide you through typical image-editing tasks, such as removing red eye in photos, adding effects to text, and creating GIF animations.

Note: To add new recipes, choose Download New Adobe Recipes from the How To palette pop-up menu.

Tutorials are available through the Help system and use sample files to take you step-by-step through the basics of working with layers, animated GIFs, and merging photos. The layers tutorial is particularly helpful, because understanding layers is an important step in mastering fundamental Photoshop Elements tools and techniques.

Using context-sensitive menus

Context-sensitive menus, which display options for tools and palettes, change depending on the item you've currently selected.

To display context menus:

1 Position the pointer over an image or palette item.

2 Right-click (Windows) or hold down Control and press the mouse button (Mac OS).

If no context-sensitive menu appears, no menu is available for that tool or palette.

Using tool tips

The tool tips feature lets you display the names of tools, buttons, or controls.

To identify a tool, button, or control:

Position the pointer over a tool, button, or control, and pause. A tool tip appears showing the name and keyboard shortcut (if any) for the item.

Note: *Tool tips are not available in most dialog boxes.*

Using Web resources

If you have an Internet connection, you can access additional resources for learning Photoshop Elements on the Adobe Systems Web site. These resources are continually updated.

To access the Adobe home page for your region:

1 Open the Adobe U.S. home page at www.adobe.com.

2 From the Adobe sites pop-up menu, choose your geographical region. Adobe's home page is customized for 20 different geographical regions.

About Adobe Online

Adobe Online provides access to the latest tutorials, quicktips, and other Web content for Photoshop Elements and other Adobe products. Adobe Online also provides bookmarks that take you quickly to noteworthy sites related to Adobe and Photoshop Elements.

Using Adobe Online

Adobe Online is constantly changing, so you should update it before you use it. Updating Adobe Online updates its bookmarks and buttons so you can access the most current content available. You can set preferences to automatically update Adobe Online daily, weekly, or monthly.

When you set up Adobe Online, you can choose to have Adobe either notify you when new information for Adobe Online is available, or automatically download and install that information to your hard disk. You can also choose Help > Updates to view and download new Adobe Online files whenever they are available.

To set preferences for Adobe Online:

1 Choose Edit > Preferences > Adobe Online (Windows and Mac OS 9) or Photoshop Elements> Preferences > Adobe Online (Mac OS X).

2 To specify how often Adobe Online checks for updates, choose an option from the pop-up menu.

3 Click OK.

To use Adobe Online:

1 In Photoshop Elements, click the icon at the top of the toolbox.

Adobe Online icon

Note: *To use Adobe Online, you must have an Internet connection and an installed Web browser.*

2 Do any of the following:

• Click Updates to access updated files.

• Click Preferences to specify how often Adobe Online checks for updates.

• Click Go Online to access the Adobe Web site.

• Click Close to return to Photoshop Elements.

Customer support

When you register your product, you may be entitled to technical support for a single incident. Terms vary depending on the country of residence and are only available for retail and upgrade versions. For more information, refer to the technical support card provided with your Photoshop Elements documentation.

Customer support on Adobe Online

Adobe Online provides access to the Support Knowledgebase, where you can find troubleshooting information that provides solutions to common problems.

Additional customer support resources

Adobe Systems also provides several forms of automated technical support:

• See the ReadMe and ReadMe First! files installed with the program for information that became available after this guide went to press.

• Explore the extensive customer support information on Adobe's World Wide Web site (www.adobe.com). To access Adobe's Web site from Photoshop Elements, choose Help > Support.

An Overview of Adobe Photoshop Elements 2.0

Adobe Photoshop Elements 2.0 makes digital imaging a breeze. Use Photoshop Elements to create high-quality images for print, e-mail, and the Web.

With a broad set of features, Photoshop Elements gives you endless ways to explore your creativity — restore old photographs, adjust color and lighting, create a new image by combining photographs, apply artistic effects, and prepare photos for sending via email or posting on the Web.

Use the tools of the trade

Based on the leading image-editing software that professionals have always relied on, Photoshop Elements 2.0 offers you an easy way to create high-quality images.

Quick Fix dialog Make instant color adjustments with just a few clicks in the Quick Fix dialog box.

Digital video frame acquisition Easily capture individual video frames from downloaded files with support for common video file formats, including MPEG2, MPEG3, and AVI.

Photomerge Automatically assemble multiple photos into one seamless panorama.

File browser Quickly preview, open, and organize all of your photos and view important metadata about each photo using the File menu Browse feature.

Red eye brush Fix unwanted red eye with a single stroke of the red eye brush.

Color variations Bring out the best in any photo by previewing various color adjustments to your photo and applying your choice with a single click.

Auto straighten/auto crop Photos are often taken or scanned at a slight angle, and may need to be cropped or rotated. You can correct skewed photos with one click.

Fill flash/adjust backlighting Instantly fix improper lighting with Fill Flash and Adjust Backlighting tools.

Broad file format support Save your images for virtually any use: print on photo paper, import into newsletters, presentations, reports, or greeting cards; attach to e-mail, post on the Web, and share as PDF (Portable Document Format) files on almost any computer or handheld device.

GIF animation Import or create GIF animations using Photoshop Elements layers and then interactively preview the results before saving.

Save for Web Compress your photos so they look sharp on the Web and download quickly.

Mac OS X and Windows XP support Take advantage of the newest operating systems including Windows XP and Mac OS X.

WIA Support (Windows only) Easily acquire photos from Windows Image Acquisition (WIA) enabled digital cameras, scanners, and other devices.

Get up to speed quickly

The intuitive design, built-in glossary, tutorials, and innovative Help features in Photoshop Elements 2.0 make it easy to learn and easy to use.

Comprehensive Help features Get immediate answers to your questions simply by typing a word in the new Help field. Linked to all Hints, Recipes, Tutorials, and the Glossary, the new Help feature does the searching for you and provides all the information you need in plain English.

Glossary Built-in glossary explains digital-imaging and computer terms.

Attach E-mail Easily attach edited pictures to e-mail using your existing e-mail program. Photoshop Elements can automatically resize and optimize the file for sending and viewing.

Graphics file management (Windows only) Use the built-in file association manager to set the file formats you want to be associated with Photoshop Elements.

Hints palette Get productive fast with illustrations and tips that show you how to use the wide variety of painting tools and palettes.

Dialog tips Tips embedded in the more complex dialogs eliminate confusion.

Web photo gallery Quickly and easily create a Web photo gallery featuring your pictures. Choose from a variety of templates that includes holiday, sports, and business themes, an old-fashioned slide show, and many other cool designs.

Batch processing Automatically rename, resize, convert the format, reorganize, or make other changes to multiple images at once using convenient Batch Processing.

History palette Work without worry knowing you can instantly undo or redo multiple steps with the History Palette.

Customizable palette well Access the tools you need quickly by organizing palettes any way you like in the palette well.

Explore digital imaging

Expand your creativity with powerful tools and effects.

Recipes Inspirational Recipes spark your imagination and describe how to perform complex editing techniques.

Selection brush Easily and precisely mask unwanted areas of a photo with the Selection Brush that lets you see feathered edges as you brush.

Editable text Type and see text right on the canvas and make changes at any time to the font, size, color.

PDF Slideshow Create PDF slide shows, complete with transitions that you can share with anyone who has Adobe Acrobat Reader—even on Palm and Pocket PC devices.

Picture package printing Lay out multiple pictures in various sizes on the same page for high-quality printouts from your home inkjet printer.

Painting tools Add creative touches to your photos using realistic paintbrush effects that simulate oils, watercolors, charcoal, pastels, and different canvas textures.

Effects Instantly apply frames, edges, and other complex effects to your photos, text, and shapes from the Effects Browser.

Filters Never run out of ways to enhance your photos. Visually scan the complete range of filter effects from a floating palette and apply any filter simply by dragging and dropping it onto your photo.

Layer styles Quickly create drop shadows, bevels, glows, and other effects by applying Layer Styles to the contents of a layer. Watch the contents instantly update anytime you edit the layer.

Liquify Create surreal effects by interactively twisting and pulling an image, or use Liquify as a touch-up tool to make subtle enhancements.

Background eraser Easily erase the background from a photo without disturbing objects in the foreground. Then paste the objects into another photo to effortlessly create composite pictures without harsh edges.

Darkroom-style tools Adjust the tone of specific areas of a photo using professional photographers' darkroom tools, including dodge, burn, and sponge.

Drawing tools Add graphic elements to your photos from a newly expanded library of shapes and symbols.

Layers Combine multiple images, text, and graphics on layers that you can move and modify independently with complete flexibility.

Contact sheet Quickly create a visual index of your photos that you can save or print for future reference.

Quickly Fix Photographs

Photoshop Elements Quick Fix

If you are new to digital photography or experienced at digital imaging, you'll find the tools you need to correct and enhance your photos in Photoshop Elements. In this tutorial you'll learn about basic tools and techniques to make your photos look their best. Be sure to look under the Help menu to read additional tutorials.

The Photoshop Elements Quick Fix dialog box gathers several image correction tools in one spot. You can fix photos that are too dark or too light, have an off-color cast, need more contrast, or need sharpening. Before and after previews let you compare adjustments to your original image before saving the changes.

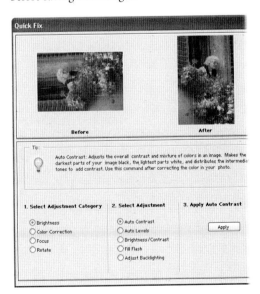

1. Open the Quick Fix dialog box.

With the file you want to fix open, choose Enhance > Quick Fix. The Quick Fix dialog box opens and presents tools for fixing photographs and tips for using the tools.

To make adjustments to your photograph:

Select an adjustment category Choose a category from the list:

- *Brightness* adjusts your photo's contrast and brightness, and quickly fixes overexposed or underexposed areas.

- *Color Correction* adjusts the saturation and color (hue) in your photo, and automatically corrects a color cast.

- *Focus* sharpens or blurs your photo.

- *Rotate* flips your image horizontally and vertically, or rotates your image at 90° or 180° angles.

Select an adjustment Each category has multiple adjustments that you can choose. The Tips provide more information for each adjustment.

Apply the adjustment If an adjustment has options to set, drag the slider to increase or decrease the value. If you selected an automatic adjustment, click Apply.

2. Rotate the photograph.

Choose Rotate from Select Adjustment Category, rotate the photo right, and then click Apply.

The photograph in our example was taken with a digital camera at a vertical orientation. The After preview shows the new orientation.

💡 *To straighten an image that was captured at an angle, or for more rotation options, choose Image > Rotate rather than Quick Fix.*

3. Correct the color and contrast.

The photograph in our example has a blue color cast, and it needs a little more contrast. We can fix both of these problems using Auto Color.

Choose Color Correction from Select Adjustment Category, select Auto Color, and then click Apply.

If your photograph needs more contrast, but the color looks fine, you could use the Auto Contrast command in the Brightness category. The Tips provide more information on when to use an adjustment.

4. Sharpen the photos.

Choose Focus from Select Adjustment Category, select Auto Focus, and then click Apply. You can click Apply multiple times for additional sharpening.

5. Accept the changes.

If you are satisfied with the adjustments click OK.

If you are not satisfied, you can undo, redo, or reset the adjustments:

- Click Undo once or multiple times for each successive adjustment you'd like to undo. Clicking Undo can undo the Reset Image option.

- Click Redo once or multiple times for each adjustment you'd like to redo that was undone.

- Click Reset Image to start over and undo all adjustments you've set in the current Quick Fix dialog box.

6. Learn more correction techniques.

The image adjustment tools in the Quick Fix dialog box are individually available in the Photoshop Elements menus. You can work in the Quick Fix dialog box or choose the tools you need individually.

In addition, you might want to become familiar with other image correction tools:

Variations to fix color casts, add color saturation, and lighten and darken images.

Levels and adjustment layers to have more control over contrast, brightness, and color adjustments.

Unsharp mask to precisely control sharpening in your photo.

Complete information for these tools is available in the Photoshop Elements Help.

Chapter 1: Looking at the Work Area

Welcome to Adobe Photoshop Elements. Photoshop Elements gives you an efficient work area and user interface to create and edit images for both print and the Web.

Getting familiar with the work area

The Photoshop Elements work area is arranged to help you focus on creating and editing images. The work area consists of the following components:

Menu bar The menu bar contains menus for performing tasks. The menus are organized by topic. For example, the Layers menu contains commands for working with layers.

Shortcuts bar The shortcuts bar displays buttons for executing common commands. (See "Using the shortcuts bar" on page 13.)

Options bar The options bar provides options for using a tool. (See "Using the options bar" on page 12.)

Toolbox The toolbox holds tools for creating and editing images. (See "Using the tools" on page 12.)

Palette well The palette well helps you organize the palettes in your work area. (See "Using the palette well" on page 13.)

Palettes Palettes help you monitor and modify images. (See "Using palettes" on page 14.)

Photoshop Elements work area
A. Toolbox B. Menu bar C. Shortcuts bar D. Options bar E. Active image area F. Search field G. Palette well H. Palettes

Using the tools

You use tools in the toolbox to select, edit, and view images; other tools let you paint, draw, and type. You can view information about any tool in the toolbox by positioning the pointer over it. The name of the tool appears below the pointer—this is called the *tool tip*. Additional information about the tool appears in the Hints palette. (See "Using the Hints palette" on page 16.)

You must select a tool in order to use it. The currently selected tool is highlighted in the toolbox. Some tools have additional tools beneath them—these are called *hidden tools*. When you see a small triangle at the lower right of the tool icon, you know that there are hidden tools.

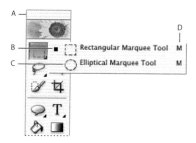

Selecting a hidden tool
A. *Toolbox* **B.** *Active tool* **C.** *Hidden tool* **D.** *Shortcut key*

To select a tool:

Do one of the following:

- Click a tool in the toolbox. If there is a small triangle at a tool's lower right corner, hold down the mouse button to view the hidden tools. Then click the tool you want to select.

- Press the tool's keyboard shortcut. The keyboard shortcut is displayed in its tool tip. For example, you can select the move tool by pressing the "v" key (see "Using keyboard commands and modifier keys" on page 19).

To move the toolbox:

Drag the toolbox by its title bar.

To set tool preferences:

1 In Windows or Mac OS 9.x, choose Edit > Preferences > General.

2 In Mac OS X, choose Photoshop Elements > Preferences > General.

3 Set one or more of the following options:

- Select Show Tool Tips to show or hide tool tips and rollover hints in the Hints palette.

- Select Use Shift Key for Tool Switch so you can hold down the Shift key in order to cycle through a set of hidden tools. When this option is deselected, you can cycle through a set of hidden tools by simply pressing the shortcut key (without holding down Shift).

4 Click OK.

Using the options bar

The first thing you should do after you select a tool is set its options in the options bar. By default, the options bar appears below the shortcuts bar at the top of the work area. The options bar is context sensitive, which means that it changes as you select different tools. Some settings in the options bar are common to several tools, and some are specific to one tool.

Options bar for lasso tool
A. *Gripper bar* **B.** *Tool icon* **C.** *Active tool* **D.** *Hidden tools*
E. *Tool options*

To use the options bar:

1 Select a tool. (See "Using the tools" on page 12.)

2 Look in the options bar to see the available options. For more information on setting options for a specific tool, search for the tool's name in online Help.

To return a tool or all tools to the default settings:

Click the tool icon in the options bar, then choose Reset Tool or Reset All Tools from the context menu.

Using the shortcuts bar

The shortcuts bar displays buttons for common commands. You can quickly click commands as you need them while you're working in Photoshop Elements. To see the name of a button, position the pointer over the button and its tool tip appears.

The shortcuts bar should always be left open in the work area so you can access all the tools and options that are available to you.

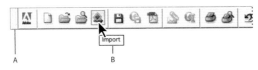

Shortcuts bar
A. *Gripper bar* **B.** *Tool tip*

You can also perform searches in the shortcuts bar. In the search field, you can enter a word or a phrase, click the Search button, and then a Search Results palette will appear. You can click on a link for more information about your search topic.

Clicking the Help Contents button ❷ in the shortcuts bar takes you directly to the Help system. In the Help system, you can search through the User Guide on-screen to help you find the answers you need. The results of your search will appear in the Search Results palette.

Using the palette well

The palette well helps you organize and manage palettes. You can store palettes that you don't frequently use in the palette well. You can still access the palettes, without having them expanded in the work area.

Palette well

Note: *The shortcuts bar must be showing in order to use the palette well. Choose Window > Shortcuts to display the shortcuts bar if it's not open.*

To use a palette in the palette well:

Click the palette's tab. The palette remains open until you click outside it or click the palette's tab.

To store palettes in the palette well:

Do one of the following:

- Drag the desired palette's tab into the palette well so that the palette well is highlighted.

- Make sure that the Close Palette to Palette Well option is selected in the palette's menu (see "Using palette menus" on page 15), and then close the palette.

To move a palette in the palette well:

Click the palette's tab and then drag it to a new location in the palette well.

To view information about a palette in the palette well:

1 Position the pointer over the palette's tab.

2 Look at the Hints palette to see a brief description of the palette. (See "Using the Hints palette" on page 16.)

Using palettes

Palettes help you monitor and modify images. There are many ways to organize palettes in the work area. You can store palettes in the palette well to keep them out of your way but easily accessible; or, you can keep frequently used palettes open in the work area. Another option is to group palettes together in the work area, or to dock one palette at the bottom of another palette.

Note: Drag a palette out of the palette well if you want to keep it open.

To display a palette:

Do one of the following:

- Click its tab.

- Choose the palette's name in the Window menu. Choosing the palette a second time hides the palette.

To change the size of a palette:

Drag any corner of the palette (Windows) or drag the size box at its lower right corner (Mac OS).

Note: Not all palettes can be resized.

To close a palette:

Do one of the following:

- If the palette is in the palette well, click outside the palette in the work area or click the palette's tab. (See "Using the palette well" on page 13.)

- Click the close icon on the palette title bar.

- If the palette is in a palette group, click the close icon on the title bar for the group.

- Choose the palette name in the Window menu.

To show or hide multiple palettes:

Do one of the following:

- To show or hide all open palettes, the options bar, the shortcuts bar, and the toolbox, press Tab.

- To show or hide all palettes in the work area (not in the palette well) press Shift+Tab.

To group palettes together:

1 Display the palettes you want to group together. If the palettes are in the palette well, drag at least one of them into the work area.

2 Drag a palette's tab onto the body of the target palette. A thick line appears around the body of the target palette when the pointer is over the correct area.

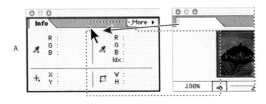

Grouping two palettes together
A. *Dragging a palette onto another open palette*
B. *Palettes grouped together*

To move a palette to another group, drag the palette's tab to that group. To separate a palette from a group, drag the palette's tab outside the group.

To dock palettes together:

Drag a palette's tab to the bottom of another palette. A double line appears at the bottom of the target palette when the pointer is over the correct area.

Note: Entire palette groups cannot be docked together at once, but you can dock the palettes from one group to another, one at a time.

To move a palette group:

Drag its title bar.

To collapse a palette group:

Double-click a palette's tab or title bar.

To reset palettes to their default positions:

Choose Window > Reset Palette Locations.

To always start with the default palette and dialog box positions:

1 In Windows or Mac OS 9.x, choose Edit > Preferences > General.

2 In Mac OS X, choose Photoshop Elements > Preferences > General.

3 Deselect Save Palette Locations. The change takes effect the next time you start the application.

Using palette menus

Palette menus are an important part of working with Photoshop Elements. Some commands in palette menus can be found in the menu bar; other commands are exclusive to palette menus.

When a palette has a palette menu, a More button appears at the top of the palette. The exact location and appearance of the More button depends on where the palette is located: in the palette well, in a palette group, or in the options bar. When a palette is docked, the More button is a sideways triangle.

Layers palette menu

To use a palette menu:

1 Select a palette. If the palette is in the palette well, click the palette's tab to open it.

2 Click the More button [More ▸] in the upper right corner of the palette.

3 Choose a command from the palette menu.

Using pop-up sliders

A number of palettes and dialog boxes contain settings that use pop-up sliders (for example, the Opacity option in the Layers palette). If there is a triangle ▣ next to the text box, you can activate the pop-up slider by clicking the triangle.

To use a pop-up slider:

Do one of the following:

• Position the pointer over the triangle next to the setting, hold down the mouse button, and drag the slider or angle radius to the desired value.

• Click the triangle next to the setting to open the pop-up slider box, and drag the slider or angle radius to the desired value. Click outside the slider box or press Enter or Return to close the slider box. To cancel changes, press the Escape key (Esc).

 To increase or decrease values in 10% increments when the pop-up slider box is open, hold down Shift and press the Up Arrow or Down Arrow.

Getting the most out of Photoshop Elements

The Photoshop Elements interface provides a variety of features to help you work efficiently and knowledgeably. Some features—such as the Hints palette and the How To palette—provide information about using tools and performing tasks. Other features—such as the Info palette and status bars—provide feedback about the current image and operation. Yet other features—such as context menus and keyboard commands—provide alternate ways to access commands.

Using the Hints palette

The Hints palette helps you learn how to use tools and palettes. As you run your mouse over a tool or select a tool, the Hints palette will give you information on using the tool.

To use the Hints palette:

1 Display the Hints palette by clicking its tab. If the Hints palette isn't showing in the palette well or the work area, choose Window > Hints to display the palette.

2 Position the pointer over a tool or palette, and look at the Hints palette to see a brief description of the item.

3 Click on one of the Related topics links for more information about an item.

Using the How To palette

The How To palette provides activities, called recipes, that guide you through different image-editing tasks. For example, you can view instructions about restoring an old photograph. Photoshop Elements will even do some of the steps for you.

To use the How To palette:

1 Display the How To palette by clicking its tab in the palette well. If the How To palette isn't showing in the palette well or the work area, choose Window > How To to display the palette.

2 Select a category of recipes, and click the recipe you want to use.

3 Follow the instructions in the recipe. When available, you can click *Do this step for me* to have Photoshop Elements perform the task for you.

Using the Info palette

The Info palette provides feedback as you use a tool. Make sure the Info palette is visible in your work area if you want to view information while dragging in the image.

To use the Info palette:

1 Display the Info palette by clicking its tab if it's in the palette well. If the Info palette isn't showing in the palette well or the work area, choose Window > Info to display the palette.

2 Select the desired tool.

3 Move the pointer in the image, or drag in the image to use the tool. The following information may appear, depending on which tool you're using:

The numeric values for the color beneath the pointer.

The x- and y-coordinates of the pointer.

The width (W) and height (H) of a marquee or shape as you drag, or the width and height of an active selection.

The x- and y-coordinates of your starting position (when you click in the image).

The change in position along the x-coordinate, ΔX, and y-coordinate, ΔY, as you move a selection, layer, or shape.

The angle (A) of a line or gradient; the change in angle as you move a selection, layer, or shape; or the angle of rotation during a transformation. The change in distance (D) as you move a selection, layer, or shape.

⊡ The percentage of change in width (W) and height (H) as you scale a selection, layer, or shape.

▱ The angle of horizontal skew (H) or vertical skew (V) as you skew a selection, layer, or shape.

To change the mode of color values displayed in the Info palette:

Do one of the following:

- Click an eyedropper icon ☌ in the Info palette, and choose a color mode from the pop-up menu.

- Choose Palette Options from the Info palette menu. Choose a color mode for First Color Readout and/or Second Color Readout, and click OK.

Actual Color displays values in the current color mode of the image; Grayscale displays the grayscale values beneath the pointer; RGB Color displays the RGB values beneath the pointer; Web Color displays the hexadecimal code for the RGB values beneath the pointer; and HSB Color displays the HSB values beneath the pointer. (See "About image modes" on page 54 for more information.)

To change the unit of measurement displayed in the Info palette:

Do one of the following:

- Click the cross-hair icon +, in the Info palette, and choose a unit of measurement from the pop-up menu.

- Choose Palette Options from the Info palette menu. Choose a unit of measurement from the Ruler Units pop-up menu, and click OK.

Using the status bar

The status bar at the bottom of the application window (Windows) or document window (Mac OS) displays useful information and is divided into three sections:

- The leftmost section displays the current magnification. (See "Magnifying and reducing the view" on page 20).

- The middle section displays information about the current file. You can change the type of information that displays.

- (Windows only) The rightmost section provides information as you use a tool. It also displays a progress bar to help you monitor operations. When an operation—such as applying a filter or using the Photomerge command—is in progress, you cannot perform other operations. However, you can interrupt the process or have the program notify you when it has finished.

To display file information in the status bar:

1 Click the triangle ▶ in the status bar.

2 Select a view option:

- Document Sizes to display information on the amount of data in the image. The number on the left represents the printing size of the image—approximately the size of the saved, flattened file in Photoshop format. The number on the right indicates the file's approximate size, including layers.

- Document Profile to display the name of the color profile used by the image. (See "About color management" on page 31.)

- Document Dimensions to display the document size of the image. (See "Changing the print dimensions and resolution of an image" on page 78.)

- Scratch Sizes to display information on the amount of RAM and scratch disk used to process the image. The number on the left represents the amount of memory that is currently being used by the program to display all open images. The number on the right represents the total amount of RAM available for processing images.

- Efficiency to display the percentage of time actually doing an operation instead of reading or writing the scratch disk. If the value is below 100%, Photoshop Elements is using the scratch disk and, therefore, is operating more slowly.

- Timing to display the amount of time it took to complete the last operation.

- Current Tool to view the name of the active tool.

To cancel operations:

Hold down Esc until the operation in progress has stopped. In Mac OS, you can also press Command+period.

To set notification for completion of operations:

1 In Windows or Mac OS 9.x, choose Edit > Preferences > General.

2 In Mac OS X, choose Photoshop Elements > Preferences > General.

3 Select Beep when Done, and click OK.

Using context menus

In addition to the menus at the top of your screen, context-sensitive menus display commands that are relevant to the active tool, selection, or palette.

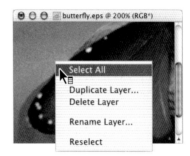

Context menu for a document window

To use a context menu:

1 Position the pointer over an image or palette item.

2 Click the right mouse button (Windows) or hold down Control and press the mouse button (Mac OS).

3 Choose a command from the menu.

Using keyboard commands and modifier keys

Keyboard commands let you quickly execute commands without using a menu; modifier keys let you alter how a tool operates. When available, the keyboard command appears to the right of the command name in the menu. You can view a list of keyboard commands and modifier keys in the Quick Reference Card section of online Help.

Using the Welcome window

The Welcome window provides options for acquiring images, as well as links to online Help and tutorials.

To display the Welcome window:

Choose Window > Welcome.

Deselect Show this screen at startup if you don't want the Welcome window to appear when you restart Photoshop Elements.

Viewing images

The hand tool, the zoom tools, the Zoom commands, and the Navigator palette let you view different areas of an image at different magnifications. The document window is where your image appears. You can open additional windows to display several views of an image at once (such as different magnifications).

Magnifying and reducing the view

You can magnify or reduce your view using various methods. The window's title bar displays the zoom percentage (unless the window is too small for the display to fit), as does the status bar at the bottom of the window.

💡 *When using the zoom tool, hold down Alt (Windows) or Option (Mac OS) to switch between zooming in and zooming out.*

To zoom in:

Do one of the following:

- Select the zoom tool 🔍, and click the Zoom In button 🔍 in the options bar. Click the area you want to magnify. Each click magnifies the image to the next preset percentage, centering the display around the point you click. When the image has reached its maximum magnification level of 1600%, the magnifying glass appears empty.

- Click the Zoom In button on the Navigator palette bar.

- Type the desired magnification in the Navigator palette bar text box.

- Choose View > Zoom In.

To zoom out:

Do one of the following:

- Select the zoom tool 🔍, and click the Zoom Out button 🔍 in the options bar. Click the center of the area of the image you want to reduce. Each click reduces the view to the previous preset percentage. When the file has reached its maximum reduction level so that only 1 pixel is visible horizontally or vertically, the magnifying glass appears empty.

- Choose View > Zoom Out to reduce to the previous preset percentage. When the image reaches its maximum reduction level, the command is dimmed.

- Enter the desired magnification level in the Zoom text box in the status bar (See "Using the status bar" on page 18) or in the Navigator palette.

- Click the Zoom Out button on the Navigator palette bar.

To magnify by dragging:

1 Select the zoom tool 🔍, and click the Zoom In button 🔍 in the options bar.

2 Drag over the part of the image you want to magnify.

Drag the zoom tool to magnify the view.

The area inside the zoom marquee is displayed at the highest possible magnification. To move the marquee around the image, begin dragging a marquee and then hold down the spacebar while dragging the marquee to a new location.

To display an image at 100%:

Do one of the following:

- Double-click the zoom tool 🔍.

- Select the zoom tool or the hand tool, and click Actual Pixels in the options bar.

- Choose View > Actual Pixels.

- Enter 100% in the Status Bar and press Enter or Return.

To change the view to fit the screen:

Do one of the following:

- Double-click the hand tool 🖐.

- Select the zoom tool or the hand tool, and click Fit on Screen in the options bar.

- Choose View > Fit on Screen.

These options scale both the zoom level and the window size to fit the available screen space.

To automatically resize the window when magnifying or reducing the view:

With the zoom tool active, select Resize Windows To Fit in the options bar. The window resizes when you magnify or reduce the view of the image.

When Resize Windows To Fit is deselected, the window maintains a constant size regardless of the image's magnification. This can be helpful when you are using smaller monitors or working with tiled views.

To automatically resize the window when magnifying or reducing the view using keyboard shortcuts:

1 In Windows or Mac OS 9.x, choose Edit > Preferences > General.

2 In Mac OS X, choose Photoshop Elements > Preferences > General.

3 Select the Keyboard Zoom Resizes Windows preference, and click OK.

Navigating the view area

If you have enlarged your image, you can navigate to bring another area of the image into view.

To view another area of an image:

Do one of the following:

• Use the window scroll bars.

• Select the hand tool  and drag to pan over the image.

> To use the hand tool while another tool is selected, hold down the spacebar as you drag in the image.

To move the view of an image using the Navigator palette:

1 Choose Window > Navigator, or click the Navigator tab in the palette well.

2 Do one of the following:

• Drag the view box in the thumbnail of the image, which represents the boundaries of the image window.

• Drag the slider in the Navigator palette.

• Click in the thumbnail of the image. The new view includes the area you clicked.

View of an image in the Navigator palette

To change the color of the Navigator palette view box:

1 Choose Palette Options from the Navigator palette menu.

2 Choose a color:

• To use a preset color, choose an option for Color.

• To specify a different color, click the color box, and choose a color. (See "Using the Adobe Color Picker" on page 131.)

• Choose Custom from the preset list.

3 Click OK.

Using the document window

You can open multiple windows to display different views of the same file. A list of open windows appears in the Window menu. Available memory may limit the number of windows per image.

To open multiple views of the same image:

Choose View > New View. Depending on the position of the first window, you may have to move the second window to view both simultaneously.

You can use the New View command when you're working with a zoomed image to see what the image will look like at 100% size in a separate window.

To arrange multiple windows:

Do one of the following:

• Choose Window > Images > Cascade to display windows stacked and cascading from the upper left to the lower right of the screen.

• Choose Window > Images >Tile to display windows edge to edge.

• Choose Window > Images > Arrange Icons to align minimized images along the bottom of the work area (Windows only).

To close windows:

Do one of the following:

• Choose File > Close to close the active window.

• Click the close icon on the title bar for the active window.

• Choose Window > Images > Close All to close all windows (Windows).

• Choose File > Close All to close all windows (Mac OS).

Duplicating images

Duplicating lets you experiment with and compare multiple versions of the same image. You can duplicate an entire image into available memory without saving to disk.

To duplicate an image:

1 Open the image you want to duplicate.

2 Choose Image > Duplicate Image.

3 Enter a name for the duplicated image.

4 To duplicate the image without layers, select Duplicate Merged Layers Only.

5 Click OK.

Viewing file information

You can view copyright and authorship information that has been added to the file. This information includes standard file information and Digimarc® watermarks. Photoshop Elements automatically scans opened images for Digimarc watermarks. If a watermark is detected, Photoshop Elements displays a copyright symbol in the image window's title bar and includes the information in the Copyright Status, Copyright Notice, and Owner URL sections of the File Info dialog box.

To view additional file information:

Choose File > File Info. For Section, choose the attribute you want to view.

To read a Digimarc watermark:

1 Choose Filter > Digimarc > Read Watermark. If the filter finds a watermark, a dialog box displays the Digimarc ID, copyright year (if present), and image attributes.

2 Click OK. If you have a Web browser installed, click Web Lookup to get more information about the owner of the image. This option launches the browser and displays the Digimarc Web site, where contact details appear for the given Digimarc ID.

Using rulers and the grid

Rulers and the grid help you position items (such as selections, layers, and shapes) precisely across the width or length of an image.

When visible, rulers appear along the top and left side of the active window. Markers in the ruler display the pointer's position when you move it. Changing the ruler origin (the (0, 0) mark on the top and left rulers) lets you measure from a specific point on the image. The ruler origin also determines the grid's point of origin.

To show or hide rulers:

If the rulers aren't visible, choose View > Rulers. Choose the command a second time to hide the rulers.

To show or hide the grid:

If the grid isn't visible, choose View > Grid. Choose the command a second time to hide the grid.

To change the rulers' zero origin:

Position the pointer over the intersection of the rulers in the upper left corner of the window, and drag diagonally down onto the image. A set of cross hairs appears, marking the new origin on the rulers. The new zero origin will be set where you release the mouse button.

Note: To reset the ruler origin to its default value, double-click the upper left corner of the rulers.

To change the rulers' settings:

1 Do one of the following:

• Double-click a ruler.

• In Windows or Mac OS 9.x, choose Edit > Preferences > Units & Rulers.

• In Mac OS X, choose Photoshop Elements > Preferences > Units & Rulers.

2 For Rulers, choose a unit of measurement.

Note: Changing the units on the Info palette automatically changes the units on the rulers. (See "Using the Info palette" on page 17.)

3 For Column size, enter values for Width and Gutter.

Some layout programs use the column width setting to specify the display of an image across columns. The Image Size and Canvas Size commands also use this setting. (See "Changing the print dimensions and resolution of an image" on page 78 and "Changing the size of the work canvas" on page 80.)

4 Click OK.

To change the grid settings:

1 In Windows or Mac OS 9.x, choose Edit > Preferences > Grid.

2 In Mac OS X, choose Photoshop Elements > Preferences > Grid.

3 For Color, choose a preset color, or select Custom to choose a custom color.

4 For Style, choose the line style for the grid. Choose Lines for solid lines, or choose Dashed lines or Dots for broken lines.

5 For Gridline every, enter a number value, and then choose the unit of measurement to define the spacing of major grid lines.

6 For Subdivisions, enter a number value to define the frequency of minor grid lines.

7 Click OK.

Undoing operations

Most operations can be undone if you make a mistake. Alternatively, you can restore all or part of an image to its last saved version. But available memory may limit your ability to use these options.

For information on how to restore your image to how it looked at any point in the current work session, see "Reverting to any state of an image" on page 26.

To undo the last operation:

Choose Edit > Undo, or click the Step Backward button ⤺ in the shortcuts bar.

If an operation can't be undone, the command dims and changes to Can't Undo.

To redo the last operation:

Choose Edit > Redo, or click the Step Forward button ⤻ in the shortcuts bar.

To free memory used by the Undo command, the Undo History palette, or the Clipboard:

Choose Edit > Purge, and choose the item type or buffer you want to clear. If already empty, the item type or buffer is dimmed.

Important: *The Purge command permanently clears from memory the operation stored by the command or buffer; it cannot be undone. Use the Purge command when the amount of information held in memory is so large that the performance of Photoshop Elements is noticeably diminished.*

To revert to the last saved version:

Choose File > Revert.

Note: *Revert is added as a history state in the Undo History palette and can be undone.*

Reverting to any state of an image

The Undo History palette lets you jump to any recent state of the image created during the current working session. Each time you apply a change to pixels in an image, the new state of that image is added to the palette.

For example, if you select, paint, and rotate part of an image, each of those states is listed separately in the palette. You can then select any of the states, and the image will revert to how it looked when that change was first applied. You can then work from that state.

Actions that do not affect pixels in the image, such as zooming and scrolling, will not appear in the Undo History palette.

About the Undo History palette

Note the following guidelines when using the Undo History palette:

- Program-wide changes, such as changes to palettes, color settings, and preferences, are not changes to a particular image and so are not added to the Undo History palette.

- By default, the Undo History palette lists 20 previous states. Older states are automatically deleted to free more memory for Photoshop Elements. You can change the number of states displayed in the Undo History palette in General Preferences. The maximum number of states is 100.

- Once you close and reopen the document, all states from the last working session are cleared from the palette.

- States are added from the top down. That is, the oldest state is at the top of the list, the most recent one at the bottom.

- Each state is listed with the name of the tool or command used to change the image.

- By default, selecting a state dims those below. This way you can easily see which changes will be discarded if you continue working from the selected state.

- Selecting a state and then changing the image eliminates all states that came after it. Likewise, deleting a state deletes that state and those that came after it.

- If you select a state and then change the image, eliminating the states that came after it, you can use the Undo command to undo the last change and restore the eliminated states.

Using the Undo History palette

You can use the Undo History palette to revert to a previous state of an image and delete an image's states.

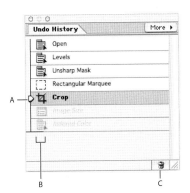

Undo History palette
A. *Undo History state slider* **B.** *History state*
C. *Trash button*

To display the Undo History palette:

Choose Window > Undo History, or click the
Undo History palette tab.

To revert to a previous state of an image:

Do any of the following:

- Click the name of the state.

- Drag the slider at the left of the state up or down
  to a different state.

- Click the Step Forward or Step Backward
  buttons on the shortcuts bar.

- Choose Step Forward or Step Backward from
  the palette menu or the Edit menu to move to
  the next or previous state.

   *To set the keyboard command for Step Forward
   and Step Backward, in Windows or Mac OS
9.x, choose Edit > Preferences > General, or in Mac
OS X, choose Photoshop Elements > Preferences >
General, and select an option for Step Back/Fwd.*

To delete one or more states of an image:

Do one of the following:

- Click the name of the state, and choose Delete
  from the Undo History palette menu to delete
  that change and those that came after it.

- Drag the state to the Trash button 🗑 to delete
  that change and those that came after it.

- Choose Clear Undo History from the palette
  menu to delete the list of states from the Undo
  History palette, without changing the image.
  This option doesn't reduce the amount of
  memory used by Photoshop Elements because
  it can be undone.

- Hold down Alt (Windows) or Option
  (Mac OS), and choose Clear Undo History from
  the palette menu to purge the list of states from
  the Undo History palette (and from the Undo
  buffer) without changing the image. If you get a
  message that Photoshop Elements is low on
  memory, purging states is useful, since the
  command frees up memory.

Important: This action cannot be undone.

- Choose Edit > Purge > Histories to purge the
  list of states from the Undo History palette for
  all open documents.

Important: This action cannot be undone.

Working with preset options

Photoshop Elements provides predefined libraries
of brushes, swatches, gradients, patterns, layer
styles, and custom shapes called *presets*. You can
use the Presets Manager to load different preset
libraries.

Presets are stored in separate library files that can be found in the Presets folder in the Photoshop Elements application folder.

Using pop-up palettes

Pop-up palettes appear in the options bar and provide access to libraries of brushes, swatches, gradients, patterns, layer styles, and custom shapes. When closed, pop-up palettes display a thumbnail image of the currently selected preset.

When you click the triangle to the right of the thumbnail image, the pop-up palette opens to show you the currently loaded preset libraries. You can change the display of a pop-up palette to view presets by their names, as thumbnail icons, or with both names and icons.

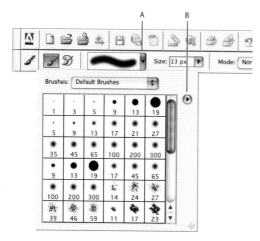

The Brush pop-up palette in the options bar.
A. Click to open the pop-up palette. *B. Click to view the pop-up palette menu.*

To select a preset in a pop-up palette:

1 Click the triangle in the upper right area of a pop-up palette.

2 Choose a preset.

To rename a brush, gradient, or pattern in a pop-up palette:

1 Select an item, click the triangle ⊙ in the upper right corner of the pop-up palette, and choose the Rename command from the palette menu.

2 Enter a new name in the dialog box provided, and click OK.

To delete a brush, gradient, or pattern from a pop-up palette:

Do one of the following:

• Select an item, click the triangle ⊙ in the upper right corner of the pop-up palette, and choose the Delete command from the palette menu.

• Hold down Alt (Windows) or Option (Mac OS) and click a brush or gradient.

To save a library of brushes, gradients, or patterns for later use:

Choose the Save command from the pop-up palette menu. Then enter a name for the library file, and click Save.

To load a library of brushes, gradients, or patterns:

Choose the Load command from the pop-up palette menu. Then select the library file you want to add to the pop-up palette, and click Load.

Note: Using the Load command will add the brush library to the brushes you have available. If you choose a preset library of brushes, the preset library will replace your current set of brushes.

To replace the current set of brushes, gradients, or patterns in a pop-up palette:

Do one of the following:

- Choose the Replace command from the pop-up palette menu. Then select the library file you want to use, and click Load.

- Choose a library file from the bottom section of the palette menu. Then click OK to replace the current list (gradients or patterns only).

To load to the default library of brushes, gradients, or patterns:

Choose the Reset command from the pop-up palette menu.

To change the display of items in a pop-up palette:

1 Click the triangle ▶ in the upper right corner of the pop-up palette to view the palette menu.

2 Select a view option:

- Text Only to display the name of each item.

- Small Thumbnail or Large Thumbnail to display a thumbnail of each item.

- Small List or Large List to display the name and thumbnail of each item.

- Stroke Thumbnail to display a sample brush stroke and brush thumbnail. (This option is available for brushes only.)

Note: Not all of the above options are available for all pop-up palettes.

Using the Preset Manager

The Preset Manager lets you manage the libraries of brushes, swatches, gradients, and patterns that come with Photoshop Elements. For example, you can create a set of favorite brushes, or you can restore the default presets. The configuration of presets in the Preset Manager corresponds to presets that appear in pop-up palettes and regular palettes.

Each type of library has its own file extension and default folder. Preset files are installed on your computer inside the Presets folder in the Photoshop Elements program folder.

To display the Preset Manager:

Choose Edit > Preset Manager.

To load a library:

1 Choose Brushes, Swatches, Gradients, or Patterns from the Preset Type menu.

2 Do one of the following:

- Click Load, then select a library from the list. If you want to load a library located in another folder, navigate to that folder, then select the library. By default, preset files are installed on your computer inside the Presets folder in the Photoshop Elements program folder.

- Click the More button ⌊ More ▶ ⌋, and choose a library from the bottom section of the pop-up menu.

3 Click the Done button when you're finished.

To restore the default library or replace the currently displayed libraries:

Click the More button ⌊ More ▸ ⌋, and choose a command from the pop-up menu:

- Reset to restore the default library for that type.

- Replace to replace the current library with the contents of another library.

To save a subset of a library:

1 Shift-click to select multiple presets. Only the selected presets will be saved to the new library.

2 Click Save Set, then enter a name for the library. If you want to save the library to a folder other than the default, navigate to the new folder before saving.

To rename a preset:

1 Do one of the following:

- Select a preset in the list, and click Rename.

- Double-click a preset in the list.

2 Enter a new name for the preset. If you selected multiple presets, you will be prompted to enter multiple names.

To delete a preset:

Select the preset you want to delete, and click Delete.

To change the display of presets in the Preset Manager:

Click the More button ⌊ More ▸ ⌋, and choose a display mode from the middle section of the pop-up menu:

- Text Only to display the name of each preset item.

- Small Thumbnail or Large Thumbnail to display a thumbnail of each preset item.

- Small List or Large List to display the name and thumbnail of each preset item.

- Stroke Thumbnail to display a sample brush stroke and brush thumbnail of each brush preset. (This option is available for brush presets only.)

Chapter 2: Setting Up Photoshop Elements

Adobe Photoshop Elements can be customized to your working environment.

About color management

Color management allows you to get consistent color between digital cameras, scanners, monitors, and printers. Color management also helps different applications, monitors, and operating systems display colors consistently.

When you create computer graphics, each piece of equipment you work with that reproduces color—such as a scanner, color monitor, and desktop printer—is called a *device*. Each type of device reproduces a different range of color, called a *color gamut*. As you move an image from one device to another, its colors can shift in appearance, sometimes resulting in dramatic changes. Color management maps colors from a device, such as a monitor, to another device, such as a printer. Color mapping ensures that colors on the monitor represent colors that the printer can reproduce.

By attaching, or tagging, a color profile to an image, you define how colors appear in the image; changing the attached profile changes how colors appear. Images without attached profiles are known as untagged images and are not color managed.

When an image has a color profile assigned to it, each device recognizes the profile, and displays colors according to the settings in the profile. This way, colors should look the same with all the devices.

Setting up color management

Photoshop Elements allows you to create color-managed images easily.

To create a color-managed image:

1 Open a file and choose Edit > Color Settings.

2 Select one of these color management options:

- No color management leaves your image untagged.

- Limited color management optimizes your images for the Web.

- Full color management tags your image with a standard ICC color profile for print optimization. The exact color profile depends on the color mode of your image.

3 Click OK.

4 Choose File > Save As, and select ICC Profile (Windows) or Embed Color Profile (Mac OS) in the Save As dialog box.

5 Finish saving the image, as described in "Saving images" on page 225.

Calibrating your monitor

Your monitor will display color more reliably if you use color management and accurate ICC (International Color Consortium) profiles. Using an ICC monitor profile helps you eliminate any color cast in your monitor, make your monitor grays as neutral as possible, and standardize image display across different monitors.

On Windows, you can use the Adobe Gamma software (installed with Photoshop Elements) to create a monitor profile. On Mac OS, you can use the Apple® calibration utility to create a monitor profile. Be sure to use only one calibration utility to display your profile; using multiple utilities can result in incorrect color.

About monitor calibration settings

Monitor calibration involves adjusting video settings, which may be unfamiliar to you. A monitor profile uses these settings to precisely describe how your monitor reproduces color.

Brightness and contrast The overall level and range, respectively, of display intensity. These parameters work just as they do on a television set.

Gamma The brightness of the midtone values. The values produced by a monitor from black to white are nonlinear—if you graph the values, they form a curve, not a straight line. The gamma value defines the slope of that curve halfway between black and white. Gamma adjustment compensates for the nonlinear tonal reproduction of output devices such as monitor tubes.

Phosphors The substance that monitors use to emit colors. Different phosphors have different color characteristics.

White point The coordinates at which red, green, and blue phosphors at full intensity create white.

Getting ready to calibrate

Before you begin calibrating:

- Make sure that your monitor is displaying thousands (16 bits) of colors or more.

- Set your desktop to display neutral grays only, using RGB values of 128. For more information, see the documentation for your operating system.

- Make sure your monitor has been on for at least 30 minutes. If your monitor isn't warmed up, the colors it displays may not be accurate.

Calibrating with Adobe Gamma (Windows)

The ICC profile you get by using Adobe Gamma uses the calibration settings to describe how your monitor reproduces color.

Note: If you're using Windows NT, some calibration options documented here may not be available.

To use Adobe Gamma:

1 Start Adobe Gamma, located in the Control Panels folder or in the Program Files/Common Files/Adobe/Calibration folder on your hard drive.

2 Do one of the following:

- To use a version of the utility that will guide you through each step, select Step by Step, and click OK. This version is recommended if you're new to color management. If you choose this option, follow the instructions described in the utility. Start from the default profile for your monitor if available, and enter a unique description name for the profile. When you are finished with Adobe Gamma, save the profile using the same description name. (If you do not have a default profile, contact your monitor manufacturer for appropriate phosphor specifications.)

- To use a compact version of the utility with all the controls in one place, select Control Panel, and click OK. This version is recommended if you have experience creating color profiles.

At any time while working in the Adobe Gamma control panel, you can click the Wizard button to switch to the wizard for instructions that guide you through the same settings as in the control panel, one option at a time.

Configuring Photoshop Elements

You can configure preferences in Photoshop Elements to best meet your needs. By setting preferences, you can control the working environment in Photoshop Elements and change how the program uses memory.

Setting preferences

Preferences settings control how Photoshop Elements displays images, cursors, and transparencies, saves files, and uses plug-ins and scratch disks. You set most of these options in the Preferences dialog box from the Edit menu.

If the preferences you set are not behaving as you expect, the preferences file may be damaged. You can restore all preferences to their defaults, then create a new file by setting new preferences.

To open the preferences dialog box:

1 Choose the desired preference set from the Edit > Preferences submenu.

2 To switch to a different preference set, do one of the following:

- Choose the preference set from the Edit > Preferences drop-down menu.

- Choose the preference set from the menu at the top of the dialog box.

- Click Next to display the next preference set in the menu list; click Prev to display the previous preference set.

For information on a specific preference option, search for the preference name in the index.

To restore all preferences to their default settings:

In Windows, press and hold Alt+Control+Shift immediately after launching Photoshop Elements. Click Yes to delete the Adobe Photoshop Elements settings file.

In Mac OS, hold down Option+Command+Shift immediately after launching Photoshop Elements. Click Yes to delete the Adobe Photoshop Elements settings file.

New preferences files are available the next time you start Photoshop Elements.

Using tool pointers

When you select most tools, the mouse pointer matches the tool's icon. The marquee pointer appears by default as cross hairs, the text tool pointer appears as an I-beam, and painting tools appear as the Brush Size icon.

To set the appearance of a tool pointer:

1 Choose Edit > Preferences > Display & Cursors.

2 Select a setting for the tool pointer:

• Standard to display pointers as tool icons.

• Precise to display pointers as cross hairs.

• Brush Size to display the painting cursors as brush shapes representing the size of the current brush. Brush Size cursors may not display for very large brushes.

3 Click OK.

The Painting Cursors options control the pointers for the eraser, pencil, airbrush, paintbrush, impressionist brush, background eraser, magic eraser, selection brush, red eye brush, clone stamp, pattern stamp, and the smudge, blur, sharpen, dodge, burn, and sponge tools.

The Other Cursors options control the pointers for the marquee, lasso, magic wand, crop, eyedropper, gradient, paint bucket, shape, hand, and zoom tools.

To toggle between standard and precise cursors of some tool pointers, press Caps Lock. Press Caps Lock again to return to your original setting.

Making previews display more quickly

Pixel Doubling speeds up an image preview by temporarily doubling the size of the pixels by halving the resolution of the preview. This option has no effect on the pixels in the file; it simply provides faster previews.

To speed up previews:

1 Choose Edit > Preferences > Display & Cursors.

2 Select Use Pixel Doubling.

3 Click OK.

Resetting all warning dialogs

In certain situations, Photoshop Elements displays messages containing warnings or prompts. You can disable the display of these messages by selecting the Don't Show Again option in the message. You can also reset Photoshop Elements to display all messages that you've disabled.

To reset the display of all warning messages:

1 Choose Edit > Preferences > General.

2 Click Reset All Warning Dialogs, and click OK.

Using plug-in modules

Plug-in modules are software programs developed by Adobe Systems and other software developers to add functionality to Photoshop Elements. A number of importing, exporting, and special-effects plug-ins come with your program; they are in folders inside the Photoshop Elements Plug-ins folder.

You can select an additional plug-ins folder to use compatible plug-ins stored with another application. You can also create a shortcut (Windows) or an alias (Mac OS) for a plug-in stored in another folder on your system. You can then add the shortcut or alias to the Plug-ins folder to use that plug-in with Photoshop Elements. Once installed, plug-in modules appear as options added to the Import or Export menu, or as file formats in the Open and Save As dialog boxes.

Photoshop Elements can accommodate a large number of plug-ins. However, if the number of installed plug-in modules becomes great enough, Photoshop Elements may not be able to list all the plug-ins in their appropriate menus. Newly installed plug-ins will then appear in the Filter > Other submenu.

To install an Adobe Systems plug-in module:

Do one of the following:

• Use the plug-in installer, if provided.

• In Windows, copy the module into the appropriate Plug-ins folder in the Photoshop Elements folder.

• In Mac OS, drag a copy of the module to the appropriate Plug-ins folder inside the Photoshop Elements folder.

Note: Before copying or dragging the plug-in files into the Plug-ins folder, make sure that the files are uncompressed.

To install a third-party plug-in module:

Follow the installation instructions that came with the plug-in module.

To select an additional plug-ins folder:

1 Choose Edit > Preferences > Plug-Ins & Scratch Disks.

2 In the Preferences dialog, do one of the following:

• In Windows, select Additional Plug-ins Directory, click Choose, and select a folder from the list. Click OK.

• In Mac OS, select Additional Plug-ins Folder, select a folder from the list. Click Select or Choose.

3 To display the contents of a folder, double-click the directory (Windows) or click Open (Mac OS).

The path to the folder appears in the preferences window.

Make sure that you do not select a location inside the Plug-ins folder for Photoshop Elements.

4 Restart Photoshop Elements to load the plug-ins.

To prevent a plug-in or folder of plug-ins from loading:

Add a tilde character (~) at the beginning of the plug-in name, folder, or directory. That file (or all files in the folder) is ignored by the application when you restart it.

To view information about installed plug-ins:

Choose Help > About Plug-In and select a plug-in from the submenu (Windows) or choose Apple menu > About Plug-In and select a plug-in from the submenu (Mac OS).

Setting memory preferences

The amount of memory (RAM) Photoshop Elements needs is approximately three to five times the file size of your open images. When the amount of memory is insufficient, the application uses any available hard-disk space. To improve the application's performance, you can increase the amount of memory reserved for the application.

If you use other applications simultaneously with Photoshop Elements, make sure you leave enough memory for the other applications to use.

To set memory preferences in Windows:

1 Choose Edit > Preferences > Memory & Image Cache.

- In the Memory Usage menu, drag the Maximum Used By Photoshop Elements slider to the right.

To set memory preferences in Mac OS:

In Mac OS, memory preferences are set outside of Photoshop Elements. Refer to your Mac OS documentation.

Assigning scratch disks

When your system does not have enough RAM to perform an operation, Photoshop Elements uses a proprietary *virtual memory* technology, also called *scratch disks*. A scratch disk is any drive or partition of a drive with free memory. By default, Photoshop Elements uses the hard drive that the operating system is installed on as its primary scratch disk.

You can change the primary scratch disk or designate a second, third, or fourth scratch disk, to be used when the primary disk is full. Your primary scratch disk should be your fastest hard disk and have plenty of defragmented space available.

The following guidelines can help you assign scratch disks:

- You can use up to four scratch disks of any size your file system supports. Photoshop lets you create up to 200 GB of scratch disk space.

- For best performance, scratch disks should be on a different drive than any large files you are editing.

- Scratch disks should be on a different drive than the one used for virtual memory.

- Scratch disks should be on a local drive. That is, they should not be accessed over a network.

- Scratch disks should be conventional (non-removable) media.

- Raid disks/disk arrays are good choices for dedicated scratch disk volumes.

- Drives with scratch disks should be defragmented regularly.

To change the scratch disk assignment:

1 Choose Edit > Preferences > Plug-Ins & Scratch Disks.

2 Select the desired disks from the Scratch Disks menu (you can assign up to four scratch disks).

3 Click OK.

4 Restart Photoshop Elements for the change to take effect.

Important: The scratch disk file that is created by Photoshop Elements must be in contiguous hard drive space. For this reason you should frequently defragment your hard drive. Adobe recommends that you use a disk tool utility, such as Windows Disk Defragmenter or Norton Speed Disk, to defragment your hard drive on a regular basis. See your Windows or Mac OS documentation for information on defragmentation utilities.

About Web access

So that you can use all of the Web-related features in Photoshop Elements, including Online Services, make sure that you've set up your computer to send e-mail and browse the Web. Refer to any documentation provided by your preferred e-mail or Internet provider for setting up Web access.

You can also adjust these settings in your operating system. Refer to the operating system's documentation if you need help with settings.

Chapter 3: Acquiring and Opening Photos

You can acquire digital images from a variety of sources—you can create new images, import them from another graphics application, or capture them using a digital camera. Often you will begin by scanning a photograph, a slide, or an image.

About this chapter

Before you begin working with your photos, it's helpful to understand a few things about digital images. In this chapter, you'll also learn about the different ways of getting your photos into Photoshop Elements.

About digital images

Computer graphics falls into two main categories—*bitmap* and *vector*. Files can contain both bitmap and vector data. Understanding the difference between the two categories helps as you create, edit, and import artwork.

Bitmap images—technically called *raster images*—use a grid of colors known as pixels to represent images. Each pixel is assigned a specific location and color value. For example, a bicycle tire in a bitmap image is made up of a mosaic of pixels in that location. When working with bitmap images, you edit pixels rather than objects or shapes.

Bitmap images are the most common electronic medium for continuous-tone images, such as photographs or digital paintings, because they can represent subtle gradations of shades and color. Bitmap images are resolution-dependent—that is, they contain a fixed number of pixels. As a result, they can lose detail and appear jagged if they are scaled on-screen or if they are printed at a lower resolution than they were created for.

300%

1600%

Bitmap images are good for reproducing subtle gradations of color, as in photographs. They can have jagged edges when printed at too large a size or displayed at too high a magnification.

Vector images are displayed according to geometric characteristics and are resolution-independent—that is, they can be scaled to any size and printed at any resolution without losing detail or clarity. Vector objects include shapes and text in Photoshop Elements. (See "About vector graphics" on page 191.)

Getting photos from a scanner

Before you scan a photo, make sure that the software necessary for your scanner has been installed. Scanner drivers are provided and supported by scanner manufacturers, not Adobe Systems Incorporated. If you have problems with scanning, make sure that you are using the latest version of the appropriate scanner driver.

If you can't import the scan using the TWAIN interface, use the scanner manufacturer's software to scan your images, and save the images as TIFF, PICT, or BMP files. Then open the files in Photoshop Elements.

Importing scanned photos

You can directly import scanned photos from any scanner that has an Adobe Photoshop Elements-compatible plug-in module. See your scanner documentation for instructions on installing the scanner plug-in. For general plug-in information, see "Using plug-in modules" on page 35.

If your scanner does not have a compatible plug-in, you can import scanned photos using the TWAIN interface. (See "Importing photos using a TWAIN device" on page 40.)

To import the scan using a plug-in module:

1 Do one of the following:

- Click the Connect to Camera or Scanner button in the Welcome window, then choose the scanner name from the Import pop-up menu in the Select Import Source dialog box.

- Choose the scanner name from the File > Import submenu.

Importing photos using a TWAIN device

TWAIN is a cross-platform interface for acquiring images captured by certain scanners, digital cameras, and frame grabbers. The manufacturer of the TWAIN device must provide a Source Manager and TWAIN Data Source for your device to work with Photoshop Elements.

You must install the TWAIN device and its software, and restart your computer before you can use it to import images into Photoshop Elements. See the documentation provided by your device manufacturer for installation information.

To import a photo using the TWAIN interface:

Do one of the following:

- Choose File > Import, and choose the device you want to use from the submenu.

- Click the Connect to Camera or Scanner button in the Welcome window, then choose the scanner name from the Import pop-up menu in the Select Import Source dialog box.

Importing photos using WIA (Windows Image Acquisition) Support

You can use WIA Support to import images from certain scanners. When you use WIA Support, Photoshop Elements works with Windows Me, Windows XP or later, and your scanner software to import images.

Note: WIA Support is only available if you are using Windows Me or Windows XP, or later.

To import images from a scanner using WIA Support:

1 Choose File > Import > WIA Support.

2 Choose a destination on your computer to save image files to.

3 Click Start.

4 Make sure Open Acquired Images in Photoshop Elements is checked. If you have a large number of images to import, or if you want to edit the images at a later time, deselect it.

5 Make sure Unique Subfolder is selected so that the imported images are put directly into a folder named with the current date.

6 Select the scanner that you want to use.

Note: If the name of your scanner does not appear in the submenu, verify that the software and drivers were properly installed and that the scanner is connected.

7 Choose the kind of image you want to scan:

- Color picture to use the default settings for scanning color images.

- Grayscale picture to use the default settings for scanning grayscale images.

- Black and White picture or Text to use the default settings.

- Click Adjust the Quality of the Scanned Picture to use custom settings.

8 Click Preview to view the scan. Crop the scan if needed by pulling the rectangle so it surrounds the image.

9 Click Scan.

10 The scanned image will be saved in the .bmp file format.

Importing photos from a digital camera

Photoshop Elements works with digital camera software to import images directly from a camera. Make sure that the software and drivers that came with your digital camera are properly installed before you import images.

There are several ways digital cameras connect to computers. Be sure to check the documentation that came with your camera before you try to import photos.

To import photos:

1 Follow the procedures in the digital camera documentation to install any software that came with your camera and to connect the digital camera to your computer.

2 Do one of the following:

- Click the Connect to Camera or Scanner button in the Welcome window, and then choose the digital camera name from the Import pop-up menu in the Select Import Source dialog box.

- Choose File > Import, and select your digital camera from the submenu.

Note: If the camera name does not appear in the submenu, verify that the software and drivers were installed properly.

3 Once the digital camera software launches, import the desired images as you would if you were downloading them to your computer.

4 Save the imported image as a Photoshop Elements file.

Importing photos from digital cameras mounted to your computer

Certain digital cameras are connected, or mounted, to your computer in such a way that they are treated as additional storage devices. You can browse the contents of your mounted digital cameras as you would a CD-ROM drive or a hard disk drive.

Note: Some cameras mounted to your computer cannot be accessed via the Import command. In that case, you can use the File > Open command and then navigate to your camera to retrieve your photos.

Some mounted cameras require that you install manufacturer's software before you can connect the camera to your computer, so check any documentation that came with your camera.

To import photos from a mounted digital camera:

1 Connect your digital camera to your computer as directed in the documentation accompanying your camera.

2 Once your camera is detected by your computer, launch Photoshop Elements.

3 Do one of the following:

- Click the Browse for File button in the Welcome window, or choose Window > File Browser to browse the contents of your digital camera and open photos.

- Choose File > Open to navigate to a specific photo.

4 Save your photos as .psd files on your computer so you can edit them in Photoshop Elements. (See "Saving images" on page 225.)

If you're using Windows XP, you can set up your computer so Photoshop Elements is automatically launched as soon as photos are detected after your digital camera is connected. See the Windows XP documentation for more help.

Importing photos using WIA (Windows Image Acquisition) Support

You can use WIA Support to import images from certain digital cameras. When you use WIA Support, Photoshop Elements works with Windows Me, Windows XP or later, and your digital camera software to import images.

Note: WIA Support is only available if you are using Windows Me, Windows XP or later.

To import images from a digital camera using WIA support:

1 Choose File > Import > WIA Support.

2 Choose a destination on your computer for saving your image files.

3 Make sure Open Acquired Images in Photoshop Elements is checked. If you have a large number of images to import, or if you want to edit the images at a later time, deselect it.

4 Make sure Unique Subfolder is selected so that the imported images are put directly into a folder named with the current date.

5 Click Start.

6 Select the digital camera from which you want to import images.

Note: If the name of your camera does not appear in the submenu, verify that the software and drivers were properly installed and that the camera is connected.

7 Choose the image or images you want to import:

- Click the image from the list of thumbnails to import the image.

- Hold down Shift and click on multiple images to import them at the same time.

- Click Select All to import all available images.

8 Click Get Picture to import the image.

Getting images from video

You can quickly and easily capture frames from your digital videos using the Frame from Video command. When you see a frame you'd like to import as a still image, click the Grab Frame button, or simply press the space bar.

Your video clips must be saved in video file formats that Photoshop Elements can open in the Frame for Video dialog box. Windows formats include .avi, .mpg, and .mpeg, and Mac OS formats include QuickTime and .mpeg.

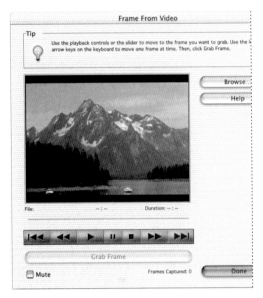

Capturing a frame from video

To acquire still frames from a video:

1 Do one of the following:

- Choose File > Import > Frame from Video.

- Click the Connect to Camera or Scanner button in the Welcome window, and then choose Frame from Video from the Import pop-up menu in the Select Import Source dialog box.

2 In the Frame from Video dialog box, click the Browse button, navigate to the video from which you want to acquire still frames, and then click Open.

3 To start the video, click the Play button ▶.

4 To import a frame of the video as a still image, click the Grab Frame button or press the space bar when the frame is visible on the screen. You can move forward and backward in the video to capture additional frames.

Note: *Some video formats don't support rewinding or fast-forwarding. In these cases, the Rewind and Fast Forward buttons are grayed out.*

5 When you have all the frames you want, click the Done button.

6 Save the still files in Photoshop Elements.

Creating new images

The New command ⬚ lets you create a blank image.

To create a new image:

1 Do one of the following:

- Click New on the Welcome window that appears when you start Photoshop Elements.

- To base the image dimensions and resolution on copied art pasted on the Clipboard, choose File > New. If the Clipboard does not contain image data, the image dimensions and resolution are based on the last image you created.

- To create an image from data on the Clipboard, select File > Create from Clipboard.

2 If desired, enter a name for the image, and set the width and height.

To match the width and height of the new image to that of any open image, choose a filename from the Window > Images menu.

3 Set the resolution and mode. (See "About image modes" on page 54.)

4 Select an option for the contents of the bottommost layer of the image:

- White to create a white background.

- Background Color to fill the background with the current background color. (See "Selecting foreground and background colors" on page 127.)

- Transparent to make the background layer transparent, with no color values. The resulting document will not have a background layer. (See "About the Background layer" on page 92.)

5 Click OK.

Using the File Browser

File Browser lets you view, sort, and process image files. You can use the File Browser to perform tasks such as creating new folders; renaming, moving, and deleting files; and rotating images. You can also view individual file information and data imported from your digital camera.

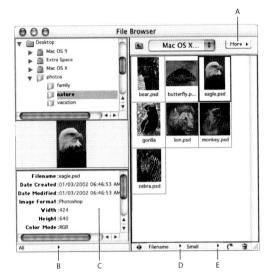

File Browser screen
A. *File Browser menu* **B.** *File information pop-up menu*
C. *File information* **D.** *Sort By pop-up menu*
E. *View By pop-up menu*

To display the File Browser:

Do one of the following:

- Click the Browse for File button in the Welcome window.

- Choose File > Browse.

- Choose Window > File Browser.

To display the File Browser menu:

Click the More button [More ▸].

Opening files from File Browser

File Browser helps you quickly locate image files and open them in the work area. You can also rotate images and view file information in the File Browser.

To open a file:

Select the file or files you want to open, and do one of the following:

- Double-click the file.

- Drag the selected file or files into the work area.

- Choose Open from the File Browser menu.

- Press Enter (Windows) or Return (Mac OS).

To rotate an image in the File Browser:

Select one or more files, and do one of the following:

- Choose a rotation option from the File Browser menu.

- Click the Rotate button ⟲ to rotate the images clockwise by 90 degrees.

- Alt-click (Windows) or Option-click (Mac OS) the Rotate button ⟲ to rotate the images counterclockwise by 90 degrees.

Note: *Using the File Browser, you can't Rotate or Batch Rename files stored on your computer desktop.*

To display file information:

Click the File Information pop-up menu at the bottom of the File Browser, and select one of the following:

- All to view all image information for a file.

- EXIF to view image information imported from your digital camera. (See "Viewing file information" on page 23).

Working with files and folders

Using File Browser, you can manage your folders and files. You can select files and folders, sort them by different criteria, and move, copy, and delete files. You can rename one file, or rename all of the files in a folder using the Batch Rename command.

To select or deselect files:

Do any of the following:

- On the right side of the palette, click a thumbnail to select a file.
- Shift-click to select multiple files.
- Control-click (Windows) or Command-click (Mac OS) to select non-contiguous images.

To select all files in the current folder:

Choose Select All from the palette menu. To deselect all files, choose Deselect All from the palette menu.

To sort files:

Click the Sort By pop-up menu at the bottom of the File Browser, and choose a sorting option.

To copy files:

Alt-drag (Windows) or Option-drag (Mac OS) files to a different folder.

To delete files:

1 Select the file or files you want to delete.

2 Do one of the following:

- Click the Trash button.
- Drag the files to the Trash button 🗑 .
- Press the Delete key.
- Choose Delete from the File Browser menu.

To create new folders:

1 Choose New Folder from the File Browser menu.

2 Type a name, and press Enter (Windows) or Return (Mac OS).

To rename files or folders:

1 On the right side of the palette, click a filename or folder name, or select a file or folder and choose Rename from the palette menu.

2 Type a new name, and press Enter (Windows) or Return (Mac OS).

Note: To move to the next filename, press Tab.
To move to the previous filename, press Shift+Tab.

To rename all the files in a folder:

1 Make sure that no files are selected.

2 To rename a subset of files in a folder, select the files you want to rename.

3 Choose Batch Rename from the File Browser menu, and set the following options:

- For Destination Folder, select where you want to place the renamed files: in the same folder or in a different folder. If you select Move to New Folder, click Browse (Windows) or Choose (Mac OS) to select a different folder.

- For File Naming, choose elements from the pop-up menus or enter text into the fields. The specified elements and text will be combined to create the new filename.

- For Compatibility, select the operating systems with which you want renamed files to be compatible. The current operating system is selected by default, and you cannot deselect it.

To change the display of files:

Do one of the following:

- Choose a thumbnail display option from the File Browser menu.

- Click the View By pop-up menu at the bottom of the File Browser and choose a display option.

To refresh the view:

Choose Refresh Desktop View from the File Browser menu. Closing and reopening the File Browser also refreshes the view.

When you rename a file, the order of files in the File Browser is not automatically updated, so you can refresh the view to see the changes you made.

To display files in Windows Explorer or Mac OS Finder:

Choose Reveal Location in Explorer (Windows) or Reveal Location in Finder (Mac OS) from the File Browser menu.

Working with the cache

The cache stores thumbnail and file information to make loading times quicker when you return to a previously viewed folder. Purging the cache frees up disk space on your computer.

To purge the cache:

Choose Purge Cache from the File Browser menu.

Opening images

You can open and import images in various file formats. The available formats appear in the Open dialog box, the Open As dialog box (Windows), or the Import submenu.

Note: *Photoshop Elements uses plug-in modules to open and import many file formats. If a file format does not appear in the Open dialog box or in the File > Import submenu, you may need to install the format's plug-in module. (See "Using plug-in modules" on page 35.)*

Opening files

The Open dialog box provides controls for locating and previewing files. You can also quickly access frequently used files with the Open Recent command.

There may be instances when Photoshop Elements cannot determine the correct format for a file. For example, transferring a file between Mac OS and Windows can cause the format to be mislabeled. In such cases, you must specify the correct format in which to open the file.

To open a file:

1 Choose File > Open .

2 Navigate to the file you want to open. If the file does not appear, select the option for showing all files from the Files of Type (Windows) or Show (Mac OS) pop-up menu.

3 (Mac OS) Click Show Preview to preview the selected file. This option requires the Apple QuickTime extension.

Note: Previews display faster if they are saved with the file. Select Always Save for Image Previews in the Saving Files preferences to always save a preview; select Ask When Saving to save previews on a file-per-file basis.

4 Click Open. In some cases, a dialog box appears, letting you set format-specific options. (See "Opening and importing PDF files" on page 48 and "Opening PostScript artwork" on page 49.)

To open a recently used file:

Choose File > Open Recent, and select a file from the submenu.

To specify the number of files that are available in the Open Recent submenu, choose Edit > Preferences > Saving Files, and enter a number in the Recent File List Contains text box.

To specify the file format in which to open a file:

Do one of the following:

- (Windows) Choose File > Open As, and select the file you want to open. Then choose the desired format from the Open As pop-up menu, and click Open.

- (Mac OS) Choose File > Open, and choose All Documents from the Show pop-up menu. Then select the file you want to open, choose the desired file format from the Format pop-up menu, and click Open.

Important: If the file does not open, then the chosen format may not match the file's true format, or the file may be damaged.

Opening and importing PDF files

Portable Document Format (PDF) is a versatile file format that can represent both vector and bitmap data and can contain electronic document search and navigation features. PDF is the primary format for Adobe Acrobat.

Photoshop Elements recognizes two types of PDF files: Photoshop PDF files and Generic PDF files. You can open both types of PDF files; however, you can only save images to Photoshop PDF format.

Photoshop PDF files Created using the Photoshop Elements Save As command, Photoshop PDF files can contain only a single image.

Photoshop PDF format supports all of the color modes and features that are supported in standard Photoshop format.

Generic PDF files Created using applications other than Photoshop Elements, such as Adobe Acrobat and Adobe Illustrator*, Generic PDF files can contain multiple pages and images. When you open a Generic PDF file, Photoshop Elements rasterizes the image.

You can also bring PDF data into Photoshop Elements using the Place command, the Paste command, and the drag-and-drop feature. (See "Placing files" on page 52, "Using drag-and-drop to copy between applications" on page 124, and "Using the Clipboard to copy between applications" on page 124.)

To open a PDF file:

1 Choose File > Open.

2 Select the name of the file, and click Open. You can change which types of files are shown by selecting an option from the Files of Type (Windows) or Show (Mac OS) pop-up menu.

3 If you are opening a Generic PDF file, do the following:

- If the file contains multiple pages, select the page you want to open, and click OK.

- Indicate the desired dimensions, resolution, and mode. If the file has an embedded ICC profile, you can choose the profile from the mode pop-up menu.

- Select Constrain Proportions to maintain the same height-to-width ratio.

- Select Anti-aliased to minimize the jagged appearance of the artwork's edges as it is rasterized.

- Click OK.

To import images from a PDF file:

1 Choose File > Import > PDF Image, select the file from which you want to import images, and click Open.

2 Select the image you want to open:

- To open a specific image, select it and click OK. You can use the arrows to scroll through the images, or click Go to Image to enter an image number.

- To open each image as a separate file, click Import All Images.

Press Esc to cancel the import operation before all images are imported.

To create a new Photoshop file for each page of a multiple-page PDF file:

1 Choose File > Automation Tools > Multi-Page PDF to PSD.

2 Under Source PDF, click the Choose button, and select the file from which you want to import images.

3 Under Page Range, specify a range of pages to import.

4 Under Output Options, specify a resolution, choose a color mode, and set the Anti-alias option for rasterizing each page of the PDF file. (To blend edge pixels during rasterization, select the Antialias option. To produce a hard-edged transition between edge pixels during rasterization, deselect the Anti-alias option.)

5 Under Destination, enter a base name for the generated files. (When Photoshop creates the new files, the base name is appended with a number that corresponds to the page number of the PDF file.) Then click the Choose button, and select the location where you want to save the generated files.

Opening PostScript artwork

Encapsulated PostScript® (EPS) can represent both vector and bitmap data and is supported by virtually all graphics, illustration, and page-layout programs. Adobe applications that produce PostScript artwork include Adobe Illustrator. When you open an EPS file containing vector art, it is *rasterized*—the mathematically defined lines and curves of the vector artwork are converted into the pixels or bits of a bitmap image.

You can also bring PostScript artwork into Photoshop Elements using the Place command, the Paste command, and the drag-and-drop feature. (See "Placing files" on page 52, "Using drag-and-drop to copy between applications" on page 124, and "Using the Clipboard to copy between applications" on page 124.)

To open an EPS file:

1 Choose File > Open.

2 Select the file you want to open, and click Open.

3 Indicate the desired dimensions, resolution, and mode. To maintain the same height-to-width ratio, select Constrain Proportions.

4 Select Anti-aliased to minimize the jagged appearance of the artwork's edges as it is opened.

💡 *Anti-aliasing lets you produce smooth-edged objects by partially filling the edge pixels, so the edges of the objects blend into the background.*

5 Click OK.

Opening Photo CD files

You can open Kodak® Photo CD™ (PCD) files, including high-resolution files from Pro Photo CDs.

Note: You cannot save files in PCD format in Photoshop Elements.

To open a Photo CD file:

1 Choose File > Open.

2 Select the PCD file you want to open, and click Open. If the file does not appear, select the option for showing all files from the Files of Type (Windows) or Show (Mac OS) menu.

3 Select options for the source image:

• Pixel Size to specify the pixel dimensions of the image. Keep in mind that the on-screen size of the opened image depends on both the pixel size and resolution you choose. (See "About image size and resolution" on page 75.)

• Profile to specify a device profile for color management. (See "Setting up color management" on page 31.)

4 Select options for the destination image:

• Resolution to specify the resolution of the opened image.

• Color Space to specify a color profile for the opened image. (See "Setting up color management" on page 31.)

• Landscape or Portrait to specify the orientation of the opened image.

5 Click OK.

Opening Raw files

The Raw format is designed to accommodate images saved in undocumented formats, such as those created by scientific applications. Compressed files, such as PICT and GIF, cannot be opened using this format.

To open a file using the Raw format:

1 Choose File > Open or File > Open As (Windows).

2 Choose Raw from the file format list, and click Open.

3 For Width and Height, enter values for the dimensions of the file.

4 To reverse the order of the width and height, click Swap.

5 Enter the number of channels.

6 Select Interleaved if the file was saved with an interlaced data option.

7 Select a color depth and, if necessary, a byte order.

8 For Header, enter a value.

9 If you are missing the dimensions or header value, you can have Photoshop Elements estimate the parameters. Either enter the correct height and width values to estimate the header size, or enter the correct header size to estimate the height and width, and then click Guess.

10 To have Photoshop Elements retain the header when you save the file, select Retain When Saving.

11 Click OK.

Importing anti-aliased PICT files (Mac OS)

Choose File > Import > Anti-aliased PICT to import object-oriented PICT files (such as those created with MacDraw and Canvas) as smooth-edged, or anti-aliased, images. Because the entire PICT file must be held in memory for this module to operate, you may not be able to use the module with large PICT files.

The Anti-aliased PICT dialog box indicates the current file size and dimensions. To change the image dimensions, enter new values for Width and Height. The file size is then updated. To maintain image proportions, select Constrain Proportions.

You can choose Grayscale or RGB color mode for an anti-aliased PICT file.

Importing PICT resources (Mac OS)

The PICT Resource module lets you read PICT resources from a file—for example, from another application. To open a PICT resource, choose File > Import > PICT Resource.

To preview a resource, click Preview. Click the arrow buttons to step forward and backward through the resources. Note that the number displayed for Resource refers to the resource's position in ascending order in the resource fork and not to the resource's identification number.

Note: In Photoshop Elements, you can also open a file in the PICT Resource file format by choosing File > Open, choosing All Documents from the Show pop-up menu, selecting the file you want to open, choosing PICT Resource from the Format pop-up menu, and clicking Open. However, the Open command automatically opens the first resource in the file and does not display any other PICT resources in the file.

Opening images in EPS TIFF or EPS PICT Preview format

These formats let you open images saved in file formats that create previews but are not supported by Adobe Photoshop Elements (such as QuarkX-Press®). An opened preview image can be edited and used like any other low-resolution file. EPS PICT Preview is available only in Mac OS.

Using the File Association Manager (Windows only)

The File Association Manager lets you decide which file types are opened in Photoshop Elements. Choosing to open digital images in Photoshop Elements can help you streamline your workflow.

To select file types:

1 Choose Edit > File Association.

2 Do one of the following to select the file types you want to open in Photoshop Elements:

• Click the box next to the file type names to add a file type. Selected file types have a check next to them.

• Click the Default button to have the suggested file types checked.

• Click the Select All button to have all available file types open in Photoshop Elements.

• Click Deselect All if you don't want any of the listed file formats to open in Photoshop Elements. This means that you would have to use the Open command to open an image file from your computer.

3 Click the OK button when you're done.

Placing files

You can use the File > Place command to place artwork into a new layer in an image. In Photoshop Elements, you can place PDF, Adobe Illustrator, and EPS files.

When you place a PDF, Adobe Illustrator, or EPS file, it is rasterized; you cannot edit text or vector data in placed artwork. Keep in mind that artwork is rasterized at the resolution of the file into which it is placed.

To place a PDF, Adobe Illustrator, or EPS file:

1 Open the Photoshop Elements image into which you want to place the artwork.

2 Choose File > Place, select the file you want to place, and click Place.

3 If you are placing a PDF file that contains multiple pages, select the page you want to place from the provided dialog box, and click OK.

The placed artwork appears inside a bounding box at the center of the Photoshop Elements image. The artwork maintains its original aspect ratio; however, if the artwork is larger than the Photoshop Elements image, it is resized to fit.

4 If desired, reposition the placed artwork by doing one or more of the following:

• Position the pointer inside the bounding box of the placed artwork, and drag.

- In the options bar, enter a value for X to specify the distance between the center point of the placed artwork and the left edge of the image. Enter a value for Y to specify the distance between the center point of the placed artwork and the top edge of the image.

5 If desired, scale the placed artwork by doing one or more of the following:

- Drag one of the handles at the corners or sides of the bounding box. Hold down Shift as you drag a corner handle to constrain the proportions.

- In the options bar, enter values for W and H to specify the width and height of the artwork. By default, these options represent scale as a percentage; however, you can enter another unit of measurement (in, cm, or px). To constrain the proportions of the artwork, click the Constrain Proportions icon ▯; the option is on when the icon has a white background.

6 If desired, rotate the placed artwork by doing one or more of the following:

- Position the pointer outside the bounding box of the placed artwork (the pointer turns into a curved arrow), and drag.

- In the options bar, enter a value (in degrees) for the Rotation option △.

7 If desired, skew the placed artwork by holding down Ctrl (Windows) or Command (Mac OS) and dragging a side handle of the bounding box.

8 Set the Anti-alias option in the options bar as desired. To blend edge pixels during rasterization, select the Anti-alias option. To produce a hard-edged transition between edge pixels during rasterization, deselect the Anti-alias option.

9 To commit the placed artwork to a new layer, do one of the following:

- Click the OK button ✔ in the options bar.

- Press Enter or Return.

To cancel the placement, click the Cancel button ⊘ in the options bar, or press Esc.

Closing files and quitting

To close a file:

1 Do one of the following:

- Choose File > Close.

- Choose Window > Close All (Windows).

- Choose File > Close All (Mac OS).

2 Choose whether or not to save the file:

- Click Yes (Windows) or Save (Mac OS) to save the file.

- Click No (Windows) or Don't Save (Mac OS) to close the file without saving it.

To exit Photoshop Elements:

1 Choose File > Exit (Windows) or File > Quit (Mac OS).

2 Choose whether or not to save any open files:

- Click Yes (Windows) or Save (Mac OS) for each open file to save the file.

- Click No (Windows) or Don't Save (Mac OS) for each open file to close the file without saving it.

Choosing an image mode

Photoshop Elements provides several image modes for displaying and printing images. The image mode you choose determines the number of colors that can be displayed in an image and can also affect the file size of the image.

About image modes

Photoshop Elements provides four image modes: RGB, Bitmap, Grayscale, and Indexed color.

RGB mode RGB is the default mode for new Photoshop images. It uses the RGB image model to assign an intensity value to each pixel ranging from 0 (black) to 255 (white) for each of the RGB components in a color image. For example, a bright red color might have an R value of 246, a G value of 20, and a B value of 50. When the values of all three components are equal, the result is a shade of neutral gray. When the value of all components is 255, the result is pure white; when the value is 0, pure black.

RGB images use three colors, or channels, to reproduce up to 16.7 million colors on-screen. In addition to being the default mode for new Photoshop images, the RGB model is used by computer monitors to display colors.

Bitmap mode This mode uses one of two color values (black or white) to represent the pixels in an image. Images in Bitmap mode are called bitmapped 1-bit images because they have a bit depth of 1.

Grayscale mode This mode uses up to 256 shades of gray. Every pixel of a grayscale image has a brightness value ranging from 0 (black) to 255 (white). Grayscale values can also be measured as percentages of black ink coverage (0% is equal to white, 100% to black). Images produced using black-and-white or grayscale scanners typically are displayed in Grayscale mode.

Indexed Color mode This mode uses at most 256 colors. When converting to indexed color, Photoshop Elements builds a color lookup table (CLUT), which stores and indexes the colors in the image. If a color in the original image does not appear in the table, the program chooses the closest one or simulates the color using available colors.

By limiting the palette of colors, indexed color can reduce file size while maintaining visual quality—for example, for a Web page. Limited editing is available in this mode. For extensive editing you should convert temporarily to RGB mode.

 For more information, see "Converting to indexed color" in online Help.

Converting between color modes

When you choose a different color mode for an image, you permanently change the color values in the image.

Consequently, before converting images, it's best to do the following:

- Edit as much as possible in RGB mode.

- Save a backup copy before converting. Be sure to save a copy of your image that includes all layers in order to edit the original version of the image after the conversion.

- Flatten the file before converting it. The interaction of colors between layer blending modes will change when the mode changes.

To convert an image to another mode:

Choose Image > Mode, and choose the mode you want from the submenu. Modes not available for the active image appear dimmed in the menu.

Note: *Images are flattened when you convert them to Bitmap or Indexed Color mode, because these modes do not support layers.*

For more information, see "Converting between Grayscale and Bitmap modes" in online Help.

Chapter 4: Fixing Your Photos

You can fix photos in Adobe Photoshop Elements by using the retouching, editing, and color adjusting features. You can correct an entire image, or portions of an image.

About fixing your photos

You may need to correct the color and tone of an image for several reasons. The original photograph may have a color cast caused by the film, lighting, or aging. Or the scan may have been imperfect—scanners can introduce color casts or artifacts. Or the colors in your original art may be out of printable range.

You can quickly fix simple image problems by using automated or simple correction features in Photoshop Elements. For example, you can easily fix underexposed photos or subtle color casts with an auto correction command or with a few simple visual adjustments. For more information, see "Quickly fixing your photos" on page 58 and "Using the Color Variations command" on page 66.

If you need more precise controls for adjusting a photo's color, highlights, and shadows, you can use more advanced features, including the Levels command. For more information, see "Adjusting the range of dark and light tones in an image" on page 62.

For more information, see "Checking scan quality and tonal range" in online Help.

To remove blemishes, such as dust and scratches, you can use filters to quickly repair the damaged areas. If the blemished areas are more complex, you can use the clone stamp tool to manually repair the photo. To fix other common issues, including red-eye, color-saturation, and exposure problems, you can use other retouching tools. For more information, see "Retouching an image" on page 70.

Workflow for fixing photos

To correct the color balance and tonal range of an image, complete the following steps:

Calibrate your monitor Use Adobe Gamma to calibrate your monitor or the display calibrator (Mac OSX only). A calibrated monitor ensures consistent color from other devices such as printers. (See "Calibrating your monitor" on page 32.)

View the image at 100% Before making any color corrections, view the image at a zoom percentage of 100%. At that percentage, Photoshop Elements displays color most accurately.

Check the scan quality and tonal range Look at the image's histogram to evaluate whether the image has sufficient detail to produce high-quality output. The greater the range of values in the histogram, the greater the detail. Poor scans and photographs without much detail can be difficult if not impossible to correct. Too many color corrections can also result in a loss of pixel values and too little detail.

For more information, see "Checking scan quality and tonal range" in online Help.

Adjust the tonal range Begin tonal corrections by adjusting the values of the extreme highlight and shadow pixels in the image, setting an overall tonal range that allows for the sharpest detail possible throughout the image. This process is known as *setting the highlights and shadows* or *setting the white and black points*. (See "Adjusting the range of dark and light tones in an image" on page 62.)

Setting the highlights and shadows typically redistributes the midtone pixels appropriately. When pixel values are concentrated at either end of the tonal range, however, you may need to adjust your midtones manually.

Adjust the color balance After correcting the tonal range, you can adjust the image's color balance to remove unwanted color casts or to correct oversaturated or undersaturated colors. (To manually fix a color cast, see "Using the Color Cast command" on page 67; or you can try the Auto Color Correction command: See "Using the Auto Color Correction command" on page 59.)

Make other special color adjustments Once you have corrected the overall color balance of your image, you can make optional adjustments to enhance colors. For example, you can increase the vividness of color in your image by increasing its saturation. (See "Adjusting color" on page 65.)

Sharpen the edges of the image As a final step, use the Unsharp Mask filter to sharpen the clarity of edges in the image. This step helps restore detail and sharpness that tonal adjustments may reduce. (See "Sharpen filters" on page 179.)

For information on viewing the range of shadows, midtones, and highlights in an image, see "Checking scan quality and tonal range" in online Help.

Quickly fixing your photos

Some image problems are simple enough that they can be quickly fixed using the automated or simple correction features in Photoshop Elements.

Using the Auto Levels command

To enhance the contrast of an image that has an average distribution of color values, use the Auto Levels command. Auto Levels defines the lightest and darkest pixels in an image, and then redistributes intermediate pixel values proportionately.

Note: Because Auto Levels adjusts each color channel (red, green, and blue) individually, it may remove or introduce color casts. If Auto Levels introduces an undesirable color cast, undo the command, and then try the Auto Contrast command instead. See "Using the Auto Contrast command" on page 59.

To use the Auto Levels command:

1 Do one of the following:

• To make adjustments to your entire image, choose Select > Deselect to make sure nothing is selected. If your image has multiple layers, select a layer to adjust in the Layers palette.

• To make adjustments to a portion of your image, make a selection in the document window. See "Selecting pixels" on page 114.

2 Do one of the following:

- Choose Enhance > Auto Levels.

- Choose Enhance > Adjust Brightness/ Contrast > Levels. In the Levels dialog box, click Auto, and then click OK.

Using the Auto Contrast command

The Auto Contrast command adjusts the overall contrast and mixture of colors in an image automatically. Because it does not adjust each color channel (red, green, and blue) individually, Auto Contrast does not introduce or remove color casts. It maps the lightest and darkest pixels in the image to white and black, which makes highlights appear lighter and shadows appear darker.

Auto Contrast can improve the appearance of many photographic or continuous-tone images. It does not improve flat-color images.

To use the Auto Contrast command:

1 Do one of the following:

- To make adjustments to your entire image, choose Select > Deselect to make sure nothing is selected. If your image has multiple layers, select a layer to adjust in the Layers palette.

- To make adjustments to a portion of your image, make a selection in the document window. See "Selecting pixels" on page 114.

2 Choose Enhance > Auto Contrast.

Using the Auto Color Correction command

The Auto Color Correction command adjusts the contrast and color by identifying shadows, midtones, and highlights in the image as a whole, rather than in individual color channels. It neutralizes the midtones and clips the white and black pixels using a default set of values.

To apply Auto Color Correction command:

1 Do one of the following:

- To make adjustments to your entire image, choose Select > Deselect to make sure nothing is selected. If your image has multiple layers, select a layer to adjust in the Layers palette.

- To make adjustments to a portion of your image, make a selection in the document window. See "Selecting pixels" on page 114.

2 Choose Enhance > Auto Color Correction.

Using the Adjust Backlighting command

When taking photos with a camera, you can use backlighting to emphasize the shape of the subject. However, backlighting can cause overexposure in the areas surrounding the subject. You can use the Adjust Backlighting command to correct this problem by darkening the overexposed areas.

The Adjust Backlighting command is especially useful for correcting overexposed skies, and other backgrounds.

Original image, and Backlighting applied   *Original image, and Fill Flash applied*

To use the Adjust Backlighting command:

1 Do one of the following:

- To make adjustments to your entire image, choose Select > Deselect to make sure nothing is selected. If your image has multiple layers, select a layer to adjust in the Layers palette.

- To make adjustments to a portion of your image, make a selection in the document window. See "Selecting pixels" on page 114.

2 Choose Enhance > Adjust Lighting > Adjust Backlighting.

3 Drag the Darker slider or enter a value in the text box to adjust the tonal variation in the image. Values can range from 0 to 100.

4 Click OK.

Using the Fill Flash command

In pictures taken in bright light, shadows are often so dark that they show little detail. You can lighten such shadows using the Fill Flash command.

To use the Fill Flash command:

1 Do one of the following:

- To make adjustments to your entire image, choose Select > Deselect to make sure nothing is selected. If your image has multiple layers, select a layer to adjust in the Layers palette.

- To make adjustments to a portion of your image, make a selection in the document window. See "Selecting pixels" on page 114.

2 Choose Enhance > Adjust Lighting > Fill Flash.

3 Drag the Lighter slider or enter a value in the text box to adjust the tonal variation in the image. Values can range from 0 to 100.

4 Click OK.

Using the Quick Fix dialog box

The Quick Fix command lets you adjust the brightness, color, sharpness, and even the rotation of your image in a single dialog box. You compare your original image without changes next to a preview of the same image with the adjustments you select.

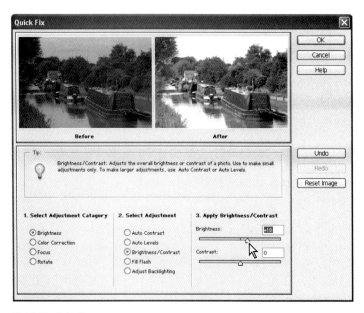

Quick Fix dialog box

To use the Quick Fix command:

1 Do one of the following:

• To make adjustments to your entire image, choose Select > Deselect to make sure nothing is selected. If your image has multiple layers, select a layer to adjust in the Layers palette.

• To make adjustments to a portion of your image, make a selection in the document window. See "Selecting pixels" on page 114.

2 To open the Quick Fix dialog box, you can either click the Quick Fix button in the Shortcuts bar or choose Enhance > Quick Fix.

3 Select an Adjustment Category in the first step of the Quick Fix dialog box:

• Brightness lets you adjust your photo's contrast, tonal range, and brightness, and quickly fix overexposed or underexposed areas.

• Color Correction lets you adjust the saturation and color (*hue*) in your photo, and automatically correct a color cast.

• Focus lets you sharpen or blur your photo.

• Rotate lets you flip your image horizontally and vertically, or rotate your image at 90° or 180° angles. (To straighten an image or for more rotation options, see "Rotating and straightening images" on page 81.)

4 Select an adjustment type in the second step of the Quick Fix dialog box. The text in the Tip section provides helpful information and instructions about using the selected adjustment.

5 Some adjustments give you options to set, and others have default options you can apply automatically. Depending on the adjustment you selected, one of the following options will be available to you in the third step of the Quick Fix dialog box:

- If there are options to set, drag the slider to the left to decrease the value, or drag it to the right to increase it.

- Click Apply to apply the default adjustment values to the preview image.

6 To undo or redo adjustments made in the Quick Fix dialog box, you can do any of the following:

- Click Reset Image to start over and undo all adjustments you've set in the current Quick Fix dialog box.

- Click Undo for each successive adjustment you'd like to undo. Note that you can click Undo to undo the Reset Image command.

- Click Redo for each adjustment you'd like to redo that was undone.

7 To apply the adjustments to your image, click OK.

Adjusting the range of dark and light tones in an image

You can adjust the tonal relationships between pixels in an image using a variety of commands with different levels of control in Photoshop Elements. Of all the features for adjusting tonal values, the Levels dialog box gives you the most precision.

Using the Levels dialog box

The Levels dialog box lets you correct the tonal range and color balance of an image by adjusting intensity levels of the image's shadows, midtones, and highlights. The Levels histogram serves as a visual guide for adjusting the image's key tones.

Note that dragging the gray slider in Levels has no effect on the black and white points of the image. You can set the highlights and shadows in an image by moving Input sliders to the first group of pixels on both ends of the Levels histogram. This maps these pixels—the darkest and lightest pixels in each channel—to black and white, increasing the tonal range of the image. The corresponding pixels in the other channels are adjusted proportionately to avoid altering the color balance. You can use the middle Input slider to change the intensity values of the middle range of gray tones without dramatically altering the highlights and shadows.

To adjust tonal range using Levels:

1 Do one of the following:

- To make adjustments to your entire image, choose Select > Deselect to make sure nothing is selected. If your image has multiple layers, select a layer to adjust in the Layers palette.

- To make adjustments to a portion of your image, make a selection in the document window. See "Selecting pixels" on page 114.

2 Do one of the following:

- Choose Enhance > Adjust Brightness/Contrast > Levels.

- Create a new Levels adjustment layer, or open an existing Levels adjustment layer. (See "Using adjustment and fill layers" on page 101.)

3 To adjust the values for the composite channels (RGB) or for a specific color channel (red, green, or blue), choose an option from the Channel menu.

4 To adjust the shadows or highlights, do any of the following:

- Drag the black and white Input Levels sliders (directly underneath the histogram) to the edge of the first group of pixels on either end of the histogram. You can also enter values directly into the first and third Input Levels text boxes.

- Drag the black and white Output Levels sliders (at the bottom of the dialog box) to adjust the shadow and highlight range. You can also enter values directly into the Output Levels text boxes.

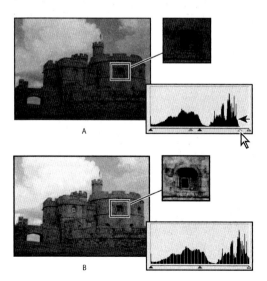

Adjusting the white Input Levels slider
A. *Original* **B**. *Resulting histogram and image*

Note: You can click Auto to move the highlight and shadow sliders automatically to the brightest and darkest points. This is the same as using the Auto Levels command and may be adequate for an average-key image. (See "Using the Auto Levels command" on page 58.)

5 If your image needs midtone corrections, use the gray Input Levels slider. Drag the slider to the right to darken the midtones; drag it to the left to lighten the midtones. You can also enter values directly in the middle Input Levels text box. (A value of 1.0 represents the current unadjusted midtone value.)

6 Click OK.

7 To view the adjusted histogram, reopen the Levels dialog box.

Gaps in the adjusted histogram do not indicate a problem unless they are large.

To use the eyedropper tool to set target colors for the lightest, darkest, and neutral gray areas in the image, see "Using the Brightness/Contrast command" in online Help.

Using the Brightness/Contrast command

The Brightness/Contrast command lets you make simple adjustments to the tonal range of an image.

To use the Brightness/Contrast command:

1 Do one of the following:

- To make adjustments to your entire image, choose Select > Deselect to make sure nothing is selected. If your image has multiple layers, select a layer to adjust in the Layers palette.

- To make adjustments to a portion of your image, make a selection in the document window. (See "Selecting pixels" on page 114.)

2 Do one of the following:

- Choose Enhance > Adjust Brightness/ Contrast > Brightness/Contrast.

- Create a new Brightness/Contrast adjustment layer, or open an existing Brightness/Contrast adjustment layer. (See "Using adjustment and fill layers" on page 101.)

3 Drag the sliders to adjust the brightness and contrast.

Dragging to the left decreases the level; dragging to the right increases it. The number at the right of each slider value displays the brightness or contrast value. Values range from –100 to +100.

4 Click OK.

Describing color

The human eye perceives color in terms of three characteristics—hue, saturation, and brightness (HSB), while computer monitors display colors by generating varying amounts of red, green, and blue (RGB) light. Photoshop Elements lets you use the HSB and RGB *color models* to select and manipulate color.

HSB model

Based on the human perception of color, the HSB model describes three fundamental characteristics of color:

- *Hue* is the color reflected from or transmitted through an object. It is measured as a location on the standard color wheel, expressed as a degree between 0 and 360. In common use, hue is identified by the name of the color such as red, orange, or green.

- *Saturation*, sometimes called *chroma*, is the strength or purity of the color. Saturation represents the amount of gray in proportion to the hue, measured as a percentage from 0 (gray) to 100 (fully saturated). On the standard color wheel, saturation increases from the center to the edge.

- *Brightness* is the relative lightness or darkness of the color, usually measured as a percentage from 0 (black) to 100 (white).

Although you can use the HSB model in Photoshop Elements to define a color in the Color Picker dialog box, there is no HSB mode available for creating and editing images.

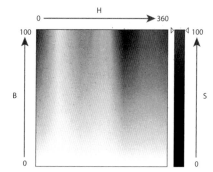

HSB model
H. *Hue* **S.** *Saturation* **B.** *Brightness*

RGB model

A large percentage of the visible spectrum can be represented by mixing red, green, and blue (RGB) colored light in various proportions and intensities. Where the colors overlap, they create cyan, magenta, yellow, and white.

Because the RGB colors combine to create white, they are also called *additive colors*. Adding all colors together creates white—that is, all light is transmitted back to the eye. Additive colors are used for lighting, video, and monitors. Your monitor, for example, creates color by emitting light through red, green, and blue phosphors.

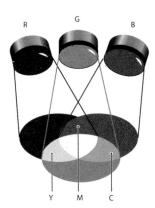

Additive colors (RGB)
R. *Red* **G.** *Green* **B.** *Blue* **Y.** *Yellow* **M.** *Magenta* **C.** *Cyan*

About the color wheel

Because there are numerous ways to achieve similar results in color balance, it's useful to consider the type of image you have and the effect you want to produce. If you're new to adjusting

color components, it helps to keep a diagram of the color wheel on hand. You can use the color wheel to predict how a change in one color component affects other colors.

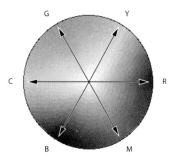

Color wheel
C. *Cyan* **G.** *Green* **Y.** *Yellow* **R.** *Red* **M.** *Magenta* **B.** *Blue*

You can decrease the amount of any color in an image by increasing the amount of its opposite on the color wheel—and vice versa. Similarly, you can increase and decrease a color by adjusting the two adjacent colors on the wheel, or even by adjusting the two colors adjacent to its opposite. For example, in an RGB image you can decrease magenta by removing red and blue or by adding green. This results in an overall color balance containing less magenta.

Adjusting color

You can quickly adjust an image's color balance to remove unwanted color casts or to correct color saturation using the Color Cast and Color Variation commands.

Using the Color Variations command

The Color Variations command lets you adjust the color balance, contrast, and saturation of an image by selecting previews that show the effect of different adjustments.

This command is most useful for average-key images that don't require precise color adjustments.

Note: You can't use the Color Variations command with images in Indexed Color mode.

To use the Color Variations command:

1 Do one of the following:

- To make adjustments to your entire image, choose Select > Deselect to make sure nothing is selected. If your image has multiple layers, select a layer to adjust in the Layers palette.

- To make adjustments to a portion of your image, make a selection in the document window. See "Selecting pixels" on page 114.

2 To open the Color Variations dialog box, you can either choose Enhance > Adjust Color > Color Variations, or click the Color Variations button 🔵 in the Shortcuts bar.

The two thumbnails at the top of the dialog box show the original image (Before) and the image with its currently selected adjustments (After). When you first open the dialog box, these two images are the same. As you make adjustments, the After image changes to reflect your choices.

3 Select what to adjust in the image:

- Shadows, Midtones, or Highlights to indicate whether you want to adjust the dark, middle, or light areas.

- Saturation to change the vividness of color in the image.

4 Drag the Adjust Color Intensity slider to determine the amount of each adjustment. Dragging the slider to the left decreases the amount, and dragging to the right increases it.

5 With either the Midtones, Shadows, or Highlights option selected, do either of the following:

- To add a color to the image, click the appropriate Increase color thumbnail.

- To subtract a color, click the appropriate Decrease color thumbnail.

Each time you click a thumbnail, all thumbnails are updated.

6 With the Saturation option selected, click either the Less Saturation or More Saturation buttons.

7 To undo or redo adjustments made in the Color Variations dialog box, you can do any of the following:

- Click Reset Image to start over and undo all adjustments you've set in the current Color Variations dialog box.

- Click Undo once or multiple times for each successive adjustment you'd like to undo. You cannot undo the Reset Image option.

- Click Redo once or multiple times for each adjustment you'd like to redo that was undone.

8 To apply the adjustments to your image, click OK.

Using the Color Cast command

The Color Cast command changes the overall mixture of colors to remove color casts in your image.

To use the Color Cast command:

1 Do one of the following:

• To make adjustments to your entire image, choose Select > Deselect to make sure nothing is selected. If your image has multiple layers, select a layer to adjust in the Layers palette.

• To make adjustments to a portion of your image, make a selection in the document window. (See "Selecting pixels" on page 114.)

2 Choose Enhance > Adjust Color > Color Cast.

3 In your image, click an area that should be neutral gray, white, or black. The image changes based on the color you selected.

To start over, and undo the changes made to the image, click the Reset button.

4 Click OK.

Adjusting color using the Levels dialog box

The Levels dialog box lets you correct the color balance and tonal range of an image by adjusting intensity levels of the image's shadows, midtones, and highlights. The Levels histogram serves as a visual guide for adjusting the image's key tones.

To use Levels to fine-tune the color balance of your image:

In the Levels dialog box, choose a single color channel from the Channel pop-up menu, and use the sliders or text boxes to adjust the intensity levels. (See "Using the Levels dialog box" on page 62.)

Using the Hue/Saturation command

The Hue/Saturation command lets you adjust the hue (color), saturation, and lightness of the entire image or of individual color components in an image. Adjusting the hue represents a move around the color wheel. Adjusting the saturation, or purity of the color, represents a move across the radius of the color wheel.

You can also use the Colorize option to add color to a grayscale image converted to RGB, or to an RGB image—for example, to make it look like a duotone by reducing its color values to one hue.

To use the Hue/Saturation command:

1 Do one of the following:

• To make adjustments to your entire image, choose Select > Deselect to make sure nothing is selected. If your image has multiple layers, select a layer to adjust in the Layers palette.

• To make adjustments to a portion of your image, make a selection in the document window. (See "Selecting pixels" on page 114.)

2 Do one of the following:

• Choose Enhance > Adjust Color > Hue/Saturation.

• Create a new Hue/Saturation adjustment layer, or open an existing Hue/Saturation adjustment layer. (See "Using adjustment and fill layers" on page 101.)

The two color bars in the dialog box represent the colors in their order on the color wheel. The upper bar shows the color before the adjustment; the lower bar shows how the adjustment affects all hues at full saturation.

3 For Edit, choose which colors to adjust:

• Choose Master to adjust all colors at once.

• Choose one of the other preset color ranges listed for the color you want to adjust. (An adjustment slider appears between the color bars, which you can use to edit any range of hues. For information on how to modify the slider's range, see "To modify the range of an adjustment slider" after step 7.)

4 For Hue, enter a value or drag the slider until the colors appear as you want.

The values displayed in the text box reflect the number of degrees of rotation around the wheel from the pixel's original color. A positive value indicates clockwise rotation, a negative value counterclockwise rotation. Values range from −180 to +180. (See "About the color wheel" on page 65.)

5 For Saturation, enter a value or drag the slider to the right to increase the saturation or to the left to decrease it.

The color shifts away from or toward the center of the wheel, relative to the beginning color values of the selected pixels. Values range from −100 to +100.

6 For Lightness, enter a value or drag the slider to the right to increase the lightness or to the left to decrease it. Values range from −100 to +100.

7 Click OK.

To modify the range of an adjustment slider:

1 In the Hue/Saturation dialog box, choose an individual color from the Edit menu.

2 Do any of the following to the adjustment slider:

• Drag one of the triangles to adjust the amount of color fall-off without affecting the range.

• Drag one of the light gray bars to adjust the range without affecting the amount of fall-off.

• Drag the dark-gray center part to move the entire adjustment slider, selecting a different color area.

• Drag one of the vertical white bars next to the dark gray center part to adjust the range of the color component. Increasing the range decreases the fall-off, and vice versa.

• To move the color bar and the adjustment slider bar together, Ctrl-drag (Windows) or Command-drag (Mac OS) the color bar.

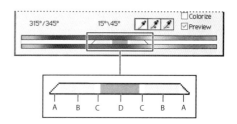

Adjustment slider
A. Adjusts fall-off without affecting range **B.** *Adjusts range without affecting fall-off* **C.** *Adjusts range of color component* **D.** *Moves entire slider*

If you modify the adjustment slider so that it falls into a different color range, the name changes to reflect this. For example, if you choose Yellow and alter its range so that it falls in the red part of the color bar, the name changes to Red 2. You can convert up to six of the individual color ranges to varieties of the same color range (for example, Red through Red 6).

Note: By default, the range of color selected when you choose a color component is 30° wide, with 30° of fall-off on either side. Setting the fall-off too low can produce banding in the image.

3 To edit the range by choosing colors from the image, select the eyedropper tool 🖋 in the dialog box, and click in the image. Use the eyedropper + tool to add to the range; use the eyedropper – tool to subtract from the range.

While the eyedropper tool is selected, you can also press Shift to add to the range or Alt (Windows) or Option (Mac OS) to subtract from it.

To colorize a grayscale image or create a duotone effect:

1 If you are colorizing a grayscale image, choose Image > Mode > RGB to convert the image to RGB.

2 Open the Hue/Saturation dialog box.

3 Select Colorize. If the foreground color isn't black or white, Photoshop Elements converts the image to the hue of the current foreground color. The lightness value of each pixel does not change.

4 Use the Hue slider to select a new color if desired. Use the Saturation and Lightness sliders to adjust the saturation and lightness of the pixels.

5 Click OK.

Using the Remove Color command

The Remove Color command converts the colors in the image to gray values. For example, it assigns equal red, green, and blue values to each pixel in an RGB image to make the image appear grayscale. The lightness value of each pixel does not change. The Remove Color command can also be used on a selected area.

This command has the same effect as setting Saturation to –100 in the Hue/Saturation dialog box.

To use the Remove Color command:

1 Do one of the following:

• To make adjustments to your entire image, choose Select > Deselect to make sure nothing is selected. If your image has multiple layers, select a layer to adjust in the Layers palette.

• To make adjustments to a portion of your image, make a selection in the document window. (See "Selecting pixels" on page 114.)

2 Choose Enhance > Adjust Color > Remove Color.

Using the Replace Color command

The Replace Color command lets you create a mask around specific colors and then replace those colors in the image. You can set the hue, saturation, and lightness of the area identified by the mask. The mask is temporary.

To use the Replace Color command:

1 Do one of the following:

- To make adjustments to your entire image, choose Select > Deselect to make sure nothing is selected. If your image has multiple layers, select a layer to adjust in the Layers palette.

- To make adjustments to a portion of your image, make a selection in the document window. (See "Selecting pixels" on page 114.)

2 Choose Enhance > Adjust Color > Replace Color.

3 Select a display option under the image thumbnail:

- Selection to display the mask in the preview box. Masked areas are black and unmasked areas are white. Partially masked areas (areas covered with a semitransparent mask) appear as varying levels of gray according to their opacity.

- Image to display the image in the preview box. This option is useful when you are working with a magnified image or have limited screen space.

4 Click the eyedropper button, and then click in the image or in the preview box to select the area exposed by the mask. Use the eyedropper + button to add areas or use the eyedropper – button to remove areas.

5 Adjust the tolerance of the mask by dragging the Fuzziness slider or entering a value. This controls the degree to which related colors are included in the selection.

6 Drag the Hue, Saturation, and Lightness sliders (or enter values in the text boxes) to change the color of the selected areas.

7 Click OK.

Retouching an image

You can retouch images using filters, and the clone stamp, red eye brush, smudge, focus, toning, and sponge tools.

Using the clone stamp tool

The clone stamp tool takes a sample of an image, which you can then apply over another image or part of the same image. Each stroke of the tool paints on more of the sample. Cross hairs mark the original sampling point.

To use the clone stamp tool:

1 Select the clone stamp tool ⬚. (For information about the pattern stamp tool ⬚, see "Using the pattern stamp tool" on page 135.)

2 Choose a brush from the pop-up palette in the options bar, and drag the Size pop-up slider to set the brush size.

3 Specify a blending mode and opacity. (See "Setting options for painting and editing tools" on page 135.)

4 Select Aligned to copy the sampled area once, regardless of how many times you stop and resume painting. This option is useful when you want to eliminate unwanted areas such as a telephone line across the skyline or a rip in a scanned photo.

If Aligned is deselected, the clone stamp tool applies the sampled area from the initial sampling point each time you stop and resume painting. This option is useful for applying multiple copies of the same part of an image to different areas within the same image or to another image.

5 To sample data from all visible layers, select Use All Layers. To sample data from only the active layer, deselect this option.

6 Position the pointer on the part of any open image you want to sample, and Alt-click (Windows) or Option-click (Mac OS). This sample point is the location from which the tool duplicates your image as you paint.

7 Drag to paint with the tool.

Using the Dust & Scratches filter

If your photo has a lot of minor imperfections, you can use the Dust & Scratches filter to quickly remove the defects. The filter reduces defects by changing dissimilar pixels. To achieve a balance between sharpening the image and hiding defects, try various radius and threshold settings. Or apply the filter to selected areas of the image.

To use the Dust & Scratches filter:

1 Do one of the following:

• To make adjustments to your entire image, choose Select > Deselect to make sure nothing is selected. If your image has multiple layers, select a layer to adjust in the Layers palette.

• To make adjustments to a portion of your image, make a selection in the document window. See "Selecting pixels" on page 114.

2 Choose Filter > Noise > Dust & Scratches, or use the Filters palette to apply the Dust & Scratches filter.

3 If you need to adjust the preview image in the Dust & Scratches dialog box, you can do any of the following:

• Click the zoom out − or zoom in + button until the area containing defects is visible.

• Drag in the preview image to view other areas in your image

• Move your pointer over your image in the document window and click in an area you want to center.

4 Drag the Threshold slider left to 0 to turn off the value, so that all pixels in the selection or image can be examined.

The Threshold determines how different the pixels' values should be before they are eliminated.

Note: The Threshold slider gives greater control for values between 0 and 128—the most common range for images—than for values between 128 and 255.

5 Drag the Radius slider left or right, or enter a value in the text box from 1 to 100 pixels. The radius determines how far the filter searches for differences among pixels.

Increasing the radius makes the image more blurry. Stop at the lowest value that eliminates the defects.

To correct large defects in your image, try using the clone stamp tool. See "Using the clone stamp tool" on page 70.

6 Increase the threshold gradually by dragging the slider to the lowest value that eliminates defects by entering a value between 1 and 255.

7 Click OK.

Using the red eye brush

Red eye occurs in photos when light from a camera flash reflects off the back of a person's eye. You can easily remove red eye from an image using the red eye brush. You can also use the red eye brush to retouch other details in an image, such as dental braces. The red eye brush tool changes the hue of the area you paint without removing detail in the image.

To use the red eye brush:

1 Select the red eye brush 🖌️ .

2 Choose a brush from the pop-up palette in the options bar, and drag the Size pop-up slider to set the brush size. A brush that is a little larger than the pupil of the eye may be the most effective size.

3 Specify a target color (the color you want to remove) by doing one of the following:

- To set the target color when you click in the image, choose First Click from the Sampling pop-up menu.

- To use the default target color, choose Current Color from the Sampling pop-up menu. Then click Default Colors.

- To pick a custom target color, choose Current Color from the Sampling pop-up menu. Then click the Current color swatch. When the Color Picker appears, click in the image on the color you want to remove. Alternately, you can choose a target color using the Color Picker.

4 Specify a replacement color by doing one of the following:

- To use the default replacement color, click Default Colors.

Note: Clicking Default Colors also resets the target color.

- To pick a custom replacement color, click the Replacement color swatch, and pick the color that you want to use for the correction.

5 Specify a value for Tolerance. This setting defines how similar in color replaced pixels must be. A low percentage replaces adjacent pixels within a range of color values very similar to the pixel you click. A high percentage replaces adjacent pixels within a broader range of color values.

If a person has pinkish skin, the red eye brush might have problems differentiating between the colors of the pupil and the face. Specifying a lower tolerance might help.

6 Click in the image over the details you want to correct and drag if necessary. Any pixels that match the target color are colorized with the replacement color.

If you want to darken the effect, try using the burn tool over the details you want to correct. See "Using the toning tools" on page 72.

Using the toning tools

The toning tools consist of the dodge tool and the burn tool. Used to lighten or darken areas of the image, the dodge and burn tools are based on a traditional photographer's technique for changing exposure on specific areas of a print. Photographers hold back light to lighten an area on the print (dodging) or increase the exposure to darken areas on a print (burning). You can use the dodge tool to bring out details in shadows and the burn tool to bring out details in highlights.

To use the dodge or burn tool:

1 Select the dodge tool 🔍 or burn tool ✍.

2 Choose a brush from the pop-up palette in the options bar, and drag the Size pop-up slider to set the brush size.

3 Select the tonal range to change in the image:

• Midtones to change the middle range of grays.

• Shadows to change the dark areas.

• Highlights to change the light areas.

4 Specify the exposure for the tool. (See "Specifying opacity, strength, exposure, or flow" on page 138.)

5 Drag over the part of the image you want to modify.

💡 *To gradually dodge or burn an area, set the tool with a low exposure value and drag several times over the area you want to correct.*

Using the sponge tool

The sponge tool subtly changes the color saturation or vividness of an area. In Grayscale mode, the tool increases or decreases contrast by moving gray levels away from or toward the neutral gray.

To use the sponge tool:

1 Select the sponge tool 🧽.

2 Choose a brush from the pop-up palette in the options bar, and drag the Size pop-up slider to set the brush size.

3 Select how to change the color:

• Saturate to intensify the color's saturation.

• Desaturate to dilute the color's saturation.

4 To set the rate of saturation change, drag the Flow pop-up slider or enter a value in the text box.

5 Drag over the part of the image you want to modify.

Using the focus tools

The focus tools consist of the blur tool and the sharpen tool. The blur tool softens hard edges or areas in an image to reduce detail. The sharpen tool focuses soft edges to increase clarity. For information on other ways to adjust sharpness, see "Sharpen filters" on page 179.

To use the blur or sharpen tool:

1 Select the blur tool 💧 or sharpen tool △.

2 Choose a brush from the pop-up palette in the options bar, and drag the Size pop-up slider to set the brush size.

3 Specify a blending mode and stroke strength. (See "Setting options for painting and editing tools" on page 135.)

4 To blur or sharpen using data from all layers visible in the document window, select Use All Layers. To affect only the active layer, deselect this option.

Drag over the part of the image you want to blur or sharpen.

Chapter 5: Resizing, Cropping, and Laying Out Images

Adjusting the resolution and size of your images is easy using the tools in Photoshop Elements.

About image size and resolution

When you take a photo with a digital camera, or scan a photo, you create an image that has specific number of pixels on each side. For example, your digital camera may make a photo that is 1024 pixels wide and 800 pixels high. These two measurements, referred to as the *pixel dimensions*, have a direct correlation to the image's file size, and both are an indication of the amount of image data in a photo.

Resolution is the number of pixels per linear unit of measure—for example, the number of pixels per inch (ppi). While a digital photo contains a specific amount of image data, it doesn't have a specific physical output size or resolution. As you change the resolution of a file, its physical dimensions change, or as you change the width and height of an image the resolution changes.

You can see the relationship between image size and resolution in the image size dialog box (choose Image > Resize > Image Size). Deselect Resample Image, because you don't want to change the amount of image date in your photo. Then change the width or the height or the resolution. Notice that as you change one value the other two values change.

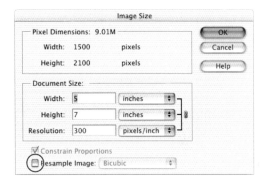

The image size dialog box with Resample Image deselected

Generally, the higher the resolution of your image, the better the printed image quality. Some printing devices may require a specific image resolution, but for a photo inkjet printer, the resolution can range from 240 to 360 ppi.

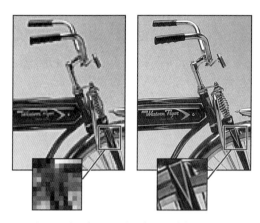

Same image printed at 72-ppi and 300-ppi; inset zoom 200%

If you need to print using a specific resolution, or you want to print an image significantly smaller or larger than the image's pixel dimensions allow, you can resample the image. Resampling involves either throwing away or adding pixels to the image. For more information, see "Resampling images" on page 77.

About printer and monitor resolution

Printer resolution refers to the number of ink dots per inch (dpi) produced by a printer. Most desktop laser printers have a resolution of 600 dpi. Inkjet printers produce a spray of ink, not actual dots; however, most inkjet printers have an approximate resolution of 720 to 2880 dpi.

Your printer's resolution is different from, but related to your image's resolution. To print a high quality photo on an inkjet printer, an image resolution of about 300 ppi should provide very good results. Depending on the image, you can get acceptable results with a resolution of 240 ppi. Using the lower resolution will let you print a slightly larger photo—if you are willing to accept some image degradation.

Your monitor's resolution is described in pixels per inch. For example, if your monitor resolution is set to 1024 x 768 and your photo's pixel dimensions are the same size, the photo will fill the screen. You should consider the lowest monitor resolution that your photo is likely to be viewed on when you are preparing images for viewing on-screen.

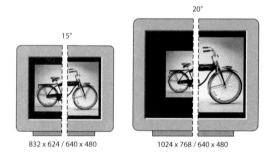

How large an image appears on-screen depends on a combination of factors—the pixel dimensions of the image, the monitor size, and the monitor resolution setting. The examples above show a 620- by 400-pixel image displayed on monitors of various sizes and resolutions.

When you work in Photoshop Elements, you can change the image magnification on-screen, so you can easily work with images of any pixel dimensions.

Changing image size and resolution

Once you have scanned or imported an image, you may want to adjust its size. The Image Size command lets you adjust the pixel dimensions, print dimensions, and resolution of an image.

Keep in mind that bitmap and vector data can produce different results when you resize an image. Bitmap data is resolution-dependent; therefore, changing the pixel dimensions of a bitmap image can cause a loss in image quality and sharpness. In contrast, vector data is resolution-independent; you can resize it without losing its crisp edges.

Displaying image size information

You can display information about the current image size using the information box at the bottom of the application window (Windows) or the document window (Mac OS). (See "Using the status bar" on page 18.)

To display the current image size:

Click the file information box, and hold down the mouse button. The box displays the width and height of the image (both in pixels and in the unit of measurement currently selected for the rulers), the number of channels, and the image resolution.

Resampling images

Changing the pixel dimensions of an image is called *resampling*. Resampling also affects the display size of your image. When you *downsample,* meaning that you decrease the number of pixels in your image, information is deleted from the image. When you *resample up,* or increase the number of pixels in your image, new pixels are added based on color values of existing pixels.

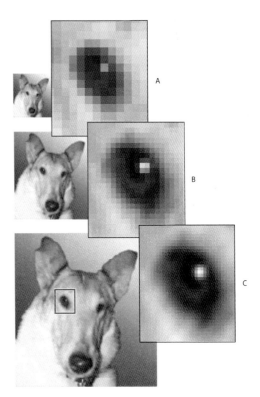

Resampling pixels that make up the dog's eye
A. Downsampled *B. Original* *C. Resampled up*
(Selected pixels displayed for each image.)

Keep in mind that resampling can result in poorer image quality. For example, when you resample an image to larger pixel dimensions, the image will lose some detail and sharpness.

💡 *Applying the Unsharp Mask filter to a resampled image can help refocus the image's details. (See "Using the focus tools" on page 73.)*

To avoid the need for resampling, scan or create the image at a high resolution. If you want to preview the effects of changing pixel dimensions on-screen or print proofs at different resolutions, resample a duplicate of your file.

Resampling affects not only the size of an image on-screen but also its image quality and its printed output—either its printed dimensions or its image resolution. (See "About image size and resolution" on page 75.)

💡 *If you're preparing images for the Web, it's useful to specify image size in terms of the pixel dimensions.*

To resample an image:

1 Choose Image > Resize > Image Size.

2 Make sure that Resample Image is selected, and choose an interpolation method:

- Bicubic is the slowest but most precise method, resulting in the smoothest tonal gradations.

- Nearest Neighbor is the fastest but least precise method. This method can result in jagged effects, which become apparent when distorting or scaling an image or performing multiple manipulations on a selection.

- Bilinear is the medium-quality method.

3 To maintain the current proportions of pixel width to pixel height, select Constrain Proportions. This option automatically updates the width as you change the height, and vice versa.

4 In Pixel Dimensions, enter values for Width and Height. To enter values as percentages of the current dimensions, choose Percent as the unit of measurement.

The new file size for the image appears at the top of the Image Size dialog box, with the old file size in parentheses.

5 Click OK to change the pixel dimensions and resample the image.

💡 *For best results in producing a smaller image, downsample and apply the Unsharp Mask filter. To produce a larger image, rescan the image at a higher resolution.*

Changing the print dimensions and resolution of an image

When creating an image for print media, it's useful to specify image size in terms of the printed dimensions and the image resolution. These two measurements, referred to as the *document size*, determine the total pixel count and therefore the file size of the image; document size also determines the base size at which an image is placed into another application. You can further manipulate the scale of the printed image in the Print Options dialog box; however, changes you make in the Print Options dialog box affect only the printed image, not the document size of the image file. (See "Positioning and scaling images" on page 238.)

If you turn on resampling for the image, you can change print dimensions and resolution independently (and change the total number of pixels in the image). If you turn resampling off, you can change either the dimensions or the resolution—Photoshop Elements adjusts the other value automatically to preserve the total pixel count. For the highest print quality, it's generally best to change the dimensions and resolution first without resampling. Then resample only as necessary.

To change the print dimensions and resolution of an image:

1 Choose Image > Resize > Image Size.

2 Change the print dimensions, image resolution, or both:

- To change only the print dimensions or only the resolution and adjust the total number of pixels in the image proportionately, make sure that Resample Image is selected. Then choose an interpolation method. (See "Resampling images" on page 77.)

- To change the print dimensions and resolution without changing the total number of pixels in the image, deselect Resample Image.

3 To maintain the current proportions of image width to image height, select Constrain Proportions. This option automatically updates the width as you change the height, and vice versa.

4 Under Document Size, enter new values for the height and width. If desired, choose a new unit of measurement. Note that for Width, the Columns option uses the width and gutter sizes specified in the Units & Rulers preferences. (See "Using rulers and the grid" on page 24.)

5 For Resolution, enter a new value. If desired, choose a new unit of measurement.

6 Click OK.

To return to the original values displayed in the Image Size dialog box, hold down Alt (Windows) or Option (Mac OS), and click Reset.

To view the print size on-screen:

Do one of the following:

- Choose View > Print Size.

- Select the hand tool or zoom tool, and click Print Size in the options bar.

The magnification of the image is adjusted to display its approximate printed size, as specified in the Document Size section of the Image Size dialog box. Keep in mind that the size and resolution of your monitor affect the on-screen print size.

Cropping images

Cropping is the process of selecting and removing a portion of an image to create focus or strengthen its composition. You can crop an image using the crop tool or the Crop command. In addition, you can use the Straighten and Crop Image command to automatically correct a skewed image. (See "Straightening images" on page 82.)

Using the crop tool to focus on the dog in the image.

To crop an image using the crop tool:

1 Select the crop tool ⊠ .

2 If you want to specify the size or resolution of the crop, enter the values in the Width, Height, or Resolution text boxes in the options bar. You can also click Front Image to enter the values of the currently active image.

3 Drag over the part of the image you want to keep. When you release the mouse button, the crop marquee appears as a bounding box with handles at the corners and sides.

4 If necessary, select the Shield cropped area option to show the cropping shield. To adjust the color and opacity of the cropping shield, use the color selection box and the opacity pop-up slider in the options bar.

5 Adjust the crop marquee:

• To move the marquee to another position, place the pointer inside the bounding box, and drag.

• To scale the marquee, drag a handle. To constrain the proportions, hold down Shift as you drag a corner handle.

• To rotate the marquee, position the pointer outside the bounding box (the pointer turns into a curved arrow ↻), and drag.

Note: You can't rotate the crop tool marquee for an image in Bitmap mode.

6 Do one of the following to crop the image:

• Click the OK button ✔ in the options bar.

• Double-click inside the crop marquee.

• Select a different tool in the toolbox.

• Press Enter (Windows) or Return (Mac OS).

Click the Cancel button ⊘ in the options bar to cancel the cropping operation.

To crop an image using the Crop command:

1 Select the part of the image you want to keep. (See "About selections" on page 113.)

2 Choose Image > Crop.

Changing the size of the work canvas

The Canvas Size command lets you add or remove work space around an existing image. You can crop an image by decreasing the canvas area. Added canvas appears in the currently selected background color or transparent as the background.

To use the Canvas Size command:

1 Choose Image > Resize > Canvas Size.

2 Choose the units of measurement you want. The Columns option measures width in terms of the columns specified in the Units & Rulers preferences.

3 Enter the dimensions in the Width and Height boxes.

4 For Anchor, click a square to indicate where to position the existing image on the new canvas.

5 Click OK.

Adding canvas to an image.

Rotating and straightening images

You can rotate, flip, and straighten an entire image using the commands in the Image > Rotate submenu.

Rotating and flipping images

Rotating an image turns it around its center point, while flipping an image inverts it across its horizontal or vertical axis.

To rotate or flip an entire image:

Choose Image > Rotate, and choose one of the following commands from the submenu:

• 90° Left to rotate the image counterclockwise by a quarter-turn.

• 90° Right to rotate the image clockwise by a quarter-turn.

• 180° to rotate the image by a half-turn.

• Custom to rotate the image by the angle you specify. If you choose this option, enter an angle between −359.99 and 359.99 in the angle text box, and then select Right or Left to rotate clockwise or counterclockwise. Click OK.

• Flip Horizontal to flip the image horizontally.

• Flip Vertical to flip the image vertically.

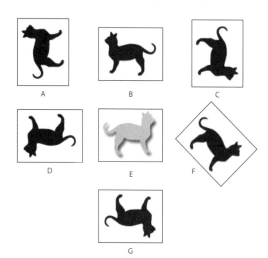

Rotating an image
A. Rotate 90° left B. Flip Horizontal C. Rotate 90° right
D. Rotate 180° E. Original image F. Free rotate
G. Flip Vertical

Straightening images

Skewed images are a common by-product of the scanning process. For example, if you lay a photograph on the scanner at an angle, the image will appear rotated when you open it in Photoshop Elements. You can quickly correct a rotated image using one of the Straighten Image commands.

To straighten an image:

Do one of the following:

• To straighten and crop the image, choose Image > Rotate > Straighten and Crop Image.

Note: The Straighten and Crop Image command may not produce good results if the edges of the rotated scan are too close to the image window boundaries. In this case, you can use the Canvas Size command to enlarge the work canvas. (See "Changing the size of the work canvas" on page 80.)

• To straighten the image and leave the canvas size the same, choose Image > Rotate > Straighten Image. Using this command results in an image with a transparent border at its edges.

Creating panoramic images using Photomerge™

The Photomerge command combines several photographs into one continuous image. For example, you can take five overlapping photographs of a city skyline, and then assemble them into a panorama. The Photomerge command is capable of assembling photos that are tiled horizontally as well as vertically.

Photomerge composition of the skyline of Chicago

Taking pictures for use with Photomerge

Your source photographs play a large role in panoramic compositions. To avoid problems, follow these guidelines when taking pictures for use with Photomerge:

Overlap images sufficiently Images should have an overlap of approximately 15% to 40% of the image area. If the overlap is less, Photomerge may not be able to automatically assemble the panorama. However, keep in mind that the images shouldn't overlap too much. If images overlap by 50% or more, it can be difficult to work with them, and blending may not be as effective. Try to keep the individual photos at least somewhat distinct from each other.

Use a consistent focal length Avoid using the zoom feature of your camera while taking your pictures.

Keep the camera level Although Photomerge can process slight rotations between pictures, a tilt of more than a few degrees can result in errors when automatically assembling the panorama. Using a tripod with a rotating head helps maintain camera alignment and viewpoint.

When photographing a panoramic scene from a high place, the natural inclination is to keep the horizon level in the viewfinder. However, this actually produces a noticeable rotation between images. Try using a tripod to keep the camera level when taking photographs in this situation.

Stay in the same position Try not to change your position as you take a series of photographs so the pictures are from the same viewpoint. If you walk to a new position while taking photographs, you'll likely disrupt the continuity of your images. Using the optical viewfinder with the camera held close to the eye helps keep the viewpoint consistent. Or try using a tripod to keep the camera in the same place.

Avoid using distortion lenses Lenses, such as fish-eye lenses, that cause noticeable distortion to the image can interfere with Photomerge.

Maintain the same exposure Avoid using the flash in some pictures and not in others. The advanced blending feature in Photomerge helps smooth out different exposures, but extreme differences make alignment difficult.

Creating a Photomerge composition

When you set up a Photomerge composition, you identify your source files, and then the assembly of the panorama is automatically done for you. Once the panorama is complete, you can still make changes to the placement of the individual photos, if necessary.

The Photomerge dialog box helps you create panoramic compositions. This dialog box contains tools for manipulating the composition, a lightbox for storing source images that are not in use, a work area for assembling the composition, and options for viewing and editing the composition.

To set up a new Photomerge composition:

1 Choose File > Create Photomerge.

2 Click the Browse button in the Photomerge dialog box. Open files are automatically added to the Source Files list.

3 Navigate to the source files and select the files for your Photomerge composition.

4 Click Open to add the files to the Source Files list in the Photomerge dialog box.

You can add more files by clicking the Browse button again and navigating to the source files. You can always remove a file from the Source Files list by selecting the file and clicking the Remove button.

5 When you've added all the source files, click OK to create the Photomerge composition. The source files will open automatically, and will be processed.

6 Once the new panorama image appears in the Photomerge dialog box, you can work with individual source files and change your view of the work area. (See "Editing a Photomerge composition" on page 85.)

If the panorama can't be automatically assembled, a message appears on-screen. You can assemble the composition manually in the Photomerge dialog box. (See "Editing a Photomerge composition" on page 85.)

7 If necessary, adjust the settings of your panorama. (See "Changing Photomerge composition settings" on page 85.)

8 Click OK to generate the panorama as a new Photoshop Elements file.

9 Save the panorama image.

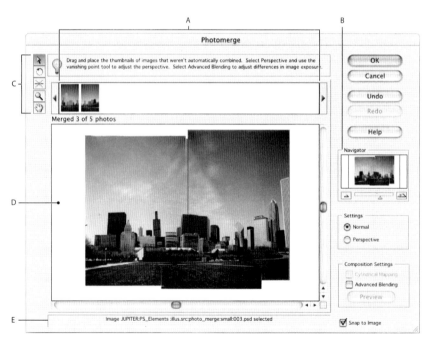

Photomerge dialog box
A. *Lightbox* **B.** *Navigator* **C.** *Toolbox* **D.** *Work area* **E.** *Status bar*

Editing a Photomerge composition

You may need to reposition an individual source file, or rotate a file in your composition. The editing tools in the Photomerge dialog box help you work with your panorama. You can also zoom in and out to better see the alignment of each file.

To reposition images in a composition:

1 Select the select image tool ⬉.

2 Do one or more of the following:

• Drag an image in the work area to reposition it.

• Drag an image from the lightbox to the work area to add it to the composition.

• Drag an image from the work area to the lightbox to remove it from the composition.

• Double-click an image in the lightbox to add it to the composition.

💡 *Make sure Snap to Image is selected to automatically snap overlapping images into place when a commonality is detected.*

To rotate an image in the work area:

1 Select the select image tool ⬉, and click on the image you want to rotate.

2 Select the rotate tool ↻.

3 Click near the edge of the image and drag in a circular motion around the center of the image.

To navigate in the Photomerge dialog box:

Do one or more of the following in the Photomerge dialog box:

• Select the hand tool ✋ and drag in the work area to move the view.

• Drag the view box or the scroll bars in the Navigator thumbnail. The view box represents the boundaries of the work area.

To zoom in:

Do one of the following:

• Click the zoom in icon ⛰ below the Navigator.

• Use the zoom tool 🔍 to zoom in.

To zoom out:

Click the zoom out icon ⛰ below the Navigator.

Changing Photomerge composition settings

How source images appear in the Photomerge dialog box depends on the settings you choose. Photoshop Elements lets you adjust the perspective and blend exposure differences to produce the best possible effect.

To change the vanishing point of a composition:

1 Select Perspective in the Settings area of the Photomerge dialog box.

2 Select the vanishing point tool ☀, and click on an image in the work area to make it the vanishing point image.

💡 *The vanishing point tool selects the vanishing point image, which changes the perspective of the composition. The middle image is the default vanishing point image (it has a blue border around it when selected). There can only be one vanishing point image in a composition.*

3 If necessary, use the Select Image Tool ➤ to adjust the position of the non-vanishing point images. A non-vanishing point image has a red border around it when selected.

When you apply perspective correction to a composition, the non-vanishing point images are linked to the vanishing point image. You can break this link by clicking the Normal button, by separating the images in the work area, or by dragging the vanishing point image back to the lightbox. Once the link is broken, images return to their original shapes.

The perspective correction only works up to an approximately 120° angle of view. For a wider angle of view, the Perspective option should be deselected.

💡 *To change the perspective of a composition, select the vanishing point tool, and click on a non-vanishing point image in the work area. Notice how the perspective of the composition changes depending on which image is the vanishing point image.*

To apply Advanced Blending or Cylindrical Mapping:

1 Select Composition options as desired:

• Cylindrical Mapping to reduce the "bow tie" distortion that can occur when you apply perspective correction. You must select the Perspective option in order to apply cylindrical mapping.

Adding Cylindrical Mapping
A. *Original* **B.** *Cylindrical Mapping applied*

• Advanced Blending to minimize color inconsistencies that result from blending images with exposure differences. When this option is selected, broad colors and tones are blended over a large area, while detailed colors and tones are blended over a smaller area.

2 Click Preview.

💡 *The Cylindrical Mapping and Advanced Blending options are used to process the final image. The results of applying these options are visible only in Preview mode or in the final, generated image.*

To preview changes to your Photomerge composition:

Click the Preview button. To return to edit mode, click Exit Preview.

Creating multiple-image layouts

You can export multiple images automatically as contact sheets and picture packages using Automate commands.

Creating picture packages

With the Picture Package command, you can place multiple copies of one or more photos on a single page, similar to the photo packages traditionally sold by portrait studios. You can choose from a variety of size and placement options to customize your package layout.

💡 *Using Picture Package is a great way to print more than one image on a single page.*

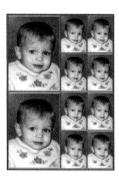

Picture package

To create a picture package from a single image:

1 Choose File > Print Layouts > Picture Package.

2 Specify the photos you want to use:

• Frontmost Document to use the currently active image.

• File to browse to a saved image.

• Folder to browse to a folder containing multiple image files.

Select Include All Subfolders to include images inside any subfolders.

3 To add other pictures to the layout, click on an image and then choose a new source image.

4 Under Document, select page size, layout, resolution, and color mode for the picture package. (A thumbnail of the selected layout is displayed on the right side of the dialog box.)

Select Flatten All Layers to create a picture package with all images and text on a single layer. Deselect Flatten All Layers to create a picture package where each image is on a separate layer and each caption is on a separate text layer.

5 For Layout, choose a preset layout option. Layout dimensions are measured in inches, and a preview of the chosen layout appears in the dialog box.

6 Under Label, select the source for label text from the Content menu (or choose None). Specify font, font attributes, and position for the labels.

7 Click OK to create the package layout.

Customizing picture package layouts

You can customize existing layouts or create new layouts using a text-editing application. The layout options in the Picture Package dialog box are determined by text files that are stored in the Layouts folder (inside the Presets folder). For example, the following text describes a layout with two 5 x 7 images:

I 8 10
(2) 5x7
0.5 0 7 5
0.5 5 7 5

First line Defines the unit of measurement and the document size.

Second line Contains the name of the layout as it appears in the Picture Package dialog box.

Subsequent lines Define the position and dimensions of each image in the layout.

To customize a new picture package layout:

1 In a text-editing application, create a new file, or open an existing file in the Layouts folder (inside the Presets folder).

2 In the first line of the file, enter the following elements (separated by a space):

- A letter for the unit of measurement: i or I (for inches), p or P (for pixels), or c or C (for centimeters). All numbers in the file use the specified unit.

- The width of the document.

- The height of the document.

Note: The width and height of the document should not exceed the printable area of the paper. For example, if you plan to print on 11 x 17 paper, specify 10 x 16 as the document size.

3 In the second line of the file, enter the name of the layout as you want it to appear in the Picture Package dialog box. You can enter up to 75 characters.

4 In the subsequent lines of the file, enter the position and dimensions for images in the layout using the following elements (separated by a space):

- The position of the image in relation to the left edge of the document (the x position of the image).

- The position of the image in relation to the top edge of the document (the y position of the image).

- The width of the image.

- The height of the image.

Enter the position and dimensions for each image in the layout on a separate line. You can specify up to 50 images per layout.

5 To add comments to the file, start the line with a semicolon (;). Lines beginning with a semicolon are ignored, as are blank lines.

6 Save the file in the Layouts folder.

Creating contact sheets

By displaying a series of thumbnail previews on a single page, contact sheets let you easily preview and catalog groups of images. You can automatically create and place thumbnails on a page using the Contact Sheet command.

Note: Make sure that the images are closed before applying this command.

To create a contact sheet:

1 Choose File > Print Layouts > Contact Sheet.

2 Click Browse (Windows) or Choose (Mac OS) to specify the folder containing the images you want to use. Select Include All Subfolders to include images inside any subfolders of the chosen folder.

3 Under Document, specify the dimensions, resolution, and color mode for the contact sheet, using the menus to specify measurement units.

4 Under Thumbnails, specify layout options for the thumbnail previews:

• For Place, choose whether to arrange thumbnails across first (from left to right, then top to bottom) or down first (from top to bottom, then left to right).

• Enter the number of columns and rows that you want per contact sheet. The maximum dimensions for each thumbnail are displayed to the right, along with a visual preview of the specified layout.

• Select Use Filename As Caption to label the thumbnails using their source image filenames. Use the menu to specify a caption font.

5 Click OK to create the contact sheet.

Creating PDF slideshows

A great way to share your pictures is to export them as a PDF slideshow. Photoshop Elements generates a PDF file of the images you select that plays like a slideshow when it's opened in Adobe Acrobat.

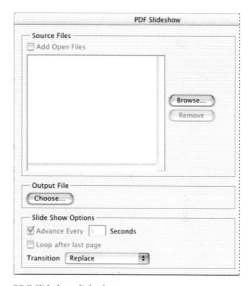

PDF Slideshow dialog box

To create a PDF slideshow:

1 Choose File > Automation Tools > PDF Slideshow.

2 Click the Browse button to navigate to the files you want to include in the slideshow.

Click Add Open Files to add the active images to the Source Files list.

3 Select the files (Shift-click to select more than one file at a time) and then click Open. The filenames will appear in the PDF Slideshow dialog box.

If you want to remove a file from the list, select the filename and then click the Remove button. To rearrange the files, click and drag them into a new position.

4 In the PDF Slideshow dialog box, click Choose to set the name and location of the slideshow file, and then click the Save button.

Note: If you want to compress your final PDF file, click the Advanced button to specify encoding options.

5 In Slide Show Options, select from the following:

- Enter the number of seconds each slide remains on the screen in the Advance Every text box.

- Select Loop After Last Page if you want the slideshow to continuously loop instead of playing through just one time.

- For Transition, choose how a new slide replaces the slide before it.

6 When you're done setting options, click the OK button to generate the slideshow.

7 Once processing is complete, a message will appear indicating the success of the generation. To see your slideshow, open the PDF file in Adobe Acrobat.

Chapter 6: Using Layers

Layers are the basis for creating and editing images in Photoshop Elements. Layers can help you customize your images, fix color and contrast, and give your images different artistic effects. Layers also make composing and managing different elements in an image much easier.

About layers

You create and manage layers using the Layers palette and the Layers menu. Layers give you the freedom to rearrange your image, adjust its color and brightness, apply special effects, edit, and add new elements to your image. With layers, all these things can be done without making permanent changes to your original image and without affecting other layers.

When you create, import, or scan an image in Photoshop Elements, the image consists of a single layer. If you're retouching the image, you can edit the original layer to make permanent changes. Alternatively, you can leave the original layer intact as a backup, and retouch a duplicate copy of the layer, or use adjustment layers to fine-tune your image.

The power of layers is that they enable you to work on one element of your image without disturbing the others, and without making tedious selections. Until you combine, or *merge*, the layers, each layer remains independent. This means you can experiment freely with different compositions without making permanent changes to your overall image. In addition, special features such as adjustment layers, fill layers, and layer styles let you create sophisticated effects.

A good way to think of layers is as sheets of transparent glass stacked one on top of the other. Where there is no image on a layer, you can see through to the layers below. Behind all of the layers is the Background layer. In the following illustration, each animal and the map are on separate layers. The map of Africa is the Background layer. Depending on how you stack and position the layers, the composition changes.

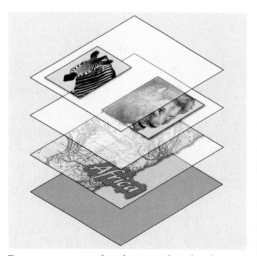

Transparent areas on a layer let you see through to the layers below.

You can also create sophisticated visual effects with layers. Grouped layers use a base layer to define the image boundaries of a layer group, and you can use layers to create a Web animation. In addition, the Layer Styles palette lets you apply special visual effects to a layer. (See "About layer styles" on page 169.)

In addition to pixel-based image layers, there are several other layer types. Fill layers are filled with a color gradient, solid color, or pattern. You can fill the entire image area or just a selected area. You can fine-tune the color, brightness, saturation of your image using Adjustment layers. Type layers and Shape layers let you create crisp vector-based text and shapes. See "Creating text" on page 196 and "Creating shapes" on page 191. When you're ready to paint on these four layer types or apply special effects to them, you must convert them to regular pixel-based image layers by *simplifying* them.

About the Layers palette

The Layers palette lists all layers in an image. The order of layers in the Layers palette indicates the stacking order of layers in the image—the topmost layer in the Layers palette is the topmost layer in the image. You can drag any layer except the Background layer up or down in the Layers palette to change the layer stacking order.

About the Background layer

When you create a new image with a color-filled background, the bottommost layer in the Layers palette is locked and labeled *Background*. You cannot change the stacking order of a Background layer, its blending mode, or its opacity. However, to do any of these things, you can convert a Background layer to a regular layer. (See "Adding layers" on page 95.)

To create a new image with transparent regions— for example, a round button with transparent edges for a Web page—select Transparent in the New dialog box. (See "Creating new images" on page 44.) In a new transparent image, the bottommost layer is called Layer 1 by default. This layer is not constrained like the Background layer; you can move it anywhere in the Layers palette and change its opacity and blending mode.

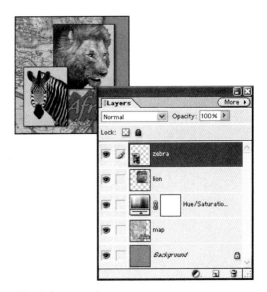

Zebra is the topmost layer.

About layers in the Layers palette

Except in the case of adjustment layers and some changes to linked layers, changes to an image affect only the selected or *active* layer, which appears highlighted in the Layers palette. To make a layer active, you can select a layer in the Layers palette. (See "Selecting layers" on page 95.) You can accomplish many tasks—such as creating, hiding, linking, locking, and deleting a layer—using the icons in the Layers palette. You can access additional commands and options in the Layers menu and in the More menu in the Layers palette.

The Layers palette uses icons to provide information about layers. The leftmost column in the palette displays an eye icon next to visible layers and no eye icon next to hidden layers.

The second column from the left shows a paintbrush icon ✐ or layer mask icon ▣ next to the active layer; layers without either of these icons can't be modified. It also shows a link icon for layers that are linked to the active layer.

The right column lists the layer's name and may display additional icons. By default, this column also shows a thumbnail image of the layer which is updated as you edit the layer. You can change the thumbnail size or choose not to show thumbnails in the Layers palette by changing the Layers palette options.

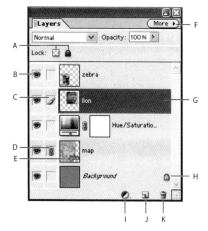

Layers palette
A. Layer lock options (from left to right): Transparency, All
B. Show/Hide layer C. Indicates active layer
D. Link/Unlink E. Layer thumbnail F. More menu
G. Highlighted layer is active layer H. Locked layer
I. Create a new fill or adjustment layer
J. Create a new layer K. Delete a layer

Note: *If you open a file that was created in Photoshop 7.0 or 6.0, the image may contain layer sets. Layer sets are indicated by a folder icon in the Layers palette and can contain multiple layers. Although Photoshop Elements doesn't support layer sets, it displays preexisting layer sets in their collapsed state. You can simplify a layer set to convert it to a single, editable raster layer. (See "Simplifying layers" on page 110.)*

Using the Layers palette

When you open Photoshop Elements for the first time, the Layers palette appears in the palette well. (See "Using the palette well" on page 13.) You can drag the palette out of the palette well to keep it on display.

Using the Layers palette, you can control whether a layer is visible and whether Photoshop Elements displays a preview, or *thumbnail,* of a layer. Turning off thumbnails or reducing their size can save space in your work area and reduce memory usage.

Note: *Only visible layers are printed.*

To display the Layers palette:

Choose Window > Layers.

To show or hide a layer in the document window:

Do one of the following:

- In the Layers palette, click the eye icon next to a layer to hide that layer. Click in the leftmost column again to redisplay the layer.

- Drag through the eye column to show or hide multiple layers.

- To display just one layer, Alt-click (Windows) or Option-click (Mac OS) the eye icon for that layer. Alt/Option-click in the eye column again to redisplay all the layers.

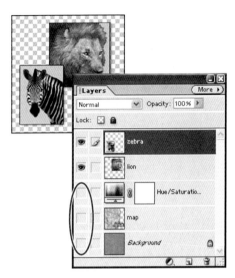

Multiple hidden layers

To change the display of layer thumbnails:

1 Choose Palette Options from the Layers palette More menu.

2 Select a size or select None to hide the thumbnails, and then click OK.

To change the transparency display:

1 Choose Edit > Preferences > Transparency or Photoshop Elements > Preferences > Transparency (Mac OS X).

2 For Grid Size, choose a pattern size. By default, the transparent areas of a document appear as a checkerboard pattern. If you choose None, transparent areas in the layer appear white.

3 For Grid Colors, choose an option:

- Light, Medium, or Dark to specify a gray pattern.

- Any other color from the list to display the checkerboard in that color.

- Custom to choose a color that does not appear in the list. Then click either of the color selection boxes to specify a custom color in the Color Picker.

4 Click OK.

Selecting layers

If your image has multiple layers, you must select what layer you want to work on. Any changes you make to the image affect only the *active* layer, except for changes made with adjustment layers, and some changes to linked layers. You select a layer to make it active, and only one layer can be active at a time.

If you don't see the desired results when you use a tool or apply a command, you may not have the correct layer selected. Check the Layers palette to make sure the desired layer is highlighted.

To select a layer:

Do one of the following:

- In the Layers palette, select a layer's thumbnail or name to make it active.

- Select the move tool, right-click (Windows) or Control-click (Mac OS) in the image, and choose the layer you want from the context menu. The context menu lists all the layers that contain pixels under the current pointer location, and all adjustment layers.

To select layers interactively as you use the move tool in the document window, select Auto Select Layer in the Move tool options bar. When this option is selected, the move tool selects the topmost layer containing opaque pixels under the pointer. (See "Moving, copying, and pasting selections" on page 122.)

Creating a layered image

Photoshop Elements lets you create up to 8000 layers in an image, each with its own blending mode and opacity. However, the amount of memory in your system may put a lower limit on the number of possible layers.

Adding layers

Newly added layers appear above the selected layer in the Layers palette. You can add layers to an image in a variety of ways:

- By creating new blank layers or turning selections into layers.

- By converting a background to a regular layer or vice versa.

- By pasting copied or cut selections into the image. (See "Copying selections or layers" on page 122.)

- By using the type tool or by using a shape tool. (See "Creating text" on page 196 and "Creating shapes" on page 191.)

- By duplicating an existing layer. See "Duplicating layers" on page 98.

To create a new transparent layer with default options:

Click the New Layer button ⬛ at the bottom of the Layers palette. The layer uses Normal mode with 100% opacity and is named according to its order of creation.

To add a new layer and specify options:

1 Do one of the following:

- Choose Layer > New > Layer.

- Choose New Layer from the Layers palette menu.

- Alt-click (Windows) or Option-click (Mac OS) the New Layer button at the bottom of the Layers palette.

2 Name the layer, and set other layer options. (See "Specifying layer blending modes" on page 100, "Specifying opacity" on page 100, and "Creating grouped layers" on page 106.)

3 Click OK.

To turn a selected area into a new layer:

1 Select an existing layer, and make a selection. (See "Selecting pixels" on page 114.)

2 Choose Layer > New, and choose one of the following commands from the submenu:

- Layer Via Copy to copy the selection into a new layer.

- Layer Via Cut to cut the selection and paste it into a new layer.

The selected area appears in a new layer in the same position relative to the image boundaries.

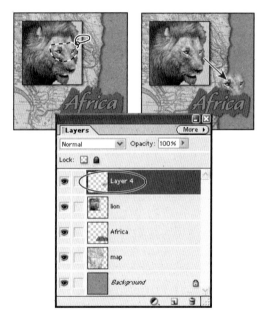

New layer created from feathered selection with Layer Via Copy command, and then moved

To create a layer from the background:

1 Do one of the following:

- Double-click the background in the Layers palette to convert it to a layer.

- Choose Layer > New > Layer from Background to convert the background to a layer.

- Select the background, and choose Duplicate Layer from the Layers palette More menu to leave the background intact and create a copy of it as a new layer.

2 Rename the layer in the New Layer dialog box, and click OK.

💡 *If you drag the background eraser tool on the background layer, the background is automatically converted to a regular layer, and erased areas become transparent.*

To convert a layer into a background:

1 Select a layer in the Layers palette.

2 Choose Layer > New > Background from Layer.

Any transparent areas in the original layer are filled with the background color.

Note: *If your image already has a background, you can't convert a layer to a background until you convert the existing background to a layer.*

Changing the stacking order of layers

The stacking order determines whether a layer appears in front of or behind other layers.

To change the order of layers by dragging:

1 In the Layers palette, select the layer that you want to move.

2 Drag the layer up or down in the Layers palette. When the highlighted line appears in the desired position, release the mouse button.

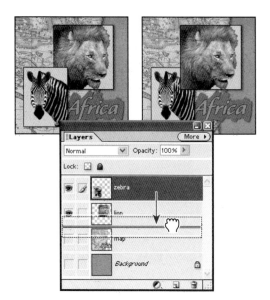

Dragging the zebra layer below the lion layer changes the stacking order

To change the order of a layer:

1 In the Layers palette, select the layer that you want to move.

2 Choose Layer > Arrange, and choose a command from the submenu to arrange the layer:

- Bring to Front to make the layer the topmost layer.

- Bring Forward to move the layer one level up in the stacking order.

- Send Backward to move the layer one level down in the stacking order.

- Send to Back to make the layer the bottommost layer in the image (except for the background).

Note: By default, the Background layer cannot be moved from the bottom of the layer list. To move the background, first convert it to a layer. (See "Adding layers" on page 95.)

Duplicating layers

You can duplicate any layer (including the background) within an image. And you can copy any layer (including the background) from one image to another.

When copying layers between images, keep in mind that the printed size of the copied layer depends on the resolution of the destination image. (See "About digital images" on page 39.)

To duplicate a layer in an image:

1 Select the layer in the Layers palette, and do one of the following to duplicate it:

- To duplicate and rename the layer, choose Layer > Duplicate Layer, or choose Duplicate Layer from the Layers palette More menu. Name the duplicate layer, and click OK.

- To duplicate without naming, select the layer and drag it to the New Layer button ▣ at the bottom of the Layers palette.

- (Windows only) Right-click on the layer name (not the thumbnail) and choose Duplicate Layer.

To copy a layer between images:

1 Open the two images you want to use.

2 In the Layers palette of the source image, select the layer that you want to copy.

3 Do one of the following:

- Choose Select > All to select all of the pixels on the layer, and choose Edit > Copy. Then make the destination image active, and choose Edit > Paste.

- Drag the layer's name from the Layers palette of the source image into the destination image.

- Use the move tool ▸⊕ to drag the layer from the source image to the destination image.

The copied layer appears in the destination image where you release the mouse button (and above the active layer in the Layers palette). If the layer you're dragging is larger than the destination image, only part of the layer is visible. You can use the move tool to drag other sections of the layer into view.

💡 *Hold down Shift as you drag a layer to copy it to the same position it occupied in the source image (if the source and destination images have the same pixel dimensions) or to the center of the destination image (if the source and destination images have different pixel dimensions).*

To copy multiple layers into another image:

1 Make sure that both the source and destination images are open, and select one of the layers you want to copy.

2 In the Layers palette, click in the column immediately to the left of any additional layers you want to copy. The link icon 🔗 appears in the column.

3 Use the move tool ➤⊕ to drag the linked layers from the source image to the destination image.

To duplicate a layer into another image or a new image:

1 Open the source image. If you plan to copy a layer to an existing image, open the destination image too.

2 In the source document's Layers palette, select the name of the layer you want to duplicate.

3 Choose Layer > Duplicate Layer, or choose Duplicate Layer from the Layers palette More menu.

4 Type a name for the duplicate layer in the Duplicate Layer dialog box, and choose a destination document for the layer:

- To duplicate the layer to an existing image, choose a filename from the Document pop-up menu.

- To create a new document for the layer, choose New from the Document pop-up menu, and enter a name for the new file. An image created by duplicating a layer has no background. (See "About the Background layer" on page 92.)

5 Click OK.

Repositioning layers

You can quickly adjust the composition of an image by repositioning its layers. Using the move tool, you can make adjustments or radically change the position of a layer. The layer's content is preserved even if you move it outside the image area.

To reposition layers:

1 In the Layers palette, select the layer that you want to reposition. To reposition multiple layers at the same time, link the layers together in the Layers palette. (See "Linking layers" on page 99.)

2 Select the move tool ➤⊕.

3 Do one of the following:

- Drag in the image to move the selected layer to the desired position.

- Press the arrow keys on the keyboard to move the layer in 1-pixel increments, or press Shift and an arrow key to move the layer in 10-pixel increments.

- Hold down Shift as you drag to move the layer directly up or down, directly to either side, or on a 45° diagonal.

Linking layers

By linking two or more layers, you can move their contents together. You can also copy, paste, merge, and apply transformations to all linked layers simultaneously.

To link layers:

1 Select a layer in the Layers palette.

2 Click in the column immediately to the left of any layers you want to link to the active layer. The link icon appears in the column.

To unlink layers:

In the Layers palette, click the link icons to remove them.

Specifying opacity and blending options

Keep in mind that a layer's opacity and blending mode interact with the opacity and mode of painting tools. For example, consider a layer that uses Dissolve mode and an opacity of 50%. If you paint on this layer with the paintbrush tool set to Normal mode with an opacity of 100%, the paint appears in Dissolve mode with a 50% opacity. Likewise, consider a layer that uses Normal mode and 100% opacity. If you use the eraser tool with an opacity of 50%, only 50% of the paint disappears from this layer as you erase.

Specifying opacity

A layer's opacity determines to what degree it obscures or reveals the layer beneath it. A layer with 1% opacity appears nearly transparent, while one with 100% opacity appears completely opaque. Transparent areas remain transparent no matter what opacity setting you use.

Map layer with 100% opacity and map layer with 50% opacity

To specify opacity for a layer:

1 Select the layer in the Layers palette.

2 In the Layers palette, enter a value between 0 and 100 for Opacity, or drag the Opacity pop-up slider.

Specifying layer blending modes

You use layer blending modes to determine how a layer blends with pixels in layers beneath it. By applying modes to layers, you can create a variety of special effects. For a description of each blending mode, see "Selecting a blending mode" on page 135.

To specify a blending mode for a layer:

1 Select the layer in the Layers palette.

2 Choose an option from the Blending Mode pop-up menu.

Right after you choose a blending mode, you can press the up or down arrows on your keyboard to try other blending mode options in the menu.

Filling a new layer with a neutral color

Some filters (such as the Lighting Effects filter) cannot be applied to layers without opaque pixels. Selecting Fill with Neutral Color in the New Layer dialog box resolves this problem by first filling the layer with a preset, neutral color. The neutral color is assigned based on the layer's blending mode and is invisible. If no effect is applied, filling with a neutral color has no effect on the image.

To fill a new layer with a neutral color:

1 Choose New Layer from either the Layers menu, or the Layers palette menu.

2 In the New Layer dialog box, choose a blending mode from the Mode pop-up menu, and then select Fill with [blending mode] Neutral Color.

Note: This option isn't available for layers that use the Normal, Dissolve, Hue, Saturation, Color, or Luminosity modes.

3 Click OK.

4 Select the neutral color layer in the Layers palette, and choose a filter, effect, or layer style from the Filters, Effects, or Layer Styles palette. (See "Using the Filters, Effects, and Layer Styles palettes" on page 165.)

Using adjustment and fill layers

Adjustment layers and fill layers add another level of flexibility to working with layers. Adjustment layers allow you to experiment with color and make tonal adjustments to an image; fill layers allow you to quickly add color, pattern, and gradient elements to an image. If you change your mind about the results, you can go back and edit or remove the adjustment or fill at any time.

About adjustment layers

Adjustment layers let you experiment with color and make tonal adjustments to an image without permanently modifying the pixels in the image. The color and tonal changes reside within the adjustment layer, which acts as a veil through which the underlying layers appear. By default, an adjustment layer affects all the layers below it. This means that you can correct multiple layers by making a single adjustment, rather than making the adjustment to each layer separately. To limit the adjustment to a portion of the image, you can select an area in your image before adding the adjustment layer. If you want the adjustment layer to only affect a single layer, you can group them together. (See "Creating grouped layers" on page 106.)

Original image, and image with levels adjustment applied

Creating adjustment layers

Adjustment layers have the same opacity and blending mode options as image layers and can be rearranged in the layer stacking order, deleted, hidden, and duplicated in the same manner as image layers. By default, adjustment layers take the name of the adjustment type.

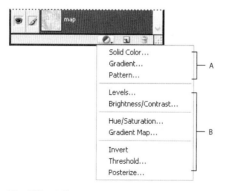

New Fill or Adjustment Layer menu
A. Fill layers B. Adjustment layers

To create an adjustment layer:

1 In the Layers palette, select the topmost layer you want to affect.

2 To confine the effects of the adjustment layer to a selected area, make a selection.

3 Do one of the following:

• To affect all the layers below the adjustment layer, click the New Fill or Adjustment Layer button ⬤ at the bottom of the Layers palette, and choose the adjustment type you want to create. (Note that the first three commands in the menu are fill layers, not adjustment layers.)

• To affect only one or more successive layers below the adjustment layer, Choose Layer > New Adjustment Layer, and choose an adjustment type from the submenu. In the New Layer dialog box, select Group With Previous Layer, and then click OK.

4 In the [adjustment type] dialog box, set the options for the adjustment type you chose:

Levels Specify values for the highlights, shadows, and midtones. (See "Using the Levels dialog box" on page 62.)

Brightness/Contrast Specify values for Brightness and Contrast. (See "Using the Brightness/Contrast command" on page 63.)

Hue/Saturation Choose which colors to edit, and specify values for Hue, Saturation, and Lightness. (See "Using the Hue/Saturation command" on page 67.)

Gradient Map Choose a gradient and set gradient options. (See "Using the Gradient Map command" on page 188.)

Invert Invert adjustment layers don't have options. (See "Using the Invert command" on page 186.)

Threshold Specify a threshold level. (See "Using the Threshold command" on page 187.)

Posterize Specify the number of tonal levels for each color channel. (See "Using the Posterize command" on page 188.)

If you chose the Group With Previous Layer option in step 3, Photoshop Elements groups the adjustment layer with the layer immediately below it and the effect is confined to the group. To add more layers to the group, press Alt (Windows) or Option (Mac OS), and position the pointer over the line dividing the bottommost layer in the group with the next layer below it (the pointer changes to two overlapping circles), and then click. For more information, see "Creating grouped layers" on page 106.

About fill layers

Fill layers let you fill a layer with a solid color, a gradient, or a pattern. Unlike adjustment layers, fill layers do not affect the layers underneath them.

Creating fill layers

Fill layers have the same opacity and blending mode options as image layers and can be rearranged in the layer stacking order, deleted, hidden, and duplicated in the same manner as image layers. By default, fill layers take the name of the fill type.

To create a fill layer:

1 In the Layers palette, select the layer you want the fill layer to be above.

2 To confine the effects of the fill layer to a selected area, make a selection.

3 Do one of the following:

• Click the New Fill or Adjustment Layer button at the bottom of the Layers palette, and choose the fill type you want to create. (Note that the first three commands in the menu are fill layers, and the rest are adjustment layers.)

• Choose Layer > New Fill Layer, and choose a fill type from the submenu. In the New Layer dialog box which appears, click OK.

4 In the [fill layer type] dialog box which appears, set the options for the fill type you chose:

Solid Color Specify a color. (See "Using the Adobe Color Picker" on page 131.)

Gradient In the Gradient Fill dialog box, click the Gradient pop-up menu arrow to choose a predefined gradient, or to edit the gradient in the Gradient Editor, click the color gradient. (See "Creating or editing gradient fills" on page 148.) You can drag in the image window to move the center of the gradient.

Set additional options in the Gradient Fill dialog box as desired:

• Style specifies the shape of the gradient.

• Angle specifies the angle at which the gradient is applied.

- Scale changes the size of the gradient.

- Reverse flips the orientation of the gradient.

- Dither reduces banding by applying dithering to the gradient.

- Align With Layer uses the bounding box of the layer to calculate the gradient fill.

Pattern Click the pattern, and choose a pattern from the pop-up palette. Set additional pattern options as desired:

- Click Scale and enter a value or drag the slider to scale the pattern.

- Click Snap to Origin to position the origin of the pattern with that of the document window. (See "Using rulers and the grid" on page 24.)

- Select Link With Layer to specify that the pattern moves with the fill layer as it is relocated. When this option is selected, you can drag in the image to position the pattern while the Pattern Fill dialog box is open.

To create a new preset pattern after editing pattern settings, click the New Preset button ⬛. For more information about creating patterns and loading pattern presets, see "Creating and editing patterns" on page 145 and "Working with preset options" on page 27.

Editing adjustment or fill layer options or layer type

Once you create an adjustment or fill layer, you can easily edit the settings, or dynamically replace it with a different adjustment or fill type.

To edit an adjustment or fill layer:

1 To open the adjustment or fill options dialog box:

- Double-click the adjustment or fill layer's leftmost thumbnail in the Layers palette.

- Choose Layer > Layer Content Options.

2 Make the desired changes, and click OK.

To change the adjustment or fill layer type:

1 Select the adjustment layer or fill layer that you want to change.

2 Choose Layer > Change Layer Content and select a different fill or adjustment layer from the list.

Editing the layer mask of adjustment or fill layers

A layer *mask* protects sections of a layer (or the entire layer) from being edited, and can be used to show or hide sections of an image or layer effect. When the layer mask is attached to an adjustment layer, it's used to control which areas of the underlying layers are affected by the adjustment layer. When the layer mask is attached to a fill layer, it's used to define the area that's filled in the fill layer.

You can edit the mask of an adjustment layer or fill layer. If you made a selection before you added the adjustment or fill layer, a mask is automatically created for the selected area. If you didn't select an area beforehand, all areas of an adjustment or fill layer are "unmasked".

Editing a mask involves painting or erasing with black, white, or shades of gray. When you select an adjustment or fill layer in the Layers palette, the color swatches in the toolbox are black and white. To add to the mask, paint with black or erase with white. The mask defines areas that aren't affected by an adjustment or fill layer. To subtract from the mask, paint with white or erase with black. Subtracting from the mask increases the area affected by an adjustment or fill layer. Painting or erasing in shades of gray will remove areas from the mask and add areas to the mask in various levels of transparency.

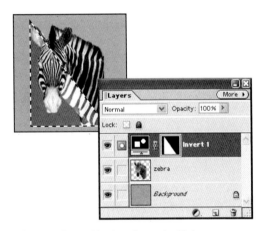

Adjustment layer with triangular mask added

To edit the layer mask for an adjustment or fill layer:

1 Select the adjustment layer or fill layer in the Layers palette.

2 Select the paintbrush tool, or any painting or editing tool.

3 Use the following methods to view the layer mask:

• Alt-click (Windows) or Option-click (Mac OS) the layer's leftmost thumbnail to view only the grayscale mask. Alt/Option-click the thumbnail again to redisplay the other layers.

• Hold down Alt+Shift (Windows) or Option+Shift (Mac OS), and click the layer's leftmost thumbnail to view the mask in a red masking color. Hold down Alt/Option+Shift and click the thumbnail again to turn off the red display.

4 To constrain editing to part of the mask, make a selection. (See "Selecting pixels" on page 114.)

5 Edit the layer mask:

• To remove areas of the adjustment effect or fill, paint the layer mask with black.

• To add areas to the adjustment effect or fill, paint the layer mask with white.

• To partially remove the adjustment effect or fill so that it shows in various levels of transparency, paint the layer mask with gray. (Double-click the foreground color swatch in the toolbox to choose a gray shade in the Color Picker.) The extent to which the effect or fill is removed depends on the tones of gray you use to paint. Darker shades are more transparent; lighter shades are more opaque.

Shift-click the mask thumbnail (the layer's rightmost thumbnail) in the Layers palette to turn off the mask; click the thumbnail again to turn on the mask.

Merging adjustment layers

You can merge an adjustment or fill layer in several ways: with the layer below it, with the layers in its own group of layers, with the layers it's linked to, and with all other visible layers. You cannot, however, use an adjustment layer or fill layer as the base or target layer for a merge.

When you merge an adjustment layer or fill layer with the layer below it, the adjustments are rasterized and permanently applied to the merged layer. Adjustment no longer affects other layers below the merged adjustment layer. (See "Merging layers" on page 111.) You can also rasterize a fill layer without merging it. (See "Simplifying layers" on page 110.)

Adjustment layers and fill layers whose masks (the layer's rightmost thumbnail in the Layers palette) contain only white values do not add significantly to the file size, so you needn't merge these adjustment layers to conserve file space.

Creating grouped layers

In grouped layers, the bottommost layer, or *base layer*, defines the visible boundaries for the entire group. For example, you might have a shape on the base layer, a photograph on the layer above it, and text on the topmost layer. If you group all three layers, the photograph and text appear only through the shape outline on the base layer; they also take on the opacity of the base layer.

Note that you can group only successive layers. The name of the base layer in the group is underlined, and the thumbnails for the overlying layers are indented. Additionally, the overlying layers display the grouped layer icon ⬐.

💡 *You can link grouped layers so they move together. See "Linking layers" on page 99.*

Africa text layer is the base layer in a layer group with the Lion layer

To create grouped layers:

1 Do one of the following:

- Hold down Alt (Windows) or Option (Mac OS), position the pointer over the line dividing two layers in the Layers palette (the pointer changes to two overlapping circles ⬤), and then click.

- In the Layers palette, select the top layer of a pair of layers you want to group, and choose Layer > Group with Previous.

- Link together the desired layers in the Layers palette. (See "Linking layers" on page 99.) Then choose Layer > Group Linked.

- When creating a new layer to group with an existing layer, select the existing layer in the Layers palette, and then choose New Layer from the Layers menu or the Layers palette menu. In the New Layer dialog box, select Group with Previous Layer, and click OK.

The grouped layer is assigned the opacity and mode attributes of the bottommost base layer in the group.

⚲ *If you need to change the stacking order of the layer group relative to other layers in the image, drag the group's base layer up or down in the Layers palette. (Dragging any other layer in the group will remove that layer from the group.)*

To remove a layer from a grouped layer:

Do one of the following:

- Hold down Alt (Windows) or Option (Mac OS), position the pointer over the line separating two grouped layers in the Layers palette (the pointer changes to two overlapping circles ⦿), and click. Ungrouping the base layer from the layer above it will ungroup all layers in the group.

- In the Layers palette, select a layer in the grouped layer, and choose Layer > Ungroup. This command removes the selected layer and any layers above it from the grouped layer.

- In the Layers palette, select any layer in the group besides the base layer, and either drag the layer below the base layer, or drag it between two ungrouped layers in the image.

To ungroup all layers:

1 In the Layers palette, select the base layer in the grouped layer, or the layer immediately above the base layer.

2 Choose Layer > Ungroup.

Editing layers

A newly created layer is transparent. You can add color values to the layer using the painting and editing tools, and then apply filters or use special effects to modify the layer. All painting and editing occurs on the active layer.

Locking layers

You can fully or partially lock layers to protect their contents. When a layer is locked, a lock displays to the right of the layer name, and the layer cannot be deleted. The lock is solid when the layer is fully locked and no editing is possible; it is hollow when only the layer's transparency is locked. Except for the background layer, locked layers can be moved to different locations in the stacking order of the Layers palette. When a layer is fully locked, you cannot edit the pixels, move it, or change its opacity, blending mode, or layer style. When only a layer's transparency is locked, painting and editing are confined to opaque areas of the layer. For example, if you lock a layer's transparency, you can edit an object without adding opaque pixels to the transparent area outside the object.

To lock all layer properties:

1 Select the layer in the Layers palette.

2 Click the Lock All icon ● at the top of the Layers palette.

To protect the transparent areas in a layer from editing:

1 Select the layer in the Layers palette.

2 Click the Lock Transparency icon ⊡ at the top of the Layers palette.

Note: For type and shape layers, transparency is locked by default and cannot be unlocked.

Painting with transparency locked

Sampling from all layers

By default, when you work with the magic wand, smudge, blur, sharpen, or clone stamp tool, you are applying color sampled only from pixels on the active layer. This means you can smudge or sample in a single layer even when other layers are visible, and you can sample from one layer and paint in another one.

Alternatively, you can choose to paint using sampled data from all the visible layers. For example, you can use the clone stamp tool to clone an area containing pixels from all the visible layers.

To sample from all visible layers:

1 Select the magic wand tool ✎, paint bucket tool ◑, smudge tool 🖑, blur tool ◐, sharpen tool △, or clone stamp tool 🛢.

2 In the options bar, select Use All Layers. If you selected the paint bucket tool, select All Layers.

Smudging all layers in the image

Selecting opaque areas on a layer

You can quickly select all the opaque areas on a layer within the layer boundaries. This is useful when you want to exclude transparent areas from a selection.

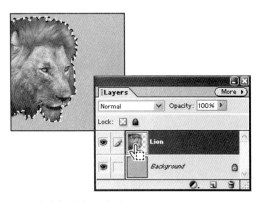

Layer pixels loaded as selection

To select all opaque areas on a layer:

Do one of the following:

- In the Layers palette, Ctrl-click (Windows) or Command-click (Mac OS) either the layer thumbnail or if the layer has a mask, the mask thumbnail.

- Right-click (Windows) on the layer thumbnail in the Layers palette, and choose Select Layer Transparency from the pop-up menu.

- To add the pixels to an existing selection, press Ctrl+Shift (Windows) or Command+Shift Mac OS), and either click the layer thumbnail in the Layers palette or, if the layer has a mask, the mask thumbnail.

- To subtract the pixels from an existing selection, press Ctrl+Alt (Windows) or Command+Option (Mac OS), and either click the layer thumbnail in the Layers palette or if the layer has a mask, the mask thumbnail.

- To load the intersection of the pixels and an existing selection, press Ctrl+Alt+Shift (Windows) or Command+Option+Shift (Mac OS), and either click the layer thumbnail in the Layers palette or if the layer has a mask, the mask thumbnail.

Managing layered images

After you add layers to an image, you can use the Layers palette to manage them. You can rename layers, delete layers, simplify layers, merge two or more layers, or flatten all layers in an image into one layer.

Renaming layers

As you add more layers to an image, it's helpful to rename layers based on their content. Using descriptive layer names allows you to easily identify layers in the Layers palette.

Note: You can't rename the Background layer unless you change it to a normal layer. See "Adding layers" on page 95.

To rename a layer:

1 Do one of the following:

- Double-click the layer's name in the Layers palette, and enter a new name.

- Double-click the layer's thumbnail in the Layers palette, and type a new name in the Layers Properties dialog box.

- Select the layer in the Layers palette, and choose Rename Layer from the Layer menu or the More menu in the Layers palette. Type a new name in the Layers Properties dialog box.

Simplifying layers

You can simplify a type layer, shape layer, solid color layer, gradient layer, pattern fill layer, or a layer set imported from Photoshop in order to convert the layer's content into a raster image. Once you simplify a layer, you can apply filters to it and edit it with the painting tools. However, you can no longer make changes to the layer using the type- and shape-editing options.

To simplify a layer:

1 In the Layers palette, select a type layer, shape layer, fill layer, or a Photoshop layer set.

2 Simplify the layer or layer set:

- If you selected a shape layer, click Simplify in the options bar.

- If you selected a type, shape, or fill layer, or a Photoshop layer set, choose Simplify Layer from either the Layer menu or the Layers palette More menu.

Tracking file size

File size depends on the pixel dimensions of an image and the number of layers contained in the image. Images with more pixels may produce more detail when printed, but they require more disk space to store and may be slower to edit and print. You should keep track of your file sizes to make sure the files are not becoming too large for your purposes. If the file is becoming too large, you can merge some layers together, remove hidden layers you don't need, flatten your image, or change the image size. (See "Merging layers" on page 111, "Flattening all layers" on page 112, and "About image size and resolution" on page 75.)

To track file size:

Choose Document Sizes from the status bar pop-up menu at the bottom of the application window. (See "Using the status bar" on page 18.)

The value on the left shows what the file size would be if you were to flatten all the layers into one. The value on the right shows the file size with all the layers intact.

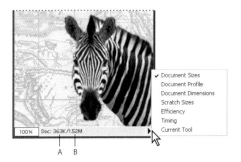

Status bar pop-up menu
A. *Flattened document size* **B.** *Document size with layers intact*

Deleting layers

Deleting layers that you no longer need reduces the size of your image file.

To delete a layer:

1 Select the layer in the Layers palette.

2 Do one of the following:

- Drag the layer to the Delete Layers button 🗑 at the bottom of the Layers palette.

- Click the Trash button at the bottom of the Layers palette, and click Yes in the delete confirmation dialog box. To bypass this dialog box, press Alt (Windows) or Option (Mac OS) as you click the Trash button.

- Choose Delete Layer from either the Layers menu or the Layers palette More menu, and click Yes.

Merging layers

When you've finalized the characteristics and positioning of two or more layers, merging these layers into one helps reduce the size of your image file. You can also choose to merge only the linked layers, only the visible layers, or only the layers in a group. (See "Creating grouped layers" on page 106.) The intersection of all transparent areas in the merged layers remains transparent.

For information on merging adjustment layers, see "Merging adjustment layers" on page 106.

To merge a layer with the layer below it:

1 Make sure an eye icon displays next to each of the two layers you want to merge. Select the top layer of the pair in the Layers palette.

2 Choose Merge Down from either the Layers menu, or from the Layers palette menu.

Note: If the bottom layer in the pair is a shape, type, or fill layer, you can't choose Merge Down until you've simplified the layer. (See "Simplifying layers" on page 110.) If the bottom layer in the pair is linked to another layer or is an adjustment layer, you also can't choose Merge Down.

To merge all visible linked layers:

1 Make sure an eye icon displays next to all layers you want to merge, and make sure they're linked together. Select one of the linked layers in the Layers palette.

2 Choose Merge Linked from either the Layers menu, or from the Layers palette menu.

To merge all the visible layers in an image:

1 Hide any layers you don't want to merge.

2 Choose Merge Visible from either the Layers menu, or the Layers palette menu.

To merge layers that are in a layer group:

1 Hide any layers you don't want to merge that are in the layer group.

2 Select the base layer in the group. If the base layer is a type, shape, solid color fill, gradient fill, or pattern fill layer, you must simplify the layer. (See "Simplifying layers" on page 110.)

3 Choose Merge Group from the Layers menu or the Layers palette menu.

To create a merged layer from all visible layers, while keeping the hidden layers intact:

1 Click the eye icon next to layers you don't want to merge.

2 Select a layer in the Layers palette on which to merge all visible layers.

3 Hold down Alt (Windows) or Option (Mac OS), and choose Merge Visible from either the Layers menu, or the Layers palette menu. Photoshop Elements merges a copy of all visible layers into the selected layer.

Flattening all layers

When you flatten an image, Photoshop Elements merges all visible layers into the background, greatly reducing the file size. Flattening an image discards all hidden layers, and fills any transparent areas with white. In most cases, you won't want to flatten a file until you've finished editing individual layers.

You can see the difference between your image's layered file size and its flattened file size by choosing Document Sizes from the status bar pop-up menu. See "Tracking file size" on page 110.

To flatten an image:

1 Make sure that the layers you want to keep in your image are visible.

2 Choose Flatten Image from either the Layers menu or the Layers palette menu.

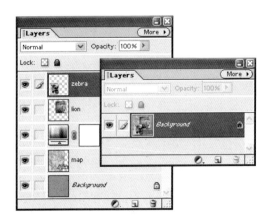

Layered file and flattened file

Chapter 7: Selecting

To modify or copy a specific area of an image in Adobe Photoshop Elements, you first select the area in the active layer. You can choose from a variety of specialized tools for creating selections.

About selections

When you want to edit a particular area of your image without affecting other areas, you select the area you want to change. You also make selections when you want to copy or duplicate an area of your image.

Photoshop Elements indicates a selected area with a border of moving dashes, also called a selection marquee or marching ants. The area outside the selection border is protected while you move, copy, paint, or apply special effects to the selected area. To make a selected area easier to distinguish from unselected areas, you can use the selection brush tool in mask mode to display unselected areas with a color overlay.

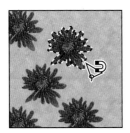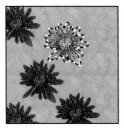

Selection made with magnetic lasso tool, color adjusted in selected area

The selection tool or command you choose depends on the nature of your image, the changes you want to make, and the area you want to select. For example, the magic wand tool is useful for quickly selecting areas of similar color, such as a clear blue sky. To select a more complex area, such as a person standing in a crowd of people, you can use the selection brush or lasso tool. To create smooth transitions between selected and unselected areas, you can use a selection tool that supports feathering.

After you make a selection, you can fine-tune the selection border in many ways. You can use commands in the Select menu to invert, expand, contract, or smooth the border. You can use a selection tool to add to or subtract from the selection. You can also move the selection border alone (see "Moving or inverting a selection border" on page 118) or move the border with the selected image area (see "Moving pixel selections within an image" on page 122.)

Note: *To select shape, type, or fill layers, you must use the shape selection tool or the move tool. To select a portion of these layer types (or to paint on or apply special effects to them) you must first simplify the layer. (See "Simplifying shape layers" on page 194 or "Simplifying type layers" on page 199.)*

Selecting pixels

You can select pixels in an image by dragging with the marquee tools, lasso tools, selection brush tool, or by targeting areas with the magic wand tool. Making a new selection replaces the existing one, unless you're using the selection brush tool, which adds to selections. You can also invert selections and expand or reduce the area of a selection.

Using the Select menu

You can use commands in the Select menu to select the entire layer, deselect everything, or to reselect an area you just deselected.

To select all pixels on a layer:

1 Select the layer in the Layers palette.

2 Choose Select > All.

To deselect selections:

Do one of the following:

• Choose Select > Deselect.

• If you are using the rectangular marquee, elliptical marquee, or lasso tool, click anywhere in the image outside the selected area.

To reselect the most recent selection:

Choose Select > Reselect.

> You can also choose selection commands from a context menu while using the marquee, lasso, or magic wand tools. To access this menu, right-click (Windows) or Ctrl+click (Mac OS) in the image window.

Showing or hiding selection borders

Selections are marked by a border of moving dashes. You can show or hide selection borders in your image.

To hide selection borders or show hidden selection borders:

Choose View > Selection.

Making rectangular or elliptical selections with the marquee tools

The marquee tools draw rectangular and elliptical selection borders.

To use the marquee tools:

1 Select a marquee tool in the toolbar:

• Rectangular marquee ⬚ to make a rectangular selection.

• Elliptical marquee ◯ to make an elliptical selection.

2 In the options bar, specify whether to create a new selection ◼, add to a selection ◪, subtract from a selection ◪, or select an area intersected by other selections ◪.

3 To soften the selection border so that it blends into the area outside the selection, enter a Feather value in the options bar. (For more information on feathering selections, see "Softening the edges of a selection" on page 121.)

4 If you chose the elliptical marquee, you can select Anti-aliased in the options bar to smooth the edges of your selection. (For more information on anti-aliasing, see "Softening the edges of a selection" on page 121.)

5 In the options bar, choose an option from the Style pop-up menu:

• Normal to visually set the size and proportions of the selection border.

> When making a Normal selection, you can press the Shift key as you drag to constrain the selection to a square or circle.

• Fixed Aspect Ratio to set a width-to-height ratio for the selection border. Enter values (decimal values can be used) for the aspect ratio. For example, to draw a marquee twice as wide as it is high, enter **2** for the width and **1** for the height.

• Fixed Size to specify values for the marquee's height and width in inches, centimeters, or pixels. If you use pixel measurements, enter values in whole numbers, and keep in mind that the number of pixels in one inch depends on the resolution of the image. (See "About image size and resolution" on page 75.)

6 Do one of the following:

• To make a Normal or Fixed Aspect Ratio selection, drag over the area you want to select.

• To make a Fixed Size selection, click in the image to set the upper left corner of the selection border.

By default, a selection border is created from one of its corners. To create a marquee from its center, press Alt (Windows) or Option (Mac OS) while making the selection.

> To reposition a marquee tool selection while dragging to define the selected area, hold down the spacebar, and drag.

Using the lasso, polygonal lasso, and magnetic lasso tools

The lasso and polygonal lasso tools let you draw both straight-edged and freehand segments of a selection border. With the magnetic lasso tool, the selection border snaps to edges you drag over in the image.

> The magnetic lasso tool is especially useful for quickly selecting objects with complex edges set against high-contrast backgrounds.

To set options for the lasso tools:

1 Select a lasso tool in the toolbar.

2 In the options bar, specify whether to create a new selection ▣, add to an existing selection ▣, subtract from a selection ▣, or select an area intersected by other selections ▣.

3 If desired, specify feather and anti-aliasing options. (See "Softening the edges of a selection" on page 121.)

4 To use the tool, see the lasso, polygonal lasso, or magnetic lasso tool instructions that follow.

To use the lasso tool:

1 Select the lasso tool ℘, and select tool options in the options bar.

2 Drag to draw a freehand selection border.

3 To draw a straight-edged selection border, hold down Alt (Windows) or Option (Mac OS), and click where segments should begin and end. You can switch between freehand and straight-edged segments.

4 To close the selection border, release the mouse button and Alt key (Windows) or Option key (Mac OS).

To use the polygonal lasso tool:

1 Select the polygonal lasso tool ⊠, and select tool options in the options bar.

2 Click in the image to set the starting point.

3 Do one or more of the following:

- To draw a straight segment, position the pointer where you want the first straight segment to end, and click. Continue clicking to set endpoints for subsequent segments.

- To draw a freehand segment, hold down Alt (Windows) or Option (Mac OS), and drag. When finished, release Alt or Option and the mouse button.

- To erase recently drawn straight segments, press the Delete key.

4 To close the selection border, do one of the following:

- Position the pointer over the starting point (a closed circle appears next to the pointer), and click.

- If the pointer is not over the starting point, double-click the pointer, or Ctrl-click (Windows) or Command-click (Mac OS).

To use the magnetic lasso tool:

1 Select the magnetic lasso tool ⊠, and then select tool options in the options bar:

- To specify the area of edge detection, enter a pixel value between 1 and 40 for Width. The magnetic lasso detects edges only within the specified distance from the pointer.

To change the magnetic lasso cursor so that it indicates the area of edge detection (the Width value), press the Caps Lock key on the keyboard. Change the cursor while the tool is selected but not in use.

- To specify the lasso's sensitivity to edges in the image, enter a value between 1% and 100% for Edge Contrast. A higher value detects only edges that contrast sharply with their surroundings; a lower value detects lower-contrast edges.

- To specify the rate at which the lasso sets fastening points, enter a value between 0 and 100 for Frequency. A higher value anchors the selection border in place more quickly.

On an image with well-defined edges, try higher Width and Edge Contrast settings, and trace the border roughly. On an image with softer edges, try lower Width and Edge Contrast settings, and trace the border more precisely.

- If you are working with a stylus tablet, select or deselect the Pen Pressure option. When the option is selected, an increase in stylus pressure causes the width of the edge detection to decrease.

2 Click in the image to set the first fastening point. Fastening points anchor the selection border in place.

3 Drag the pointer along the edge you want to trace. (You can also drag with the mouse button depressed.)

As you move the pointer, the active segment snaps to the strongest edge in the image, based on the Width and Edge Contrast options. Periodically, the magnetic lasso tool adds fastening points to the selection border to anchor segments, using the rate set by the Frequency option.

4 If the border doesn't snap to the desired edge, click once to add a fastening point manually. Continue to trace the edge, and click to add fastening points as needed.

5 To switch temporarily to the other lasso tools, do one of the following:

- To activate the lasso tool, hold down Alt (Windows) or Option (Mac OS), and drag with the mouse button depressed.

- To activate the polygonal lasso tool, hold down Alt (Windows) or Option (Mac OS), and click.

6 To erase recently drawn segments and fastening points, press the Delete key until you've erased the fastening points for the desired segment.

7 To close the selection border, do one of the following:

- To close the border manually, drag back over the starting point (a closed circle appears next to the pointer), and click.

- To close the border with a freehand magnetic segment, double-click, press Enter or Return, or click anywhere outside the document window.

- To close the border with a straight segment, hold down Alt (Windows) or Option (Mac OS), and double-click.

Using the Selection Brush tool

The selection brush tool lets you drag with a variety of soft-edged or hard-edged brushes to define selected areas. You can drag to either define the selected area or define a mask (unselected areas).

To use the selection brush tool:

1 Select the selection brush tool in the toolbox.

2 In the options bar, choose a brush from the brush presets pop-up palette (See "Using pop-up palettes" on page 28).

3 To set the brush size, drag the Size pop-up slider, or enter a pixel value in the Size text box.

4 From the Mode menu, choose one of the following:

- Selection to drag over the area you want to select, and to display a selection border with moving dashes. If a selection already exists, this option adds to the selection. To remove from the selection, press Alt (Windows) or Option (Mac OS) while dragging.

- Mask to drag over the area you want outside the selection, and to display a color overlay over that area. If a selection already exists, this option subtracts from the selection. To add to the selection, press Alt (Windows) or Option (Mac OS) while dragging.

5 To adjust the brush tip's hardness, drag the Hardness pop-up slider, or enter a number between 0 and 100.

6 If the Mode option is set to Mask, set the color and opacity of the overlay color:

- To set the color, click the Overlay Color swatch and select a color in the Color Picker.

- To set the opacity, drag the Overlay Opacity pop-up slider, or enter a percentage between 0 and 100 in the text box.

If you use a soft-edged brush with the selection brush tool, changing the Mode option to Mask can help you see the soft edges of the selection.

Using the magic wand tool

The magic wand tool lets you select an area of similar colors (for example, a blue sky) without having to trace its outline. You specify the color range, or *tolerance*, for the magic wand tool's selection.

To use the magic wand tool:

1 Select the magic wand tool .

2 In the options bar, specify whether to create a new selection ▣, add to an existing selection ▣, subtract from a selection ▣, or select an area intersected by other selections ▣.

3 For Tolerance, enter a value between 0 to 255. Enter a low value to select colors very similar to the pixel you click, or enter a higher value to select a broader range of colors.

4 To define a smooth selection edge, select Anti-aliased. (See "Softening the edges of a selection" on page 121.)

5 To select only adjacent areas using the same colors, select Contiguous. When this option is deselected, pixels using the same colors are selected throughout the entire image.

6 To select colors using data from all the visible layers, select Use All Layers. When this option is deselected, the magic wand tool selects colors from only the active layer.

7 In the image, click the color you want to select. If Contiguous is selected, all adjacent pixels within the tolerance range are selected.

To add to the selected area, you can Shift+click unselected areas, or choose Select > Grow.

Adjusting selection borders

You can adjust and refine your selection borders using the selection tools and a variety of commands in the Select menu.

In addition, you can apply geometric transformations to change the shape of a selection border. (See "Transforming objects in three dimensions" on page 157.)

Moving or inverting a selection border

You can move or hide a selection border, and you can invert a selection to select the opposite part of the image. Moving the selection border repositions just the border and doesn't alter the image. To move the selected image area, see "Moving pixel selections within an image" on page 122.

To move a selection border:

1 Using any selection tool, select New Selection ▣ in the options bar, and position the pointer inside an existing selection border. The pointer changes to indicate that you can move the selection ▸.

2 Drag the border to enclose a different area of the image. You can drag a selection border partly beyond the canvas boundaries. You can also drag the selection border to another image window.

To control the movement of a selection:

- To move the selection in 1-pixel increments, use an arrow key.

- To move the selection in 10-pixel increments, hold down Shift, and use an arrow key.

- To constrain the direction to multiples of 45°, begin dragging, and then hold down Shift as you continue to drag.

To select the unselected areas of an image:

In an image with an existing selection border, choose Select > Inverse.

You can use this command to easily select an object that appears against a solid-colored area. Select the solid color using the magic wand tool, and then choose Select > Inverse.

Adjusting selections manually

You can use the selection tools to add to or subtract from existing pixel selections.

For consistent results when manually adding to or subtracting from a selection, use the same feather and anti-aliasing settings used for the original selection. (See "Softening the edges of a selection" on page 121.)

To add to a selection:

1 Select a selection tool, and do one of the following:

- Select the Add to Selection option ▣ in the options bar, and make another selection.

- Hold down Shift (a plus sign appears next to the pointer), and make another selection.

To subtract from a selection:

1 Select a selection tool, and do one of the following:

- Select the Subtract from Selection option ▣ in the options bar, and select an area to subtract from the selection.

- Hold down Alt (Windows) or Option (Mac OS) so that a minus sign appears next to the pointer, and select an area to subtract from the selection.

To select only areas intersected by an existing selection:

1 Select a selection tool, and do one of the following:

- Select the Intersect with Selection option ▣ in the options bar, and select an area that intersects the existing selection.

- Hold down Alt+Shift (Windows) or Option+Shift (Mac OS) so that cross hairs appear next to the pointer, and select an area that intersects the existing selection.

Adjusting selections numerically

You can use commands in the Select menu to increase or decrease the size of an existing selection and to clean up stray pixels left inside or outside a color-based selection.

To expand or contract a selection by a specific number of pixels:

1 Use a selection tool to make a selection.

2 Choose Select > Modify > Expand or Contract.

3 For Expand By or Contract By, enter a pixel value between 1 and 100, and click OK.

The border is increased or decreased by the specified number of pixels. Any portion of the selection border that runs along the canvas's edge is unaffected.

To frame an existing selection with a new selection border:

1 Use a selection tool to make a selection.

2 Choose Select > Modify > Border.

3 Enter a value between 1 and 200 pixels in the Width text box, and click OK. The new selection frames the original selected area.

The Border command creates a soft-edged, anti-aliased selection border. (See "Softening the edges of a selection" on page 121.) To paint a hard-edged border around a selection, use the Stroke command on a selection that lacks feathering or anti-aliasing. (See "Filling and tracing selections and layers" on page 144.)

To expand a selection to include areas with similar color:

Do one of the following:

- Choose Select > Grow to include all adjacent pixels falling within the tolerance range specified in the magic wand options. A higher Tolerance value adds a broader range of colors.

- Choose Select > Similar to include pixels throughout the image, not just adjacent ones, that fall within the tolerance range.

To increase the selection incrementally, choose either command multiple times.

Note: You cannot use the Grow and Similar commands on images in bitmap mode.

To clean up stray pixels left inside or outside a color-based selection:

1 Choose Select > Modify > Smooth.

2 For Sample Radius, enter a pixel value between 1 and 100, and click OK.

Photoshop Elements searches around each selected pixel for unselected pixels within the specified range. For example, if you enter 16 for Sample Radius, Photoshop Elements searches 16 pixels on each side of every selected pixel. If most pixels in that range are selected, any unselected pixels are added to the selection. If most pixels in that range are unselected, any selected pixels are removed from the selection.

Note: The relationship between physical distance and the pixel distance depends on the resolution of the image. For example, 5 pixels is a longer distance in a 72-ppi print than in a 300-ppi print. (See "About image size and resolution" on page 75.)

Softening the edges of a selection

You can smooth the hard edges of a selection by anti-aliasing or feathering, or by using a soft-edged brush with the selection brush tool. Feathering lets you smooth an edge subtly with small transitions of just a few pixels or create more visible transitions up to 250 pixels wide.

Anti-aliasing   Smooths the jagged edges of a selection by softening the color transition between edge pixels and background pixels. Since only the edge pixels change, no detail is lost. Anti-aliasing is useful when cutting, copying, and pasting selections to create composite images.

In the options bar, you can select anti-aliasing for the lasso, polygonal lasso, magnetic lasso, elliptical marquee, and magic wand tools. To use anti-aliasing, you must select this option before using these tools; you cannot add anti-aliasing to an existing selection.

Feathering   Blurs edges by building a transition between the selection and surrounding pixels. This blurring can cause some loss of detail at the edge of the selection.

You can create a feathered selection with the elliptical marquee, rectangular marquee, lasso, polygonal lasso, or magnetic lasso tool. You can also add feathering to an existing selection by using the Select menu. Feathering effects are apparent when you move, cut, copy, or fill the selection.

To view the boundaries of an existing feathered selection, select the selection brush tool, and choose Mask in the options bar. Unselected areas display with a color overlay. See "Using the Selection Brush tool" on page 117.

To use anti-aliasing:

1 Select the lasso, polygonal lasso, magnetic lasso, elliptical marquee, or magic wand tool.

2 Select Anti-aliased in the options bar.

3 Make a selection in the image window.

To define a feathered edge for a selection tool:

1 Do one of the following:

- Select any of the lasso or marquee tools, and enter a Feather value from 1 to 250 pixels in the options bar. This value defines the width of the feathered edge.

- Select the selection brush tool, and select a soft-edged brush from the brushes popup palette in the options bar.

2 Make a selection in the image window.

To define a feathered edge for an existing selection:

1 Use a selection tool to make a selection.

2 Choose Select > Feather.

3 Enter a value between .2 and 250 in the Feather Radius text box, and click OK. The feather radius defines the width of the feathered edge.

Note: If you make a small selection with a large feather radius, Photoshop Elements displays the message "No pixels are more than 50% selected." If you click OK, Photoshop Elements creates a selection with invisible edges. To avoid this situation, either decrease the feather radius, or increase the selection's size.

Selections without and with feathering
A. *Selection with no feather, same selection filled with gray pattern* **B**. *Selection with feather, same selection filled with with gray pattern*

Moving, copying, and pasting selections

You can move or copy selections within or between images—and also between images in other applications. If you want to move an entire layer, see "Repositioning layers" on page 99.

Moving pixel selections within an image

The move tool lets you drag a pixel selection to a new location in the image. With the Info palette open, you can track the exact distance of the move.

To specify move tool options:

1 Select the move tool ▸⊕.

2 Select any of the following in the options bar:

- Auto Select Layer to select the topmost layer that has pixels under the move tool, rather than the selected layer.

- Show Bounding Box to display the bounding box around the selected item.

To move a pixel selection:

1 Select the move tool ▸⊕.

2 Move the pointer inside the selection border, and drag the pixel selection to a new position. If you've selected multiple areas, all pixel selections move as you drag.

Note: To move just the selection border, see "Moving or inverting a selection border" on page 118.

To activate the move tool when another tool is selected, hold down Ctrl (Windows) or Command (Mac OS). (This technique does not work with the hand tool 🖑.)

Copying selections or layers

You can use the move tool to copy selections as you drag them within or between images, or you can copy and paste selections using the Copy, Copy Merged, Cut, Paste, or Paste Into commands in the Edit menu.

Copying with the move tool within a single image saves memory because the Clipboard isn't used, but once you deselect the copied selection, you can't move it again. The Paste command creates a new layer for the copied selection, which you can move freely at any time.

Depending on your color management settings and the color profile associated copied data, Photoshop Elements may ask you how to convert copied colors. For more information, see "Setting up color management" on page 31.

Using the Paste Into command
A. Window panes selected **B.** Copied image **C.** Paste Into command **D.** Pasted image repositioned

Note: *Keep in mind that when a selection or layer is pasted between images with different resolutions, the pasted data retains its original pixel dimensions. This can make the pasted portion appear out of proportion to the new image. Use the Image Size command to make the source and destination images the same resolution before copying and pasting.*

To copy a selection:

1 Select the area you want to copy.

2 Do one of the following:

- Choose Edit > Copy to copy the selection to the Clipboard.

- Choose Edit > Copy Merged to copy all layers in the selected area to the Clipboard.

To copy a selection while dragging:

1 Do one of the following:

- Select the move tool , and press Alt (Windows) or Option (Mac OS) while dragging the selection you want to copy and move.

- With any tool, press Ctrl+Alt (Windows) or Command+Option (Mac OS) to activate the move tool, and drag the selection you want to copy and move.

2 To make additional copies of the same selection, do one of the following:

- Hold down the keys used in step 1 while dragging the selection to each new location.

- To offset the duplicate by 1 pixel, hold down the keys in step 1, and press an arrow key.

- To offset the duplicate by 10 pixels, press Alt+Shift (Windows) or Option+Shift (Mac OS), and press an arrow key.

When copying between images, drag the selection from the active image window into the destination image window. A border highlights the destination image window when you can drop the selection into it.

To paste one selection into another selection border:

1 Use the Cut or Copy command to copy the part of the image you want to paste.

2 Make a selection in the image into which you want to paste the copied image.

Note: The copied image appears only within the selection border. You can move the copied image within the border, but if you move it completely out of the border, it won't be visible.

3 Choose Edit > Paste Into.

4 With your pointer within the selection border, drag the pasted image to the proper location.

5 When you're satisfied with the results, deselect the pasted image to lock the layer.

Using drag-and-drop to copy between applications

The drag-and-drop feature lets you copy and move images between Photoshop Elements and other applications. In Windows, the other application must be OLE-compliant.

To duplicate an entire image by dragging and dropping, use the move tool to drag the image to the other open application. If your image has multiple layers, you must link the layers first to drag all of them together. (See "Linking layers" on page 99.) To copy an OLE object that contains .psd data, use the OLE Clipboard. (See your Windows documentation.)

In Mac OS, the application must support Mac OS Drag Manager, and you must be running System 9.1 or later.

When you drag vector shapes or text to Photoshop Elements from an application that uses Adobe Illustrator Clipboard, Photoshop Elements rasterizes the vector artwork—converting its mathematically defined lines and curves into the pixels of a bitmap image.

Using the Clipboard to copy between applications

You can often use the Cut or Copy command to copy selections between Photoshop Elements and other applications. The cut or copied selection remains on the Clipboard until you cut or copy another selection.

In some cases, the contents of the Clipboard can be converted to a *raster* image. Photoshop Elements prompts you to paste the vector artwork as pixels or as a shape layer.

Note: The image is rasterized at the resolution of the file into which you paste it.

To change the Export Clipboard preference:

1 Choose Edit > Preferences > General (Windows, Mac OS 9.x) or Photoshop Elements > Preferences > General (Mac OS X).

2 Select Export Clipboard to save copied data from Photoshop Elements on the Clipboard when you exit from Photoshop Elements. If this option is deselected, the contents are deleted when you exit from the application.

3 Click OK.

To paste PostScript artwork from another application:

1 In the other application, select the artwork, and choose Edit > Copy. Applications that produce PostScript artwork include Adobe Photoshop, Adobe Illustrator (versions 5.0 through 10), Adobe Dimensions®, and Adobe Streamline™. (See "Saving images in different file formats" on page 226.)

2 In Photoshop Elements, select the image into which you want to paste the selection.

3 Choose Edit > Paste.

4 In the dialog box, select from the following options:

• Paste as Pixels to rasterize the artwork as it is pasted. Rasterizing converts mathematically defined vector artwork to pixels.

• Paste as Shape Layer to create a new shape layer that uses the path as a layer clipping path.

5 If you chose Paste as Pixels in the previous step, you can choose Anti-alias in the options bar to make a smooth transition between the edges of the selection and surrounding pixels. (See "Softening the edges of a selection" on page 121.)

6 Click OK.

Saving and loading selections

You can save selections with an image and load them for reuse in the same image. You can also modify saved selections by replacing, adding to, or subtracting from them.

Note: Some file formats, including JPEG and GIF, cannot save selections.

To save a new selection:

1 Make a selection in your image.

2 Choose Select > Save Selection.

3 In the Save Selection dialog box, choose New from the Selection pop-up menu.

4 Enter a name for the selection in the Name textbox, and then click OK.

To modify a saved selection:

1 Make a selection in your image.

2 Choose Select > Save Selection.

3 In the Save Selection dialog box, choose a selection name from the Selection menu.

4 Select one of the following operations:

• Replace Selection to replace the saved selection with the current selection.

- Add To Selection to add the current selection to the saved selection.

- Subtract From Selection to subtract the current selection from the saved selection.

- Intersect With Selection to replace the saved selection with the intersection between the current selection and the saved selection.

5 Click OK.

To load a saved selection:

1 Open an image that contains a saved selection.

2 Choose Select > Load Selection.

3 Choose the saved selection from the Selection menu.

4 To invert the selected area, select Invert.

5 Click OK.

To modify a selection with a saved selection:

1 Open an image that contains a saved selection.

2 Make a new selection in your image.

3 Choose Select > Load Selection.

4 Choose a saved selection from the Selection menu.

5 Select one of the following operations:

- Add To Selection to add the saved selection to the current selection.

- Subtract From Selection to subtract the saved selection from the current selection.

- Intersect With Selection to replace the current selection with the intersection between the current selection and the saved selection.

6 To invert the selected area, select Invert.

7 Click OK.

To delete a saved selection:

1 Choose Select > Delete Selection.

2 Choose a saved selection from the Selection menu, and click OK.

Deleting selected areas

To delete a selected area in your image, choose Edit > Clear, or press Backspace (Windows) or Delete (Mac OS). To cut a selection to the Clipboard, choose Edit > Cut.

If you delete a selection on a background layer or a layer that uses the Lock Transparency option (located in the Layers palette), Photoshop Elements replaces the selected area with the current background color, which appears in the toolbox.

Chapter 8: Painting

You can paint, erase, and fill areas of your image with several different tools in Adobe Photoshop Elements. By customizing the options for these tools, you can create sophisticated effects. Other tools and commands let you transform and stylize an image.

About painting and drawing

When you create graphics in Photoshop Elements, there is a distinction between painting and drawing. *Painting* involves changing the colors of pixels using a painting tool. *Drawing* involves creating shape layers, type layers, and fill layers. These layer types contain vector graphics, which are defined by geometric characteristics rather than by pixels. For example, if you draw a circle shape using the ellipse tool, the circle is defined by a specific radius, location, and color. To paint on these layers and apply certain layer effects to them, you must first convert the vector data to bitmap data by *simplifying* the layer (see "Simplifying layers" on page 110).

Photoshop Elements provides many ways to creatively enhance your images. You can paint, fill, or trace with preset colors, patterns, and color gradients, or with customized patterns and gradients you create.

When you want to transform your image without adding new colors or patterns, a few tools allow you to change the image details with stylized brush strokes. When you want to remove areas from your image, you can select from several different eraser tools.

After you choose a painting or erasing tool, you can set tool options to control blending mode, opacity, brush style and size, and other options that are unique to each tool.

Selecting foreground and background colors

The toolbox displays a *foreground* color and a *background* color in two overlapping color boxes. Photoshop Elements uses the foreground color to paint, fill, and trace selections and shapes, and it uses the background color to create fills, such as gradient fills and fills in erased areas of the image background. The foreground and background colors are also used by some special effects filters.

Foreground and background color boxes in toolbox
A. *Foreground color box* **B.** *Default colors icon*
C. *Switch colors icon* **D.** *Background color box*

You can change the foreground or background color by using the eyedropper tool, the Swatches palette, the icons in the toolbox, or the Adobe Color Picker.

Using color settings in the toolbox

In the toolbox, the current foreground color appears in the topmost color selection box; the current background color appears in the bottom box.

The Info palette and the Adobe Color Picker let you display color values using a number of color models. (See "Choosing an image mode" on page 54.)

To change the foreground or background color:

1 Do one of the following:

- To change the foreground color, click the topmost color box in the toolbox.

- To change the background color, click the bottom color box in the toolbox.

2 Choose a color in the Adobe Color Picker, and click OK. (See "Using the Adobe Color Picker" on page 131.)

To switch the color in the foreground and background boxes:

Click the Switch Colors icon ↱ in the toolbox.

To set the foreground and background color boxes to black and white:

Click the Default Colors icon ◨ in the toolbox.

Using the eyedropper tool

The eyedropper tool samples color from an image to designate a new foreground or background color. You can sample from the active image or from another open image. (When you're using the eyedropper, you can click in another image without making it the active image.) You can even sample color anywhere on your computer screen including the desktop and within the application window.

You can also specify the size of the area that the eyedropper tool samples. For example, you can set the eyedropper to sample the color values of a 5-by-5 or 3-by-3 pixel area under the pointer.

Selecting a foreground color with the eyedropper tool
A. *Point Sample* **B.** *5 x 5 average sample*

To select the foreground or background color:

1 Select the eyedropper tool 🖋.

2 To change the sample size of the eyedropper, choose an option from the Sample Size menu:

- Point Sample to get the precise value of the pixel you click.

- 3 by 3 Average or 5 by 5 Average to get the average value of the specified number of pixels within the area you click.

3 Select a color:

- To select a new foreground color from an image, click the desired color in your image. To select a color that appears elsewhere on your computer screen, click inside your image and drag away from it.

- To select a new background color from an image, Alt-click (Windows) or Option-click (Mac OS) the color you want. To select a color that appears elsewhere on your computer screen, click inside your image and drag away from it.

As you click and drag the eyedropper tool, the foreground color selection box changes dynamically. Alt-click and drag (Windows) or Option-click and drag (Mac OS) to activate the background color selection box. Release the mouse button to pick the new color.

To use the eyedropper tool temporarily while using most painting tools, hold down Alt (Windows) or Option (Mac OS).

Using the Swatches palette

You can select a foreground or background color from the Swatches palette, or you can add or delete colors to create a custom swatch library. You can also save a library of swatches and reload them for use in another image. Although you can add many colors to the Swatches palette, you should manage its size and organization to improve performance.

To display the Swatches palette:

Choose Window > Color Swatches, or click the Swatches palette tab in the palette well.

To change the thumbnail display in the Swatches palette:

In the Swatches palette, choose either Small Thumbnail or Small List from the More menu.

To select a foreground or background color:

Do one of the following:

- To choose a foreground color, click a color in the Swatches palette.

- To choose a background color, Ctrl-click (Windows) or Command-click (Mac OS) a color in the Swatches palette.

To choose a swatch library:

In the upper left corner of the Swatches palette, choose a swatch library name from the Swatches pop-up menu.

Managing swatches

The Swatches palette can hold many different color swatches and different libraries of color swatches. Creating libraries can help you group related or special swatches and manage palette size. The Adobe Photoshop Elements application folder includes a Color Swatches folder inside the Presets folder to contain the various swatch libraries. When you create custom libraries, saving them to the Color Swatches folder causes them to automatically appear in the palette libraries pop-up menu.

You can also load or save swatches using the Preset Manager. (See "Using the Preset Manager" on page 29.)

To add a color to the Swatches palette:

1 Set the foreground color in the toolbox to the color you want to add. (For information on setting the foreground color, see "Using color settings in the toolbox" on page 128, or "Using the eyedropper tool" on page 128.)

2 Do one of the following in the Swatches palette:

- Click the New Swatch button at the bottom of the Swatches palette. The color swatch is added and named Swatch.

- Choose New Swatch from the More menu in the Swatches palette.

- If the palette is in thumbnail view, position the pointer over an empty space in the bottom row of the palette (the pointer turns into the paint bucket tool), and click to add the color.

- If the palette is in list view, position the pointer over an empty space in the rightmost column of the palette (the pointer turns into the paint bucket tool), and click to add the color.

3 Enter a name for the new color and click OK.

Note: To save swatches you add to a library, you must save the entire library. See "To save and use custom swatch libraries" below.

To save and use custom swatch libraries:

Choose one of the following commands in the Swatches palette:

- To save a library of swatches, choose Save Swatches from the More menu. To make the set appear in the palette's swatch libraries pop-up menu, save the file to the Color Swatches folder inside the Presets folder of the Photoshop Elements application folder. (To see the new swatch set in the menu, you must restart the application.)

- To select and load a swatch library, choose Load Swatches from the More menu in the palette.

- To replace the current swatch library with a different library, choose Replace Swatches from the More menu in the palette, and select a library.

You can also load or save swatches using the Preset Manager. (See "Using the Preset Manager" on page 29.)

To delete a color in the Swatches palette:

Do one of the following:

- Drag the color swatch to the Trash button in the palette.

- Press Alt (Windows) or Option (Mac OS) to change the pointer to a scissors icon ✂, and click a color in the Swatches palette.

Note: To permanently remove swatches you delete, you must resave the library that contained them.

To reset a swatch library to its default color swatches:

1 Choose a swatch library from the pop-up menu in the Swatches palette.

2 From the More menu in the Swatches palette, choose Preset Manager.

3 In the Preset Manager dialog box, choose Swatches from the Preset Type menu.

4 Choose Reset Swatches from the More menu, and click Done.

Using the Adobe Color Picker

You can use the Adobe Color Picker to select the foreground or background color by choosing from a color spectrum or by defining colors numerically. In addition, you can select colors based on HSB or RGB color models, or choose to select only Web-safe colors.

To display the Adobe Color Picker:

In the toolbox, click the foreground or background color selection box.

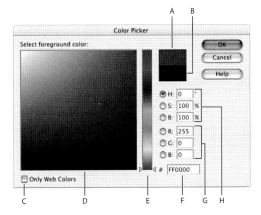

Adobe Color Picker
A. Adjusted color B. Original color C. Web Colors option
D. Color field E. Color slider F. Hexadecimal color value
G. RGB color values H. HSB color values

Specifying a color using the color field and color slider

To select a color in the HSB (Hue, Saturation, and Brightness) or RGB (Red, Green, Blue) color modes, you can use the color field or the color slider in the Color Picker dialog box. The color slider displays the range of color levels available for the selected color component (for example, R, G, or B). The color field displays the range for the remaining two components—one on the horizontal axis, one on the vertical. (For more information about HSB and RGB color modes, see "Describing color" on page 64.)

For example, if the current color is black and you select the red radio button (R) using the RGB color mode, the color slider displays the range of color for red (0 is at the bottom, and 255 is at the top). The color field displays blue values along its horizontal axis and green values along its vertical axis.

To specify a color using the color field and color slider in the Color Picker dialog box:

1 Select a radio button next to an HSB or RGB value.

2 Select a color:

• Drag the white triangles along the slider.

• Click inside the color slider.

• Click inside the color field.

When you click in the color field, a circular marker indicates the color's position in the field, and the numerical values change to reflect the new color.

The color rectangle to the right of the color slider displays the new color in the top section of the rectangle. The original color appears at the bottom of the rectangle.

Specifying a color using numeric values

In the Adobe Color Picker, you can select a color by specifying numeric values for each color component.

To specify a color using numeric values:

Do one of the following:

- In RGB color mode (the mode your monitor uses), specify component values from 0 to 255 (0 is no light, and 255 is the brightest light).

- In HSB color mode, specify saturation and brightness as percentages; specify hue as an angle from 0° to 360° that corresponds to a location on the color wheel. (See "About the color wheel" on page 65.)

Using Web-safe colors

The *Web-safe colors* are the 216 colors used by browsers on both the Windows and Mac OS platforms. By working only with these colors, you ensure that colors in art you prepare for the Web display accurately on a system set to display 256 colors.

To identify Web-safe colors in the Adobe Color Picker:

- Select Only Web Colors in the lower left corner of the Color Picker, and then choose any color in the Color Picker. When this option is selected, any color you pick is Web-safe.

- Choose a color in the Color Picker. If you choose a color that isn't Web-safe, an alert cube appears next to the color rectangle in the upper right area of the Color Picker. Click the alert cube to select the closest Web-safe color. (If no alert cube appears, the color you chose is Web-safe.)

Using other color pickers

In addition to the default Adobe Color Picker, you can select colors by using the built-in color pickers on your system or a plug-in color picker. These color pickers appear in the General Preferences dialog box. For information on installing and using a plug-in color picker, see the documentation that came with the plug-in.

To use the Windows Color Picker (Windows):

1 Choose Edit > Preferences > General.

2 Choose Windows from the Color Picker menu, and click OK.

For more information, see your Windows documentation.

To use the Apple Color Picker (Mac OS):

1 Choose Edit > Preferences > General.

2 For Color Picker, choose Apple, and click OK.

For more information, see your Mac OS documentation.

To return to the Adobe Color Picker after using another color picker:

1 Choose Edit > Preferences > General.

2 Choose Adobe from the Color Picker menu, and click OK.

Using the painting tools

You can use the brush, pencil, pattern stamp, or smudge tool to paint color on an image. The impressionist brush and smudge tools can also paint using the existing colors in an image. The five tools create different effects:

- The brush tool creates soft or hard strokes of color and can simulate airbrush techniques.

- The pencil tool creates hard-edged freehand lines.

- The smudge tool either smudges the existing colors in your image or smears new color through your image.

- The pattern stamp tool paints with a pattern defined from your image, another image, or a preset pattern.

- The impressionist brush tool repaints the existing colors and details in your image using stylized brush strokes.

Using the brush or pencil tools

Use the brush tool to paint with soft or hard strokes of color and to paint with special effects such as strokes that fade out. Use the pencil tool to paint hard-edged lines of color.

To use a painting tool:

1 Select a color to paint by setting the foreground color. (See "Selecting foreground and background colors" on page 127.)

2 Select the brush tool ✎ or pencil tool ✎.

3 Click the inverted arrow ▾ next to the brush sample, choose a brush category from the Brushes pop-up menu, and then select a brush thumbnail. To learn more about using the brush presets, see "Using pop-up palettes" on page 28.

4 To set the brush size in the options bar, drag the Size pop-up slider or enter a size in the text box.

5 Choose a blending mode to control how painting affects existing pixels in the image. (See "Selecting a blending mode" on page 135.)

6 To set the color opacity, drag the pop-up slider or enter an opacity value. (See "Specifying opacity, strength, exposure, or flow" on page 138.)

7 Set additional tool-specific options:

- For the brush tool, select airbrush to enable airbrush capabilities. This option applies gradual tones to an image, simulating traditional airbrush techniques. Click the More Options button to specify additional options. (See "Specifying brush dynamics" on page 138.)

- For the pencil tool, select Auto Erase to paint the background color over areas containing the foreground color.

8 Drag in the image to paint.

To draw a straight line with a painting tool, click a starting point in the image. Then hold down Shift and click an ending point.

Using the impressionist brush tool

The impressionist brush tool lets you re-create your image as if it were painted with stylized strokes. By experimenting with different style, area size, and tolerance options, you can simulate the texture of painting with different artistic styles. The impressionist brush tool doesn't add new color or use the foreground and background colors.

Original image and with impressionist brush strokes

To use the impressionist brush tool:

1 Select the impressionist brush tool.

2 Click the inverted arrow ▾ next to the brush sample, choose a brush category from the Brushes pop-up menu, and then select a brush thumbnail. To learn more about using the brush presets, see "Using pop-up palettes" on page 28.

3 To set the brush size in the options bar, drag the Size pop-up slider or enter a size in the text box.

4 Choose a blending mode to control how the brush affects existing pixels in the image. (See "Selecting a blending mode" on page 135.)

5 To set the opacity, drag the pop-up slider or enter an opacity value. (See "Specifying opacity, strength, exposure, or flow" on page 138.)

6 Click the More Options button to specify the following options:

- Choose a style to control the shape of the paint stroke.

- For Area, enter a value to specify the area covered by the paint strokes. The greater the size, the larger the covered area and the more numerous the strokes.

- For Tolerance, enter a value or drag the slider to limit the regions where paint strokes are applied. A low spacing tolerance affects pixels within a range of color values very similar to the pixel you click. A high spacing tolerance affects pixels within a broader range of color values.

7 Drag in the image to paint.

Using the smudge tool

The smudge tool simulates the actions of dragging a finger through wet paint. The tool picks up color where the stroke begins and pushes it in the direction you drag. You can smudge existing colors in your image, or smear foreground color on the image.

To use the smudge tool:

1 Select the smudge tool.

2 Click the inverted arrow ▾ next to the brush sample, choose a brush category from the Brushes pop-up palette, and then select a brush thumbnail. To learn more about using the brush presets, see "Using pop-up palettes" on page 28.

3 To set the brush size in the options bar, drag the Size pop-up slider or enter a size in the text box.

4 Specify a blending mode and strength. (See "Setting options for painting and editing tools" on page 135.)

5 Select Use All Layers to smudge using color data from all layers visible in the image window. If this option is deselected, the smudge tool uses colors from only the active layer.

6 Select Finger Painting to smear the foreground color at the beginning of each stroke. If this option is deselected, the smudge tool uses the color under the pointer at the beginning of each stroke.

7 Drag in the image to smudge color.

To temporarily use the Finger Painting option as you drag with the smudge tool, press Alt (Windows) or Option (Mac OS).

Using the pattern stamp tool

The pattern stamp tool lets you paint with a pattern. You can select a pattern from the pattern libraries or create your own patterns.

To use the pattern stamp tool:

1 Select the pattern stamp tool 🏷️.

2 In the options bar, click the inverted arrow ▼ next to the brush sample, choose a brush category from the Brushes pop-up palette, and then select a brush thumbnail. To learn more about using the brush presets, see "Working with preset options" on page 27.

3 To set the brush size in the options bar, drag the Size pop-up slider or enter a size in the text box.

4 Specify a blending mode and opacity. (See "Setting options for painting and editing tools" on page 135.)

5 Choose a pattern from the Pattern pop-up palette in the options bar.

To load additional pattern libraries, select a library name from the pop-up palette menu, or choose Load Patterns and navigate to the folder where the library is stored. To learn more about patterns and pattern libraries, see "Creating and editing patterns" on page 145.

6 Select Aligned to repeat the pattern as contiguous, uniform tiles. The pattern is aligned from one paint area to the next.

If Aligned is deselected, the pattern is centered on the pointer each time you stop and resume painting.

7 Select Impressionist to apply the pattern with an impressionistic effect.

8 Drag in the image to paint with the tool.

Setting options for painting and editing tools

You set options for a painting or editing tool in the options bar.

Selecting a blending mode

The blending mode specified in the options bar controls how pixels in the image are affected by a painting or editing tool. It's helpful to think in terms of the following colors when visualizing a blending mode's effect:

- The *base color* is the original color in the image.

- The *blend color* is the color being applied with the painting or editing tool.

- The *result color* is the color resulting from the blend.

To select a blending mode for a tool:

Choose from the Mode menu in the options bar.

Normal Edits or paints each pixel to make it the result color. This is the default mode. (Normal mode is called *Threshold* when you're working with an image in Bitmap or Indexed Color mode.)

Dissolve Edits or paints each pixel to make it the result color. However, the result color is a random replacement of the pixels with the base color or the blend color, depending on the opacity at any pixel location. This mode works best with the brush tool and a large brush.

Behind Edits or paints only on the transparent part of a layer. This mode works only on layers with Lock Transparency deselected, and is analogous to painting on the back of transparent areas on a sheet of glass.

Clear Edits or paints each pixel and makes it transparent. You must be on a layer with Lock Transparency deselected in the Layers palette to use this mode.

Darken Looks at the color information in each channel and selects the base or blend color—whichever is darker—as the result color. Pixels lighter than the blend color are replaced, and pixels darker than the blend color do not change.

Multiply Looks at the color information in each channel and multiplies the base color by the blend color. The result color is always a darker color. Multiplying any color with black produces black. Multiplying any color with white leaves the color

unchanged. When you're painting with a color other than black or white, successive strokes with a painting tool produce progressively darker colors. The effect is similar to drawing on the image with multiple felt-tipped pens.

Color Burn Looks at the color information in each channel and darkens the base color to reflect the blend color. Blending with white produces no change.

Linear Burn Looks at the color information in each channel and darkens the base color to reflect the blend color by decreasing the brightness. Blending with white produces no change.

Lighten Looks at the color information in each channel and selects the base or blend color—whichever is lighter—as the result color. Pixels darker than the blend color are replaced, and pixels lighter than the blend color do not change.

Screen Looks at each channel's color information and multiplies the inverse of the blend and base colors. The result color is always a lighter color. Screening with black leaves the color unchanged. Screening with white produces white. The effect is similar to projecting multiple photographic slides on top of each other.

Color Dodge Looks at the color information in each channel and brightens the base color to reflect the blend color. Blending with black produces no change.

Linear Dodge Looks at the color information in each channel and brightens the base color to reflect the blend color by increasing the brightness. Blending with black produces no change.

Overlay Multiplies or screens the colors, depending on the base color. Patterns or colors overlay the existing pixels while preserving the highlights and shadows of the base color. The base color is mixed with the blend color to reflect the lightness or darkness of the original color.

Soft Light Darkens or lightens the colors, depending on the blend color. The effect is similar to shining a diffused spotlight on the image.

If the blend color (light source) is lighter than 50% gray, the image is lightened as if it were dodged. If the blend color is darker than 50% gray, the image is darkened as if it were burned in. Painting with pure black or white produces a distinctly darker or lighter area but does not result in pure black or white.

Hard Light Multiplies or screens the colors, depending on the blend color. The effect is similar to shining a harsh spotlight on the image.

If the blend color (light source) is lighter than 50% gray, the image is lightened as if it were screened. This is useful for adding highlights to an image. If the blend color is darker than 50% gray, the image is darkened as if it were multiplied. This is useful for adding shadows to an image. Painting with pure black or white results in pure black or white.

Vivid Light Burns or dodges the colors by increasing or decreasing the contrast, depending on the blend color. If the blend color (light source) is lighter than 50% gray, the image is lightened by decreasing the contrast. If the blend color is darker than 50% gray, the image is darkened by increasing the contrast.

Linear Light Burns or dodges the colors by decreasing or increasing the brightness, depending on the blend color. If the blend color (light source) is lighter than 50% gray, the image is lightened by increasing the brightness. If the blend color is darker than 50% gray, the image is darkened by decreasing the brightness.

Pin Light Replaces the colors, depending on the blend color. If the blend color (light source) is lighter than 50% gray, pixels darker than the blend color are replaced, and pixels lighter than the blend color do not change. If the blend color is darker than 50% gray, pixels lighter than the blend color are replaced, and pixels darker than the blend color do not change. This mode is useful for adding special effects to an image.

Difference Looks at the color information in each channel and subtracts either the blend color from the base color or the base color from the blend color, depending on which has the greater brightness value. Blending with white inverts the base color values; blending with black produces no change.

Exclusion Creates an effect similar to but lower in contrast than the Difference mode. Blending with white inverts the base color values. Blending with black produces no change.

Hue Creates a result color with the luminance and saturation of the base color and the hue of the blend color.

Saturation Creates a result color with the luminance and hue of the base color and the saturation of the blend color. Painting with this mode in an area with zero saturation (a neutral gray area) causes no change.

Color Creates a result color with the luminance of the base color and the hue and saturation of the blend color. This preserves the gray levels in the image and is useful for coloring monochrome images and for tinting color images.

Luminosity Creates a result color with the hue and saturation of the base color and the luminance of the blend color. This mode creates an inverse effect from that of the Color mode.

Specifying opacity, strength, exposure, or flow

You can specify opacity, pressure, flow, tolerance, or exposure for a variety of tools:

- Opacity is used by the gradient, pencil, eraser, magic eraser, brush, clone stamp, pattern stamp, paint bucket, and impressionist brush tools.

- Strength of stroke is used by the smudge, blur, and sharpen tools.

- Amount of exposure is used by the dodge and burn tools.

- Flow is used by the sponge tool to set the rate of saturation change.

- Tolerance is used by the background eraser, impressionist bush, paint bucket, magic wand, and the red eye brush tools. The tolerance percentage defines how similar in color a pixel must be to be affected by the tool. A low tolerance value affects pixels within a range of color values very similar to the pixel you click. A high tolerance affects pixels within a broader range of color values.

To specify opacity, pressure, exposure, tolerance, or flow:

In the options bar, enter a value, or drag the pop-up slider for Opacity, Pressure, Exposure, Tolerance, or Flow.

The value can range from 1% to 100%. For transparent paint or a weak effect, specify a low percentage value; for more opaque paint or a strong effect, specify a high value.

Specifying brush dynamics

If you don't have a stylus or art tablet, you can still simulate actual brush strokes by setting the rates at which the brush tool strokes fade out. You can specify which options dynamically change over the course of a brush stroke including stroke scattering, size, and color. The brush thumbnail in the options bar reflects the brush changes as you adjust the brush dynamics options.

To set brush dynamics:

1 Select the brush tool in the toolbox.

2 Click the More Options button ✎ in the options bar.

3 Set any of the following options:

Spacing Controls the distance between the brush marks in a stroke. To change the spacing, type a number, or use the slider to enter a value that is a percentage of the brush diameter. (The brush thumbnail in the options bar dynamically changes to reflect your spacing adjustments.)

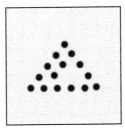

Increasing the spacing makes the brush skip.

Paint stroke without and with color jitter

Fade Sets the number of steps until the paint flow fades to nothing. A low value makes the paint stroke fade away very quickly, and a value of zero creates no fading effect. Each step is equal to one mark of the brush tip. Possible values range from 0 to 9999. For example, entering 10 for Fade produces a fade in 10 increments. For smaller brushes, you may want to set a value of 25 or larger. If strokes fade too quickly, increase the values.

Hardness Controls the size of the brush's hard center. Type a number, or use the slider to enter a value that's a percentage of the brush diameter.

Brush strokes with different hardness values

Fade showing setting of 40, 60, and 80 steps

Scatter Brush scattering determines how brush marks are distributed in a stroke. A low value produces a denser stroke with less paint scattering, and higher values increase the scattering area.

Color jitter Sets the rate at which the stroke color switches between the foreground and background colors. Higher values cause more frequent switches between the two colors than lower values. (To set the colors used by the color jitter option, see "Selecting foreground and background colors" on page 127.)

Brush stroke with low and high scatter values

Angle Specifies the angle by which an elliptical brush's long axis is offset from horizontal. Type a value in degrees, or drag the arrowhead in the angle icon to mark the desired angle.

Angled brushes create a chiseled stroke.

Roundness Specifies the ratio between the brush's short and long axes. Enter a percentage value, or drag a dot in the angle icon away from or toward the arrow. A value of 100% indicates a circular brush, a value of 0% indicates a linear brush, and intermediate values indicate elliptical brushes.

Adjusting roundness affects the shape of a brush tip.

Setting tablet support

Photoshop Elements is compatible with most pressure-sensitive digitizing tablets, such as the Wacom® tablets. With a software control panel for your tablet installed, you can vary brush tool properties based on the chosen Pen Pressure brush and the amount of pressure you apply with your stylus.

To enable tablet support:

1 Select the brush tool in the toolbox.

2 In the options bar, click the More Options ✎ button, and select Tablet Support.

3 Select the brushes pop-up palette, choose Pen Pressure Brushes from the Brushes pop-up menu, and then select a brush from the list.

Pen Pressure brush names that include the words *opacity, scatter,* or *size* change only that property when you apply more or less pressure to the pen. Other Pen Pressure brushes change several different properties.

Note: *If the highest pressure of your stylus does not reach 100%, contact your tablet vendor. This problem is caused by the driver software, not Photoshop Elements.*

Creating and editing brushes

You can create new brushes and delete brushes you no longer need, and you can use part of an image to create a custom brush. You can also create a temporary brush that you only expect to use one time.

Brush options in options bar
A. Brush pop-up palette and brush thumbnail
B. Brush size pop-up slider and text box

To add a new brush to the brush library:

1 Click the inverted arrow ▼ next to the brush sample to display the pop-up palette in the options bar; choose a category from the Brushes pop-up menu, and then select a brush to modify in the brush list.

2 Use the options bar to modify the original brush and then click OK. (See "Setting options for painting and editing tools" on page 135.)

3 Click the inverted arrow next to the brush sample to display the pop-up palette, and then choose New Brush from the palette menu.

4 Enter a name in the Brush Name dialog box and click OK.

The new brush is selected in the options bar, and is added at the bottom of the brushes pop-up palette.

To create a temporary brush or temporarily change a brush:

1 Select a brush from the brushes pop-up palette in the options bar.

2 Set the brush options. (See "Specifying brush dynamics" on page 138.)

3 Paint or erase in the image.

To delete a brush:

Do one of the following:

- Click the inverted arrow ▼ next to the brush sample to display the brushes pop-up palette in the options bar, press Alt (Windows) or Option (Mac OS) to change the pointer to scissors ✄, and then click the brush you want to delete.

- Select the brush in the pop-up palette, and choose Delete Brush from the palette menu.

- Choose Preset Manager from the palette menu, select Brushes from the Preset Type list, select the brush from the list in the dialog box, and click Delete.

To create a custom brush shape:

1 Select a selection tool in the toolbox, and select part of an image to use as a custom brush. (See "Selecting pixels" on page 114.)

The brush shape can be up to 1024 pixels by 1024 pixels in size. To define brushes with soft edges, select brush shapes composed of pixels with gray values. (Colored brush shapes appear as gray values.)

2 Choose Define Brush from the Edit menu.

3 Name the brush and click OK.

Selection defined as custom brush, and brush stroke using custom brush set with 100% spacing

You can easily save, load, replace, or delete brushes using the pop-up palette menu. You can also customize the view of the pop-up palette. (See "Using pop-up palettes" on page 28.) You can also load or save brushes using the Preset Manager. (See "Working with preset options" on page 27.)

Exiting Photoshop Elements saves the contents of the current pop-up palette in the Preferences file.

Managing brush libraries

The brush sizes and shapes available for painting and editing appear in the pop-up palette in the options bar for the painting and editing tools. You can customize the brushes and settings for each of the painting tools (airbrush, brush, eraser, and pencil) and editing tools (clone stamp, smudge, focus, toning, and red eye brush).

In Photoshop Elements, you can save libraries, load, replace, save, rename brushes in libraries, reset, or delete new brushes or libraries of brushes using the Preset Manager. (See "Working with preset options" on page 27.)

Erasing

The eraser, background eraser, and magic eraser tools let you erase areas of an image to transparency. The eraser tool also lets you erase to the background color in a Background layer or a layer with locked transparency. You can use the background eraser and magic eraser tools to erase a Background layer to transparency and convert it to a regular layer.

You can also use the Auto Erase option with the pencil tool to erase the foreground color to the background color as you paint, unless the area does not contain the foreground color. In that case the area is painted with the foreground color.

Using the eraser tool

The eraser tool changes pixels in the image as you drag through them. If you're working on the Background layer or on a layer with locked transparency, erased pixels change to the background color; otherwise, erased pixels become transparent.

To use the eraser tool:

1 Select the eraser tool ✐.

2 Click the inverted arrow ▾ next to the brush sample, choose a brush category from the Brushes pop-up menu, and then select a brush thumbnail. To learn more about using the brush presets, see "Using pop-up palettes" on page 28.

3 To set the brush size in the options bar, drag the Size pop-up slider or enter a size in the text box.

4 Choose the mode you want the eraser to use: brush, pencil, or block.

5 Specify an opacity to define the strength of the erasure. An opacity of 100% erases pixels to complete transparency on a layer and to the background color on the Background layer. A lower opacity erases pixels to partial transparency on a layer and paints partially with the background color on the Background layer. (This option isn't available for block mode.)

6 Drag through the area you want to erase.

Using the magic eraser tool

When you click in a layer with the magic eraser tool, the tool automatically changes all similar adjacent pixels. If you're working in a layer with locked transparency, the pixels change to the background color; otherwise, the pixels are erased to transparency. You can choose to erase contiguous pixels only or all similar pixels on the current layer.

Erasing similar pixels

Note: *When used on a Background layer, the magic eraser and the background eraser tools convert the Background layer to a regular layer. To erase on the Background layer without converting it, use the eraser tool. See "Using the eraser tool" on page 142.*

To use the magic eraser tool:

1 Select the magic eraser tool 🖉 .

2 Enter a tolerance value in the options bar. This setting defines the range of colors that can be erased. A low tolerance erases pixels within a range of color values very similar to the pixel you click. A high tolerance erases pixels within a broader range.

3 Select Anti-aliased to smooth the edges of the area you erase.

4 Select Contiguous to erase only pixels that are adjacent to the one you click. Deselect this option to erase all similar pixels in the image.

5 Select Use All Layers to sample the erased color using combined data from all visible layers.

6 Specify an opacity to define the strength of the erasure. An opacity of 100% erases pixels to complete transparency on a layer and to the background color on a locked layer. A lower opacity erases pixels to partial transparency on a layer and paints partially with the background color on a locked layer.

7 Click in the area of the layer you want to erase.

Using the background eraser tool

The background eraser samples the color in the brush center, also called the *hotspot*, and deletes that color wherever you drag the brush. This approach allows you to erase the background while maintaining the edges of an object in the foreground. The background eraser also performs color extraction at the edges of any foreground objects, so that color halos are not visible if the foreground object is later pasted into another image.

Note: *The background eraser overrides the Lock Transparency setting of a layer.*

To use the background eraser tool:

1 In the Layers palette, select the layer containing the areas you want to erase.

2 Select the background eraser tool 🖉 .

3 To set the brush size in the options bar, drag the Size pop-up slider or enter a size in the text box.

4 Choose a Limits mode:

• Discontiguous to erase the sampled color wherever it occurs under the brush.

• Contiguous to erase areas that contain the sampled color and are connected to one another.

5 For Tolerance, enter a value or drag the slider. A low tolerance limits erasure to areas that are very similar to the sampled color. A high tolerance erases a broader range of colors.

6 Drag through the area you want to erase. The tool pointer for the background eraser is a brush shape with a cross hair indicating the tool's hotspot ⊕.

Using the Auto Erase option

The Auto Erase option for the pencil tool lets you paint with the background color if your stroke begins in an area that contains the foreground color.

To use the Auto Erase option:

1 Specify foreground and background colors. (See "Selecting foreground and background colors" on page 127.)

2 Select the pencil tool ✐.

3 Select Auto Erase in the options bar.

4 Drag over the image.

If you begin dragging over areas in your image that contain the foreground color, the pencil tool paints with the background color. If you begin dragging from an area that doesn't contain the foreground color, the tool paints with the foreground color.

Filling and tracing selections and layers

Photoshop Elements provides a variety of ways to fill and trace selections and layers. You can fill them with colors and patterns, or you can paint a border around them.

Filling a selection or layer with colors or patterns

You can fill a selection or layer with the foreground color, the background color, or a pattern. In Photoshop Elements, you can use patterns from the provided pattern libraries or create your own patterns. When you use fill layers to fill a selection, you can easily change the type of layer being used. (See "About the Layers palette" on page 92 and "Creating fill layers" on page 103.) To increase the contrast between your image and the surrounding area in the image window, you can fill the area with a color.

♀ *To fill opaque pixels with the foreground color, press Alt+Shift+Backspace (Windows) or Option+Shift+Delete (Mac OS). To fill opaque pixels with the background color, press Ctrl+Shift+Backspace (Windows) or Command+Shift+Delete (Mac OS).*

To fill a selection or a layer with a pattern, foreground color, or background color:

1 Specify a foreground or background color. (See "Selecting foreground and background colors" on page 127.)

2 Select the area you want to fill. To fill an entire layer, select the layer in the Layers palette.

3 Choose Edit > Fill to fill the selection or layer.

4 In the Fill dialog box, choose one of the following options from the Use pop-up menu:

• Foreground Color, Background Color, Black, 50% Gray, or White to fill the selection with the specified color.

• Pattern to fill the selection with a pattern. Click the Custom Pattern pop-up menu, and then select a pattern from the pop-up palette. You can create or load additional patterns, see "Creating and editing patterns" on page 145.

5 Specify the blending mode and opacity for the paint. (See "Setting options for painting and editing tools" on page 135.)

6 To fill only areas opaque pixels on a layer, choose Preserve Transparency.

7 Click OK to fill the selection.

To fill the area surrounding the work canvas:

1 In the toolbox, set the foreground color you want to use. (See "Selecting foreground and background colors" on page 127.)

2 Drag the image window corners away from your image so that the image window dimensions are greater than your image dimensions.

3 Select the paint bucket tool 🪣.

4 In the options bar, set Fill to Foreground.

5 Hold down Shift, and click in the area surrounding your image.

Note that these steps affect all images in Photoshop Elements.

Filling the area surrounding the work canvas with color

Creating and editing patterns

In addition to using the libraries of patterns provided with Photoshop Elements, you can create your own custom patterns. Once you've created patterns, you can save them in a library, and then load and manage libraries of patterns using the Preset Manager. This allows you to easily use multiple patterns in an image. You can also use the pattern stamp tool to paint with a pattern. (See "Using the pattern stamp tool" on page 135).

To add a custom pattern to the pattern picker:

1 To create a pattern from part of the image, make a rectangular selection with Feather set to 0 px. Or, to create a pattern from the entire image, deselect everything. (Note that large patterns may become hard to manage.)

2 Choose Edit > Define Pattern.

3 Enter a name for the pattern in the Pattern Name dialog box.

4 To deselect the rectangle, choose Select > Deselect.

Note: If you apply a pattern from one image to another in a different color mode, Photoshop Elements converts the pattern's color mode to the current image's color mode.

To use a preset pattern from the PostScript Patterns folder:

1 Choose File > Open. Each preset file in the PostScript Patterns folder (located in Photoshop Elements 2/Presets/Patterns/PostScript Patterns/) contains a single pattern in the Adobe Illustrator format. You can scale and render these patterns at any resolution.

2 Select the pattern file you want to use, and click Open.

3 Select any rasterizing options. (See "Using the File Browser" on page 44.)

4 Click OK.

5 Choose Select > All, or make a rectangular selection around the pattern with Feather set to 0 px in the options bar.

6 Choose Edit > Define Pattern. The pattern is defined as an Adobe Photoshop Elements pattern.

7 Enter a name for the pattern in the Pattern Name dialog box.

8 Click OK.

Managing patterns

To manage patterns, you use the Pattern pop-up palette, which appears in the options bar for the pattern stamp tool and the paint bucket tool. You can change how that palette displays patterns (See "Using pop-up palettes" on page 28.), and you can load or save patterns using the Preset Manager. (See "Working with preset options" on page 27.)

Exiting Photoshop Elements saves the contents of the Pattern pop-up palette in the Preferences file.

Tracing a selection or layer with color

You can use the Stroke command to automatically trace a colored border around a selection or layer.

To stroke a selection or layer:

1 Select the area or layer you want to stroke.

2 Choose Edit > Stroke.

3 In the Stroke dialog box, specify the width of the hard-edged border. Values can range from 1 to 250 pixels.

4 To set the stroke color, click the color swatch to select a color in the color picker.

5 For Location, specify whether to place the border inside, outside, or centered over the selection or layer boundaries.

6 Specify a blending mode and an opacity. (See "Setting options for painting and editing tools" on page 135.)

7 To stroke only areas containing opaque pixels on a layer, select Preserve Transparency. (If your image has no transparency, this option isn't available.)

8 Click OK to stroke the selection or layer.

Using the paint bucket tool

The paint bucket tool fills an area that is similar in color value to the pixels you click. You can fill an area with the foreground color or a pattern.

Note: If you don't want to fill transparent areas on a layer, lock the layer's transparency in the Layers palette. (See "Locking layers" on page 107.)

To use the paint bucket tool:

1 Specify a foreground color. (See "Selecting foreground and background colors" on page 127.)

2 Select the paint bucket tool ⬧.

3 In the options bar, choose whether to fill the selection with the foreground color, or with a pattern. (See "Filling and tracing selections and layers" on page 144.)

4 If you chose to fill the selection with a pattern, click the inverted arrow ▾ next to the pattern sample, and select a pattern for the fill. (See "Using adjustment and fill layers" on page 101.)

5 Specify a blending mode and opacity for the paint. (See "Setting options for painting and editing tools" on page 135.)

6 Enter the tolerance for the fill.

The tolerance defines how similar in color filled pixel must be. Values can range from 0 to 255. A low tolerance fills pixels with color values very similar to the pixel you click. A high tolerance fills pixels that have a broader range of colors.

7 To smooth the edges of the filled selection, select Anti-aliased. (See "Softening the edges of a selection" on page 121.)

8 To fill only pixels in a contiguous group with the one you click, select Contiguous. Deselect this option to fill all similar pixels in the image.

9 To fill pixels based on all layers visible in the document window, select All Layers. (See "Sampling from all layers" on page 108.)

10 Click the part of the image you want to fill. All specified pixels within the specified tolerance are filled with the foreground color or pattern.

Using the gradient tools

The gradient tools create a gradual blend between multiple colors. You can choose from existing gradient fills or create your own.

Linear gradient ▭ Shades from the starting point to the ending point in a straight line.

Radial gradient ▭ Shades from the starting point to the ending point in a circular pattern.

Angle gradient ◣ Shades in a counterclockwise sweep around the starting point.

Reflected gradient ▭ Shades using symmetric linear gradients on either side of the starting point.

Diamond gradient ◆ Shades from the starting point outward in a diamond pattern. The ending point defines one corner of the diamond.

Applying a gradient fill

You fill an area with a gradient by dragging in the image or in a selection. The distance between the starting point (where you press and hold the mouse button) and ending point (where you release the mouse button) affects the gradient appearance, as does the gradient type.

To apply a gradient fill:

1 To fill part of the image, select the desired area. Otherwise, the gradient fill is applied to the entire active layer.

2 Select the gradient tool ▦.

3 In the options bar, click the desired gradient type (linear ▦, radial ▦, angle ◣, reflected ▭, or diamond ◈).

4 Choose a gradient fill from the Gradient Picker pop-up palette in the options bar. (See "Using pop-up palettes" on page 28.)

5 Specify a blending mode and opacity for the paint. (See "Setting options for painting and editing tools" on page 135.)

6 To reverse the order of colors in the gradient fill, select Reverse.

7 To create a smoother blend with less banding, select Dither.

8 To use a transparency mask for the gradient fill, select Transparency. (See "Specifying the gradient transparency" on page 150.)

9 In the image, position the pointer where you want to set the starting point of the gradient, and drag to define the ending point. To constrain the gradient angle to a multiple of 45°, hold down Shift as you drag.

Creating or editing gradient fills

The Gradient Editor dialog box lets you define a new gradient by modifying a copy of an existing gradient. You can also edit fills by either adding intermediate colors to a gradient, or creating a blend between three or more colors.

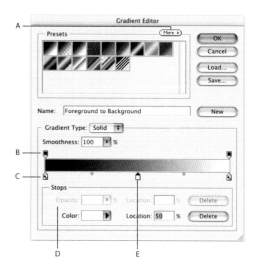

Gradient Editor dialog box
A. Palette menu B. Opacity stop C. Color stop D. Adjust values or delete the selected opacity or color stop E. Midpoint

To create a gradient:

1 Select the gradient tool ▦.

2 To display the Gradient Editor dialog box, do one of the following:

- Click the Edit button next to the gradient sample.

- Click the gradient sample in the options bar.

3 In the Presets section of the Gradient Editor dialog box, select a gradient on which to base your new gradient.

4 To define the starting color of the gradient, click the left color stop under the gradient bar. The triangle above the stop turns black, indicating that you're editing the starting color.

5 To choose a color, do one of the following:

- Double-click the color stop, or click the color swatch below the gradient bar. Choose a color, and click OK. For information on choosing a color, see "Using the Adobe Color Picker" on page 131.

- Choose foreground from the color pop-up menu in the Gradient Editor dialog box to use the current foreground color.

- Choose background from the color pop-up menu to use the current background color.

- Position the pointer over the gradient bar (the pointer turns into the eyedropper), and click to sample a color, or click anywhere in the image to sample a color.

6 To define the ending color, click the right color stop under the gradient bar. Then choose a color as described in step 5.

7 To adjust the location of the starting point or ending point, do one of the following:

- Drag the corresponding color stop left or right to the location you want.

- Click the corresponding color stop, and enter a value for Location. A value of 0% places the point at the far left end of the gradient bar, a value of 100% at the far right end.

8 To adjust the location of the midpoint (where the gradient displays an even mix of the starting and ending colors), drag the diamond below the gradient bar to the left or right, or click the diamond and enter a value for Location.

9 To delete the color stop you are editing, click Delete.

Note: Gradients require at least two color stops.

10 To set the color transition's smoothness, enter a percentage in the Smoothness text box, or drag the pop-up slider.

11 If desired, set transparency values for the gradient. (See "Specifying the gradient transparency" on page 150.)

12 To save the gradient to the gradient presets, enter a name for the new gradient, and then click New.

13 Click OK to exit the dialog box; the newly created gradient is selected and ready to use.

To add intermediate colors to a gradient:

In the Gradient Editor dialog box, click below the gradient bar to define another color stop. Specify the color and adjust the location and midpoint for the intermediate point as you would for a starting or ending point. To remove an intermediate color, drag the color stop down and off the gradient bar, or select the color stop and press Delete.

Applying gradient fill to text

You can fill text using the gradient tool.

To apply gradient fill to text:

1 Do one of the following:

- Select the Horizontal Type tool to enter horizontal text.

- Select the Vertical Type tool to enter vertical text.

2 Enter the type you want, and then in the options bar, click the Commit Text button ✔ to commit changes to the text.

3 Choose Layer > Simplify Layer to convert the vector text to a bitmap image. (For more information on simplifying type, see "Simplifying type layers" on page 199.)

4 Control-click (Windows) or Command-click (Mac OS) on the text layer in the Layers palette to select the text.

5 Select the Gradient tool.

6 In the options bar, click the desired gradient type (linear, radial, angular, reflected, or diamond).

7 Choose a gradient fill from the Gradient Picker pop-up palette.

8 Position the pointer on the text where you want to set the starting point of the gradient, and drag to define the ending point.

Specifying the gradient transparency

Each gradient fill contains settings that control the opacity of the fill at different locations on the gradient. For example, you can set the starting color to 100% opacity and have the fill gradually blend into an ending color with 50% opacity. The checkerboard pattern indicates the amount of transparency in the gradient preview.

To specify the gradient transparency:

1 Create a gradient as described in steps 1 through 10 of "Creating or editing gradient fills" on page 148.

2 To adjust the starting opacity in the Gradient Editor, click the left opacity stop above the gradient bar. The triangle below the stop turns black, indicating that you're editing the starting transparency.

3 Set the Opacity by doing one of the following:

- Enter a value between 0 (fully transparent) and 100% (fully opaque).

- Drag the arrow on the Opacity pop-up slider.

4 To adjust the opacity of the endpoint, click the right transparency stop above the gradient bar. Then set the opacity as described in step 3.

5 To adjust the location of the starting or ending opacity, do one of the following:

- Drag the corresponding opacity stop to the left or right.

- Select the corresponding opacity stop, and enter a value for Location.

6 To adjust the location of the midpoint opacity (the point midway between the starting and ending opacities), do one of the following:

- Drag the diamond above the gradient bar to the left or right.

- Select the diamond, and enter a value for Location.

7 To delete the opacity stop you are editing, click Delete.

Note: Gradients require at least two opacity stops.

8 To add an intermediate opacity, click above the gradient bar to define a new opacity stop. You can then adjust and move this opacity as you would a starting or ending opacity. To remove an intermediate opacity, drag its transparency stop up and off the gradient bar, or select the stop and click the Delete button.

9 To save the gradient to the gradient presets, enter a new name in the Name text box, and then click New. This creates a new gradient preset with the transparency setting you specified.

10 Click OK to exit the dialog box and select the newly created gradient.

Creating noise gradient fills

In addition to creating smooth gradients, the Gradient Editor dialog box lets you define a new noise gradient. A noise gradient is a gradient that contains randomly distributed colors within a range of colors that you specify.

Noise gradients with different noise values
A. 10% noise B. 50% noise C. 90% noise

To create a noise gradient:

1 Select the gradient tool ▭.

2 To display the Gradient Editor dialog box, either click the Edit button or click in the gradient sample in the options bar.

3 Choose Noise from the Gradient Type menu.

4 To set the roughness for the gradient, enter a value, or drag the pop-up slider.

5 Choose a color model from the Color Model list. (See "Describing color" on page 64.)

6 To define the range of colors in the gradient, drag the sliders for each color component. For example, if you choose the HSB model, you can restrict the gradient to blue-green hues, high saturation, and medium brightness.

7 To prevent oversaturated colors, select Restrict Colors. To add transparency to random colors, select Add Transparency.

8 To randomly create a gradient that conforms to your settings, click the Randomize button until you find a gradient you like.

9 Enter a name for the new gradient.

10 To create a new gradient preset, with the settings you specified, click New.

11 Click OK to exit the dialog box and select the newly created gradient.

Managing gradients

By saving and loading libraries of gradients, you can customize the gradient presets that appear in the gradient options bar and the Gradient Editor dialog box. You can also manage gradients by using the Preset Manager. (For more information on the Preset Manager, see "Working with preset options" on page 27.)

To display gradient presets in different ways, you can change the view of the pop-up palette in the options bar and the list box in the Gradient Editor dialog box. (See "Using pop-up palettes" on page 28.)

Chapter 9: Transforming and Distorting Images

You can transform a layer in many ways by making subtle changes to retouch an image, or by making drastic distortions to create an artistic effect. For example, you can scale, rotate, or apply perspective to a selection, and make areas of a layer look like they've been melted.

Transforming layers, selections, and shapes

You can scale, rotate, skew, distort, and apply perspective to entire layers, selected parts of layers, and shapes. Some memory-intensive transformations cause Photoshop Elements to display a progress indicator in the status bar (Windows) or progress bar (Mac OS) to mark the time remaining until the transformation is applied.

Specifying what to transform

You can apply a transformation to a selection on a layer or to an entire layer. You can also transform multiple layers in an image simultaneously.

To specify what to transform:

Do one of the following:

- To transform an entire layer or a type layer, deselect everything, and then select the layer in the Layers palette.

- To transform the background layer, select the layer in the Layers palette and choose Select > All. Some areas of the background layer may display the background color after you apply a transformation. Alternatively, you can convert a background layer to a regular layer before applying a transformation. (See "Adding layers" on page 95.)

- To transform part of a layer, select the layer in the Layers palette, and then use any selection tool to select an area in the layer. (See "Selecting pixels" on page 114).

- To transform multiple layers simultaneously, link the layers together in the Layers palette. (See "Linking layers" on page 99.)

- To transform a shape on a layer, use the shape selection tool ▶ to select the shape. (See "Transforming shapes" on page 194.)

Rotating layers, selections, and shapes

Rotating a layer, a selection on a layer, or a shape turns it around its center point.

To rotate or flip a layer, selection, or shape:

1 Select the layer, area, or shape you want to transform. (See "Specifying what to transform" on page 153.)

2 Choose Image > Rotate, and choose one of the following commands from the submenu:

- Layer/Selection 90° Left to rotate counter-clockwise by a quarter-turn.

- Layer/Selection 90° Right to rotate clockwise by a quarter-turn.

- Layer/Selection 180° to rotate by a half-turn.

- Flip Layer/Selection Horizontal to flip horizontally.

- Flip Layer/Selection Vertical to flip vertically.

To freely rotate a layer, selection, or shape:

1 Select the layer, area, or shape you want to rotate. (See "Specifying what to transform" on page 153.)

2 Choose Image > Rotate > Free Rotate Layer/Selection. A bounding box appears in the image.

3 By default, the rotation occurs around the center of your selection. To change this behavior, click a square on the reference point locator ▦ in the options bar.

Each square on the reference point locator represents a point on the bounding box. For example, to set the reference point to the top left corner of the bounding box, click the top left square on the reference point locator.

4 Do one of the following:

- Move the pointer outside of the bounding border (it becomes a curved, two-sided arrow) ↰, and then drag. To constrain the rotation to 15° increments, hold down Shift as you drag.

- Type an angle of rotation (−180 to 180) in the angle degree ∠ text box of the options bar. A positive value rotates clockwise, and a negative value rotates counterclockwise.

5 Do one of the following:

- To commit the transformation, double-click inside the bounding box, click the Commit button ✔ in the options bar, or press Enter (Windows) or Return (Mac OS).

- To cancel the transformation, click the Cancel button ⊘ in the options bar, or press Esc.

💡 *To simultaneously apply several transformations, including rotate, use the Free Transform command. (See "Using the Free Transform command" on page 156.)*

Scaling layers, selections, and shapes

Scaling a layer, a selection on a layer, or a shape enlarges or reduces it relative to its center point. You can scale horizontal and vertical dimensions separately or simultaneously.

Scaling a layer

To scale a layer, selection, or shape:

1 Select the layer, area, or shape you want to scale. (See "Specifying what to transform" on page 153.)

2 Choose Image > Resize > Scale.

3 Do one of the following:

- To maintain the relative proportions as you scale, click the Maintain Aspect Ratio button in the options bar, and then drag a corner handle. Alternatively, you can hold down Shift as you drag a corner handle.

- To scale only the height or the width, drag a side handle.

- Enter a percentage for the Width, Height, or both in the options bar. To scale both dimensions proportionately, select the Maintain Aspect Ratio button .

4 Do one of the following:

- To commit the transformation, double-click inside the bounding box, click the Commit button ✔ in the options bar, or press Enter (Windows) or Return (Mac OS).

- To cancel the transformation, click the Cancel button ⊘ in the options bar, or press Esc.

💡 *To simultaneously apply several transformations, including scale, use the Free Transform command. (See "Using the Free Transform command" on page 156.)*

Skewing, distorting, and setting perspective

Skewing, distorting, and applying perspective change the geometry of a layer, selection, or a shape. Skewing lets you slant things vertically and horizontally; distorting lets you stretch things

in any direction; applying perspective makes things appear to go backward or forward in three-dimensions.

Correcting perspective

To skew, distort, or apply perspective to a layer, selection, or shape:

1 Select the layer, area, or shape you want to transform. (See "Specifying what to transform" on page 153.)

2 Do one of the following:

- To skew an image, choose Image > Transform > Skew, and drag a handle in the middle of any side to slant the bounding box.
  If you are transforming a shape with the shape tool selected, choose Image > Transform Shape > Skew.

- To distort an image, choose Image > Transform > Distort, and drag a corner handle to stretch the bounding box. If you are transforming a shape with the shape tool selected, choose Image > Transform Shape > Distort.

• To give your image perspective, choose Image > Transform > Perspective, and drag a corner handle to apply perspective to the bounding box. If you are transforming a shape with the shape tool selected, choose Image > Transform Shape > Perspective.

3 Do one of the following:

• To commit the transformation, double-click inside the bounding box, click the Commit button ✔ in the options bar, or press Enter (Windows) or Return (Mac OS).

• To cancel the transformation, click the Cancel button ⃠ in the options bar, or press Esc.

💡 *To simultaneously apply several transformations, including skew, distort, and perspective, use the Free Transform command. (See "Using the Free Transform command" on page 156.)*

Using the Free Transform command

The Free Transform command lets you apply transformations (rotating, scaling, skewing, distorting, and applying perspective) in one continuous operation. Instead of choosing different commands, you simply hold down a key on your keyboard to switch between transformation types.

To freely transform a layer:

1 Select the layer, area, or shape you want to transform. (See "Specifying what to transform" on page 153.)

2 By default, any rotation occurs around the center of your selection. To change this behavior, click a square on the reference point locator 🔳 in the options bar.

Each square on the reference point locator represents a point on the bounding box. For example, to set the reference point to the top left corner of the bounding box, click the top left square on the reference point locator.

3 Choose Image > Transform > Free Transform. If you are transforming a shape with the custom shape tool selected, choose Image > Transform Shape > Free Transform Shape.

4 Do one or more of the following:

• To scale, drag any handle on the bounding box. To scale the width and height proportionally, either press Shift as you drag a corner handle, or click the Maintain Aspect Ratio button 🔘 in the options bar and then drag a corner handle.

• To rotate, move the pointer outside of the bounding box (it becomes a curved, two-sided arrow ↰, and then drag. Press Shift to constrain the rotation to 15° increments.

• To distort freely, press Ctrl (Windows) or Command (Mac OS), and drag any handle. When positioned over a handle, the pointer becomes a gray arrowhead ▷.

• To skew, press Ctrl+Shift (Windows) or Command+Shift (Mac OS), and drag a handle in the middle of a side of the bounding box. When positioned over a side handle, the pointer becomes a gray arrowhead with a small double arrow ▷↔.

- To apply perspective, press Ctrl+Alt+Shift (Windows) or Command+Option+Shift (Mac OS), and drag a corner handle. When positioned over a corner handle, the pointer becomes a gray arrowhead ▶.

 To undo the last handle adjustment, choose Edit > Undo.

5 Do one of the following:

- To commit the transformation, double-click inside the bounding box, click the Commit button ✔ in the options bar, or press Enter (Windows) or Return (Mac OS).

- To cancel the transformation, click the Cancel button ⊘ in the options bar, or press Esc.

Transforming objects in three dimensions

The 3D Transform filter lets you manipulate a flat, two-dimensional image as if it were a solid, three-dimensional object. Take, for example, a perspective photograph of a cereal box. You specify the corners of the box using a wire frame, and you can then manipulate the box as if it were a three-dimensional object. You can reposition the box, turn or rotate it, shrink or enlarge it, and change its field of view.

Using the 3D Transform filter

You can transform a two-dimensional object into a cube, sphere, or cylinder and manipulate it using wire frames based on that shape. Cylinders can include anything from simple objects, such as a can of soup, to more complex shapes, such as a bottle or a lamp.

You can create and manipulate any grouping of cubes, spheres, and cylinders in the same image. For example, you can create and rotate a box, three spheres, and a bottle together in the same image.

3D Transform Filter
*A. Image of 2D label **B.** Cylinder wireframe in 3D transform preview **C.** Tilting the bottle by using Track Ball tool **D.** Completed Image with Lens Flare effect applied*

To transform and manipulate an object in three dimensions:

1 Select the layer, area, or shape you want to transform.

2 Choose Filter > Render > 3D Transform.

3 Select one of the tools in the dialog box:

- Cube ⬡ to map the image (such as a file cabinet) to a cubic surface.

- Sphere ⬤ to map the image (such as a globe or ball) to a spherical surface.

- Cylinder ⬓ to map the image (such as a can or bottle) to a cylindrical surface.

4 Drag to create a cubic, cylindrical, or spherical wire frame over the image.

5 Move or reshape the wire frame, as described later in this section. The anchor points should line up with the corners of the box, or the top and bottom of the sphere or cylinder you want to manipulate.

6 Manipulate the object in three dimensions, as described later in this section.

7 Click OK.

To move or reshape the wire frame:

1 Do either of the following:

- To move the entire frame, select the selection tool ▸ in the 3D Transform dialog box and drag an edge of the wire frame.

- To move an anchor point, select the direct selection tool ▸ in the 3D Transform dialog box and drag an anchor point on the wire frame.

Note: The wire frame turns red if you try to make a wire frame that is impossible to re-create in three dimensions.

2 If you are creating a complex cylinder, do any of the following:

- To add an anchor point, select the add anchor point tool ⬦⁺ in the dialog box, and click the right side of the wire frame. For example, you can add an anchor point to more closely fit the cylindrical wire frame to a picture of a bottle.

- To change an added anchor point from a smooth anchor point to a corner anchor point and vice versa, select the convert anchor point tool ⋀, and click the point. A smooth anchor point creates a gentle curve when you adjust it; a corner anchor point creates a sharp corner.

- To delete an added anchor point, select the delete anchor point tool ⬦⁻, and click the point. You can delete only round or diamond-shaped points.

3 For Field of View, enter a value between 1 and 130. Alternatively, drag the pop-up slider to the left to increase the apparent field of view, or to the right to decrease it. This technique can make the wire frame fit the image better. If you know the field of view angle used to photograph the image, you can enter it here.

To manipulate the object in three dimensions:

Do any of the following in the 3D Transform dialog box:

- To move the object, click the pan camera tool ⬥ in the dialog box, and drag the object.

- To rotate the object in any direction, click the trackball tool , and drag the object.

- With any of the bottom four tools selected in the dialog box, enter a value between 0 and 99 for Dolly Camera. Alternatively, drag the slider to the left to magnify the transformed object, to the right to shrink it. This has the same effect as dollying, or moving, the camera further from or closer to the image.

- With any of the bottom four tools selected in the dialog box, enter a value between 1 and 130 for Field of View. Alternatively, drag the slider to the left to increase the apparent field of view, to the right to decrease it.

The 3D Transform dialog box previews only the active layer.

To delete a wire frame:

1 Select the selection tool in the 3D Transform dialog box.

2 Select the wire frame, and press Backspace (Windows) or Delete (Mac OS).

Modifying the preview image

Use the zoom and hand tools in the 3D Transform dialog box to change your preview of an image. These actions do not modify the transformation itself, only your view of it.

To magnify or shrink the preview image:

1 Select the zoom tool in the 3D Transform dialog box.

2 Click the image to zoom in, or Alt-click (Windows) or Option-click (Mac OS) to zoom out.

To move the view of the preview image:

Select the hand tool in the 3D Transform dialog box, and drag the preview image. This technique works only if you are zoomed in on the image.

Setting 3D rendering options

You can set the resolution and anti-aliasing of rendered images and specify whether to show the background from the original image in the 3D preview.

To set 3D rendering options:

1 Click Options in the 3D Transform dialog box.

2 Do any of the following:

- For Resolution, choose the quality of the rendered image. This setting has little effect on the image quality of cubes, but produces smoother curved surfaces in cylinders and spheres.

- For Anti-aliasing, choose the level of anti-aliasing to apply to the rendered image.

- Select Display Background to include the portions of the original image outside of the wire frame in the preview and the rendered image. Turn this option off to separate the transformed object from the original background.

3 Click OK.

Using Distort filters to transform an image

Many of the Distort filters let you apply 3D effects to a layer and reshape a layer or selection in your image. You work with a preview of the filter's effect on your image to set the filter options.

Using the Liquify filter

The Liquify filter makes it easy to manipulate areas of an image as if those areas had been melted. You work with a preview image of the current layer, using special tools to warp, twirl, expand, contract, shift, and reflect areas of the image. You can make subtle changes to retouch an image or drastic distortions to create an artistic effect.

Using the Liquify filter to distort and reconstruct

To use the Liquify filter:

1 Select the layer or area you want to distort.

2 Choose Filter > Distort > Liquify.

Note: *If a type layer is selected, you must simplify the layer before applying the Liquify filter. See "Simplifying type layers" on page 199. Alternatively, to distort type without simplifying the type layer, click the Warp Text button in the type tool's option bar.*

3 To zoom in or out on the image preview, do one of the following:

- Choose a zoom level from the pop-up menu in the bottom left area of the dialog box.

- Select the zoom tool from the toolbox in the dialog box, and click in the image to zoom in, or Alt-click (Windows) or Option-click (Mac OS) to zoom out. You can also use the zoom tool to drag over an area of the preview you want to magnify.

4 In the Tool Options section, adjust the brush size and pressure of the tools, as needed:

- To change the brush size, drag the pop-up slider, or enter a brush size value from 1 to 600 pixels.

- To change the brush pressure, drag the pop-up slider, or enter a brush pressure value from 1 to 100.

  A low brush pressure makes more gradual changes.

- If you're using a stylus tablet, select Stylus Pressure.

5 Use any of the following tools to distort the preview image:

- The warp tool to push pixels forward as you drag.

- The turbulence tool to smoothly scramble pixels and create fire, clouds, waves, and similar effects. To adjust the smoothness, drag the Turbulent Jitter pop-up slider in the Tool Options section, or enter a value between 1 and 100 in the text box. Higher values increase smoothness.

- The twirl clockwise tool ⟳ to rotate pixels clockwise as you hold down the mouse button or drag.

- The twirl counterclockwise tool ⟲ to rotate pixels counterclockwise as you hold down the mouse button or drag.

- The pucker tool 🔅 to move pixels toward the center of the brush area as you hold down the mouse button or drag.

- The bloat tool ◇ to move pixels away from the center of the brush area as you hold down the mouse button or drag.

- The shift pixels tool ▨ to move pixels perpendicularly to the stroke direction. Drag to move pixels to the left, and Alt-drag (Windows) or Option-drag (Mac OS) to move pixels to the right.

- The reflection tool ▨ to copy pixels to the brush area. Drag to reflect the area perpendicular to the direction of the stroke (to the left of or below the stroke). Alt-drag (Windows) or Option-drag (Mac OS) to reflect the area in the direction opposite to that of the stroke (for example, the area above a downward stroke). Use overlapping strokes to create an effect similar to a reflection in water.

- To fully or partially reverse the changes, use the reconstruct tool. See "To restore a preview image to a previous state" in the next set of procedures.

💡 *To create the effect of dragging in a straight line between the current point and the previous point that you clicked, Shift-click with the warp, shift pixels, and reflection tools.*

6 To apply the changes in the preview image to the actual image, click OK.

To restore a preview image to a previous state:

Do one of the following:

- Select the reconstruct tool 🖌, and hold down the mouse button or drag over the distorted areas. The restoration occurs more quickly at the brush center. Shift-click to reconstruct in a straight line between the current point and the previous point that you clicked.

- To restore the entire preview image to its state when you opened the dialog box, Alt-click (Windows) or Option-click (Mac OS) Reset. Alternatively, click Revert to restore the original image and reset the tools to their previous settings.

Using the Displace filter

The Displace filter uses an image, called a *displacement map*, to determine how to distort a selection. For example, using a parabola-shaped displacement map, you can create an image that appears to be printed on a cloth held at its corners.

This filter requires a displacement map file composed of either a flattened image saved in Photoshop format (see "Flattening all layers" on page 112) or an image in Bitmap mode. You can use your own files or the files included in the Photoshop Elements 2 / Plug-Ins / Displacement Maps folder or the Photoshop Elements 2 / Presets / Textures folder.

To use Displace:

1 Choose Filter > Distort > Displace.

2 To define the magnitude of the displacement, enter a value between –999 and 999 in the Horizontal and Vertical Scale text boxes.

When the horizontal and vertical scales are 100%, the greatest displacement is 128 pixels (because middle gray produces no displacement).

3 If the displacement map is not the same size as the selection, select how the map will fit the image:

- To resize the map, select Stretch to Fit.
- To fill the selection by repeating the map in a pattern, select Tile.

4 Select how to fill voids that are created by the filter in the image:

- To fill voids with content from the opposite edge of the image, select Wrap Around.
- To extend the colors of pixels along the image's edge in the direction specified, select Repeat Edge Pixels.

5 Click OK.

6 Select and open the displacement map.

Photoshop Elements applies the map to the image.

Applying the Pinch filter

The Pinch filter squeezes a selection or layer inward or outward.

To pinch a layer or selection:

1 Select the layer or area you want to pinch.

2 Choose Filter > Distort > Pinch.

3 Drag the slider to the right, into positive values, to pinch a selection inward toward its center; or to the left, into negative values, to shift a selection outward.

4 Click OK.

Applying the Shear filter

The Shear filter distorts an image along a curve.

To shear a layer or selection:

1 Select the layer or area you want to shear.

2 Choose Filter > Distort > Shear

3 To define a distortion curve, do one of the following in the Shear dialog box:

- Click anywhere on either side of the vertical line.
- Click on the vertical line, and then drag the new curve point.

You can drag any point along the curve to adjust the distortion, and you can add additional curve points.

4 Select one of the following in the Undefined Areas options:

- Wrap Around fills new voids in the image with content from the opposite side of the image.
- Repeat Edge Pixels extends the colors of pixels. Banding may result if the edge pixels are different colors.

You can click Defaults to start over and return the curve to a straight line.

Applying the Spherize filter

The Spherize filter gives objects a 3D effect by wrapping a selection around or inside a spherical shape, distorting and stretching the image.

For more options and control, use the 3D Transform filter. See "Using the 3D Transform filter" on page 157.

To spherize a layer or selection:

1 Select the layer or area you want to spherize.

2 Choose Filter > Distort > Spherize.

3 Drag the slider to the right, into positive values, to stretch the image outward as if it's wrapped around a sphere. Drag the slider to the left, into negative values, to stretch the image inward as if it's wrapped inside a sphere.

Applying the Twirl filter

The Twirl filter rotates a selection more sharply in the center than at the edges. Specifying an angle produces a twirl pattern. Select the layer or area you want to twirl, and then choose Filter > Distort > Twirl.

To apply the Twirl filter:

1 Select the layer or area you want to twirl.

2 Choose Filter > Distort > Twirl.

3 Drag the slider to the right into positive values to twirl the image clockwise, drag to the left into negative values to twirl counterclockwise, or enter a value between –999 and 999.

Applying the Wave filter

The Wave filter creates an undulating pattern on a layer or selection. You can set the wave pattern type, and fine tune various wave properties.

To apply the Wave filter:

1 Select the layer or area you want to undulate.

2 Choose Filter > Distort > Wave.

3 Select a wave type in the Type section: Sine (creates a rolling wave pattern), Triangle, or Square.

4 To set the number of wave generators, drag the slider or enter a number between 1 and 999.

5 Drag the minimum and maximum Wavelength sliders to set the distance from one wave crest to the next. Set both sliders to the same value to create a consistent pattern of wave crests.

6 Drag the minimum and maximum Amplitude sliders to set the wave strength.

7 Drag the horizontal and vertical Scale sliders to set the height and width of the wave effect.

8 To apply random results based on the set of values in the dialog box, click Randomize. You can click Randomize multiple times to get more results.

9 Select the Wrap Around option to fill the voids in the image with content from the opposite edge of the image, or select Repeat Edge Pixels to extend the colors of pixels along the image's edge in the direction specified.

10 Click OK.

Applying the ZigZag filter

The ZigZag filter distorts a selection radially, depending on the radius of the pixels in your selection.

To apply the ZigZag filter:

1 Select the layer or area you want to affect.

2 Choose Filter > Distort > ZigZag.

3 Drag the Amount slider to set the level and direction of distortion.

4 Drag the Ridges slider to set the number of direction reversals for the zigzag from the center of to the edge of the selection.

5 Choose a displacement option from the Style pop-up menu:

- Around Center rotates the pixels around the center of the selection.

- Out From Center produces a rippling effect toward or away from the center of the selection.

- Pond Ripples produces a rippling effect that distorts the selection to the upper left or lower right.

6 Click OK.

Chapter 10: Applying Filters, Effects, and Layer Styles

A photographer can place filters over a camera lens to create interesting visual effects. Adobe Photoshop Elements provides filters, layer styles, and effects you can use to enhance your photos, simulate photographic effects, and create visual effects beyond the bounds of traditional photography.

Using the Filters, Effects, and Layer Styles palettes

The Filters, Effects, and Layer Styles palettes let you view thumbnail examples of each visual effect and apply a filter, layer style, or effect to your image. In addition, many filters have specific options you can access with the Filters palette or Filter menu.

Working with the Filters, Effects, and Layer Styles palettes

From any palette, you can choose from a variety of categories to apply to your images. You can also change how the categories are displayed on a palette.

You can combine the different categories of filters, effects, and layer styles to create unique images from a simple photograph. For example, you can create a dramatic look by combining the Outer Glow category from the Layer Styles palette with Neon Nights from the Image Effect category in the Effects palette.

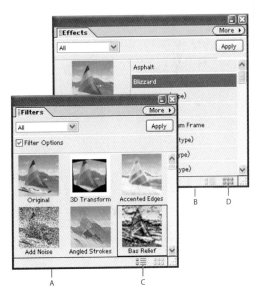

Filters and Effects palettes
A. Filters palette B. Effects palette C. List View button
D. Thumbnail View button

To display the Filters, Effects, or Layer Styles palettes:

Do one of the following:

• Choose a palette name from the Window menu.

- Click the Filters, Layer Styles, or Effects tab in the palette well.

To change categories in the Filters, Layer Styles, or Effects palettes:

Choose a category from the pop-up menu at the top of the palette.

To change how filters, layer styles, or effects are displayed in the palette:

Do one of the following:

- To view the visual effects by their names, click the List View button ▤ at the bottom of the palette. When you select a name, the left side of the palette displays thumbnails with and without the filter or effect.

- To view the visual effects as thumbnails, click the Thumbnail View button ▦ at the bottom of the palette.

Using filters

Filters let you apply special visual effects to your images, such as mosaic tile, lighting, and three-dimensional effects. You can also use some filters to clean up or retouch your photos.

Filter sets appear in the Filters palette and in the Filter menu. In addition, some third-party filters appear at the bottom of the Filter menu. Keep in mind the following guidelines when choosing a filter:

- Filters affect the active, visible layer or a selected area of the layer.

- You can't use some filters on images in Grayscale mode, or any filters on images in Bitmap or Indexed Color mode.

- The last filter you applied will appear at the top of the Filter menu and can be reapplied with the same filter settings you last used.

Displaying filter options and applying filters

Applying filters to an image—especially to a large image—can be time-consuming. It's quicker to view an example of the filter's effect in the Filters palette instead. Most filters also let you preview their effect on your image in the Filter Options dialog box and the document window. See "Choosing a filter" on page 172 for more information about the effects you can expect from a filter.

💡 *To save time when testing the effect of various filters, select a small, representative part of your image.*

To set filter options and apply a filter:

1 To apply a filter to an entire layer, deselect any selected areas, and then select the layer in the Layers palette.

2 To apply a filter to a portion of a layer, use any selection tool to select an area.

3 Do one of the following:

- Choose a filter from a submenu in the Filter menu. If a filter name is followed by ellipses (…), a Filter Options dialog box appears.

- In the Filters palette, select the filter you want to apply.

4 To set filter options and preview the filter, select Filter Options at the top of the Filters palette. Or, to apply the preset filter settings deselect Filter Options. (Filter Options and preview windows are not available for all filters.)

5 To apply the filter to your image, double-click the filter, drag the filter into the image, or click Apply in the Filters palette.

6 If a dialog box appears, enter values or select options. (Read more about each filter and setting filter options later in this chapter.)

To start over, and reset the filter options, press the Alt (Windows) or Option (Mac OS) key, and click Reset in the dialog box.

7 If available, select the Preview option to preview the filter effect in the document window. Use one of the following methods to preview the effect:

- Use the + or – button under the preview window to zoom in or zoom out on the preview.

- Drag in the preview window to center a specific area of the image in the window.

Note: A flashing line beneath the preview size indicates that the preview is being rendered.

8 Click OK to apply the filter.

In some cases, a progress indicator marks the time remaining until the filter is applied.

Defining undistorted areas

The Displace, Shear, and Wave filters in the Distort submenu and the Offset filter in the Other submenu let you treat areas undefined by the filter.

See "Transforming layers, selections, and shapes" on page 153 for more information.

Using texture and glass surface controls

The Conté Crayon, Glass, Rough Pastels, Texturizer, and Underpainting filters have texturizing options. These options make images appear as if they are painted onto textures such as canvas and brick or viewed through glass blocks.

To use texture and glass surface controls:

Do one of the following:

- Choose the filter from the appropriate submenu in the Filter menu.

- Use the Filters palette to apply the desired filter (make sure Filter Options is selected in the Filters palette before you apply the filter).

1 For Texture, choose a texture type or choose Load Texture to specify a Photoshop file.

2 Drag the Scaling slider to enlarge or reduce the effect on the image surface.

3 Drag the Relief slider (if available) to adjust the depth of the texture's surface.

4 For Light Angle (if available), choose the direction of the light source on the image.

5 Select Invert to reverse the surface's light and dark colors.

6 Click OK.

Tips for applying filters

Try the following techniques to create special visual effects with filters.

Feather the filter edges If you're applying a filter to a selected area, you can soften the edges of the filter effect by feathering the selection before you apply the filter. See "About selections" on page 113 for more information on defining a feathered edge.

Apply filters to multiple layers Apply filters to individual layers or to several layers in succession to build up an effect. You can choose different blending modes in the Layers palette to blend the effect. (See "Specifying layer blending modes" on page 100.) For a filter to affect a layer, the layer must be visible and must contain pixels.

Create textures and backgrounds By applying filters to solid-color or grayscale images, you can generate a variety of backgrounds and textures. You can then blur these textures if desired. Although some filters (for example, the Glass filter) have little or no visible effect when applied to solid colors, others produce interesting effects. For such colors, you can use Add Noise, Chalk & Charcoal, Clouds, Conté Crayon, Difference Clouds, Glass, Graphic Pen, Halftone Pattern, Mezzotint, Note Paper, Pointillize, Reticulation, Rough Pastels, Sponge, or Underpainting. You can also use any of the filters in the Texture submenu.

Improve image quality and consistency You can disguise faults, alter or enhance images, or make a series of images look similar by applying the same filter to each.

Using effects

The Effects palette lets you quickly create different looks for your images.

If an effect name is followed by (Selection), (Layer), or (Type), the effect can only be applied to a selected portion of your image, to a selected layer, or to a type layer, respectively. Some effects are automatically applied to a copy of the selected layer, while other effects can only be applied to a flattened image. You cannot preview layer effects or change options for the effects.

💡 *Many of the choices in the Effects palette are modified versions of filters—giving you a default value of a filter. See "Choosing a filter" on page 172 to decide whether to use an Effect or a Filter.*

To apply an effect:

1 Do one of the following:

• To apply an effect to an entire layer, deselect any selected areas in the image, and then select the layer in the Layers palette.

• To apply an effect to a portion of a layer, use any selection tool to select the area.

• To apply a Text effect, use the text tool to enter the text you want.

2 Do one of the following in the Effects palette:

• Double-click an effect.

• Select an effect, and click Apply.

• Drag an effect to the image.

Note: In some cases, when applying an effect to an image with multiple layers, you are prompted to flatten the image first.

Frames effects

Frames effects apply a variety of effects to the edges of a selected layer, or to a portion of a layer.

The Vignette effect, for example, creates a separate layer from a selected portion of an image. Using any selection tool, select a portion of the image and apply the Vignette effect. The results are two new layers added to the image—a white layer appearing to frame the new vignette layer. You can either flatten the image, or drag the vignette layer to another image.

Textures effects

Texture effects apply texture layers to an image. You can add texture to a new, blank image as a background, or add a texture to an existing image. By arranging layers, and working with opacity and other layer tools, you can create interesting and attractive images.

Text effects

Text effects apply text effects to text layers you have added to your image.

To apply text effects:

1 Select the text tool and type a caption or message in your image. (The text is added as a new layer.)

2 Choose a Text effect and drag it to the text in your image. You can reposition the text if needed.

Image effects

Image effects apply an effect to a copy of a selected layer. Adding the Blizzard effect to an image makes it look like it's snowing. The Neon Glow effect turns the image into a dramatic neon picture. You can use Image effects such as Oil Pastel or Soft Focus to soften colors or blur an image. You can also combine Image effects, but you may be prompted to flatten layers first.

Using layer styles

Layer styles let you quickly apply visual effects to an entire layer. You can scan through a variety of predefined layer styles in the Layer Styles palette and apply a style with just a click of the mouse.

The Layer Styles Palette, Patterns category

About layer styles

Layer styles allow you to apply visual effects—such as drop shadows and bevels—to a layer. The boundaries of the effect are automatically updated when you edit that layer. For example, if you apply a drop shadow style to a text layer, the shadow changes automatically when you edit the text.

Layer styles are cumulative, which means that you can create a complex effect by applying multiple styles to a layer. You can also change a layer's style settings to adjust the final effect.

Applying layer styles

When you apply a style to a layer, an "f" icon ⦿ appears to the right of the layer's name in the Layers palette. Layer styles are linked to the layer contents. When you move or edit the contents of the layer, the effects are modified correspondingly.

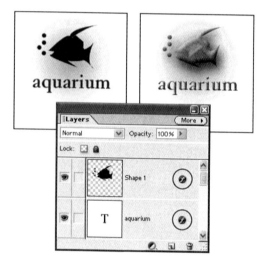

Layer style added

To remove a layer style, click the Step Backward button ↩ in the shortcuts bar.

To apply a layer style to a layer:

1 Select a layer from the Layers palette.

2 Click a style in the Layer Styles palette.

💡 *You can also drag the style to the image, where it is applied to the selected layer.*

To hide or show all layer styles in the image:

1 Choose one of the following:

• Layer > Layer Style > Hide All Effects.

• Layer > Layer Style > Show All Effects.

Editing layer styles

You can edit a layer's style settings to adjust the effect. You can also copy style settings between layers and remove a style from a layer.

To edit a layer's style settings:

1 Do one of the following:

• Double-click the "f" icon ⦿ in the Layers palette.

• Choose Layer > Layer Style > Style Settings.

2 To preview the changes in your image, select Preview.

3 Adjust one or more of the following settings, and click OK. If a setting is dimmed, it is not available for the effect you are using.

Lighting Angle Specifies the lighting angle at which the effect is applied to the layer.

Use Global Light Applies the lighting angle to all styles in the image. Using a global angle gives the appearance of a consistent light source shining on the image.

Shadow Distance Specifies the distance of a drop shadow from the layer's content.

Outer Glow Size Specifies the size of a glow that emanates from the outside edges of the layer's content.

Inner Glow Size Specifies the size of a glow that emanates from the inside edges of the layer's content.

Bevel Size Specifies the size of beveling along the inside edges of the layer's content.

Bevel Direction Specifies the direction of the bevel, either up or down.

To change the scale of a layer style:

You can only change the scale of Shadow Distance, Outer Glow or Inner Glow Size, and Bevel Size.

1 In the Layers palette, select the layer containing style effects you want to scale.

2 Choose Layer > Layer Style > Scale Effect.

3 To preview the changes in your image, select Preview.

4 Specify how much you want to scale the effects. For example, if you are increasing the size of an outer glow, 100% is the current scale; 200% doubles the glow size.

5 Click OK.

To copy style settings between layers:

1 In the Layers palette, select the layer containing the style settings you want to copy.

2 Choose Layer > Layer Style > Copy Layer Style.

3 Select the destination layer in the Layers palette, and choose Layer > Layer Style > Paste Layer Style.

To remove a layer style:

1 In the Layers palette, select the layer containing the style you want to remove.

2 Do one of the following:

• Choose Layer > Layer Style > Clear Layer Style.

• Click Clear Style in the Layer Styles palette.

Improving performance with filters and effects

Some filters and effects are memory-intensive, especially when applied to a high-resolution image. You can use these techniques to improve performance:

• Try out filters and settings on a small selected area of the image.

• Try filters and settings on a smaller, resized copy of your image. When you're satisfied with the results, apply the filter with the same settings to your original image.

• Free up memory before running the filter or effect by using the Purge command. (See "Undoing operations" on page 25.)

• Allocate more RAM to Photoshop Elements. (See "Setting memory preferences" on page 36). If necessary, exit from other applications to make more memory available to Photoshop Elements.

- Adjust filter settings to make memory-intensive filters less complex. Memory-intensive filters include Lighting Effects, Cutout, Stained Glass, Chrome, Ripple, Spatter, Sprayed Strokes, and Glass. (For example, to reduce the complexity of the Stained Glass filter, increase cell size. To reduce the complexity of the Cutout filter, increase Edge Simplicity, decrease Edge Fidelity, or both.)

Choosing a filter

The filters are grouped into categories. Any third-party filters appear at the bottom of the Filter menu.

Artistic filters

Choose an Artistic filter to simulate painterly effects on traditional media, and to create unique visual effects. For example, use the Rough Pastels filter to simulate pastels on a painter's canvas, or use Plastic Wrap to give your image a plastic sheen.

Colored Pencil Redraws an image using colored pencils on a solid background. Retains important edges and gives them a rough crosshatch appearance; the solid background color shows through the smoother areas. You can set the pencil width, stroke pressure, and paper brightness in the filter options.

For a parchment effect, change the background color before applying the Colored Pencil filter to a selected area.

Cutout Portrays an image as though it is made from roughly cut-out pieces of colored paper. High-contrast images appear as if in silhouette, while colored images are built up from several layers of colored paper. You can set the tonal levels, edge simplicity, and edge fidelity in the filter options.

Dry Brush Paints an image using a dry brush technique (between oil and watercolor). The filter simplifies an image by reducing its range of colors to areas of common color. You can set the brush size, brush detail, and texture amount in the filter options.

Film Grain Applies an even, grainy pattern to an image. Adds a smoother, more saturated pattern to the image's lighter areas. This filter is useful for eliminating banding in blends and visually unifying elements from various sources. You can set the grain amount, highlight area range, and intensity level in the filter options.

Fresco Paints a layer in a coarse style using short, rounded, and hastily applied dabs. You can set the brush size, brush detail, and texture in the filter options.

Neon Glow Uses the foreground color, background color, and glow color to colorize an image while softening its look. You can set the glow size, glow brightness, and glow color in the filter options. Lower glow size values restrict the glow color to the shadow areas, and higher values move the glow color to the midtones and highlight areas of a layer. To select a glow color, click the Glow Color box, and select a color in the color picker.

Paint Daubs Makes an image look painted. You can set the brush size, image sharpness, and brush types in the filter options.

Palette Knife Reduces detail in an image to give the effect of a thinly painted canvas that reveals the texture underneath. You can set the stroke size, stroke detail, and edge softness in the filter options.

Plastic Wrap Renders a layer as if it is coated in shiny plastic, accentuating the surface detail. You can set the highlight strength, plastic wrap detail, and plastic smoothness in the filter options.

Poster Edges Reduces the number of colors in an image according to the posterization option you set, finds the edges of the image, and draws black lines on them. Large broad areas of the image receive simple shading while fine dark details are distributed throughout the image. You can set the edge thickness, edge intensity, and posterization in the filter options.

Rough Pastels Makes an image appear as if it was stroked with colored pastel chalk on a textured background. In areas of bright color, the chalk appears thick with little texture; in darker areas, the chalk appears scraped off to reveal the texture. You can set the stroke length, stroke detail, and texture in the filter options. For more information on setting the Texture options, see "Transforming layers, selections, and shapes" on page 153.

Smudge Stick Softens an image using short diagonal strokes to smudge or smear the darker areas of the images. Lighter areas become brighter and lose detail. You can set the stroke length, highlight area, and intensity in the filter options.

Sponge Paints a layer with highly textured areas of contrasting color. You can set the brush size, image definition, and edge smoothness in the filter options.

Underpainting Paints a layer as if it exists on a textured background. You can set the brush size, texture coverage area, and texture options in the filter options.

Watercolor Paints an image in a watercolor style, simplifying details in an image by using a medium brush loaded with water and color. Where significant tonal changes occur at edges, the filter saturates colors. You can set the brush detail, shadow intensity, and texture in the filter options.

Blur filters

The Blur filters soften a selection or an image, and are useful for retouching. They smooth transitions by averaging the color values of pixels next to the hard edges of defined lines and shaded areas.

Note: Before applying a Blur filter, deselect the Lock transparent pixels option in the Layers palette. (See "Locking layers" on page 107.)

Blur and Blur More Eliminate noise where significant color transitions occur in an image. Blur filters smooth transitions by averaging the color values of pixels next to the hard edges of defined lines and shaded areas. The Blur More filter produces an effect several times stronger than that of the Blur filter.

Gaussian Blur Quickly blurs a selection by an adjustable amount. Gaussian refers to the bell-shaped curve that Photoshop Elements generates when it applies a weighted average to the pixels. The Gaussian Blur filter adds low-frequency detail and can produce a hazy effect. You can set the blur radius in the filter options to determine how far the filter searches for dissimilar pixels to blur.

Motion Blur Blurs in a particular direction (from −360º to +360º) and at a specific distance (from 1 to 999). The filter's effect is analogous to taking a picture of a moving object with a fixed exposure time. You can set the blur angle, and distance in the filter options.

Radial Blur Simulates the blur of a zooming or rotating camera to produce a soft blur. Drag the Amount slider to control the blur amount. Choose Spin to blur along concentric circular lines, and then specify a degree of rotation; or choose Zoom, to blur along radial lines, as if zooming in or out of the image, and then specify an amount from 1 to 100. Blur quality ranges from Draft for fast but grainy results to Good and Best for smoother results, which are indistinguishable except on a large selection. Specify the origin of the blur by dragging the pattern in the Blur Center box.

Smart Blur Precisely blurs an image. You can specify a radius to determine how far the filter searches for dissimilar pixels to blur, a threshold to determine how different the pixels' values must be before they are eliminated, and a blur quality. You also can set a mode for the entire selection (Normal) or for the edges of color transitions (Edge Only and Overlay Edge). Where significant contrast occurs, Edge Only applies black-and-white edges, and Overlay Edge applies white.

Brush Stroke filters

Like several of the Artistic filters, the Brush Stroke filters give a painterly or fine-arts look using different brush and ink stroke effects. Some of the filters add grain, paint, noise, edge detail, or texture to an image for a pointillist effect.

Accented Edges Accentuates the edges of an image. When the edge brightness control is set to a high value, the accents resemble white chalk; when set to a low value, the accents resemble black ink. You can set the edge width, edge brightness, and smoothness in the filter options.

Angled Strokes Repaints an image using diagonal strokes. The lighter areas of the image are painted in strokes going in one direction, while the darker areas are painted in strokes going the opposite direction. You can set the stroke direction balance, stroke length, and sharpness in the filter options.

Crosshatch Preserves the details and features of the original image while adding texture and roughening the edges of the colored areas in the image with simulated pencil hatching. You can set the stroke length, sharpness, and strength (the number of hatching passes) in the filter options.

Dark Strokes Paints dark areas of an image closer to black with short, tight strokes, and paints lighter areas of the layer with long, white strokes. You can set the stroke balance, and black and white intensity levels in the filter options.

Ink Outlines Redraws an image with fine narrow lines over the original details, in pen-and-ink style. You can set the stroke length, and dark and light intensity levels in the filter options.

Spatter Replicates the effect of a spatter airbrush. You can set the spray radius, and smoothness in the filter options.

Sprayed Strokes Repaints a layer using its dominant colors with angled, sprayed strokes of color. You can set the stroke length, spray radius, and stroke direction in the filter options.

Sumi-e Redraws a layer with a Japanese style, as if with a wet brush full of black ink on rice paper. The effect is soft blurry edges with rich blacks. You can set stroke width, stroke pressure, and contrast in the filter options.

Distort filters

The Distort filters geometrically distort an image, creating three-dimensional or other reshaping effects. Note that these filters can be very memory-intensive.

See "Transforming layers, selections, and shapes" on page 153 for more information about using the Distort filters.

Noise filters

The Noise filters add or remove *noise*, or pixels with randomly distributed color levels. This helps to blend a selection into the surrounding pixels. Noise filters can create unusual textures or remove problem areas, such as dust and scratches, from an image.

Add Noise Applies random pixels to an image, simulating the effect of shooting pictures on high-speed film. The Add Noise filter can also be used to reduce banding in feathered selections or graduated fills, to give a more realistic look to heavily retouched areas, or to create a textured layer. You can set the amount of noise, the type of noise distribution, and color mode in the filter options.

Uniform creates a subtle distribution effect, and Gaussian creates a speckled distribution effect. The Monochromatic option applies the filter using the existing tones of the image without changing the colors.

Despeckle Detects the edges in a layer (areas where significant color changes occur) and blurs all of the selection except those edges. This blurring removes noise while preserving detail. You can use this filter to remove banding or visual noise that often appear in scans of magazines or other printed materials.

Dust & Scratches Reduces visual noise by changing dissimilar pixels. See "Using the Dust & Scratches filter" on page 71.

Median Reduces noise in a layer by blending the brightness of pixels within a selection. The filter searches for pixels of similar brightness, discarding pixels that differ too much from adjacent pixels, and replaces the center pixel with the median brightness value of the searched pixels. This filter is useful for eliminating or reducing the effect of motion on an image, or undesirable patterns that may appear in a scanned image.

Pixelate filters

The Pixelate filters sharply define an image or selection by clumping pixels of similar color values.

Color Halftone Simulates the effect of using an enlarged halftone screen on the layer. The filter divides the image into rectangles and replaces each rectangle with a circle. The circle size is proportional to the brightness of the rectangle.

To use the Color Halftone filter:

1 Either choose Filter > Pixelate > Color Halftone, or use the Filters palette to apply the Color Halftone filter. (If using the palette, select Filter Options before applying the filter.)

2 Enter a value for the maximum radius of a halftone dot, from 4 to 127 pixels.

3 Enter a screen-angle value between -360 and 360 (the angle of the dot from the true horizontal) for one or more channels:

- For Grayscale images, enter a value in channel 1. Values in the other channel text boxes do not affect the filter.

- For color images, use channels 1, 2, 3, and 4, which correspond to CMYK channels (Cyan, Magenta, Yellow, and Black).

- Click Defaults to return all the screen angles to their default values.

4 Click OK.

Crystallize Redraws a layer as polygon-shaped clumps of color. You can set the cell size of the crystals in the filter options.

Facet Redraws a layer as blocks of solid color. You can use this filter to make a scanned image look hand painted or to make a realistic image resemble an abstract painting.

Fragment Redraws a layer so it appears offset and blurred.

Mezzotint Redraws a layer as a random pattern of black-and-white areas in a grayscale image, or fully saturated colors in a color image. You can choose a dot, line, or stroke pattern in the filter options.

Mosaic Redraws a layer as square blocks of color. You can set the mosaic cell size in the filter options.

Pointillize Redraws a layer as randomly placed dots, as in a pointillist painting, and uses the background color in the toolbox as a canvas area between the dots. You can set the cell size in the filter options.

Render filters

The Render filters create 3D shapes, cloud patterns, refraction patterns, and simulated light reflections in an image. You can also manipulate objects in 3D space, create 3D objects (cubes, spheres, and cylinders), and create texture fills from grayscale files to produce 3D-like effects for lighting.

3D Transform Maps images to cubes, spheres, and cylinders, which you can then rotate in three dimensions. (See "Transforming objects in three dimensions" on page 157.)

Clouds Generates a soft cloud pattern using random values that vary between the foreground and the background color in the toolbar.

To generate a starker cloud pattern, hold down Alt (Windows) or Option (Mac OS) as you choose Filter > Render > Clouds.

Difference Clouds Uses randomly generated values that vary between the foreground and background color in the toolbox to produce a cloud pattern. The first time you choose this filter, portions of the image are inverted in a cloud pattern. Applying the filter several times creates rib and vein patterns that resemble a marble texture.

Lens Flare Simulates the light refraction caused by shining a bright light into a camera lens. You can set the flare brightness, flare location, and flare shape (the lens type) in the filter options. Click inside the preview window in the dialog box to set the flare location.

Lighting Effects Lets you produce myriad lighting effects on RGB images by varying 17 light styles, three light types, and four sets of light properties. You can also use textures from grayscale files called *texture maps* to produce 3D-like effects, and save your own styles for use in other images. (See "Using the Lighting Effects filter" on page 177.)

Using the Lighting Effects filter

The Lighting Effects filter lets you produce sophisticated lighting effects on RGB images. You can create multiple lights, set individual light properties, and easily drag lights around in the preview window to test different lighting setups. You can also use textures from grayscale files called *texture maps* to produce 3D-like effects, and save your own styles for use in other images.

To use the Lighting Effects filter:

1 Either choose Filter > Render > Lighting Effects, or use the Filters palette to apply the Lighting Effects filter. (If using the palette, select Filter Options before applying the filter.)

2 Choose a lighting effects style from the Style menu.

 For more information, see "Choosing a Lighting Effects style" in online Help.

Note: *If the style you choose has multiple lights, you must select and set the options for each light individually.*

3 Choose a Light Type from the pop-up menu. For more information on adjusting lights in the preview window, see "Adjusting omni lights, directional lights, and spotlights" on page 178.

4 If your lighting effects style uses multiple lights, you can turn a light off by selecting it in the preview window and deselecting On.

5 To add or remove lights in the preview window, see "Creating and deleting lights" on page 179.

6 Drag the Intensity and Focus sliders to decrease or increase these values.

7 To change the color of the light, click the color box in the Light Type section of the dialog box to display the Color Picker.

8 To set light properties, drag the corresponding slider for the following options:

• Gloss determines how much the surface reflects light, from Matte (low reflectance) to Shiny (high reflectance).

- Material determines whether the light or the object on which the light is cast reflects more light. Plastic reflects the light's color; Metallic reflects the object's color.

- Exposure increases the light (positive values) or decreases the light (negative values). A value of 0 has no effect.

- Ambience diffuses the light as if it were combined with other light in a room, such as sunlight or fluorescent light. Choose a value of 100 to use only the light source, or a value of −100 to completely diffuse the light source. To change the color of the ambient light, click the color box and use the Color Picker that appears.

9 To use a texture map, choose a color or layer from the Texture Channel pop-up menu.

The Texture Channel option lets you manipulate how light reflects off an image. You can create a texture effect based on the light and dark areas of the red, green, and blue color information in your image. You can also choose to use the layer transparency of the active layer to create a texture effect.

10 Select White Is High to raise the light parts of the channel from the surface. Deselect this option to raise the dark parts.

11 Drag the Height slider to vary the depth of the texture from Flat (0) to Mountainous (100).

12 Click OK.

Adjusting omni lights, directional lights, and spotlights

You can choose from several light types.

- Omni shines light in all directions from directly above the image—like a light bulb over a piece of paper.

- Directional shines light from one angle—like the parallel light rays of the sun.

- Spotlight casts an elliptical beam of light. The line in the preview window defines the light direction and angle, and the handles define the edges of the ellipse.

To adjust an Omni light:

Do any of the following:

- To move the light, drag the center circle.

- To increase or decrease the size of the light (like a light moving closer or farther away), drag one of the handles defining the edges of the light.

To adjust the angle and height of the Directional light using the preview window:

Do any of the following:

- To move the light, drag the center circle.

- To change the direction of the light, drag the handle at the end of the line to rotate the light's angle. Ctrl-drag (Windows) or Command-drag (Mac OS) to keep the light's height constant.

- To change the light's height, drag the handle at the end of the line. Shorten the line for a bright light, lengthen it for a less intense one. A very short line produces pure white light, a very long one no light. Shift-drag to keep the angle constant and change the light's height (line length).

To adjust the angle and height of the Spotlight using the preview window:

Do any of the following:

- To move the light, drag the center circle.

- To increase the light angle, drag the handle at the end of the line to shorten the line. To decrease the light angle, drag to lengthen the line.

- To stretch the ellipse or rotate the light, drag one of the handles. Shift-drag to keep the angle constant and change only the size of the ellipse. Ctrl-drag (Windows) or Command-drag (Mac OS) to keep the size constant and change the angle or direction of the spotlight.

- To set the light focus (or spotlight intensity) and control how much of an ellipse is filled with light, drag the Intensity slider: a full intensity value of 100 is brightest; normal intensity is about 50; 0 intensity produces no light; and negative intensity takes away light. Use the Focus slider to control how much of the ellipse is filled with light.

Creating and deleting lights

You can create your own lighting style by adding lights to an existing style or removing lights. The Lighting Effects filter requires at least one light source.

To add a light:

Do one of the following in the Lighting Effects dialog box:

- To create a new light, drag the light icon at the bottom of the dialog box into the preview area. Repeat as desired for a maximum of 16 lights.

- To copy an existing light, select a light in the preview window, press Alt (Windows) or Option (Mac OS), and drag to a new location.

To delete a light:

Do one of the following in the Lighting Effects dialog box:

- Select a light in the preview window, and press delete on the keyboard.

- Drag a light by its center circle to the Trash button at the bottom right of the preview window.

To save a lighting style:

1 In the Lighting Effects dialog box, click Save.

2 Name the style, and then click OK.

Saved styles include all of the settings for each light and appear in the Style menu whenever you open an image in Photoshop Elements.

To delete a style:

In the Lighting Effects dialog box, choose a style, and then click Delete.

Note: Default styles cannot be deleted.

Sharpen filters

The Sharpen filters focus blurry images by increasing the contrast of adjacent pixels.

Sharpen and Sharpen More Add focus to a selection and improve its clarity. The Sharpen More filter applies a stronger sharpening effect than the Sharpen filter.

Sharpen Edges and Unsharp Mask Find the areas in the image where significant color changes occur and sharpen them. The Sharpen Edges filter sharpens only edges while preserving the overall smoothness of the image. Use this filter to sharpen edges without specifying an amount. For professional color correction, use the Unsharp Mask filter to adjust the contrast of edge detail and produce a lighter and darker line on each side of the edge. This process emphasizes the edge to create the illusion of a sharper image. (See "Using the Unsharp Mask filter to sharpen photos" on page 180.)

Using the Unsharp Mask filter to sharpen photos

Unsharp masking, or *USM,* is a traditional film technique used to sharpen edges in an image. The Unsharp Mask filter corrects blurring introduced during photographing, scanning, resampling, or printing. It is useful for images intended for both print and online viewing.

Unsharp Mask locates pixels that differ from surrounding pixels by the threshold you specify and increases the pixels' contrast by the amount you specify. In addition, you specify the radius of the region to which each pixel is compared. The effects of the Unsharp Mask filter are far more pronounced on-screen than in high-resolution printed output. If your final destination is printed output, experiment to determine what settings work best for your image.

For information on other filters for sharpening images, see "Sharpen filters" on page 179.

To use Unsharp Mask to sharpen an image:

1 Choose Filter > Sharpen > Unsharp Mask, and select the Preview option.

Click the preview window in the Unsharp Mask dialog box window to see how the image looks without sharpening. Drag in the preview window to see different parts of the image, and click + or – to zoom in or out.

2 Do one of the following:

• Drag the Amount slider or enter a value to determine how much to increase the contrast of pixels. For high-resolution printed images, an amount between 150% and 200% is usually recommended.

• Drag the Radius slider or enter a value to determine the number of pixels to sharpen around edges. For high-resolution images, a radius between 1 and 2 is usually recommended. A lower value sharpens only the edge pixels, whereas a higher value sharpens a wider band of pixels. This effect is much less noticeable in print than on-screen, because a 2-pixel radius represents a smaller area in a high-resolution printed image.

• Drag the Threshold slider or enter a value to determine how different pixels must be from the surrounding area before they are considered edge pixels and sharpened. To avoid introducing noise (in images with flesh tones, for example), experiment with Threshold values between 2 and 20. The default Threshold value (0) sharpens all pixels in the image.

3 Click OK.

Sketch filters

Filters in the Sketch submenu add texture to images, often for a 3D effect. These filters are also useful for creating a fine-art or hand-drawn look. Many of the Sketch filters use the foreground and background color as they redraw the image.

Bas Relief Transforms an image to appear carved in low relief and lit to accent the surface variations. Dark areas of the image take on the foreground color, light areas use the background color. You can set relief detail and smoothness in the filter options.

Chalk & Charcoal Redraws an image's highlights and midtones with a solid midtone gray background drawn in coarse chalk. Shadow areas are replaced with black diagonal charcoal lines. The charcoal is drawn in the foreground color, the chalk in the background color. You can set stroke pressure, and the charcoal and chalk areas in the filter options.

Charcoal Redraws an image to create a smudged effect. Major edges are boldly drawn, while midtones are sketched using a diagonal stroke. Charcoal is the foreground color, and the paper is the background color. You can set the charcoal thickness, level of image detail, and light/dark balance in the filter options.

Chrome Gives the image a polished chrome surface using highlights as high points and shadows as low points in the reflecting surface. You can set the level of chrome surface detail and smoothness in the filter options.

After applying the Chrome filter, use the Levels dialog box to add more contrast to the image. (For more information on adjusting levels, see "Using the Levels dialog box" on page 62.)

Conté Crayon Replicates the texture of dense dark and pure white Conté crayons on an image. The Conté Crayon filter uses the foreground color for dark areas and the background color for light areas. In the filter options, you can set the level of foreground and background emphasis, and texture options. For more information on setting the texture options, see "Using texture and glass surface controls" on page 167.

For a more realistic effect, change the foreground color to one of the common Conté Crayon colors (black, sepia, sanguine) before applying this filter. For a muted effect, change the background color to white with some foreground color added to it.

Graphic Pen Uses fine, linear ink strokes to capture the details in the original image and is especially striking with scanned images. The filter replaces color in the original image, using the foreground color for ink and background color for paper. You can set the stroke length and direction, and the light/dark balance in the filter options.

Halftone Pattern Simulates the effect of a halftone screen while maintaining the continuous range of tones. You can set the halftone size, contrast, and pattern type in the filter options.

Note Paper Simulates the texture of handmade paper by combining the effects of the Emboss and Grain filters. Dark areas of the image appear as holes in the top layer of paper, revealing the background color. You can set the image balance, graininess, and relief in the filter options.

Photocopy Simulates the effect of photocopying an image. Large areas of darkness tend to copy only around their edges, and midtones fall away to either solid black or white. You can set the level of detail and darkness in the filter options.

Plaster Molds the layer into a 3D plaster effect, and then colorizes the result using the foreground and background color. Dark areas are raised, light areas are sunken. You can set the image balance, smoothness, and light direction in the filter options.

Reticulation Simulates the controlled shrinking and distorting of film emulsion to create an image that appears clumped in the shadow areas and lightly grained in the highlights. You can set the density, foreground, and background levels in the filter options.

Stamp Is best used with black-and-white images. Simplifies the image so it appears stamped with a rubber or wood stamp. In the filter options, you can set the smoothness, and the balance between light and dark.

Torn Edges Is particularly useful for images consisting of text or high-contrast objects. Reconstructs the image as ragged, torn pieces of paper, and then colorizes the image using the foreground and background color. You can set the image balance, smoothness, and contrast in the filter options.

Water Paper Uses blotchy daubs that appear to be painted onto fibrous, damp paper, causing the colors to flow and blend. You can set the paper's fiber length, brightness, and contrast in the filter options.

Stylize filters

The Stylize filters produce a painted or impressionistic effect on a selection by displacing pixels and heightening contrast in an image.

Diffuse Shuffles pixels in a selection to make the selection look less focused according to the option you select: Normal moves pixels randomly, ignoring color values; Darken Only replaces light pixels with darker pixels; Lighten Only replaces dark pixels with lighter pixels; and Anistropic softens all pixels.

Emboss Makes a selection appear raised or stamped by converting its fill color to gray and tracing the edges with the original fill color. You can set the embossing angle, height, and a percentage for the amount of color within the selection.

Extrude Gives a 3D texture to a selection or layer. See "Extrude Filter" on page 183 for more information.

Find Edges Identifies areas of the image with significant transitions and emphasizes edges. Like the Trace Counter filter, Find Edges outlines the edges of an image with dark lines against a white background and is useful for creating a border around an image.

After using filters like Find Edges and Trace Contour that highlight edges, you can apply the Invert command to outline the edges of a color image with colored lines or a grayscale image with white lines (see "Using the Invert command" on page 186.)

Glowing Edges Identifies the edges of color and adds a neon-like glow to them. You can set the edge width, brightness, and smoothness in the filter options.

Solarize Blends a negative and a positive image—similar to exposing a photographic print briefly to light during development.

Tiles Breaks up an image into a series of tiles, offsetting the selection from its original position. In the filter options, you can set the number of tiles and the offset percentage. You can also choose one of the following to fill the empty area between the tiles: Background Color, Foreground Color, Inverse Image, or Unaltered Image, which puts the tiled version on top of the original and reveals part of the original image underneath the tiled edges.

Wind Creates tiny horizontal lines in the image to simulate a wind effect. You can set the wind strength and direction in the filter options.

Extrude Filter

The Extrude filter gives a three-dimensional texture to a selection or layer.

To use the Extrude filter:

1 Either choose Filter > Stylize > Extrude, or use the Filters palette to apply the Extrude filter. (If using the palette, select Filter Options before applying the filter.)

2 Choose a 3D type:

- Blocks creates objects with a square front face and four side faces.

- Pyramids creates objects with four triangular sides that meet at a point.

3 Enter a value in the Size text box to determine the length of the object's base, from 2 to 255 pixels.

4 Enter a value in the Depth text box to indicate how far the tallest object appears to protrude from the screen, from 1 to 255.

5 Choose a depth option:

- Random to give each block or pyramid an arbitrary depth.

- Level-based to make each object's depth correspond to its brightness—bright objects protrude more than dark.

6 Select Solid Front Faces to fill the front face of each block with an averaged color of the block. Deselect Solid Front Faces to fill the front face of each block with the image. This option is not available for Pyramids.

7 Select Mask Incomplete Blocks to hide any object extending beyond the selection.

8 Click OK.

Trace Contour

Trace Contour finds the transitions of major brightness areas and thinly outlines them for an effect similar to the lines in a contour map.

To use the Trace Contour filter:

1 Either choose Filter > Stylize > Trace Contour, or use the Filters palette to apply the Trace Contour filter. (If using the palette, select Filter Options before applying the filter.)

2 Select an Edge option to outline areas in the selection: Lower outlines where the color values of pixels fall below the specified level, and Upper outlines where the color values fall above.

3 Drag the Level slider to specify the edge level for evaluating color values. Experiment to see what values bring out the best detail in the image.

💡 *Use the Info palette in Grayscale mode to identify a color value that you want traced. Then enter the value in the Level text box. (See "Using the Info palette" on page 17.)*

4 Click OK.

Texture filters

Use the Texture filters to give an image the appearance of depth or substance, or to add an organic look.

Craquelure Paints an image onto a high-relief plaster surface, producing a fine network of cracks that follow the contours of the image. Use this filter to create an embossing effect with images that contain a broad range of color or grayscale values. You can set crack spacing, depth, and brightness in the filter options.

Grain Adds texture to an image by simulating different kinds of grain. The sprinkles and stippled grain types use the background color. You can set grain intensity, contrast, and type in the filter options.

Mosaic Tiles Draws the image as if it were made up of small chips or tiles and adds grout between the tiles. (In contrast, the Pixelate > Mosaic filter breaks up an image into blocks of different-colored pixels.) You can set the tile size, grout width, and grout highlights in the filter options.

Patchwork Breaks up an image into squares filled with the predominant color in different areas of the image. The filter randomly reduces or increases the tile depth to replicate the highlights and shadows. You can set the square size and relief in the Patchwork filter options.

Stained Glass Repaints an image as single-colored adjacent cells outlined in the foreground color. You can set cell size, border thickness, and light intensity in the filter options.

Texturizer Allows you to simulate different texture types or select a file to use as a texture. (For more information on setting texture options, see "Using texture and glass surface controls" on page 167.)

Video filters

The Video filters restrict the gamut of colors to those acceptable for television reproduction, and smooth moving images captured on video.

De-Interlace Smooths moving images captured on video by removing either the odd or even inter-laced lines in a video image. You can choose to replace the discarded lines by duplication or inter-polation.

NTSC Colors Restricts the gamut of colors to those acceptable for television reproduction to prevent oversaturated colors from bleeding across television scan lines.

Other filters

Filters in the Other submenu let you create your own filter effects, use filters to modify masks, offset a selection within an image, and make quick color adjustments.

Custom Lets you design your own filter effect. With the Custom filter, you can change the brightness values of each pixel in the image according to a predefined mathematical operation known as *convolution*. Each pixel is reassigned a value based on the values of surrounding pixels.

You can save the custom filters you create and use them with other Photoshop images.

To apply a Custom filter effect:

1 Either choose Filter > Other > Custom, or use the Filters palette to apply the Custom filter. (If using the palette, select Filter Options before applying the filter.)

2 Select the center text box, which represents the pixel being evaluated. Enter the value by which you want to multiply that pixel's brightness value, from –999 to +999.

3 Select a text box representing an adjacent pixel. Enter the value by which you want the pixel in this position multiplied.

For example, to multiply the brightness value of the pixel to the immediate right of the current pixel by 2, enter 2 in the text box to the immediate right of the center text box.

Note: To avoid turning the image completely white or black, the sum of the values in the matrix should equal 1.

4 Repeat steps 2 and 3 for all pixels you want to include in the operation. You don't have to enter values in all the text boxes.

5 For Scale, enter the value by which to divide the sum of the brightness values of the pixels included in the calculation.

6 For Offset, enter the value to be added to the result of the scale calculation.

7 Click OK. The custom filter is applied to each pixel in the image, one at a time.

Use the Save and Load buttons to save and reuse custom filters.

High Pass Retains edge details in the specified radius where sharp color transitions occur and suppresses the rest of the image. (A radius of 0.1 pixel keeps only edge pixels.) The filter removes low-frequency detail in an image and has an effect opposite to that of the Gaussian Blur filter.

This filter is useful for extracting line art and large black-and-white areas from scanned images. When doing so, apply the High Pass filter before using the Image > Adjustment > Threshold command or converting the image to Bitmap mode.

Minimum and Maximum The Minimum filter has the effect of applying a spread—spreading out black areas and shrinking white areas. The Maximum filter has the effect of applying a choke—spreading out white areas and choking in black areas. Like the Median filter, the Maximum and Minimum filters look at individual pixels in a selection. Within a specified radius, the Maximum and Minimum filters replace the current pixel's brightness value with the greatest or least brightness value of the surrounding pixels.

Offset Moves a selection a specified amount to the right horizontally or down vertically, leaving an empty space at the selection's original location. Depending on the size of the selection, you can fill the empty area with a transparent background, with the edge pixels, or with pixels from the right or bottom edges of an image. (See "Defining undistorted areas" on page 167.)

About plug-in filters

You can install plug-in filters developed by non-Adobe software developers. Once installed, the plug-in filters appear at the bottom of the Filter menu unless the developer has specified another location. For previews to appear in the Filters palette, plug-in filters must be specially designed for Photoshop Elements.

If you are interested in creating plug-in modules, contact Adobe Systems Developer Support. (See "Using plug-in modules" on page 35.)

Note: *If you have problems or questions about a third-party plug-in, contact the plug-in's manufacturer for support.*

Applying special color effects to images

The Invert, Equalize, Threshold, and Posterize commands change colors or brightness values in an image but are typically used for enhancing color and producing special effects, rather than for correcting color.

Using the Invert command

The Invert command inverts the colors in an image. You might use this command to make a positive black-and-white image negative or to make a positive from a scanned black-and-white negative.

Note: *Because color print film contains an orange mask in its base, the Invert command cannot make accurate positive images from scanned color negatives. Be sure to use the proper settings for color negatives when scanning film on slide scanners.*

When you invert an image, the brightness value of each pixel in the channels is converted to the inverse value on the 256-step color-values scale. For example, a pixel in a positive image with a value of 255 is changed to 0, and a pixel with a value of 5 is changed to 250.

To use the Invert command:

Do one of the following:

• Choose Image > Adjustments > Invert.

• Create an Invert adjustment layer. (See "Using adjustment and fill layers" on page 101.)

Using the Equalize command

The Equalize command redistributes the brightness values of the pixels in an image so that they more evenly represent the entire range of brightness levels. When you apply this command, Photoshop Elements finds the brightest and darkest values in the composite image and remaps them so that the brightest value represents white and the darkest value represents black. Photoshop Elements then attempts to equalize the brightness—that is, to distribute the intermediate pixel values evenly throughout the grayscale.

You might use the Equalize command when a scanned image appears darker than the original and you want to balance the values to produce a lighter image. Using Equalize together with the Histogram command lets you see before-and-after brightness comparisons.

To use the Equalize command:

1 Choose Image > Adjustments > Equalize.

2 If you selected an area of the image, select what to equalize in the dialog box, and click OK:

• Equalize Selected Area Only to evenly distribute only the selection's pixels.

• Equalize Entire Image Based on Selected Area to evenly distribute all image pixels based on those in the selection.

Using the Threshold command

The Threshold command converts grayscale or color images to high-contrast, black-and-white images. You can specify a certain level as a threshold. All pixels lighter than the threshold are converted to white; and all pixels darker are converted to black. The Threshold command is useful for determining the lightest and darkest areas of an image.

To use the Threshold command to convert images to black and white:

1 Do one of the following:

• Choose Image > Adjustments > Threshold.

• Create a new Threshold adjustment layer, or open an existing Threshold adjustment layer. (See "Using adjustment and fill layers" on page 101.)

The Threshold dialog box displays a histogram of the luminance levels of the pixels in the current selection.

2 Drag the slider below the histogram until the threshold level you want appears at the top of the dialog box, and click OK. As you drag, the image changes to reflect the new threshold setting.

To use the Threshold command to identify representative highlights and shadows:

1 Open the Threshold dialog box.

2 Select Preview.

3 To identify a representative highlight, drag the slider to the far right until the image becomes pure black. Drag the slider slowly toward the center until some solid white areas appear in the image.

4 To identify a representative shadow, drag the slider to the far left until the image becomes pure white. Drag the slider slowly toward the center until some solid black areas appear in the image. These represent the darkest pixels areas in the image.

5 Reset the dialog box by pressing Alt (Windows) or Option (Mac OS).

6 Click Cancel to close the Threshold dialog box without applying changes to the image.

Using the Posterize command

The Posterize command lets you specify the number of tonal levels (or brightness values) for each channel in an image and then maps pixels to the closest matching level. For example, choosing two tonal levels in an RGB image gives six colors, two for red, two for green, and two for blue.

This command is useful for creating special effects, such as large, flat areas in a photograph. Its effects are most evident when you reduce the number of gray levels in a grayscale image. But it also produces interesting effects in color images.

💡 *If you want a specific number of colors in your image, convert the image to grayscale and specify the number of levels you want. Then convert the image back to the previous color mode, and replace the various gray tones with the colors you want.*

To use the Posterize command:

1 Do one of the following:

• Choose Image > Adjustments > Posterize.

• Create a new Posterize adjustment layer, or open an existing Posterize adjustment layer. (See "Using adjustment and fill layers" on page 101.)

2 Enter the number of tonal levels you want, and click OK.

Using the Gradient Map command

The Gradient Map command maps the equivalent grayscale range of an image to the colors of a specified gradient fill. If you specify a two-color gradient fill, for example, shadows in the image map to one of the endpoint colors of the gradient fill, highlights map to the other endpoint color, and midtones map to the gradations in between.

To use the Gradient Map command:

1 Do one of the following:

• Choose Image > Adjustments > Gradient Map.

• Create a new Gradient Map adjustment layer, or open an existing Gradient Map adjustment layer. (See "Using adjustment and fill layers" on page 101.)

2 Specify the gradient fill you want to use:

• To choose from a list of gradient fills, click the triangle to the right of the gradient fill displayed in the Gradient Map dialog box. Click to select the desired gradient fill, and then click in a blank area of the dialog box to dismiss the list. (See "Working with preset options" on page 27 for information on customizing the gradient fill list.)

• To edit the gradient fill currently displayed in the Gradient Map dialog box, click the gradient fill. Then modify the existing gradient fill or create a new gradient fill. (See "Creating or editing gradient fills" on page 148.)

By default, the shadows, midtones, and highlights of the image are mapped respectively to the starting (left) color, midpoint, and ending (right) color of the gradient fill.

3 Select either, none, or both of the Gradient Options:

• Dither adds random noise to smooth the appearance of the gradient fill and reduce banding effects.

• Reverse switches the direction of the gradient fill, reversing the gradient map.

4 Click OK.

Chapter 11: Creating Shapes and Text

Adobe Photoshop Elements lets you add text and shapes to images with flexibility and precision.

About vector graphics

In Photoshop Elements, shapes and text are *vector* graphics, which means they are made up of lines and curves defined by their geometric characteristics. Vector graphics are resolution-independent—that is, they can be scaled to any size and printed at any resolution without losing detail or clarity. You can move, resize, or change them without losing the quality of the graphic.

Because computer monitors display images on a pixel grid, vector data is displayed as pixels on-screen.

Composition using vector objects, including text and shapes found in Photoshop Elements

About shapes

You use the shape tools to draw lines, rectangles, rounded rectangles, polygons, ellipses, and custom shapes in an image. You can change the color of a shape by editing its fill layer and applying layer styles to it.

💡 *The shape tools provide an easy way to create buttons, navigation bars, and other items used on Web pages.*

Shapes are created in shape layers. A shape layer can contain a single shape or multiple shapes, depending on the shape area option you select.

If you want a new shape to be in its own layer, make sure Create new shape layer ▪ is selected in the options bar. You can also choose to have more than one shape in a layer (see "Creating multiple shapes in one layer" on page 192).

Creating shapes

You create shapes by selecting one of the shape tools, and then dragging in your image. The shape tools are located in the options bar and in the toolbox, where the active shape tool is visible and the rest are hidden. To select a hidden shape tool, position the pointer on the visible tool and hold down the mouse button until the tools list appears. Then click the tool you want.

In the options bar, you can choose the following options for the shape tools:

- Click the color swatch to choose the color with which you want to fill the shape. (See "Using the Adobe Color Picker" on page 131.)

- Set tool-specific options. (See "Setting shape tool options" on page 195.)

To create a rectangle:

1 Select the rectangle tool ▭.

2 Drag in your image to draw the rectangle.

To create a rounded rectangle:

1 Select the rounded rectangle tool ▢.

2 Enter a value in the Radius text box in the options bar to determine the radius of the curved corners of the rounded rectangle.

3 Drag in your image to draw the rounded rectangle.

To create an ellipse:

1 Select the ellipse tool ◯.

2 Drag in your image to draw the ellipse.

To create a polygon:

1 Select the polygon tool ◯.

2 In the options bar, enter the number of sides in your polygon in the Sides text box.

3 Drag in your image to draw the polygon.

To create a line:

1 Select the line tool ＼.

2 In the options bar, enter a pixel width for the line in the Weight text box.

3 Drag in your image to draw the line.

Creating custom shapes

The custom shape tool ▱ provides many different shape options for you to use in your images. When you select the custom shape tool, you can access these shapes from the Shape pop-up palette in the options bar.

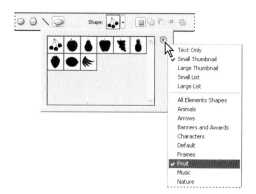

Custom shape tool pop-up menu

To create a custom shape:

1 Select the custom shape tool ▱.

2 In the options bar, select a shape from the Shape pop-up palette.

3 Drag in your image to draw the shape.

Creating multiple shapes in one layer

You can create multiple shapes in one layer by changing a few settings in the options bar.

To create multiple shapes in the same layer:

1 Select a shape layer in the Layers palette or create a new shape layer.

2 If you want to create a different type of shape, select a different shape tool.

3 Before you draw, select a shape area option to determine how shapes should overlap:

- Add to add an additional shape to the existing shape. The combined shape will cover the entire area of the shapes you drew using the Add option.

- Subtract to remove the area where shapes overlap. The rest of the shapes' areas are be preserved.

- Intersect to show only the area where shapes intersect. The other areas will be removed.

- Exclude to remove the overlapping areas in the consolidated new and existing shape areas.

4 Drag in the image to draw new shapes.

Editing shapes

You can select, move, and combine shapes, change the color of shapes, and apply layer styles to shapes with just a few clicks. You can also simplify a shape layer to convert it to a bitmap layer.

Changing the color of shapes

You can change the color of a shape by double-clicking its thumbnail in the Layers palette.

To change the color of all shapes on a layer:

1 In the Layers palette, double-click the shape layer.

2 Use the Color Picker to select a new color. (See "Using the Adobe Color Picker" on page 131.)

If the color of a shape doesn't change when you pick a new color for it, check to see if the layer has a layer style (represented by an "f" icon in the Layers palette). Some layer styles override the base color of a shape. For information on clearing layer styles, see "Editing layer styles" on page 170.

Using the shape selection tool

The shape selection tool allows you to select shapes with one click. After you select a shape, you can move, resize, and rotate the shape.

Note: After you convert a shape to a bitmap image by simplifying the layer, the shape selection tool will no longer select the shape. You can still move the entire simplified layer using the move tool.

To use the shape selection tool:

Do one of the following:

- Select the shape selection tool in the toolbox.

- If another shape tool is active, click the shape selection tool in the options bar.

Moving shapes

If a layer contains multiple shapes, you can reposition all the shapes together using the move tool. However, if you want to reposition a specific shape in a layer, you must use the shape selection tool.

To move a shape:

1 Select the shape selection tool .

2 Drag the shape to a new position in the image.

Transforming shapes

You can alter a shape by applying transformations to it. For example, you can scale, rotate, skew, distort, and apply perspective to a shape.

To transform a shape:

1 Select the shape selection tool ⬧.

2 Do one of the following:

- Double-click the shape you want to transform.

- Select the shape you want to transform, choose Image > Transform Shape, and choose a transformation command.

3 Transform the shape as described in "Transforming objects in three dimensions" on page 157.

Simplifying shape layers

Simplifying a shape layer converts it to a regular bitmap layer. Simplifying a layer is necessary when you want to paint on a shape or apply filters to it.

To simplify a shape layer:

1 Select a shape layer in the Layers palette.

2 Do one of the following:

- Choose Layer > Simplify Layer.

- If a shape tool is selected, click Simplify in the options bar.

Applying layer styles to shapes

You can apply effects—such as drop shadows and bevels—to shapes quickly and easily using layer styles. Keep in mind that a layer style is applied to all shapes on a layer. For example, if you apply a drop shadow style to a layer that contains multiple shapes, all of the shapes will display a drop shadow.

Original vector art (left) and the same art with a style applied to the leaf layer (right)

To apply a layer style to a shape:

1 Select the shape with the shape selection tool. (See "Using the shape selection tool" on page 193.)

2 Click the Layer Styles thumbnail in the options bar.

3 Scroll through the layer styles in the palette. To view additional layer styles, choose a category from the drop-down list.

4 Apply the style to the shape:

- Drag a style from the pop-up palette onto a shape in the image.

- Click a style to apply it to the shape layer.

Setting shape tool options

Each shape tool provides specific options; for example, you can set options that allow you to draw a rectangle with fixed dimensions or a line with arrowheads.

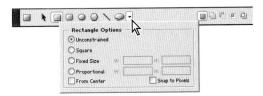

Select a shape in the options bar, and click the inverted arrow to display options for the selected shape.

To set tool-specific options:

1 Select a shape tool.

2 In the options bar, set the options that are available for the active shape tool. Click the inverted arrow ▼ next to the shape buttons to view additional options for the active tool.

Arrowheads Start and End Renders a line with arrowheads. Select Start, End, or both to specify on which end of the line arrows are rendered. The shape options appear in the pop-up dialog box. Enter values for Width and Length to specify the proportions of the arrowhead as a percentage of the line width (10% to 1000% for Width, and 10% to 5000% for Length). Enter a value for the concavity of the arrowhead (from −50% to +50%). The concavity value defines the amount of curvature on the widest part of the arrowhead, where the arrowhead meets the line.

Circle Constrains an ellipse to a circle.

Defined Proportions Renders a custom shape based on the proportions with which it was created.

Defined Size Renders a custom shape based on the size at which it was created.

Fixed Size Renders a rectangle, rounded rectangle, ellipse, or custom shape as a fixed shape based on the values you enter in the Width and Height text boxes.

From Center Renders a rectangle, rounded rectangle, ellipse, or custom shape from the center.

Indent Sides By Turns a polygon into a star. Enter a percentage in the text box to specify the depth of the star's indentations.

Proportional Renders a rectangle, rounded rectangle, or ellipse as a proportional shape based on the values you enter in the Width and Height text boxes.

Radius For rounded rectangles, specifies the corner radius. For polygons, specifies the distance from the center of a polygon to the outer points.

Sides Specifies the number of sides in a polygon.

Smooth Corners or Smooth Indents Renders a polygon with smooth corners or indents.

Snap to Pixels Snaps edges of a rectangle or rounded rectangle to the pixel boundaries.

Square Constrains a rectangle or rounded rectangle to a square.

Unconstrained Lets you set the width and height of a rectangle, rounded rectangle, ellipse, or custom shape by dragging.

Weight Determines the width of a line in pixels.

Creating text

In Photoshop Elements, you use the horizontal and vertical type tools to create and edit text. Text appears directly on-screen so you can always see how it looks in your composition.

You can also use type mask tools to create a selection in the shape of text. You can then create different effects and cut-outs with the text.

When you select a type tool, you can choose from several settings in the options bar. You can set the font, style, size, and color of the type in the options bar.

Clicking in an image with a type tool puts the type tool in edit mode so you can enter and edit text. You must commit changes to the type before you can perform other operations, like selecting menu commands. To determine if the type tool is in edit mode, look in the options bar—if you see the OK button ✔ and Cancel button ⊘, the type tool is in edit mode.

Entering text

You can enter text horizontally or vertically, depending on which type tool you select. Each line of text you enter is independent—the length of a line grows or shrinks as you edit it, but it doesn't wrap to the next line (you have to press the Enter or Return key to create a new line of text).

To enter type:

1 Select the horizontal type tool T or the vertical type tool ⌊T.

2 Click in the image to set an insertion point for the type. The small line through the I-beam marks the position of the type *baseline*. For horizontal type, the baseline marks the line on which the type rests; for vertical type, the baseline marks the center axis of the type characters.

3 Select additional type options in the options bar. (See "Formatting text" on page 199.)

4 Enter the characters you want. To begin a new line, press the Enter key (Windows) or Return key (Mac OS) to begin a new line.

5 Commit the type layer by doing one of the following:

- Click in the image, select a tool in the toolbox, or click in a palette.
- Click the OK button ✔ in the options bar.
- Press the Enter key on the numeric keypad.

The type you entered appears in a new type layer.

Note: To discard the type layer, click the Cancel button ⊘.

Working with type layers

Once you create a type layer, you can edit the type and apply layer commands to it. You can change the orientation of the type, apply anti-aliasing, and warp the type into a variety of shapes. You can move, restack, copy, and change the layer options of a type layer as you do for a normal layer. You can also make the following changes to a type layer and still edit its text:

- Apply transformation commands, except for Perspective and Distort.

Note: To apply the Perspective or Distort commands, or to transform part of the type layer, you must simplify the type layer, making the type uneditable.

- Use layer styles.

Editing text in type layers

You can insert new text, change existing text, and delete text in type layers. If any styles are applied to a type layer, all text inherits the attributes of those styles.

To edit text in a type layer:

1 Select the horizontal type tool T or the vertical type tool ↓T. (When you click in an existing type layer, the type tool changes at the insertion point to match the orientation of the layer.)

2 Select the type layer in the Layers palette, or click in the text flow to automatically select a type layer.

3 Position the insertion point in the text, and do one of the following:

- Click to set the insertion point.
- Select one or more characters you want to edit.

4 Enter text as desired.

5 Commit the changes to the type layer. (See "Entering text" on page 196.)

Changing type layer orientation

The orientation of a type layer determines the direction of type lines in relation to the document window. When a type layer is vertical, the type lines flow up and down; when a type layer is horizontal, the type lines flow from left to right.

To change the orientation of a type layer:

1 Select the type layer in the Layers palette.

2 Do one of the following:

- Select a type tool, and click the Flip Orientation button ↓T in the options bar.
- Choose Layer > Type > Horizontal, or choose Layer > Type > Vertical.

Specifying anti-aliasing

Anti-aliasing lets you produce smooth-edged type by partially filling the edge pixels, so the edges of the type blend into the background.

A   B

C   D

Applying anti-aliasing
*A. Anti-aliasing off **B.** Close up*
*C. Anti-aliasing on **D.** Close up*

Because anti-aliasing greatly increases the number of colors in an image, you may want to turn anti-aliasing off when designing for the Web. In Web images, anti-aliasing can make file sizes larger and cause stray colors to appear along the edges of type. To avoid these issues, you may prefer to leave text with jagged edges.

To turn anti-aliasing on:

Select the type layer in the Layers palette and do one of the following:

- Choose Layer > Type > Anti-Alias On, or choose Layer > Type > Anti-Alias Off.

- Select the Anti-aliased button ᵃₐ in the options bar.

To turn anti-aliasing off:

Select the type layer in the Layers palette and do one of the following:

- Choose Layer > Type > Anti-Alias Off.

- Deselect the Anti-aliased button ᵃₐ in the options bar.

Warping type layers

Warping allows you to distort type to conform to a variety of shapes; for example, you can warp type in the shape of an arc or a wave. Warping applies to all characters on a type layer—you cannot warp individual characters. The warp style you select determines the basic shape of the warped layer, while warping options let you control the orientation and perspective of the warp effect.

Type layers with warp applied

Note: You can't warp to text that uses faux bold formatting.

To warp type:

1 Select a type layer.

2 Do one of the following:

- Select a type tool, and click the Warp button ⬥ in the options bar.

- Choose Layer > Type > Warp Text.

3 Choose a warp style from the Style pop-up menu.

4 Select an orientation for the warp effect—Horizontal or Vertical.

5 If desired, specify values for additional warping options:

- Bend to specify the amount of warp.

- Horizontal Distortion and Vertical Distortion to apply perspective to the warp.

6 Click OK.

To unwarp type:

1 Select a type layer that has warping applied to it.

2 Select a type tool, and click the Warp button 🛠
in the options bar; or choose Layer > Type > Warp
Text.

3 Choose None from the Style pop-up menu,
and click OK.

Simplifying type layers

Simplifying a type layer converts it to a regular,
bitmap layer. Simplifying a type layer is necessary
when you want to paint on type or apply filters to
it. Once you simplify a type layer, you can no
longer edit its text.

To simplify a type layer:

1 Select a type layer in the Layers palette.

2 Choose Layer > Simplify Layer.

In the Layers palette, the layer thumbnail changes
from the type icon T to a thumbnail of the
simplified text.

Formatting text

Photoshop Elements gives you precise control over
individual characters in type layers, including
font, size, and color. You can set type attributes
before you enter characters, or reset them to
change the appearance of selected characters in a
type layer.

*Note: Selecting and formatting characters in a type
layer puts the type tool into edit mode. You must
commit the changes before you can perform other
operations. (See "Entering text" on page 196.)*

Selecting characters for formatting

Before you can format individual characters,
you must select them. You can select one character,
a range of characters, or all characters in a
type layer.

💡 *To select all the characters in a layer without
positioning the insertion point in the text flow,
select the type layer in the Layers palette, and then
double-click the layer's type icon* T.

To select characters:

1 Select a type tool.

2 Select the type layer in the Layers palette,
or click in the text flow to automatically select a
type layer.

3 Position the insertion point in the text, and do
one of the following:

- Drag to select one or more characters.

- Double-click to select a single word.

- Triple-click to select an entire line of text.

- Click in the text and then Shift-click to select a
range of characters.

- Choose Select > All to select all the characters in
the layer.

- To use the arrow keys to select characters,
hold down Shift and press the Right Arrow or
Left Arrow key.

Choosing a font

A font is a set of characters— letters, numbers, or symbols—that share a common weight, width, and style. When you select a font, you can select the *font family* and its *type style* independently. A type style is a variant version of an individual font in the font family (for example, Regular, Bold, or Italic). The range of available type styles varies with each font.

If a font doesn't include the style you want, you can apply *faux* (fake) versions of bold and italic. A faux font is a computer-generated version of a font that approximates an alternative typeface design, used only if there is no corresponding font for a given style.

To choose a font family and style:

1 If you're working with an existing layer, select one or more characters whose font you want to change. To change the font of all characters in a layer, select the type layer in the Layers palette, and then select a type tool.

2 In the options bar, choose a font family from the Font Family pop-up menu.

You can choose a font family and style by typing the desired name in the text box. As you type, the name of the first font or style beginning with that letter appears. Continue typing until the correct font or style name appears. (Be sure to deselect the font name before entering new type in the image.)

3 Do one of the following:

• Choose a font style from the Font Style pop-up menu in the options bar.

• If the font family you chose does not include a bold or italic style, click the Faux Bold button **T**, Faux Italic button *T*, or both; then click OK.

Changing the type color

The type you enter gets its color from the current foreground color; however, you can change the type color before or after you enter type. When editing existing type layers, you can change the color of individual characters or all type in a layer. You can also apply a gradient to text in a type layer. (See "Applying gradient fill to text" on page 149.)

To change the type color:

1 If you're working with an existing layer, select one or more characters whose color you want to change. To change the color of all characters in a layer, select the type layer in the Layers palette, and then select a type tool.

2 In the options bar, click the color selection box, and select a color using the Color Picker.

Applying underline and strikethrough

You can apply a line under horizontal type or to the right side of vertical type. You can also apply a line through horizontal or vertical type. The line is always the same color as the type color.

To apply an underline or strikethrough:

1 If you're working with an existing layer, select one or more characters whose font you want to change.

2 Do one or both of the following in the options bar:

- Click the Underline button T to apply a line below horizontal type or on the left side of vertical type.

- Click the Strikethrough button T to apply a line through the middle of the type.

Aligning type

You can *align* type to change its relationship to the initial cursor position (where you clicked when you first entered the type). Alignment affects all type on a layer.

To specify alignment:

1 If you're working with an existing layer, select the type layer in the Layers palette and then select a type tool.

2 In the options bar, click an alignment option.

The options for horizontal type are:

Aligns the left edge of each type line in the layer to the initial cursor position.

Aligns the center of each type line in the layer to the initial cursor position.

Aligns the right edge of each type line in the layer to the initial cursor position.

The options for vertical type are:

Aligns the top edge of each type line in the layer to the initial cursor position.

Aligns the center of each type line in the layer to the initial cursor position.

Aligns the bottom edge of each type line in the layer to the initial cursor position.

Choosing a type size

The type size determines how large the type appears in the image. The default unit of measurement for type is points. However, you can change the unit of measurement in the Units & Rulers section of the Preferences dialog box.

The physical size of the font depends on the resolution of the image. 72-point text is approximately 1-inch high in an image that is 72 dpi. Higher resolutions reduce the effective size of a given text point size because the pixels are packed more tightly in higher resolution images.

To choose a type size:

1 If you're working with an existing layer, select one or more characters whose size you want to change. To change the size of all characters in a layer, select the type layer in the Layers palette, and then select a type tool.

2 In the options bar, enter or select a new value for Size. To use an alternate unit of measurement, enter the unit (in, cm, pt, px, or pica) after the value in the Size text box.

The value you enter is converted to the default unit of measurement. You can enter a size larger than 72 points.

To specify the default unit of measurement for type:

1 Choose Edit > Preferences > Units & Rulers.

2 In Windows or Mac OS 9.x, choose Edit > Preferences > Units & Rulers.

3 In Mac OS X, choose Photoshop > Preferences > Units & Rulers.

4 Select a unit of measurement for Type.

Creating a text selection border

When you use the horizontal type mask tool ⟨T⟩ or vertical type mask tool ⟨T⟩, you create a selection in the shape of the type. Type selections appear on the active layer, and can be moved, copied, filled, or stroked just like any other selection. You can also warp the text created with the type mask tools.

To create a type selection border:

1 Select the layer on which you want the selection to appear. For best results, don't create the type selection border on a type layer.

2 Select the horizontal type mask tool ⟨T⟩ or the vertical type mask tool ⟨T⟩.

3 Select additional type options, and enter your text.

The type selection border appears in the image on the active layer.

💡 *You can have fun with text selection borders by cutting text out of an image to show the background, or pasting the selected text into a new image. Experiment with different options to personalize your images and compositions.*

Horizontal type mask with type warp applied to create filled selection

Setting options for Asian type

Photoshop Elements provides several options for working with Asian type. Asian fonts are often referred to as *double-byte fonts* or *CJK fonts,* meaning Chinese, Japanese, and Korean fonts.

Displaying Asian text options

In order to view and set options for working with Chinese, Japanese, and Korean type, you must select Show Asian Text Options in the Preferences dialog box. You can also control whether font names are displayed in English or in the Asian languages.

To display Asian type options:

Choose Edit > Preferences > General, and select Show Asian Text Options.

To display Asian font names in English:

Choose Edit > Preferences > General, and select Show Font Names in English.

Adjusting tsume

Tsume reduces the space around a character by a specified percentage value. The character itself is not stretched or squeezed as a result. Instead, the space around the character is compressed. When tsume is added to a character, spacing around both sides of the character is reduced by an equal percentage.

The greater the percentage, the tighter the compression between characters. At 100% (the maximum value), there is no space between the character's bounding box and its em box.

To reduce spacing between characters:

1 If you're working with an existing layer, select the type layer in the Layers palette and then select a type tool.

2 Select the characters you want to adjust.

3 Click the Show Asian Text Options button あ in the options bar.

4 Select a percentage for Tsume from the pop-up menu, and press the Enter or Return key.

Note: *An em box is a space whose height and width roughly correspond to the width of the letter "M," also called a mutton.*

Using tate-chuu-yoko

Tate-chuu-yoko (also called *kumimoji* and *renmoji*) is a block of horizontal type laid out within a vertical type line.

Before and after tate-chuu-yoko is applied

To turn on or turn off tate-chuu-yoko:

1 If you're working with an existing layer, select the type layer in the Layers palette and then select a type tool.

2 Select the characters that you want to rotate.

3 Click the Asian Text Options button あ in the options bar.

4 Select Tate-Chuu-Yoko, and press the Enter or Return key.

Note: *Using tate-chuu-yoko does not prevent you from editing and formatting type; you can edit and apply formatting options to rotated characters as you do with other characters.*

Using mojikumi

Mojikumi determines spacing between punctuation, symbols, numbers, and other character classes in Japanese type. When mojikumi is turned off, full-width spacing is applied to these characters. When mojikumi is on, half-width spacing is applied to these characters.

Mojikumi on, and Mojikumi off

To turn on or turn off mojikumi:

1 If you're working with an existing layer, select the type layer in the Layers palette and then select a type tool.

2 Click the Asian Text Options button あ in the options bar.

3 Select Mojikumi, and press the Enter or Return key.

Chapter 12: Optimizing Images for the Web and E-mail

Adobe Photoshop Elements lets you optimize the display and file size of your images for effective Web publishing and for sharing through e-mail.

About creating images for the Web and e-mail

Optimization is the process of compressing an image and setting display options for use on the World Wide Web or in e-mail. When you distribute images via these mediums, creating graphics with small file sizes is very important. In general, the file size of an image should be small enough to allow reasonable download times from a Web server but large enough to represent desired colors and details in the image.

There are three major graphic file formats used on the Web: GIF, JPEG, and PNG. You can optimize images in these formats using one of the following methods:

- To create a Web site for your portfolio of images, you can use the Web Photo Gallery command, which automates the entire process for you. Photoshop Elements produces thumbnail-sized versions of your portfolio for viewers to preview, Web pages for every image, and links between the pages. For more information, see "Creating Web photo galleries" on page 220.

- To precisely optimize an image for use in a Web page authoring application, such as Adobe GoLive®, you can use the Save for Web command. The Save for Web dialog box lets you preview your image in different file formats and with different optimization settings. You can also set transparency and animation settings. For more information, see "Using the Save For Web dialog box" on page 205.

- For basic optimization, you can use the Save As command. Depending on the file format, you can specify image quality, background transparency or matting, color display, and downloading method. For more information, see "Saving images in different file formats" on page 226.

Using the Save For Web dialog box

You use the Save For Web dialog box to choose Web file formats, select compression and color options, and preview your optimized image. In addition, you can preserve background transparency or set background matting, and change the image size.

To display the Save For Web dialog box:

Choose File > Save for Web, or click the Save for Web button 🖳 in the shortcuts bar.

Viewing images during optimization

You use a dual-image window to see both your original and optimized images in the Save For Web dialog box. This view lets you compare the two images and determine which optimization settings work best. If some areas of an image aren't visible, you can use the hand tool to bring those areas into view. You can also use the zoom tool to magnify or reduce the view.

To navigate in a view:

1 Select the hand tool 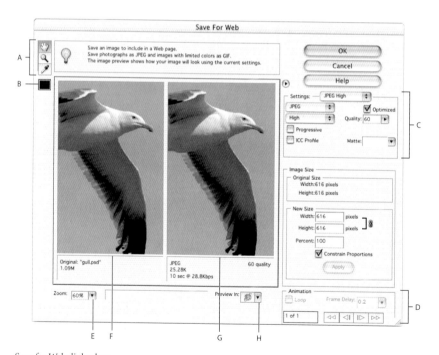 in the Save For Web dialog box, or hold down the spacebar.

2 Drag in the view area to pan over the image.

To zoom in or zoom out:

Do one of the following:

- Select the zoom tool in the Save For Web dialog box, and click in a view to zoom in.

- Hold down Alt (Windows) or Option (Mac OS) and click in a view to zoom out.

- Choose a magnification level from the Zoom pop-up menu, or enter a value in the Zoom text box, and then press Tab on your keyboard.

Save for Web dialog box
A. *Toolbox* *B.* *Color Picker* *C.* *Optimization settings* *D.* *Animation options* *E.* *Zoom level menu* *F.* *Original image*
G. *Optimized image* *H* *Browser Preview menu*

Viewing optimization information

Underneath your image in the Save For Web dialog box, the annotation area provides valuable optimization information. The annotation for the original image shows the file name and file size. The annotation for the optimized image shows the current optimization settings, the size of the optimized file, and the estimated download time based upon the selected internet access speed.

To view your image's estimated download time:

1 Click the triangle ⊙ located to the right of the optimized image to view the Preview pop-up menu.

2 Choose an Internet access speed, including modem, ISDN, cable, or DSL internet access.

When you change the internet access speed, the estimated download time in the annotation area is updated. If the download time seems too long, try different optimization settings or change the image size in the Save for Web dialog box.

Previewing variations in color display

When optimizing an image for the Web, consider how the image will appear on different monitors. In general, an image appears darker on Windows system than on Mac OS computers You can simulate cross-platform display differences in the Save For Web dialog box.

To preview variations in color display:

1 Click the triangle ⊙ to the right of the optimized image to view the Preview pop-up menu.

2 Choose a display option:

- Uncompensated Color (the default option) to view the image with no color adjustment.

- Standard Windows Color to view the image with color adjusted to simulate a standard Windows monitor.

- Standard Macintosh Color to view the image with color adjusted to simulate a standard Macintosh monitor.

- Document Color Profile to view the image with its color profile if one exists for it. For more information on color profiles, see "Setting up color management" on page 31.

Note: These preview options adjust color display only in the Save For Web dialog box; they don't change colors in the original or optimized image.

Choosing a file format for the Web

The file format you choose for a Web image is determined by the color, tonal, and graphic characteristics of the original image. In general, continuous-tone images, such as photographs, should be compressed as JPEG files. Illustrations with large areas of solid colors and crisp details, such as type, should be compressed as GIF or PNG-8 files. In addition, to animate an image, you must save it as a GIF file.

PNG-24 file format is suitable for continuous-tone images. However, PNG-24 files are often much larger than JPEG files of the same image. PNG-24 format is recommended only when you are working with a continuous-tone image that includes multilevel transparency. (Unlike the PNG-24 format, the JPEG format doesn't support transparency. See "Making transparent and matted images" on page 214.)

A photograph suitable for compression as a JPEG or PNG-24 image, and artwork suitable for compression as a GIF or PNG-8 image

Choose a format that contains sufficient bit depth to display the colors in the image. PNG-8 and GIF files support 8-bit color, so they can display up to 256 colors. JPEG and PNG-24 files support 24-bit color, so they can display up to 16 million colors. Depending on the format, you can specify image quality, background transparency or matting, color display, and how browsers display the image while it downloads.

The appearance of an image on the Web also depends on the colors displayed by the computer platform, operating system, monitor, and browser. Preview images in different browsers on different platforms to see how they will appear on the Web.

About JPEG format

The JPEG format supports 24-bit color, so it preserves the broad range and subtle variations in brightness and hue found in photographs and other continuous-toned images. A *progressive* JPEG file displays a low-resolution version of the image in the Web browser while the full image is downloading. JPEG is supported by most browsers.

JPEG format compresses file size by selectively discarding data. Because it discards data, JPEG compression is referred to as *lossy*. A higher quality setting results in less data being discarded, but the JPEG compression method may still degrade sharp detail in an image, particularly in images containing type or vector art.

Note: *Artifacts, such as wave-like patterns or blocky areas of banding, are created each time you save an image in JPEG format. Therefore, you should always save JPEG files from the original image, not from a previously saved JPEG.*

Original image, and optimized JPEG with Low quality setting

The JPEG format does not support animation or transparency. When you save an image as a JPEG file, transparent pixels are filled with the Matte color specified in the Save For Web dialog box. To simulate the effect of background transparency, you can match the Matte color to the Web page background color. If your image contains transparency and you do not know the Web page background color, or if the background is a pattern, you should use a format that supports transparency (GIF, PNG-8, or PNG-24).

About GIF format

The GIF format uses 8-bit color and efficiently compresses solid areas of color while preserving sharp details like those in line art, logos, or type. You also use the GIF format to create an animated image and preserve transparency in an image. GIF is supported by most browsers.

The GIF format uses LZW compression, which is a *lossless* compression method. However, because GIF files are limited to 256 colors, optimizing an original 24-bit image as an 8-bit GIF can subtract colors from an image.

GIF image with Selective color, and GIF image with Web color

You can choose the number of colors in a GIF image and select options to control how colors dither in a browser. GIF supports background transparency or background matting, in which you blend the edges of the image with a Web page background color. (See "Previewing and controlling dithering" on page 216.)

About PNG-8 format

The PNG-8 format uses 8-bit color. Like the GIF format, PNG-8 efficiently compresses areas of solid color while preserving sharp detail like those in line art, logos, or type.

Because PNG-8 is not supported by all browsers, you may want to avoid this format when your image must be accessible to a wide audience. For more information on browser support for PNG, see your browser's documentation.

The PNG-8 format uses a more advanced compression schemes than GIF, so a PNG-8 file can be 10% to 30% smaller than a GIF file of the same image, depending on the image's color patterns. Although PNG-8 compression is lossless, optimizing an original 24-bit image as an 8-bit PNG file can subtract colors from the image.

Note: *With certain images, especially those with simple patterns and few colors, GIF compression can create a smaller file than PNG-8 compression. View optimized images in GIF and PNG-8 format to compare file size.*

As with the GIF format, you can choose the number of colors in an image and select options to control how colors dither in a browser. The PNG-8 format supports background transparency and background matting, in which you blend the edges of the image with a Web page background color. (See "Previewing and controlling dithering" on page 216.)

PNG-8 with 256 colors and no dither, and PNG-8 with 16 colors and dithering

About PNG-24 format

The PNG-24 format supports 24-bit color. Like the JPEG format, PNG-24 preserves the broad range of colors and subtle variations in brightness and hue found in photographs. Like the GIF and PNG-8 formats, PNG-24 preserves sharp details like those in line art, logos, or type.

The PNG-24 format uses the same lossless compression method as the PNG-8 format. For that reason, PNG-24 files are usually larger than JPEG files of the same image. PNG-24 browser support is similar to that for PNG-8, so you may want to avoid this format when your image must be accessible to a wide audience.

In addition to supporting background transparency and background matting, the PNG-24 format supports multilevel transparency. Multilevel transparency allows you to preserve up to 256 levels of transparency, so you can blend the edges of an image smoothly with any background color. However, multilevel transparency is not supported by all browsers.

Optimizing Web images

Optimization settings appear on the right side of the Save For Web dialog box. You can quickly choose predefined settings, or select format-specific options to fine-tune the results of optimization.

Using predefined optimization settings

You can quickly and easily optimize an image for the Web by choosing a predefined optimization setting. Predefined settings are tailored to meet the optimization needs of different types of images. (See "Choosing a file format for the Web" on page 207.)

The name of each predefined setting reflects its file format and quality level. For example, choose JPEG High to optimize an image in JPEG format with High image quality and low compression. Choose GIF 32 Dithered to optimize an image in GIF format, reduce the number of colors to 32, and apply dithering.

When you change the options in a predefined setting, the Settings menu displays the term "Custom." You cannot save a custom setting; however, the current settings appear in the Save for Web dialog box the next time you display it.

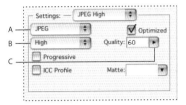

Optimization options for JPEG format
A. *Optimization format* **B.** *Compression Quality pop-up menu* **C.** *Compression Quality slider*

To optimize an image in JPEG format:

1 Choose JPEG for the optimization format.

2 To create an enhanced JPEG with a slightly smaller file size, select Optimized. The Optimized JPEG format is recommended for maximum file compression; however, some older browsers do not support this feature.

3 Do one of the following to specify the compression level:

- Choose an option from the Quality pop-up menu.

- Drag the Quality pop-up slider. (See "Using pop-up sliders" on page 16.)

- Enter a value between 0 and 100 in the Quality text box.

The higher the Quality setting, the more detail is preserved in the optimized image. However, a high Quality setting results in a larger file size than a low Quality setting. View the optimized image at several quality settings to determine the best balance of quality and file size.

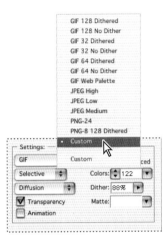

Predefined Web optimization settings

To apply a predefined optimization setting to an image:

1 Choose a setting name from the Settings pop-up menu, and click OK.

2 In the Save Optimized As dialog box, type a filename, and click Save.

Setting optimization options for JPEG format

JPEG is the standard format for compressing continuous-tone images such as photographs. (See "About JPEG format" on page 208.)

4 Select Progressive to create an image that displays progressively in a Web browser. Progressive images display first at a low resolution, and then at progressively higher resolutions as the image downloads. If you chose Optimized to create a smaller file, the Progressive option won't be available.

Note: Progressive JPEGs are not supported by some browsers.

5 To preserve the ICC profile of the original image with the optimized file, select ICC Profile.

ICC profiles are used by some browsers for color correction. The ICC profile of the image depends on your current color setting. (See "About color management" on page 31.)

6 If the original image contains transparency, select a Matte color that matches the background of your Web page. Transparent areas in your original image are filled with the Matte color. (See "Making transparent and matted images" on page 214.)

7 To save your optimized image, click OK. In the Save Optimized As dialog box, type a filename, and click Save.

Setting optimization options for GIF and PNG-8 formats

GIF is the standard format for compressing images with large areas of solid colors and crisp details like those in line art, logos, or type. (See "About GIF format" on page 209.) Like the GIF format, PNG-8 supports transparency, and efficiently compresses

areas of solid color while preserving sharp detail; however, not all Web browsers can display PNG-8 files. (See "About PNG-8 format" on page 209.)

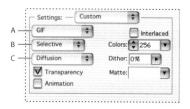

Optimization options for GIF format:
A. Optimization format B. Color reduction algorithm C. Dither algorithm

GIF format and PNG-8 format can use up to 256 colors to describe an image. The process of determining which colors to use is called *indexing*, so images in GIF and PNG-8 formats are sometimes called *indexed color* images. To convert an image to indexed color, Photoshop Elements builds a color lookup table, which stores and indexes the colors in the image. If a color in the original image does not appear in the color lookup table, the application either chooses the closest color in the table or simulates the color using a combination of available colors.

To optimize an image in GIF or PNG-8 format:

1 Choose GIF or PNG-8 for the optimization format.

2 Select Interlaced to create an image that displays at low-resolution in a browser while the full-resolution image is downloading. Interlacing can make downloading time seem shorter and assures viewers that downloading is in progress.

3 Choose a color reduction algorithm for generating the color lookup table:

- Perceptual to create a custom color table by giving priority to colors for which the human eye has greater sensitivity.

- Selective to create a color table similar to the Perceptual color table, but favoring broad areas of color and the preservation of Web colors. This color table usually produces images with the greatest color integrity. (Selective is the default choice.)

- Adaptive to create a custom color table by sampling colors from the spectrum appearing most commonly in the image. For example, an image with only shades of green and blue produces a color table made primarily of greens and blues. Most images concentrate colors in particular areas of the spectrum.

- Web to use the standard, Web-safe 216-color color table common to the 8-bit (256-color) palettes of Windows and Mac OS. This option ensures that no browser dither is applied to colors when the image is displayed using 8-bit color. If your image has fewer than 216 colors, unused colors are removed from the table. (See "Previewing and controlling dithering" on page 216.)

- Custom to preserve the current color table as a fixed palette that does not update when you change the image.

4 To specify the maximum number of colors in the color palette, select a number from the Colors pop-up menu, enter a value in the text box, or click the arrows to change the number of colors. If the image contains fewer colors than the palette, the color table reflects the smaller number of colors that are in the image.

If you chose either Web or Custom for the color reduction algorithm, you can choose Auto in the Colors menu. Choose Auto if you want Photoshop Elements to determine the optimal number of colors in the color table based on the frequency of colors in the image.

5 Choose a dithering algorithm option from the pop-up menu. If you choose Diffusion, specify a percentage for Dither. (See "Previewing and controlling dithering" on page 216.)

6 If the image contains transparency, select Transparency to preserve transparent pixels; deselect Transparency to fill fully and partially transparent pixels with the matte color. (See "Making transparent and matted images" on page 214.)

7 To create an animated GIF, select Animate. See "Setting up animated GIFs" on page 219.

8 To save your optimized image, click OK. In the Save Optimized As dialog box, type a filename, and click Save.

Setting optimization options for PNG-24 format

PNG-24 format is suitable for compressing continuous-tone images. However, PNG-24 files are often much larger than JPEG files of the same image. PNG-24 format is recommended only when working with a continuous-tone image that includes multilevel transparency. (See "About PNG-24 format" on page 210.)

To optimize an image in PNG-24 format:

1 Choose PNG-24 for the optimization format.

2 Select Interlaced to create an image that displays at low-resolution in a browser while the full-resolution image is downloading. Interlacing can make downloading time seem shorter, and assures viewers that downloading is in progress.

3 If the image contains transparency, select Transparency to preserve transparent pixels; deselect Transparency to fill fully and partially transparent pixels with the Matte color. (See "Making transparent and matted images" on page 214.)

4 To save your optimized image, click OK. In the Save Optimized As dialog box, type a filename, and click Save.

Making transparent and matted images

Transparency makes it possible to create non rectangular images for the Web. Background transparency, supported by the GIF and PNG formats, preserves transparent pixels in the image. These pixels allow a Web page background color or background image to show through the transparent areas of your image.

Web button without transparency and with transparency

Background matting, supported by the GIF, PNG, and JPEG formats, simulates transparency by filling or blending transparent pixels with a matte color that can match the Web page background. Background matting works best if the Web page background is a solid color and if you know what that color is.

To create background transparency or background matting in the optimized image, the original image must contain transparency. You can create transparency when you create a new layer or use the eraser tools. (See "Adding layers" on page 95 and "Erasing" on page 142.)

Preserving transparency in GIF and PNG images

GIF and PNG-8 formats support one level of transparency—pixels can be fully transparent or fully opaque, but not partially transparent. PNG-24 format, however, supports multilevel transparency, letting you preserve up to 256 levels of transparency in an image.

To preserve background transparency in a GIF or PNG image:

1 Open or create an image that contains transparency, and choose File > Save for Web.

2 In the Save For Web dialog box, select GIF, PNG-8, or PNG-24 as the optimization format.

3 Select Transparency.

4 For GIF and PNG-8 format, specify how to treat partially transparent pixels in the original image. You can blend these pixels with a matte color, or you can create hard-edged transparency. (See "Creating background matting in GIF and PNG images" on page 215, and "Creating hard-edged transparency in GIF and PNG-8 images" on page 215.)

Creating background matting in GIF and PNG images

When you know the background color of the Web page on which an image will be displayed, you can use the matting feature to fill or blend transparent pixels with a matte color that matches the Web page background.

The results of matting GIF and PNG-8 images depend on the Transparency option:

- If you select Transparency, partially transparent pixels are filled with the matte color, and fully transparent pixels remain transparent. When you place the image on a Web page, the edges of the image blend with the background, which shows through the fully transparent pixels. This option prevents the halo effect that results when you place an anti-aliased image on a Web page background that differs from the image background. This option also prevents the jagged edges of hard-edged transparency.

- If you deselect Transparency, fully transparent pixels are filled with the matte color, and partially transparent pixels are blended with the matte color.

To create a matted GIF or PNG image:

1 Open or create an image that contains transparency, and choose File > Save for Web.

2 In the Save For Web dialog box, select GIF, PNG-8, or PNG-24 as the optimization format.

3 For GIF and PNG-8 format, do one of the following:

- To keep fully transparent pixels transparent, and blend partially transparent pixels with the matte color, select Transparency.

- To fill transparent pixels with the matte color and blend partially transparent pixels with the matte color, deselect Transparency.

4 Select a color from the Matte pop-up menu: Eyedropper (to use the color in the eyedropper sample box), White, Black, or Other (to select a color using the Color Picker).

Creating hard-edged transparency in GIF and PNG-8 images

When working with GIF or PNG-8 files, you can create hard-edged transparency. With hard-edge transparency, all pixels that are more than 50% transparent in the original image are fully transparent in the optimized image, and all pixels that are more than 50% opaque in the original image are fully opaque in the optimized image. Use hard-edged transparency when you don't know the background color of a Web page, or when the Web page background contains a texture or pattern. However, keep in mind that hard-edged transparency can cause jagged edges in the image.

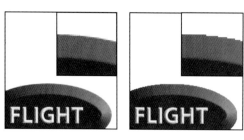

GIF without hard-edged transparency, and with hard-edged transparency

To create hard-edged transparency in a GIF or PNG-8 file:

1 Open or create an image that contains transparency, and choose File > Save for Web.

2 In the Save For Web dialog box, select GIF or PNG-8 as the optimization format.

3 Select Transparency.

4 Select None from the Matte pop-up menu.

Creating background matting in JPEG images

Though the JPEG format does not support transparency, you can specify a matte color to simulate the appearance of transparency in the original image. The matte color fills fully transparent pixels and blends with partially transparent pixels. When you place the JPEG on a Web page with a background that matches the matte color, the image appears to blend with the background.

To create a matted JPEG image:

1 Open or create an image that contains transparency, and choose File > Save for Web.

2 In the Save For Web dialog box, select JPEG as the optimization format.

3 Select a color from the Matte pop-up menu: None, Eyedropper (to use the color in the eyedropper sample box), White, Black, or Other (to select a color using the color picker).

Note: When you select None, white is used as the matte color.

Previewing and controlling dithering

Most Web images are created by designers using using 24-bit color displays (which display over 16 million colors), but some users view Web pages on computers with 8-bit color displays (which display only 256 colors). As a result, Web images often contain colors not available on some computers. Computers use a technique called *dithering* to simulate colors they can't display. Dithering uses adjacent pixels of different colors to give the appearance of a third color. For example, a red color and a yellow color may dither in a mosaic pattern to produce the illusion of an orange color that the 8-bit color palette doesn't contain.

When optimizing images, keep in mind that two kinds of dithering can occur:

• *Application dither* occurs in GIF and PNG-8 images when Photoshop Elements attempts to simulate colors that aren't in the current color table. You can control application dither by choosing a dithering pattern, or you can try to avoid application dither by adding more colors to the table.

- *Browser dither* occurs when a Web browser using an 8-bit color display (256-color mode) attempts to simulate colors that aren't in the 8-bit color palette. Browser dither can occur with GIF, PNG, or JPEG images. In Photoshop Elements, you can control the amount of browser dither by shifting selected colors in the image to Web-safe colors. You can also specify Web-safe colors when choosing a color in the Adobe Color Picker.

Previewing and controlling application dither

You can preview application dither in GIF and PNG-8 images. The Dither Algorithm pop-up menu lets you choose a dithering method for the image. Images with primarily solid colors may work well without dithering. Conversely, images with continuous-tone color (especially color gradients) may require dithering to prevent color banding.

GIF image without dithering produces banding, GIF image with Diffusion dither set to 100% dither simulates continuous tones

To control application dither:

1 Choose an option from the Dither Algorithm pop-up menu:

- No Dither to apply no application dither to the image.

- Diffusion to apply a random pattern that is usually less noticeable than Pattern dither. The dither effects are diffused across adjacent pixels.

- Pattern to apply a halftone-like square pattern to simulate any colors not in the color table.

- Noise to apply a random pattern similar to the Diffusion dither method, but without diffusing the pattern across adjacent pixels. Unlike the Diffusion method, no seams appear with the Noise dither method.

If you chose Diffusion as the dithering algorithm, drag the Dither slider, or enter a value to select a dithering percentage.

The Dither percentage controls the amount of dithering that is applied to the image. A higher dithering percentage creates the appearance of more colors and more detail in an image, but can also increase the file size. For optimal compression and display quality, use the lowest percentage of application dither that provides the color detail you require.

Previewing browser dither

You can preview browser dither directly in Photoshop Elements or in a browser that uses an 8-bit color display (256-color mode).

To preview browser dither:

Choose Browser Dither from the document panel menu in the Save For Web dialog box. (To view the menu, click the triangle near the upper right corner of the document panel.)

To preview browser dither in a browser:

1 Set your computer's color display to 8-bit color (256 colors). See your computer operating system's documentation for information on changing the color display.

2 Select a browser from the Preview pop-up menu in the Save For Web dialog box.

Minimizing browser dither

Using colors in the Web palette ensures that colors won't dither when displayed on Windows or Macintosh systems capable of displaying 256 colors. When creating an original image, you can use the Color Picker to choose Web-safe colors. (See "Using Web-safe colors" on page 132.)

Previewing an image in a browser

You can preview an optimized image in any Web browser installed on your system. The browser preview displays the image with a caption listing the image's file type, pixel dimensions, file size, compression specifications, and other HTML information.

To preview an optimized image in a Web browser:

In the Save For Web dialog box, choose a browser from the Preview In pop-up menu, or click the browser icon to launch your default Web browser.

To add a browser to the Preview pop-up menu:

1 Create a shortcut (Windows) or alias (Mac OS) for the browser you want to add to the menu. (For more information on creating shortcuts or aliases, see your operating system documentation.)

2 Drag the icon for the shortcut or alias into the Preview In folder, located in the Helpers folder in the Photoshop Elements program folder.

3 Restart Photoshop Elements.

Saving optimized images

You must save an optimized image before you can use it on the Web.

To save an optimized image:

1 Apply optimization settings in the Save For Web dialog box, and click OK. (See "Optimizing Web images" on page 210.)

2 Type a filename, and choose a location for the optimized file.

3 Click Save.

Creating animated GIFs

Some animations that you view in a Web browser are called *animated GIFs*. Animated GIFs create the illusion of movement by displaying a sequence of images, or *frames*, over time. Photoshop Elements provides a powerful, easy way to create animated GIFs from a multiple-layer image.

Setting up animated GIFs

To create an animated GIF file, you work with layers. Each layer becomes a frame when Photoshop Elements generates an optimized animation. For more information about working with layers, see "About layers" on page 91.

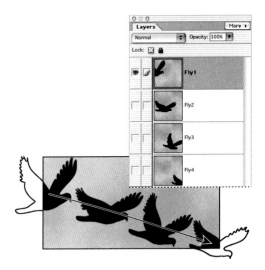

Images in separate layers can be sequenced together to create an animation

To set up an animated GIF:

1 Place the images you want to appear in each frame of the animation on separate layers. For example, to create an animation of an eye blinking, you would place an image of the open eye on one layer, and an image of the eye closed on another layer.

2 Choose File > Save for Web, or click the Save for Web button 🔲 in the shortcuts bar.

Note: *If your image has multiple layers, you can also open the Save for Web dialog box from the Save As dialog box by choosing CompuServe GIF format and selecting Layers As Frames.*

3 Optimize the image in GIF format. (See "Using predefined optimization settings" on page 210 or, "Setting optimization options for GIF and PNG-8 formats" on page 212.)

4 Select Animate.

5 Set additional options in the Animation section of the dialog box:

• Loop to continuously repeat the animation in a Web browser.

• Frame Delay to specify the number of seconds that each frame is displayed in a Web browser. Use a decimal value to specify fractions of a second. For example, use .25 to specify one-quarter of a second.

Previewing animated GIFs

You can preview an animation in the Save For Web dialog box or in a Web browser. The Save For Web dialog box shows the animation as still frames. You must preview the animation in a browser to view the frames in timed sequence.

To preview an animation in the Save For Web dialog box:

Do one of the following:

- Click the Next Frame button ▷ to view the next frame in the animation.

- Click the Previous Frame button ◁ to view the previous frame in the animation.

- Click the Last Frame button ▷▷ to view the last frame in the animation.

- Click the First Frame button ◁◁ to view the first frame in the animation.

To preview an animation in a Web browser:

1 Choose a browser from the Preview pop-up menu, or click the browser icon to launch your default Web browser.

2 Use the browser's Stop and Refresh or Reload commands to stop or replay the animation.

Opening animated GIFs

You can open an existing animated GIF file using the Open command. For each frame in the file, Photoshop Elements creates a layer. To view a specific frame in the document window, make the layer for that frame visible in the Layers palette, and hide other layers. (See "Using the Layers palette" on page 94.)

Creating Web banners

You use the Web Banner preset size to design an image banner with dimensions that are suitable for Web viewing.

To create a Web banner:

1 Choose File > New.

2 Choose 468 x 60 Web Banner from the Preset Sizes pop-up menu.

3 To modify the banner size, enter new dimensions in the Width and Height text boxes.

4 Click OK.

5 To create an animated Web banner, see "Creating animated GIFs" on page 218.

6 When you're done designing your Web banner, optimize the image using the Save For Web dialog box. (See "Optimizing Web images" on page 210.)

Creating Web photo galleries

You use the Create Web Photo Gallery command to automatically generate a Web photo gallery from a set of images. A Web photo gallery is a Web site that features a home page with thumbnail images and gallery pages with full-size images. Each page contains links that allow visitors to navigate the site. For example, when a visitor clicks a thumbnail image on the home page, a gallery page with the associated full-size image loads.

Photoshop Elements provides a variety of gallery styles, which you can select using the Create Web Photo Gallery command. After creating a photo gallery in Photoshop Elements, you can customize the Web pages in any Web page authoring program such as Adobe GoLive.

To create a Web photo gallery:

1 Choose File > Create Web Photo Gallery.

2 Choose a gallery style from the Styles pop-up menu. A preview of the home page for the chosen style appears on the right side of the dialog box.

3 To display your e-mail address in the gallery, enter your e-mail address in the textbox.

Note: Some gallery styles don't display e-mail addresses.

4 In the Folders section, click Browse (Windows) or Choose (Mac OS). Then select the folder containing the images that you want to appear in the gallery, and click OK. Select Include All Subfolders to include images inside any subfolders of the selected folder.

5 Click Destination. Then select a folder to contain optimized images and HTML pages for the gallery, and click OK.

6 If you chose Table from the Styles pop-up menu, you can click Background to select a JPEG image for the table's background.

7 If the Options section is unavailable, skip to step 12. (Some gallery styles don't have options.)

8 To set options for the text banner that appears on each page in the gallery, choose Banner from the Options pop-up menu. Then do the following:

• For Site Name, enter the title of the gallery. The title also appears in the browsers title bar.

• For Photographer, enter the name of the person or organization that deserves credit for the photos in the gallery.

• For Contact Info, enter the photographer or organization's contact information, such as an address, phone number, and e-mail address.

• For Date, enter the date that you want to appear on each page of the gallery. By default, Photoshop Elements uses the current date.

• For Font and Font Size, choose options for the banner text.

9 To set options for the gallery pages that display full-sized images, choose Large Images from the Options pop-up menu. Then do the following:

• To resize the source images on the gallery pages, select Resize Images, and then choose a preset image size from the pop-up menu, or enter a specific size in pixels. To keep the width and height proportional, choose Both from the Constrain menu; to resize only one dimension choose Width or Height. To set JPEG Quality, choose an option from the pop-up menu, enter a value between 0 and 12, or drag the File Size slider (higher values produce better image quality but increase file size).

• To create a border around each image, enter the width in pixels in the Border Size text box.

• To label gallery pages, select from the Titles Use options: Filename, Title, Caption, and Copyright Notice. (You specify an image's title, caption, and copyright notice in the File Info dialog box. See "Adding file information" on page 234.)

• From the Font and Font Size pop-up menus, choose options for the label text.

10 To set options for the home page, choose Thumbnails from the Options pop-up menu. Then do the following:

• For Size, choose a preset option from the pop-up menu or enter a specific width in pixels.

- If you chose the Simple, Table, or Wet gallery style in step 2, you can enter the number of columns and rows for the thumbnails in the Columns and Rows text boxes.

- To create a border around each thumbnail, enter the width in pixels in the Border Size text box.

- To label thumbnails, select options from the Titles Use options: Filename, Title, Caption, and Copyright Notice. (You specify an image's title, caption, and copyright notice in the File Info dialog box. See "Adding file information" on page 234.)

- From the Font and Font Size pop-up menus, choose options for the label text.

11 To color elements in the gallery, choose Custom Colors from the Options pop-up menu. To change the color of a particular element, click its color swatch, and then select a new color using the Color Picker. For example, to change the background color of each page, click the Background swatch; to change the background color of the text banner, click the banner swatch.

12 To superimpose copyright information over the full-sized images, choose Security from the Options pop-up menu. From the Content pop-up menu, choose either Custom Text to enter text or another option to include text from the File Info dialog box. (To learn how to use the File Info dialog box, see "Adding file information" on page 234.) To set how the security text appears, use the Font, Font Size, Color, Opacity, Position, and Rotate pop-up menus. To choose a custom color, click the color swatch or choose Custom from the Color menu to select a color in the color picker.

13 Click OK to create the gallery.

Photoshop Elements places the following HTML and JPEG files in your destination folder:

- A home page for your gallery named index.htm. Open this file in any Web browser to preview your gallery.

- JPEG images inside an images subfolder.

- HTML pages inside a pages subfolder.

- JPEG thumbnail images inside a thumbnails subfolder.

- Additional Web files for some gallery styles.

Sending images with an e-mail message

When you want to share your photos and images with friends and family, you can quickly attach images to an e-mail message with the click of a button.

Note: This feature works with your existing internet account and e-mail application. If you haven't setup your internet access and an e-mail account, your system may prompt you to do so. See you operating system, internet access, or e-mail application documentation.

To attach an image to an e-mail message:

1 In Photoshop Elements, open the image you want to e-mail.

2 Click the Attach To E-mail button 🖼 in the shortcuts bar, or choose File > Attach to E-mail.

Note: *If you've made any changes to your image, Photoshop Elements prompts you to save your image before you e-mail it.*

3 If your image is not in JPEG format, is larger than 1200 pixels in either dimension, or includes properties that aren't supported by the JPEG format, the Attach To E-mail dialog box appears. Click one of the following:

• Auto Convert to save a copy of your original image as a JPEG file with medium compression.

• Send As Is to e-mail your image in its current format, size, and color mode.

4 In your default e-mail application, a new e-mail message appears with your image attached to it. Enter an e-mail address in the To text box, and send the message.

Chapter 13: Saving Images

Adobe Photoshop Elements supports a variety of file formats to suit a wide range of output needs. You can save or export your image to any of these formats.

Saving images

Photoshop Elements can save images to various file formats. (See "Saving images in different file formats" on page 226.) While you're developing an image, you should always save your work in Photoshop (PSD) format. This practice ensures that all of the image data is saved.

When you're finished developing an image, you can save it in an alternate file format. The file format you choose depends on how you plan to use the image.

You can use the following commands to save images:

Save to save changes you've made to the current file in the current format. (If the file has never been saved before, you get the Save As dialog.)

Save As to save an image to a different location, filename, and/or format. The available options vary depending on the format you choose. See "Setting file saving options" on page 225 for more information.

Save for Web to save an image optimized for the Web. (See "Saving optimized images" on page 218.)

To save changes to the current file:

Choose File > Save, or click the Save button 💾 in the shortcuts bar.

To save an image with a different name and location:

1 Choose File > Save As.

2 Type a filename, and choose a location for the file.

3 Apply any appropriate file saving options. See "Setting file saving options" on page 225 for available options.

4 Click Save.

Setting file saving options

In the Save As dialog box, select one or more of the following options:

As a Copy Saves a copy of the file while keeping the current file open in Photoshop Elements. The copy is saved to the same directory as the current open file.

Layers Preserves all layers in the image. If this option is disabled or unavailable, there are no layers in the image. If you see the warning icon ⚠ at the Layers check box the layers in your image are automatically flattened or merged for the selected format. To preserve layers, select another format.

ICC Profile (Windows), or Embed Color Profile (Mac OS) Embeds a color profile in the image for certain formats.

Thumbnail (Windows) Saves thumbnail data for the file. In order to select or deselect this option, you must choose Ask When Saving for the Image Previews option in the Preferences dialog box. (See "Setting preferences for saving files" on page 233.)

Image Previews options (Mac OS) Saves thumbnail data for the file. Thumbnails display in the Open dialog box. You can set these image preview options:

• Icon to use the preview as a file icon on the desktop.

• Full Size to save a 72-ppi version for use in applications that can only open low-resolution Photoshop Elements images.

• Macintosh Thumbnail to display the preview in the Open dialog box.

• Windows Thumbnail to save a preview that can display on Windows systems. Keep in mind that Windows thumbnails increase the size of files as delivered by Web servers.

Use Lower Case Extensions (Windows) makes the file extension lowercase.

File Extension options (Mac OS) specifies the file extension for the selected file format. Select Append to add the format's extension to the filename and Use Lower Case to make the extension lowercase.

About File Extensions Unix file servers are often used to help send information over networks and the Internet. Some of these Unix servers do not recognize uppercase extension. To make sure your images arrive at their destinations, use lower case extensions.

Saving images in different file formats

Different file formats cater to the needs of different applications. The file format you choose depends on the content of your image and how you plan to use it. For example, you're saving an image for use on the Web, you should choose JPEG, GIF, or PNG format.

You can save individual images in different formats using File > Save As. You can convert several images to the same file format, or the same size and resolution, using the Batch command. See "Using the Batch command" on page 234.

Until you've finished creating an image and have decided how you want to use it, you should save the image in Photoshop format (PSD) which is the default file format. Saving your image in the Photoshop format guarantees that you will be able to access all of the image data when you reopen the image.

If you choose a format that does not support all of the data in an image, a warning appears at the bottom of the Save As dialog box. If you see this warning, save a copy of the file in Photoshop format in order to support all of the image data.

To save an image in a different file format:

1 Choose File > Save As.

2 Specify a filename and location.

3 Choose a format from the following "Saving in..." topics. With some image formats, a format-specific dialog box appears after you click save.

Saving in BMP format

BMP is a standard Windows image format on Windows-compatible computers. You can specify either Microsoft® Windows or OS/2® format and a bit depth for the image. For 4-bit and 8-bit images using Windows format, you can also specify RLE compression (see "About file compression" on page 232).

Saving in Filmstrip format

Filmstrip format lets you open, edit, and save movie files created in Adobe Premiere®. (To use this feature, Adobe Premiere must be installed on your system.) If you resize, resample, change the color mode, or change the file format of a Filmstrip file, or save a selection, in Photoshop Elements, you won't be able to save it back to Filmstrip format. For further guidelines, see the *Adobe Premiere User Guide.*

Saving in GIF format

Graphics Interchange Format (GIF) is the file format commonly used to display graphics and images, and to create and display small animations, in Web pages. GIF is an LZW-compressed format designed to minimize file size and electronic transfer time. For information on when to use GIF format to optimize images, see "Choosing a file format for the Web" on page 207.

You can save an image as one or more GIF files using the Save for Web command. (See "Optimizing Web images" on page 210.)

To save a file in GIF format:

1 Choose File > Save As, and choose CompuServe GIF Format from the format list.

2 Specify a location, select saving options (as described in "Saving images" on page 225), and click Save.

3 Your image as automatically saved as a copy (unless it's already in Indexed Color mode), in the specified directory.

4 If necessary, deselect the Layers as Frames option.

5 Specify a filename and location, and click Save.

6 For RGB images, the Indexed Color dialog box appears. Specify conversion options as described in "Choosing an image mode" on page 54, and click OK.

7 In the GIF Options dialog box, select a row order for the GIF file and click OK:

- Normal to create an image that displays in a browser only when it is fully downloaded.

- Interlaced to create an image that displays as low-resolution versions in a browser while the full image file is downloading. Interlacing can make downloading time seem shorter and assures viewers that downloading is in progress. However, interlacing also increases file size.

To save an animated GIF file:

1 Choose File > Save As, and choose CompuServe GIF from the format list.

2 Select the Layers as Frames option, specify a filename and location, and click Save.

When the Save for Web dialog box appears, set optimization options as described in "Optimizing Web images" on page 210.

Saving in JPEG format

Joint Photographic Experts Group (JPEG) format is commonly used to save photographs and other continuous-tone images. JPEG format retains all color information in an image but compresses file size by selectively discarding data. You can choose what level of compression you want. A higher level of compression results in lower image quality and a smaller file size; a lower level of compression results in better image quality and a larger file size.

JPEG is one of the standard formats for displaying images over the World Wide Web and other online services. For information on when to use JPEG format to optimize images, see "Choosing a file format for the Web" on page 207.

To save a file in JPEG format:

1 Choose File > Save As, and choose JPEG from the format list.

Note: You cannot save Indexed Color and Bitmap mode images in JPEG format.

2 Specify a filename and location, select saving options (as described in "Saving images" on page 225), and click Save, which opens the JPEG Options dialog box.

3 If the image contains transparency, select a Matte color to simulate the appearance of background transparency. (See "Making transparent and matted images" on page 214.)

4 Do one of the following to specify the image quality:

- Choose an option from the Quality menu.
- Drag the Quality pop-up slider.
- Enter a value between 1 and 12 in the Quality text box.

5 Select a format option:

- Baseline ("Standard") to use a format that is recognizable to most Web browsers.
- Baseline Optimized to optimize the color quality of the image and produce a slightly smaller file size. This option is not supported by all Web browsers.
- Progressive to create an image that displays gradually as it is downloaded to a Web browser—in a series of scans (you specify how many) showing increasingly detailed versions of the entire image. Progressive JPEG images files are slightly larger in size, require more RAM for viewing, and are not supported by all applications and Web browsers.

6 To view the estimated download time of the image, select a modem speed from the Size pop-up menu. (The Size preview is only available when Preview is selected.)

Note: If you find that a Java application cannot read your JPEG file (in any color mode), try saving the file without a thumbnail preview.

7 Click OK.

Saving in Photoshop EPS format

You can use Encapsulated PostScript (EPS) format to share Photoshop files effectively with many graphic, illustration, and page-layout programs. For best results, print documents with EPS images to PostScript-enabled printers.

To save a file in Photoshop EPS format:

1 Choose File > Save As, and choose Photoshop EPS from the format list.

2 Specify a filename and location, select saving options (as described in "Saving images" on page 225), and click Save.

3 For Preview (Windows and Mac OS), choose TIFF (8 bits/pixel) or (Mac OS-only) Macintosh 8-bits/pixel for better display quality. For a smaller file size, choose (Windows and Mac OS) TIFF 1-bit/pixel or Macintosh 1-bit/pixel (Mac OS-only). To add a 24-bit preview (Mac OS-only), choose Macintosh (JPEG).

4 For Encoding, choose an encoding method: ASCII, Binary, or a JPEG option. (See "Choosing a print encoding method" on page 239.)

5 To display white areas in the image as transparent, select Transparent Whites. This option is available only for images in Bitmap mode.

6 Select Image Interpolation if you want to anti-alias the printed appearance of a low-resolution image.

7 Click OK.

Saving to PCX format

PCX is a bitmap format widely supported on a variety of platforms.

To save a file in PCX format:

1 Choose File > Save As, and choose PCX from the format list.

2 Specify a filename and location, select saving options (as described in "Saving images" on page 225), and click Save.

The new image is saved in the specified folder.

Saving in Photoshop PDF format

Portable Document Format (PDF and PDP) is a flexible, cross-platform, cross-application file format. PDF files accurately display and preserve fonts, page layouts, and both vector and bitmap graphics.

Note: PDF and PDP are the same except that PDPs are opened in Photoshop and PDFs are opened in Acrobat.

To save a file in Photoshop PDF format:

1 Choose File > Save As, and choose Photoshop PDF from the format list.

2 Specify a filename and location, select saving options (as described in "Saving images" on page 225), and click Save.

3 Select an encoding method. (See "Choosing a print encoding method" on page 239.)

Note: Bitmap-mode images are automatically encoded using CCITT compression—the PDF Options dialog box does not appear.

4 Select Save Transparency if you want to preserve transparency when the file is opened in another application that supports PDF transparency.

5 Select Image Interpolation if you want to anti-alias the printed appearance of a low-resolution image.

6 Click OK.

Saving in PICT File format

PICT File format is widely used among Mac OS graphics and page-layout applications to transfer images between applications. PICT File format is especially effective at compressing images with large areas of solid color.

When saving an RGB image in PICT File format, you can choose either 16-bit or 32-bit pixel resolution. For a grayscale image, you can choose from 2, 4, or 8 bits per pixel. On Mac OS, you can save 32-bit PICT or PICT Resource files with four levels of JPEG compression. To retain a saved selection with the file, choose the 32-bit option.

Saving in PIXAR format

PIXAR format is designed specifically for exchanging files with PIXAR image computers. PIXAR workstations are designed for high-end graphics applications, such as those used for three-dimensional images and animation. PIXAR format supports RGB and grayscale images.

Saving in PNG format

Developed as a patent-free alternative to GIF, Portable Network Graphics (PNG) format is used for lossless compression and for display of images on the World Wide Web. Unlike GIF, PNG supports 24-bit images and produces background transparency without jagged edges; however, some Web browsers do not support PNG images. PNG preserves transparency in grayscale and RGB images. For information on when to use PNG format to optimize images, see "Choosing a file format for the Web" on page 207.

To save a file in PNG format:

1 Choose File > Save As, and choose PNG from the format list.

2 Specify a filename and location, select saving options (as described in "Saving images" on page 225), and click Save.

3 Select an Interlace option:

• None to create an image that displays in a Web browser only after downloading is complete.

• Interlaced to create an image that displays low-resolution versions in a browser while the full image file is downloading. Interlacing can make downloading time seem shorter and assures viewers that downloading is in progress. However, interlacing also increases file size.

4 Click OK.

Saving in Raw format

Raw format is a flexible file format for transferring images between applications and computer platforms. Raw format consists of a stream of bytes describing the color information in the image. You can specify the file extension (Windows), file type (Mac OS), file creator (Mac OS), and header information.

You can save the image in an interleaved or noninterleaved order. If you choose interleaved, the color values (red, green, and blue, for example) are stored sequentially. Your choice depends on requirements of the application that will open the file.

The header parameter specifies how many bytes of information appear in the file before actual image information begins. This value determines the number of zeros inserted at the beginning of the file as placeholders. By default, there is no header (header size = 0). You can save the file without a header and then use a file-editing program, such as HEdit (Windows) or Norton Utilities® (Mac OS), to replace the zeros with header information.

Saving in Scitex CT format

The Scitex CT file format is a common file format used in the prepress industry.

To save a file in Scitex format:

1 Choose File > Save As, and choose Scitex CT from the format list.

2 Specify a filename and location, select saving options (as described in "Saving images" on page 225), and click Save.

The new image is saved as a copy to the specified directory.

Saving in Targa format

TGA (Targa®) format is designed for systems using the Truevision® video board and is commonly supported by MS-DOS color applications. When saving an RGB image in this format, you can choose a pixel depth of 16, 24, or 32 bits per pixel. You can also choose Compress RLE.

Saving in TIFF format

Tagged-Image File Format (TIFF) is used to exchange files between applications and computer platforms. TIFF is a flexible bitmap image format supported by most paint, image-editing, and page-layout applications. Also, virtually all desktop scanners can produce TIFF images.

Photoshop Elements provides advanced TIFF options for image and layer compression. To make these options available, choose Enable advanced TIFF save options in the Saving Files preferences. (See "Setting preferences for saving files" on page 233.)

To save a file in TIFF format:

1 Choose File > Save As, and choose TIFF from the format list.

2 Specify a filename and location, select saving options, and click Save.

3 In the TIFF Options box, select the options you want, and click OK.

Image Compression Specifies a method for compressing the composite image data. (See "About file compression" on page 232.) ZIP and JPEG compression are only available when Enable Advanced TIFF Save Options is selected in the Saving Files preferences. (See "Setting preferences for saving files" on page 233.)

Byte Order Photoshop and most recent applications can read files using either byte order. However, if you don't know what kind of program the file may be opened in, select the platform on which the file will be read.

Save Image Pyramid Preserves multiresolution information. Photoshop Elements does not provide options for opening multiresolution files; the image opens at the highest resolution within the file. However, Adobe InDesign® and some image servers provide support for opening multi-resolution formats.

Save Transparency Preserves transparency as an additional alpha channel when the file is opened in another application. (Transparency is always preserved when the file is reopened in Photoshop Elements or ImageReady.)

Layer Compression Specifies a method for compressing data for pixels in layers (as opposed to composite data). Layer compression options are only available when Enable Advanced TIFF Save Options is selected in the Saving Files preferences. (See "Setting preferences for saving files" on page 233.)

Many applications cannot read layer data and will skip over it when opening a TIFF file. Photoshop, however, can read layer data in TIFF files. Although files that include layer data are larger than those that don't, saving layer data alleviates the need to save and manage a separate PSD file to hold the layer data. For more information on RLE and ZIP compression, (see "About file compression" on page 232). Choose Discard Layers and Save a Copy to flatten the image.

About file compression

Many image file formats use compression techniques that reduce the size of files. Compression techniques differ in the way detail and color are removed from the images. *Lossless* techniques compress image data without removing detail; *lossy* techniques compress images by removing detail.

The following are commonly used compression techniques:

RLE (Run Length Encoding) is a lossless compression technique that will compress the transparent portions of each layer in images with multiple layers containing transparency.

LZW (Lemple-Zif-Welch) is a lossless compression technique that provides the best results in compressing images that contain large areas of single color, such as screenshots or simple paint images.

JPEG (Joint Photographic Experts Group) is a lossy compression technique that provides the best results with continuous-tone images, such as photographs.

CCITT is a family of lossless compression techniques for black-and-white images. CCITT is an abbreviation for the French spelling of International Telegraph and Telekeyed Consultive Committee.

ZIP encoding is a lossless compression technique. Like LZW, ZIP compression is most effective for images that contain large areas of a single color.

Setting preferences for saving files

In Photoshop Elements, you can set preferences for saving image previews, using file extensions, and maximizing file compatibility.

To set file saving preferences:

Choose Edit > Preferences > Saving Files, and set the following options:

Image Previews Choose an option for saving image previews: Never Save to save files without previews, Always Save to save files with specified previews, or Ask When Saving to assign previews on a file-by-file basis.

In Mac OS, you can also select one or more of the following preview types (to speed the saving of files and minimize file size, select only the previews you need):

- Icon to use the preview as a file icon on the desktop.

- Macintosh Thumbnail to display the preview in the Open dialog box.

- Windows Thumbnail to save a preview that can display on Windows systems.

- Full Size to save a 72-ppi version of the file for use in applications that can only open low-resolution Photoshop Elements images. For non-EPS files, this is a PICT preview.

File Extension (Windows) Choose an option for the three-character file extensions that indicate a file's format: Use Upper Case to append file extensions using uppercase characters or Use Lower Case to append file extensions using lowercase characters.

Append File Extension (Mac OS) File extensions are necessary for files that you want to use on or transfer to a Windows system. Choose an option for appending extensions to filenames: Never to save files without file extensions, Always to append file extensions to filenames, or Ask When Saving to append file extensions on a file-by-file basis. Select Use Lower Case to append file extensions using lowercase characters.

In Mac OS, to append a file extension to the current file, hold down Option as you choose a file format from the Save As dialog box.

Enable advanced TIFF save options Select this option to enable layer compression options and additional image compression options when saving a TIFF file.

Recent File List Contains: _ Files Enter a value from 0 to 30 to specify how many files are available in the File > Open Recent submenu. (See "Opening files" on page 47.)

To display a preview file icon (Windows only):

1 Save the file in Photoshop format with a thumbnail preview.

2 Right-click the file on the desktop (or in any Windows or Photoshop Elements dialog box that displays a file list), and choose Properties from the context menu that appears.

3 Click the Photoshop Image tab.

4 Select an option for generating thumbnails, and click OK.

Preview icons appear on the desktop and in file lists (when the view is set to Large Icons).

Adding file information

In Windows, you can add file information to files saved in Photoshop, TIFF, JPEG, EPS, and PDF formats. In Mac OS, you can add file information to files in any format. You can add information such as the image title and a caption, and copyright information.

Note: File information cannot be saved in GIF format when converting a file from a different format.

To enter information about a file:

1 Choose File > File Info.

2 Enter the desired information in the File Info dialog box:

• Caption to enter text that can be printed under an image or displayed in a Web browser's title bar. To print the caption, choose File > Print Preview, and select Caption. Then print as usual. (See "Setting print options" on page 237 for more information.)

• Choose Copyrighted Work from Copyright Status to display a copyright symbol in the image window's title bar. Enter the desired text in the Copyright Notice text box. Specify a URL in the Owner URL text box if information about an image can be found on a web site. Click Go To URL to test the link.

Note: If Photoshop Elements detects a Digimarc watermark in the image, the Copyright & URL section is automatically updated.

• EXIF to view information imported from your digital camera, such as the date and time the picture was taken, resolution in ppi, the ISO speed rating, f/stop, compression, and exposure time. For more information about EXIF annotations, see your digital camera documentation.

3 When you've finished entering file information, click OK.

Using the Batch command

You can automatically convert multiple images to the same file format, or to the same size and resolution, using the Batch command. This is especially useful when importing images from a digital camera or scanner, or when processing images for use on the Web.

Note: *If the plug-in module for your camera or scanner does not support importing multiple images, it may not work optimally during batch-processing. Contact the plug-in's manufacturer for further information.*

To batch-process files using the Batch command:

1 Choose File > Batch Processing.

2 For Files to Convert, specify which files you want to process:

- Folder to process files already stored on your computer. Click Source to locate and select the folder. Select Include All Subfolders to process files in subfolders.

- Import to import and process images from a PDF file, a digital camera, or a scanner. Select an import option from the From pop-up menu. The available options depend on which plug-in modules are installed on your computer.

- Opened Files to process all the open files.

3 For Conversion Options, choose the format to which you want to convert files. For more information about file formats, see "Saving images in different file formats" on page 226.

4 To change the size and/or resolution of processed images, select Convert Image Size. Then do one or both of the following:

- Specify the width and height of the processed images. To keep the aspect ratio (the ration of width to height) of the images the same, select Constrain Aspect Ratio. Then enter a value in

either the Width text box or the Height text box. To change the aspect ratio of the images, deselect Constrain Aspect Ratio and enter values in both the Width and Height text boxes.

- Choose the resolution to which you want to convert the images from the Resolution pop-up menu.

5 To save modified versions of the files with new names (leaving the originals unchanged), select Rename Files and set naming options:

- Select items from the pop-up menus or enter text into the fields to be combined into the default names for all files. Elements include document name, serial number or letter, file creation date, and file extension. The fields let you change the order and formatting of the filename parts. You must include at least one field that is unique for every file (for example, filename, serial number, or serial letter) to prevent files from overwriting each other.

- For File Name Compatibility, choose Windows, Mac OS, and UNIX to make filenames compatible with Windows, Mac OS, and UNIX operating systems.

6 Click Destination to locate and select a destination folder for the processed files.

7 Click OK.

Chapter 14: Printing

Setting up your image files for printing is easy with Adobe Photoshop Elements. You can adjust the positioning, scaling, and output options for your image. You can also use color management to help ensure a close match between on-screen and printed colors.

Printing images

You can use the Print dialog box to print your images in just a few steps.

Before printing, make sure the file is sized for your printer. Some printers can print very large files, while others cannot, and some may take a long time to print. Check your printer documentation for size limitations. To make files smaller, consider:

- Choosing Layers > Flatten Image to flatten the file.

- Choosing Image > Resize> Resize Image to reduce resolution or Height and Width.

To print an image:

Do one of the following:

1 Choose File > Print, or click the Print button 🖨 in the shortcuts bar.

2 When the Print dialog box appears, select the name of the printer you want to use from the pop-up menu at the top of the dialog box.

3 If you are printing more than one copy, enter the number of copies.

4 Click OK to print your file.

Note: By default, Photoshop Elements prints a composite of all visible layers. To print an individual layer, make it the only visible layer in the Layers palette before choosing the Print command. (See "Selecting layers" on page 95.)

Setting print options

You can use the Print Preview dialog box to preview how your image is going to look when it's printed. You can change settings for the file as well.

To access all of the settings in the Print Preview dialog box, check the Show More Options box.

To set print options:

1 Choose File > Print Preview.

2 When the Print Preview dialog box appears, click the Page Setup button.

3 In the Page Setup dialog box, select the paper size, source, and orientation.

4 If you are printing to a printer other than your default printer, click Printer to choose the correct printer and to set printer properties if needed. Click OK.

5 Click OK to close the Page Setup dialog box.

6 Adjust the position and scale of the image in relation to the selected paper size and orientation. (See "Positioning and scaling images" on page 238.)

7 Select any output options you may need (see "Setting output options" on page 238).

8 Select an Encoding method, if desired (see "Choosing a print encoding method" on page 239.)

9 Do one of the following:

• Click Print.

• Click OK to save the print options for the image.

Positioning and scaling images

You can adjust the position and scale of an image in the Print Preview dialog box to preview how the image will look when it's printed. Scaling an image in the Print Preview dialog box changes the size and resolution of the printed image only. The file size of an image won't change.

The shaded border at the edge of the white printable area represents the margins of the selected paper. Photoshop Elements cannot override the borders settings for your printer's unprintable areas. Inkjet printers commonly have a 1/8- to 1/4-inch border around the perimeter of all printed pages onto which the printers cannot print.

To reposition an image:

1 Choose File > Print Preview.

2 Do one of the following:

• Click Center Image to center the image in the printable area. If the Center Image check box is dimmed, uncheck Scale to Fit Media.

• Click Show Bounding Box, and drag the image to a new location in the preview area.

• Enter values for Top and Left to position the image numerically. If these boxes are dimmed, uncheck Center Image.

To scale the print size of an image:

1 Choose File > Print Preview.

2 Do one of the following:

• Click Scale to Fit Media to fit the image within the printable area of the selected paper.

• Select Show Bounding Box, and drag a bounding box handle in the preview area to achieve the desired scale.

• Enter values for Height and Width to rescale the image numerically. If the Scale, Height, and Width boxes are dimmed, uncheck Scale to Fit Media.

Setting output options

Output options let you select items that print in addition to the image, like a border around the image. Show More Options (located below the image preview area) must be checked before you can see the output options. Options that aren't supported by your selected printer are dimmed.

To set output options:

1 Choose File > Print Preview.

2 Click Show More Options and choose Output from the pop-up menu.

3 Select one or more of the following options:

Background adds a background color printed on the page around the image. To use this option, click Background, and then select a color when the Color Picker appears. The background will only appear in the printed image. It won't affect the image file on your computer.

Border prints a black border around an image. Type in a number and choose inches, millimeters (mm) or points to specify the width of the border.

Caption prints any caption text entered in the File Info dialog box. (See "Adding file information" on page 234.) Caption text always prints as 9-point Helvetica plain type.

Corner Crop Marks prints crop marks where the page is to be trimmed.

Choosing a print encoding method

Encoding methods determine how image data is sent to a printer. By default, the printer driver transfers binary information to printers, but you can choose to transfer image data using JPEG or ASCII encoding.

Note that some printers only accept binary and JPEG-encoded image data through their AppleTalk or Ethernet ports, not their parallel or serial ports. Check the documentation that came with your printer if you need more information.

To choose an encoding method:

1 Choose File > Print Preview.

2 Click Show More Options if it's not checked.

3 Select an option from the Encoding menu"

ASCII encoding gives a two-byte value to each pixel of your image, which means that ASCII files are twice as large and require about twice as much time to print as binary files. ASCII files can be sent over a wide variety of network printing protocols, so select ASCII if binary or JPEG encoding is not supported your printer.

Binary encoding gives a one-byte value to each pixel of your image. Binary encoded files are smaller than ASCII files and print more quickly. However, binary data can be misinterpreted by some network printing protocols, which may cause a printer to respond slowly.

JPEG encoded files are smaller than binary files, so they require less time to print, but using JPEG encoding decreases the image quality. Only PostScript Level 2 (or higher) printers support JPEG encoding, so sending a JPEG-encoded file to a PostScript Level 1printer may result in PostScript language errors.

Using color management when printing

Photoshop Elements uses pixels to represent images. When you view an image on your monitor, pixels are displayed using red, green, and blue light. When you print an image on a printer, pixels are reproduced using colored inks. Because your monitor operates in a different *color space* than your printer, the colors you see on your monitor can vary drastically from those in the printed image. Color management provides a solution to this dilemma by using *color profiles* to ensure that the colors remain consistent. (See "About color management" on page 31.)

Converting colors to a different color space involves translating the source or image colors to accommodate the color space of the destination printer. These translation methods are known as *rendering intents* because each technique is optimized for a different intended use of color graphics.

To color-manage an image while printing:

1 Choose File > Print Preview.

2 Make sure Show More Options (located below the image preview area) is checked.

3 Choose Color Management from the pop-up menu. The Source Space section of the dialog box displays the image's color profile.

4 In the Print Space section of the dialog box, choose an option for Profile:

- Choose Same As Source if you want the printer to print the color of the image's color profile without converting it. This option will not take any printer profiles into account.

- Choose Printer Color Management or PostScript Color Management if you want to manage color conversions using the print driver. PostScript Color Management is only available when printing to a PostScript device.

- If available, choose a predefined color profile for your printer. These profiles are installed with graphics applications and print drivers. Choosing a predefined profile will result in an automatic color conversion when printing.

5 Under Print Space, for Intent, choose a rendering intent:

Perceptual is most suitable for photographic images. Perceptual preserves the visual relationship between colors that is perceived as natural to the human eye, although the color values themselves may change.

Saturation is suitable for business graphics, where the exact relationship between colors is not as important as having bright saturated colors. Saturation creates vivid color at the expense of accurate color.

Absolute Colorimetric is useful when you want to match the color of one kind of paper on another kind of paper, and have the most accurate match of all the colors. For example, you'd use Absolute Colorimetric to reproduce the appearance of a sheet of newsprint onto a sheet of bright white paper. The bright white paper would be printed over with a dingy gray to simulate the actual newsprint appearance.

Relative Colorimetric is useful when you want to match inks printed on various paper types. For example, you can use this option to match inks printed on newsprint, but not the color of newsprint itself.

Using online services

The Online Services feature allows you to send images from Photoshop Elements to remote service providers, such as Photo Printing partners and Online Sharing companies. The service list may be updated each time you select the Online Services command, so check it occasionally for new services.

To select an online service:

1 Choose File > Online Services.

2 Choose a service from the list.

Index

Photography Credits

The following photographers and stock agencies have supplied the photographs and artwork seen throughout this book.
CMCD, Inc.: Bike (page 39, 76)
Eyewire Photography: Filter and effects gallery; Sailboat (page 165)
George Matthews: Chicago skyline (page 82, 84)
John Peterson: Lakeview (page 86)